W9-AYL-852

COSMOPOLITAN'S GUIDE TO

FORTUNE -TELLING

Foreword: By Helen Gurley Brown

COSMOPOLITAN BOOKS/N.Y.

© MCMLXXIV, MCMLXXVII That Cosmopolitan Girl
Library, Inc.

Manufactured in the United States of America.
All rights reserved. No part of this book may be
reproduced without the written permission
of the publisher.

ISBN 0-87851-111-3
Library of Congress Catalogue Card No. 76-8040

ACKNOWLEDGEMENTS

Chapter Three: Part of this material originally appeared
in Cosmopolitan magazine as
"One . . . Two . . . Three . . . Four . . . Numerology!"
by Cathy Cash and K.T. Maclay. © 1974
The Hearst Corporation.
Chapter Five: Selections from *The I Ching:*
Or Book of Changes, trans. by Richard Wilhelm,
rendered into English by Cary F. Baynes,
Bollingen Series XIX
(copyright © 1950 & 1967 by Bollingen Foundation),
reprinted by permission of Princeton University Press;
also by permission
of Routledge & Kegan Paul, London, Eng.
Selections from *Sappho: A New Translation,*
by Mary Barnard (copyright © 1958
by the Regents of the University of California);
originally published by the University of California Press;
reprinted by permission of the Regents
of the University of California.
Chapter Six: The Psychological Dream Glossary
originally appeared, in longer form,
in the Cosmo Girl's Dream Book
© 1972 The Hearst Corporation.

PHOTOGRAPHIC AND ART CREDITS

Cover: photographer, J. Frederick Smith;
P. 3, *Symbols, Signs & Signets,*
by Ernst Lehner (Dover Publications, Inc.;
New York, 1950).
P. 31, *Symbols, Signs & Signets.*
P. 79, French Tarot cards—
courtesy of U.S. Games Systems, Inc.
Pp. 270-271, *Symbols, Signs & Signets.*
All Tarot cards are from the Rider Pack,
designed by Pamela Colman Smith
under the direction of Edward Arthur Waite,
reprinted by permission of U.S. Games Systems, Inc.,
New York 10016.
Playing cards, U.S. Playing Card Co.
Additional drawings by Dorris Crandall.

Have you ever watched people at a party drift toward someone who happens to murmur that, yes, she might be willing to try a few readings with her Tarot cards? Have you listened to a girlfriend recount a dream (or awakened from one yourself) and felt you could *almost* grasp the meaning? Have you ever traced the palm of a man you were holding hands with—and suddenly wished you could tell him all sorts of clever, sweet secrets about the meaning of his Love Line?

I've experienced all those things—but the mysteries of what everybody calls "the occult" have always *remained* mysterious to me. Though I faithfully read my Aquarius horoscope in the newspaper every day, as well as the astrological prediction that Cosmopolitan runs once a month (there just *could* be something to it!), I wouldn't know how to tell you if Scorpios and Capricorns are emotionally compatible without phoning Linda Goodman for a quick, expert consultation!

Well, when Cosmopolitan decided to publish this Guide to Fortune Telling, we were determined to *reveal* all the secrets of the most popular ways of predicting the future. And I discovered (and know you will, too) that fortune-telling methods are simply techniques for bringing out, and building on, what we've always called "intuition." Perhaps that's why so many occult practicioners (sibyls, sorceresses, priestesses) have been *female*. We have traditionally been the keepers of deep truths about the heart—and those truths are what *make* the future.

Whether you believe all this passionately and seriously, or as a tantalizing possibility, or just as a basis for sophisticated social games, this book will tell you how to make fortune-telling work for you, now. To help you feel confident, the following pages detail everything you'll need to know. You'll find step-by-step guides to the methods themselves (with many illustrations). And we've spent a good deal of time concentrating on *you*—how you'll look, the setting you'll create, the ambience that can make fortune-telling more intimate than any old parlor game.

You'll also find out which methods are right for your personality. Perhaps you're a sultry gypsy—your hands will give that old poker deck a new fascination. Are you a bit aloof? The aristocratic-sounding *I Ching* and Tarot cards will both suit you. Are you a cuddly at-home girl, basking in the sensual warmth of the fireside? You'll love tea-leaf reading. A girl who's a bit of a siren—frankly sexy—might opt for the most *physical* methods: palmistry, phrenology, and automatic writing.

No matter what methods you choose—and it's fun to go beyond your basic type—I hope you'll find fortune-telling much more than a way to see into the future. Isn't the *present* really the most compelling time of all? And the paradoxical thing about fortune-telling is that it offers the chance to use your most intuitive and intimate perceptions, about yourself and others, right now—to attract people you find attractive, to provide insights where glancing social observations don't go deep enough. Fortune-telling is also a terrific way to move closer physically, using all your best equipment—body, mind, emotions. (Touching a man's hand becomes doubly exciting if you're also offering to understand him and predict his future!)

So do play with all these marvelous methods, enjoy them, and let them draw you closer to those you love. Being female, you're probably a fabulous seeress already!

Helen Gurley Brown

CONTENTS

Chapter One

TEA LEAVES
AND OTHER
RANDOM SIGNS

The reading of tea leaves, coffee grounds, candle drippings, and other haphazard details of everyday life is one of the oldest—and easiest—forms of fortune-telling. Most other methods started out as public rituals with religious overtones, or as secret studies by philosophers dabbling in magic. But some people have always known that the intimate details of their lives—random signs in the home and in nature—could be used to predict the future.

Of course, the intimate and the mysterious are often very closely related. The warmth of communication over a dinner table can produce the perfect atmosphere for premonition. So each of the methods you'll learn in this chapter depends most directly upon your contact with the sitter—the person whose fortune is to be told. It is the sitter who turns the teacup, swirls the coffee grounds, holds the candle to let the wax drip. In the intimacy of his own home or that of a trusted friend—you—his real fears, needs, and hopes will show in the movements of his hand, the tremors of his arm muscles, the expression on his face. Part of what you, the reader, will see in the "random" sign will be a subliminal communication from the sitter.

TEA LEAVES

The reading of tea leaves is one of the best ways to begin fortune-telling, because it requires very little special equipment and is best done in the most comfortable and cozy situation possible. Whether in the warm afternoon sunlight following a high tea over the weekend, or in the candlelit afterglow of a good dinner, a relaxed simplicity of surroundings is most likely to produce good results. The emphasis should be on the natural, the easy, never on the mysterious or the exotic.

Remember: Not only gypsies in tearooms read tea leaves. Everyone from the parlormaid to the duchess's daughter has been gazing knowingly into drained teacups since tea was introduced to the British Isles in the late eighteenth century. Because it was imported from the East, it was considered exotic; fabulous chests were built to transport it, expensive, beautiful boxes were designed to contain the valued leaves, and rituals grew up around its brewing and serving. No wonder it became a medium for reading the future!

THE MYSTIC MOOD
You must decide what circumstances will enhance a tea-leaf reading for your sitters. Some people will be most responsive in that period of contentment following an elegant brunch or high tea. (Never served high tea before? Read on for the details.) For others, the receptive hours are the languid ones after a good dinner—when tea can be a lighter change-of-pace from coffee. And

you never can tell—your quick reading of tea leaves at breakfast might just replace the morning paper's horoscope for someone!

One of the very best reasons for thinking of tea as an essentially *English* beverage—rather than an exotic Eastern one—is that in England, "tea" often means an entire (lavish) meal. Try the approaches that follow to make your reading *sensual:*

THAT GREAT
BRITISH TRADITION
IN TWO
SMASHING VERSIONS

AFTERNOON TEA

Served at four—or at whatever hour *feels* like four to you—afternoon tea should be elegant, rich, and refreshing. Serve one of the pale amber Chinese teas, or a lightly spiced tea like Constant Comment, along with a rich rum cake or iced *petits fours* (find a really dedicated French pastry shop) and fresh fruit. Or make hot biscuits from packaged prepared dough (out of the grocer's dairy case), serve with butter and honey with the fruit. (The English tend to present three rich cakes and a hot bread, but that's *too* lavish with calories.)

For the tea itself, use a pretty pot (not that chipped old brown one) and provide a thinly sliced lemon (with all seeds removed and a clove centered in each slice), milk, and sugar cubes. (Never serve *cream* with tea—the English say it "coats" the tea, and *I* say it just tastes too buttery.) Have a shallow bowl ready to hold the dregs from the bottom of each cup, so that the next may be fresh and hot. (Of course, you'll want to keep the dregs of the *final* cup for reading.) Pour the tea through a fine mesh strainer into the cup. When the tea grows tepid, or shows signs of being overbrewed (it can get bitter and musty-tasting), brew another pot at once.

It's basically a simple ritual—but a delightful one, and so *energizing* that if your sitter is one friendly male, you may not get around to the reading until much, much later!

HIGH TEA

High tea is usually served anytime from four until early in the evening. (The working classes in England have it instead of dinner, and *everyone* occasionally substitutes it for lunch, or dinner, or both.) For *you*, it can be the ideal alternative to brunch—a kind of lunch-and-dinner meal, to be followed much later by supper.

The menu for high tea can vary, but the classic one is for a mixed grill, which can be pretty various itself. The one that follows is typical and delicious:

Mixed Grill for High Tea

4 slices thick-cut bacon	¼ lb. of calf's liver in two pieces
2 lamb chops	1 large tomato
6 link sausages	Fresh parsley
1 calf's kidney, washed and sliced, or	¼ lb. butter

Preheat the oven to lowest temperature, and put two large plates in to warm.

Cook the bacon in a large skillet until well done but not crisp; put it on the plates in the oven to keep warm. Pour away most of the bacon fat, turn up the heat, and add the chops. When they're nicely browned, add the link sausages, and cook until the sausages are well done and the lamb is a rich pink inside (about 5 to 8 minutes). Add to the plates in the oven. Lower heat under pan as far as possible. If the pan is a little dry, add a bit of butter, and toss in the sliced kidney or calf's liver. Cook over *very* low heat until *just* done (about 2 minutes on each side); it should be pink inside, too. Add to the plates. Add more butter to the pan, turn up the heat until the butter froths, and then add the tomato, cut in half, cut side down. Let it brown until it sizzles, then turn it over and brown lightly on the other side. Remove the plates from the oven, arrange the meats nicely, add the tomato, and pour the remaining pan juices over all. Decorate with chopped parsley, and serve to two people who are absolutely *ravenous*.

With it: freshly brewed tea (English breakfast tea or an Irish tea) and thick slices of fresh buttered toast or buttered English muffins. If it's early evening, you might serve ale with the grill and have the tea after—and the reading after *that*. Of course, no one can improve on the American tipple *before* the meal—Bloody Marys, Orange Blossoms, or Screwdrivers.

The way you look: The atmosphere you create for your reading can have a psychological effect on your guest. Naturally, if you're peering into a morning teacup to see what the day will offer, you won't need any more of a costume than your laciest peignoir, and the sunlight over your shoulder will be setting enough. But for an afternoon or after-dinner reading, a little *planning* can turn tea-leaf reading from a whimsical joke into an intimate event with impact.

Afternoon is a casual time, when tea can be a-little-something-before-we-go-out, or a response to I'm-starving-after-the-zoo/matinée/ramble-in-the park. So it's probably the best time for your very first try at tea-leaf reading; your sitter will be relaxed, and so will you—making a tentative technique less noticeable.

For afternoon readings, you might try the English look: pale, heathery tweeds with a sweater set, or for summer, a wrap-around cotton frock flowered like an English garden. They'll give you that Breck-girl look that inspires confidence and trust. Keep make-up warm—pink blusher, fresh pastel eyeshadow. (Don't forget your hands! Because they will be handling the teacup, turning it and holding it, they'll be a focus of attention. No startling polish, please, and no rings so heavy that they obscure the delicate movements of your hands.)

You'll look like anything *but* that hackneyed old notion of a fortune-teller—and so your subject will be even more delighted with the fascinating results of your gazing into his teacup.

As for the setting, your tea service is the centerpiece, set on a low table or in the dining area (and if your mother or a dear aunt insisted that you take that *lovely* old silver teapot for your new apartment, now is the time to get it out and polish it), or wherever the cups and napkins and plates of food will catch the afternoon sun. Use only the sun for light, if there's enough in your apartment; turn on soft-shaded lamps with pink-hued bulbs when the natural illumination begins to wane—and *that's* the best time to propose a reading.

Tea after dinner is no fixed habit on either side of the Atlantic—so you'd do best to propose it as a special occasion to honor your newly acquired skill. You can go a little gypsy—but only a *little*, and only if your coloring makes it feasible. If you're very fair, the best alternative to the gypsy is the pale lady—an image that can be every bit as devastating.

For the gypsy look: Concentrate on make-up and jewelry, your coloring heightened with a bronze-tinted foundation, glowing blusher, and red lipstick; the eyes very dark, emphatically lined and shadowed; curly, back-combed hair, with perhaps a scarn knotted behind the ear; simple hoop earrings. Make your dress décolleté, with ruffles at the neck, perhaps in a dark jewel color.

The pale lady: Dreamy and ethereal, she is the blonde's answer to the gypsy. Wear a long dress—chiffon silk, or transparent cotton, in mauve or grey or pink or palest blue, or an art-nouveau print; a fringed silk shawl in another—but equally subtle—shade. Leave your hair smooth, long and waving over your shoulders. (Use a fall if you've gone all short and curly recently.) If you have a cameo, wear it between your breasts. Make-up should be pale and luminous, touched with moon colors—silvery eyeshadow, silver-grey mascara, the palest of eyebrows, the most ethereal blusher, and translucent lipstick. You should positively *shimmer* at the edges! Do your nails in a silvery frosted enamel; your rings should be simple bands and twists of silver. As you pick up the teacup, let the fringe of your shawl drape over your fingers. Irresistible!

Create a special *setting* for your after-dinner reading, too. Move to the living room for tea, and brew it there. (You can bring the kettle boiling from the kitchen, or try the ceremony of boiling water over an alcohol lamp— available in housewares departments.) The lights should be low, but bright enough to illuminate the tiniest leaf in the bottom of the cup. If you want a *really* romantic, supercharged atmosphere, don't use electric light at all, but put *masses* of candles on the coffee and end tables. Flowers can be an important touch—two or three of the darkest red roses in a silver bud vase near the gypsy, a low arrangement of pale pink sweethearts for the pale lady. They'll scent the air and let you perform this opening ritual: Pluck a single petal from a rose and drop in into *your* cup, before beginning the reading. Say simply, "To give the reader luck," and go on with the first steps.

TEA VARIETIES
AND THEIR
FLAVORS

The two major tea-producing areas in the world were originally India and China, and almost all teas are called either Indian or Chinese, even though they can now be grown elsewhere. Indian tea is black—not because the leaf is originally black, but because it has been fermented and dried. The Chinese allowed only a semi-fermentation before drying, which leaves the tea a fine bronze color called oolong. (Japanese tea, which came late to the West, is unfermented and dried quickly after picking, so it stays green. But Japanese teas, while mild and delicious, will not do for a reading: The leaf shape is long and wiry, and will not produce the traditional designs in the bottom of the cup.)

The authorities say that the classic teas for reading are Chinese: oolong, Keemun, and Lapsang souchong. But any of the teas listed below will produce a nice pattern in the cup. (For buying information, see pages 276-277.)

Black Teas

Assam Grown in Assam Province, northeast India, it is full-bodied, robust. Good plain or with a little sugar, in the afternoon.

Ceylon Delicate and fragrant. Best in the afternoon, plain or with lemon.

Darjeeling An Indian tea grown in the Himalayas. Delicate in color and flavor. Very good after dinner, or in the morning if your palate needs pampering.

Earl Grey Black tea from India and Ceylon. Aromatic and smoky in flavor, pale in color. Definitely an afternoon tea, best taken plain. Milk kills the smokiness.

English breakfast A blend of black teas. Its name is perfectly descriptive: It is robust, makes a fast brew of rich, dark color, and is perfect with milk and sugar at breakfast.

Irish Even more hearty than English breakfast. If you've always felt that tea is just, well, *weaker* than coffee, no matter how strong you brew it, try a pot of good strong Irish tea. In Dublin they say you can "walk a spoon on it."

Keemun Excellent plain, but will take lemon or sugar.

Lapsang souchong A favorite of real tea lovers. Even smokier than Earl Grey, its flavor is very much in the aroma. A perfect afternoon tea, excellent plain.

Oolong and Mixed Teas

Formosa oolong Originally a China tea, now made in Formosa. Subtle flavor and important bouquet. To be drunk plain or with a little lemon. Aromatic. Has been called the champagne of teas.

Jasmine An oolong flavored with jasmine flowers. Good plain or with a touch of lemon or lime. Lovely in the afternoon or after dinner, especially delicious if you've served fruit for dessert.

Brand-Name Teas

Lipton Mild and not very characterful, Lipton will adapt to just about any situation, but won't leave much of a memory.

Tetley No much more interesting than Lipton's but a bit heartier.

Swee-Touch-Nee A smokier blend, more robust; produces a somewhat murky brew that tends to be a bit bitter.

Red Rose Almost as hearty and full-bodied as Irish tea. Perfect for breakfast, and makes a good pattern for readings.

Materials and Brewing

No matter what time of day you choose for your reading, the method of brewing will be the same. Not so the tea: There are teas that taste best in the evening after dinner, others that are better for breakfast or brunch, and still others that are most delicious in the afternoon. (See the preceding list for a description of the various teas and when they are best served.)

Now to the question of equipment—some of which you probably have on hand already. The pot should be an English-style teapot of at least six-cup capacity, with the holes leading from the body to the spout large enough to allow a generous number of leaves to flow through. If you have a teapot, check the spout for hole sizes; you may have to buy another for tea-leaf reading. Avoid the Japanese pots—they're associated with green tea and handleless cups that just won't do for a reading. But if you really want a fancier pot, you'll find that they're available in an endless variety of shapes and colors, patterns and sizes.

The perfect cup for a reading is the kind that was originally called a *teacup*—as opposed to the *coffee cup*, which has a narrow base and is much taller. The teacup is very broad at the top, and fairly shallow, so that after the cup has been turned over, the tea leaves adhere easily to the sides almost up to the rim. Originally, the shallowness was considered desirable so that the color of the tea might be appreciated. Here are sketches of both kinds of cup:

Try to find cups that are as much as possible the shape shown in sketch A, and that are either white or of a plain pastel color. A dark color will make it hard to see the pattern of the leaves, and any conflicting pattern *inside* the cup will make the job nearly impossible.

As for brewing, the method is time-honored, and agreed upon by all the experts from the Tea Council to every Irish grandmother on either side of the water.

Start with a large kettleful of freshly boiling water. Scald the pot (that is, rinse it well with boiling water), then place in it a teaspoonful of tea for every cup you want to make, plus one "for the pot." To get the right number of leaves for a reading, you'll need to make at least four cups. Swirl so that the leaves are distributed around the bottom and sides of the wet pot, to let the boiling water hit them all at the same time. Then pour the water (which should be at a fast, *rolling* boil) quickly over the tea. Let steep for five minutes in a warm place or under a tea cozy (a cloth cover for teapots). Just before you pour, swirl the pot again gently so that the leaves will be stirred up enough to flow through the spout and into the cup.

The sitter should be served first; the first cup is the "future's cup." Milk, sugar, or lemon won't affect the reading.

Preparing the Cup

The preparation of the cup—the first phase of the reading—is controlled by, and therefore tells the most about, the sitter. He should be in a relaxed but serious mood, ready to accept both the reading and *you*. Never begin a reading unless you're sure that the sitter is receptive—or you're not likely to get good results. "Read" the sitter before you read the leaves.

Now, wait until his cup is drained almost to the dregs—there should be no more than a spoonful of tea left. Ask him to take up the cup by the handle and swirl the tea three times—each time in a full circle, using his right hand, and turning the cup counterclockwise. Then, using his *left* hand, he is to up-end the cup quickly on the saucer, letting all the liquid drain away.

Take the cup (in your right hand) to begin studying the pattern that the leaves have made on its bottom and sides. (Remember: With this, as with *all* fortune-telling methods, you should practice a few times in advance to know roughly what to expect when looking at the leaf patterns.) Do take your *time* in examining the cup. The patterns are often hard to see at first, and the symbols difficult to make out; also, you want to give the occasion a ritual *seriousness*. Be leisurely . . . examine the cup from all directions, in a good light. If you have looked over the symbols and meanings that you'll find on the following pages, and are fully familiar with the meaning of the teacup's shape (we'll tell you about that in a minute), you'll have no trouble finding the sitter's fortune.

The Symbols and Their Placement in the Cup

When you read the leaves you will be looking at two things: at the patterns formed by the leaves themselves, and at the shape of the cup's inside. Of course, the leaf pattern will be different with every fortune; but the cup is a *constant*, and plays an important part in the reading.

First of all, the cup handle indicates the sitter. For instance, if a trail of leaves seems to lead from the handle of the cup toward the rim or the center, it will mean that the sitter will make a journey away from home, or that someone at his home will journey away from him. If a trail leads *toward* the handle, then he can expect visitors, or if he is away from home, can expect to return shortly.

The *body* of the teacup is also significant in the reading. Signs on the bottom refer to the *remote* future; as they move up toward the rim, they come closer and closer to the *present*.

The bottom and rim also affect the *meaning* of a symbol. For instance, a dog seen toward the rim of the cup means faithful friends; in the middle, friends are untrustworthy; at the bottom of the cup, secret enemies.

So, armed with this knowledge of the leaves' background—the cup— you are ready to see the pattern and to interpret it intelligently. Usually, the leaves fall into the outlines of various objects; figuring out these shapes is the largest and most delicate part of the reading. On the following pages, you'll find an alphabetical list of the most common tea-leaf symbols. Some of these are so important, however, that we will go into detail about them here.

KEY OBJECT-SYMBOLS AND WHAT THEY MEAN

The following patterns are shaped like objects, but they can often help you link a number of seemingly unrelated, simpler symbols:

ANCHOR: a lucky sign; success in business and constancy in love. If cloudy and indistinct, the meaning is reversed. An anchor on the *bottom* of the cup means great good fortune and happiness. Sometimes, in conjunction with other signs, such as a ship, a cannon, or a flag, it can mean news of someone in the navy or at sea.

BIRDS: good news. If the birds are flying, the news will come quickly; if at rest, it will be found on a fortunate journey.

BOTTLE: a very mixed sign. One bottle stands for pleasure. A row of bottles indicates sickness. Or, the

bottles may stand for someone whose work involves bottles, like a wine merchant, a chemist, a doctor.

BUILDING: generally considered to mean a move for the sitter or someone close to him. It may also refer to some specific building in the sitter's life (his house, for instance) or to some institution (the school he works in, if he is a teacher; his hospital, if he's a doctor). Position in the cup is very important—he may be going to or from the place in question; the journey may mean good or ill. A building with a flag close to it means connection with the government or entry into the army. A building with a tree on top means long life and prosperity for the home and family.

CLOCK: illness, death. If the clock face is cloudy, it means merely illness or anxiety about the future. If a seven or a nine can be seen on the clock face, there will certainly be a death in the family; even the sitter cannot feel safe. But if the hands read twelve, a secret meeting is planned.

LETTER or PARCEL: sign of news, good or bad. This is one of the most common designs, and one of the hardest to interpret. Any square or oblong shape can be read as a letter or parcel (depending on its size in relation to other designs), and only the context of the entire pattern in the cup can determine whether the news is good or bad. Near a cross, it is always bad; with a crown above, always good; near a circle or surrounded by a circle, a gift of money in the mail. The list is endless; be careful to interpret the sign by reference to the other signs nearby.

MOUNTAIN: a frequent symbol, may be interpreted many ways. A single one may mean powerful friends; many, equally powerful enemies. Sometimes, in conjunction with other signs, it means a spiritual journey for the sitter, a great psychic upheaval. It may also mean the changing of professions.

RING: usually means marriage; if an initial is found nearby, it will be that of the future spouse. If clouds are near the ring, or if it is indistinct, the marriage will be unhappy; if the ring is clearly formed and there are no adverse signs nearby, a good marriage. A ring down in the bottom of the cup means the wedding will be postponed; opposite the handle, it will not take place. Sometimes a ring will be large enough in relation to the other designs to be a circle, surrounding other objects; this can symbolize the family, or one's circle of friends. If it surrounds good omens, it means that friends are loyal and the sitter will be happy; that the family will find happiness. If the circle is broken or the other signs are bad, it can mean disloyalty, family tragedy, broken homes. Many small

circles are not seen as rings, but are interpreted differently.
(See **DOTS**, page 93.)

SNAKES: a complicated and invariably evil sign. A single snake may mean illness, bad luck, or a spiteful enemy; or it may mean anxiety due to repressed sexuality; or an evil and treacherous lover. Many snakes are a sign of impending disaster; great caution must be used to avert it.

TREES: almost always a good sign, denoting prosperity and long life. A single tree indicates recovery from illness; surrounded by dots, convalescence in the country with possibly a legacy to follow. A group of trees close together means impending trouble will be avoided. Many trees scattered over the cup mean general good luck. *Oak tree*: long life, good health, profitable business, and a happy marriage. *Palm tree*: success in any undertaking. A sign of children to a wife, and of a coming marriage to a young woman. *Pine tree*: continuous happiness.

OTHER TEA-LEAF SYMBOLS AND THEIR MEANINGS

Acorn: improvement in health, continued health; strength; good fortune
Airplane: unexpected journey; unsuccessful projects
Angel: good news, especially good fortune in love
Apples: long life; success in business
Arch: a journey abroad
Arrow: bad news in a letter
Axe: difficulties overcome
Balloon: temporary worries
Basket: an addition to the family; any pregnancy
Bat: fruitless journey, pointless tasks
Bear: a long journey
Beasts: (other than those specifically listed): misfortune

9

Beehive: business success; if bees are flying around it, great profit
Beetle: scandal
Bell: unexpected news; if more than one bell—a wedding
Bird cage: something in the way of happiness; if the cage door is open, an obstacle passing
Bird's nest: happiness in the home
Boat: a visit from a friend
Bouquet: one of the luckiest symbols—staunch friends, success, a happy marriage
Boomerang: someone is plotting
Boots: success at the end of a hard journey
Bow, or bow and arrow: scandal arising from a star-crossed love; adultery
Box: if the lid is closed, something that has been lost will soon be found; if the lid is open, trouble in love will pass
Bridge: a favorable journey; an opportunity leading to success
Bugle: hard work
Bull: slander by some powerful enemy
Bush: new friends
Butterfly: success and pleasure; if the other symbols are adverse, inconstancy
Camel: unexpected news; a burden to be patiently borne
Candle: sickness
Cannon: good fortune; news of a soldier
Car, carriage: approaching wealth, visits from friends
Cat: quarrels; treachery
Chain: an engagement
Chair: unexpected visitor
Castle: unexpected fortune
Chimney: risks in what you are about to do
Church: a legacy
Cigar: a new friend
Clouds: serious trouble; if surrounded by dots, financial success
Clover: a very lucky sign—happiness and prosperity; toward the rim of the cup, soon to arrive; toward the bottom, more distant

Coat: a parting
Coffin: long sickness or death of a near relation or great friend
Comb: a false friend
Comet: misfortune and trouble
Corkscrew: trouble caused by curiosity
Crab: an enemy
Cow: peaceful contentment
Crescent: a railroad trip
Crown: success and honor
Cup: success is at hand
Dagger: favors from friends
Dog: a favorable sign; toward rim of cup, faithful friends; in middle of cup, untrustworthy friends; at the bottom, secret enemies
Donkey: a legacy long awaited; bravery and patience needed
Dove: a lucky symbol—progress in affections
Dragon: great and sudden changes
Drum: a journey about new work; an important job interview
Duck: luck in business speculation
Eagle: a change for the better
Egg: new plans and hopes; news of a birth
Elephant: a lucky sign; good health; a trustworthy friend
Eye: triumph over a difficulty
Fan: a flirtation on the way
Fish: good news from abroad
Flag: danger from wounds inflicted by an enemy; the army, a soldier
Flowers: good fortune, success; an interesting marriage; a happy affair
Fountain: great success; generosity
Frog: success through change of work
Gallows: a sign of good luck; triumph over your enemies
Girafte: mischief caused by thoughtlessness
Goat: enemies; misfortune to a sailor
Gondola: a love affair at sea
Grasshopper: a great friend to become a soldier
Greyhound: a good end reached by hard work
Gun: disaster

10

Hammer: triumph over adversity; work that is not congenial

Hand: a good friend or loyal lover; if clenched, a quarrel; if pointing, look carefully to what it points at

Handcuffs: trouble

Harp: the beginning of an affair

Hat: a gift

Heart: pleasures to come; if surrounded by dots, through money; if accompanied by a ring, through marriage

Hen: increase in riches; a pregnancy

Hoe: work outdoors; hard work

Horse: desires fulfilled through a prosperous journey

Horseshoe: a lucky journey; success in choosing a partner

Hourglass: dangerous delays; imminent peril

Indian: news from afar

Ivy: honor and happiness through faithful friends

Jug: good health; a gathering of old friends

Kangaroo: a rival in business or love

Kettle: death or illness

Key: a change in occupation

Kite: years of travel ending in honor and dignity

Knife: broken friendship or parted lovers

Ladder: a rise in life

Leaf: encouragement for the future

Leaves: good fortune approaching

Lily: at top of cup, health and happiness, a virtuous wife or husband; at bottom, anger and strife

Lion: greatness through powerful friends

Man: a speedy visitor. If the arm is held out, he brings a present. If figure is clear, he is dark; if indistinct, he is blond.

Monkey: deception in love

Mushroom: a professional obstacle; a lovers' quarrel

Needle: talk about something you have done

Octopus: a danger signal; plotting for your downfall

Ostrich: trip by air over land and sea

Owl: an evil omen—sickness, poverty, disgrace, a warning against commencing any new enterprise. If the sitter is in love, he or she will be deceived

Padlock: if open, a surprise; if closed, a warning

Pear: fruition of long labors; a rich, passionate love affair

Pig: good and bad luck mixed; a faithful lover but envious friends

Pipe: thoughts of a man

Rabbit: success in a big city; a long journey; the return of an absent friend

Rider: good news from overseas regarding money

Rose: friendship

Saw: trouble brought about by strangers

Scissors: a misunderstanding in which an old friendship will be broken

Scale: a lawsuit; a divorce

Sheep: always a good omen

Shell: good news

Ship: a successful journey; thoughts of someone at sea

Shoe: a new job

Spider: money coming

Square: comfort, an easy life

Star: good luck on the way

Swan: good luck; ownership of land, perhaps with a body of water on it

Sword: antagonism between lovers; if broken, victory of an enemy

Telephone: trouble caused by forgetfulness

Tent: a lover's hideaway

Thimble: changes at home

Umbrella: annoyance and trouble; trivial difficulties

Unicorn: a secret marriage

Vase: news of recovery from illness

Violin: gaiety and good company; may refer to a musician

Wagon: a wedding trip in foreign lands; a sign of approaching poverty

Wheel: fulfillment of desire; an inheritance lost

Windmill: success in a precarious enterprise

Zebra: travel and adventure in foreign lands

THE CONNECTIVE
AND INTERPRETIVE SIGNS

These are not objects, but more abstract symbols. They can help you link a group of object-symbols into a meaningful pattern.

Cross: a sign of trouble and delay; it can even mean death. Much depends upon the context: For instance, a cross in conjunction with a parcel and an initial C may mean only that a parcel from a person whose initial is C will be delayed; or, if there are other and more ominous signs present, it may mean that a parcel bearing news of C's illness or death is on the way. In conjunction with a good-luck sign like the bouquet or the tree, it can mean conflict or the difficult achievement of happiness. Sometimes the cross modifies a good-luck symbol: For instance, with a crown (good fortune), it signifies death resulting in good fortune. When reading the leaves, the cross is one of the first signs to look for, not only because it is important in itself, but because of its effect upon the other signs.

Triangle & circle: both signs of *material* good fortune: gifts of money, or an unexpected legacy . . . . at the very least, presents or a visit from rich uncle!

Dots: extremely various in meaning. Because all teas are full of small particles, almost tea-dust, dots are likely to show around or near many symbols. They change the meanings of nearby symbols in a number of ways. They can indicate the country, as in dots surrounding a building. They can indicate money or good fortune: Dots surrounding a tree mean that a legacy will come from the country; surrounding a letter or parcel, the receipt of money or good news. When dots overlay or cloud another symbol, they indicate delay, or that the meaning of the symbol is reversed.

Line of dots: *Wavy line*— losses and annoyances; their importance depends upon how *numerous* the dots are, how *heavy*. Wavy lines with large breaks in them mean the relief of hardship. *Straight line*—a journey, usually pleasant. The length of the journey is measured by the length of the line; for the means of the journey, look for other symbols—a car, ship, airplane.

Number & initial: very important in indicating the specific content of the reading; its direct connection with the sitter. *Numbers* can tell you the dates when events will happen; can make doubtful signs clear by showing his lucky or unlucky numbers; can even, if seen on the hands of a clock or in conjunction with an hourglass, show you the time of day an event will occur. Some numbers are ambiguous—for instance, the birth date of the sitter (month or day) may mean good luck at that time, or may be a premonition of death. So that you can read intelligently, be sure that you ask the sitter what his birthday is. (He needn't tell you the year if he's determinedly vain, but it's best to have it.) *Initials* are most important because they connect the reading to people in the sitter's life. Be sure you know your sitter's full name (first, last, middle, nicknames), and try to know before the reading the initials of the people most important to him (his parents, his boss, his wife or former wife, and especially friends who are separated from him geographically), and look for them in the cup. Don't, by the way, forget that *you* may be a "significant other" to the sitter—keep your *own* initials in mind, too!

ith these major symbols (plus the glossary of simpler ones above), you're well on your way to an accurate understanding of what is going *on* in the sitter's teacup. *Don't* be intimidated by the seemingly *endless* possibilities. Yes, tea leaves can appear in patterns that will remind you of almost *any* object. But as you've seen from our lists, they do tend to fall into certain designs quite consistently, and many of the meanings are quite logical—just common sense. (Obviously a bouquet of flowers is a good omen, perhaps suggesting a wedding; and a coat means a parting, because what do you put *on* when you *leave?*)

Don't be afraid to let your imagination run free in interpreting a symbol that isn't listed here; and don't fear that you'll seem "unprofessional" if you look at this book during a reading. (Simply say, with an air of authority, that you must consult your charts.) After you've done a number of readings, you'll have the "feel" of how the patterns look and what they mean, and won't need to check the lists so often.

A final word about symbols: Whatever their "official" meanings, you must try to relate them to the sitter's personality and life. (This will be especially true for a symbol that isn't listed here—you'll be on your own and will need to be especially tuned in to the sitter's "vibes.") After all, the *sitter* is the one who drank from the cup and turned it to form the pattern of leaves. Be on the lookout not only for the designs listed here, but for the private symbols of the sitter's life. Tea-leaf reading is, above all, a *personal* art.

READING THE SYMBOLS—
THE ART OF INTERPRETATION

Now that you're familiar with the sitter's presence, the meanings of the cup shape and the symbols, it's time to read the leaves and see in them a coherent fortune, a line into the future and into the sitter's inner life.

This is the challenge of any fortune-telling method: to combine all the skeins of your knowledge into a whole that is both enlightening and entertaining—and perhaps even mysteriously accurate!

Do remember how important it is to go slowly in your interpretation. Give yourself plenty of time to see all that the cup shows you. Look at the general pattern, at its relation to the cup's handle, rim, bottom. If the leaves are bunched up near the handle, chances are the events of the fortune will occur close to the consultant, and will be largely concerned with his simple daily life. If the leaves are gathered at the side opposite the handle, geographically distant events will be foretold. A scattered all-over pattern indicates that the sitter's whole life will be affected. And don't forget the present-to-future rule: Check to see whether the leaves are more numerous toward the rim or on the bottom of the cup.

Once you've determined the over-all pattern of the leaves with relation to the cup, you are ready to pick out the major symbols formed by the leaves. Be sure to look for the large formations first, then go on to smaller designs. The large symbols are the most important; the small ones will modify the large ones.

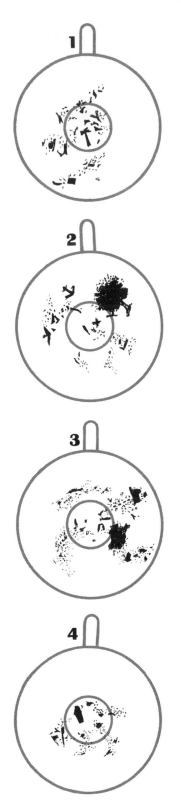

SAMPLE CUPS

1 *The most prominent symbol here is the axe in the bottom of the cup. Remember that the bottom is the remote future; the sitter's problems will be overcome then. Note, too, the many triangles—money may solve these problems! The hat (left) means a gift; and the rectangle near the bottom rim may be a letter. All in all, progressive good luck!*

2 *An immense tree is a super sign! This sitter is due for long life and prosperity, beginning soon (the tree is not far from the rim). But this fortune is modified a bit by the cross in the bottom of the cup—a bit of trouble in the distant future. The anchor and the flying bird (left) suggest a lucky piece of news, maybe with regard to money (all those coin-like dots).*

3 *This sitter may develop a relationship with someone who has the initial U (two in bottom of cup). A small p is also visible—check out the significance of these letters for him. Many other initials are scattered throughout, moving toward the present; are any of them his? The large mass (upper right) near rim looks like a house surmounted by a small tree—a sign of prosperity, and pleasantly near the present time! The large mass below reminds me of a Muppet— you'll use your own intuition.*

4 *Best to skip over this one quickly! The coffin in the bottom bodes ill, but the trails of dots lead away from the sitter (the handle), thank heavens!*

After you have a good grasp of what the larger symbols are and what their placement in the cup might mean, you must look carefully for connective signs—which bring the fortune together and connect it to the consultant. For instance, if you see a building, note whether there are dots around it (countryside), or if it has a straight line of dots leading toward or away from it (indicating a journey to or from the building). If there is a clear good-luck sign, try to find its modifying signs: Is it surrounded by dots? clear or cloudy? near an initial? near a number? Is there a clear line of dots, straight or wavy, linking it with any other sign? Or is it close to another major sign?

One of the most challenging situations in a reading is to find a major good-luck symbol near a major bad-luck symbol. The trick is to decide, in the light of the other elements in the cup, which is the dominant sign and which the modifier.

Finding the pattern and its major symbols may at first seem as hard as trying to find a pattern in the shifting leaves of a tree on a windy day. So to help you, we've included (on page 15) drawings of sample teacups with their contents, and accompanying descriptions and interpretations. They should help you find the patterns in your first reading.

Once you have a clear notion of the major elements present in the leaf-pattern, you can begin your interpretation. *Don't* simply stare silently at the cup for minutes at a time and then plunge into a fast and breathless interpretation. Your presentation will be hurried, and you'll give the impression of having given insufficient thought and attention to the sitter. Besides, such an approach will rob you of one of a fortune-teller's most valuable assets—the aid of the sitter. Getting helpful information from the sitter is not a trick, or a way to cheat him; *every* good fortune-teller freely admits that the co-operation of the sitter is the single most important element in a reading—except for the mechanics of the method itself.

After all, the fortune you're reading is the sitter's—and he knows a lot about himself. So—with the elements of the pattern firmly in mind, but with your mind *open* to the reactions, emotions, and vibrations of the sitter—begin presenting his fortune with a *tentative* authority. That is, be *definite* about the *information* you give, but do not immediately insist on its interpretation. Avoid expressions like, "I don't know what this means," or "I can't make this out at all." Start by pointing to a major symbol you're sure of, and then look inquiringly at the subject—he'll probably know how it relates to his life. For instance, you may see a large building in the bottom of the cup, surrounded by dots, as the biggest major design in the cup. Begin by saying, "In the distant future—perhaps over a year" (an inquiring look here), "I see a major move in your life, probably from city to country. From the size of the building" (point it out to him), "I would guess it means a change of job rather than a move to the suburbs, but let's see how the rest of the fortune works out." That last bit gives you a point of transition to the next major symbol, and leaves the sitter with an idea to exercise his intuition on—whether he has any feelings about a future change of job or move to the country.

Pause for a moment, looking into the cup, to let the information sink in, and then go on to the next symbol. If you've found a flower on the bottom near the building: "Of course, the flower here indicates that the move will be a happy one, perhaps the result of a promotion or a great new job, though flowers more often mean purely *personal* happiness. It seems that this move can give you *more* than just professional satisfaction."

By now, the sitter is probably ready to *inundate* you with comment. He may say that he's always dreamed of living and working in the country, or that he'd rather *die* than leave Detroit, or that he *hopes* he'll get the offer of a new job because he's beginning to go stale in the one he has. No matter *what* he says, listen carefully. Try to imagine how his current attitudes are likely to affect his future. What he says *now* should affect your reading. You may sense that though he *says* he'd want a change, he's really pretty settled and is unlikely to make much effort to move. In that case, you might modify your prediction of a move, indicate that perhaps he's going to undergo a great *psychic* upheaval instead; or, you might say that the move *will* occur, in fact, but that it will be a surprise to the sitter himself!

When modifying a previous reading, always use a symbol *in the cup* as a starting point. Don't be too *obvious* about responding to the sitter's suggestions and intuitions. Instead, *incorporate* them subtly and gently into the running commentary of your reading.

As you can see, a reading is really a collaboration between seer and sitter. It's very important for the sitter to believe the fortune-telling method is accurate *in itself*. If he believes that, his imagination and intuition are set free; if he's skeptical, he won't give you much feedback to help you. He must know, too, that *you* are the guiding force for the method (as of course you will be); but you should encourage him to feel that his observations and responses are important, that he is participating in the telling of his own fortune. This is just basic psychology—people are always more committed to something they've participated in than in something laid on them arbitrarily.

Tea-leaf reading is an especially collaborative method, since it is a domestic, *warm* ritual. Your authority does not depend upon your distance and aloofness, but upon your ability to involve the sitter with the method and your own personality. Since it begins with a friendly social activity—the brewing and drinking of tea—you've already come a long way toward winning his trust and faith. Add a large dash of your own warmth and interest, plus a firm sense of your faith in the authority of the leaves' pattern, and you can't fail to convince him of the power of the fates—and of your own charm and power as a real earth mother.

COFFEE GROUNDS

Coffee grounds, the near relatives of tea leaves, also give you the chance to tell a fortune in an atmosphere of warmth and domesticity—but they provide the added pleasures of the exotic, the unfamiliar—especially if the coffee is Turkish. Americans drink much more coffee than they do tea; it is not just a familiar drink—for some people, it is the familiar drink. Nevertheless, the ritual of brewing and drinking Turkish coffee will most likely be unfamiliar to your guests, unless they are frequenters of Near or Middle Eastern restaurants. Even so, they've probably never seen it brewed in someone's home. So you start with two advantages—the comfortable, and the mysterious.

THE MYSTIC MOOD

If you've been out to dinner and want to end the evening (or begin it?) with brandy and coffee, or dessert and coffee, at your place, you might want to do nothing more in the way of setting than just brew the coffee in the living room (see below for brewing instructions) and slip into something loose and alluring—like a caftan—to set the mood. The moment for fortune-telling grows naturally out of that time when one is looking into the heavy dregs at the bottom of the cup . . . it can be as easy as asking, "Penny for your thoughts?"

Of course, a full-dress affair to introduce your friends to your newly acquired knowledge and expertise might be more exciting—and with the resources of the East at your command, you can make quite an evening of it. Begin with the lighting of a fruity incense over drinks. (Never use a sweet or heavily spicy incense before a meal; and always remember to remove the incense *before* dinner is served.) If you're in the throes of redecorating, you might want to buy one of those fantastic hammered-brass tray-tables (or borrow one) and seat your guests around it on large pillows.

Dinner itself should be hearty and in the style of the Near East: baked kibbe (lamb pillows) with rice or wheat *pilaf; pita* (flat bread); a green salad with chick-peas and a lemon-and-mint dressing; for dessert, baklava, then Turkish coffee, and *you* as the desert seer. (See pages 19-20 for recipes, and page 277 for where to buy.)

After the dessert is cleared, light the incense again, and serve brandy or some other dry after-dinner drink (liqueurs are just *too* sweet after the heavy-honey taste of baklava). By the time your guests are thinking about a second brandy, they should be done with their coffee and ready for you to foretell their futures from the bottom of the cup.

Of course, you should *dress* the part, since this particular part is so exotic. By now, it's pretty much accepted that you don't have to be an Arab to wear a caftan, or to have been born east of Constantinople to wear harem pants. So, pick whichever of these looks suits your style. (It *is* true that small girls look better in harem pants, and of course we've seen how grand big girls look in caftans.) Whichever look you like, take some pains to make it more authentic than you would otherwise.

A Near Eastern specialty store will have *authentic* caftans, striped and tasseled. With it, don't overdo the make-up, except on the eyes; they should be as large and dark as you can get them. (Lately, some girls are going back to the old-fashioned look of kohl to get this effect, and several cosmetics companies make a kohl-like product.) Use brown or plum shadow, darken your brows slightly, and use dark-brown mascara heavily but smoothly. Wear a pale ivory base, but no blusher or highlighter: What you're after is a smooth, pale look under great, all-seeing eyes. Jewelry should be massive and fine—a silver horse-collar and band bracelet, perhaps.

The harem-girl effect can be much brighter. Use mascara color-keyed to eyeshadow, vivid rouge and highlighter. Don't *trivialize* the look, however—if you're going to be taken seriously as a fortune-teller, you can't come on as a bubble-headed forty-fifth concubine. (And come to think of it, why would you want to do that, anyway?) If you're small, and like the effect, you might want to do your hair in a close-curled twenties frizz, and wear a headache band—the band will suggest both the harem and the gypsy cara-van, and call attention to your eyes, which should be as prominent, in their brighter way, as the Arab lady's. The harem girl can, of course, wear bangles—but not too many! (You don't want to *jingle* as you hold the coffee cup.) Enhance bare feet with an ankle chain or toe ring. And if you're *brave*, try a face jewel—a tiny fake stone pasted on the side of your nose, just over the bridge of the nose, or at the edge of the bone just under your eyebrow.

The styles of dress we've described are really designed to fit two types of personality and two ways of telling fortunes with the coffee grounds. If you wear the caftan, you will probably be quieter, and so want to tell your fortunes from a greater distance, closer to the fates, farther from your subject. The harem girl is warmer, more intimate—a Scheherazade of a seer, telling fortunes as if there were a thousand and one nights and all of them were to be filled with pleasure. If you choose the style that suits you, you'll have no trouble convincing your consultant that you speak with the authority of the future, because you will be speaking out of an image that's *real* to you.

TURKISH COFFEE

To brew *perfect* Turkish coffee, you need just three things: the coffee itself, an *ibruk* (or long-handled brass pot), and some plain demitasse cups (no complicated patterns please).

Turkish coffee comes in several can-sizes. (Never buy more than the small, half-pound tins, and store in refrigerator to keep fresh). In consistency, it's somewhere between old-fashioned instant coffee and the finest-grind fresh-roasted coffee: Actually, it is stone-ground to a powder, which will sink to the bottom of the cups and become the medium for your reading.

Ibruks come in several sizes, from the two-cup to the eight-cup. It's a good thing to have a couple: one for *café-à-deux,* another for larger crowds. Actually the larger size is more useful. Buy a four-or six-cup pot. Because the coffee made in an *ibruk* is so strong and (usually) so sweet, you'll want to serve it in demitasse cups—plain or pale-colored ones if you'll tell fortunes from the grounds. Cups should also be round-bottomed (so that the grounds will adhere properly to the bottom *and* rim for a good clear reading) and, if possible, slightly bigger than average, for a clear view of the inside.

To make Turkish coffee: **1**/Pour a demitasse cup of water for each cup of coffee into the *ibruk*, and heat to lukewarm. (It should just begin to steam at the surface.) **2**/Add a heaping teaspoon of coffee for each cup of water. (The Turks and the Arabs and the Greeks and all people who drink their coffee this way also add a heaping teaspoon of sugar for each cup of water. The coffee

comes out syrupy-sweet and even stronger-tasting. However, *you* may want to leave out the sugar and let your guests sugar to taste in the cup. Over to you.) **3**/Stir the coffee into the water and heat over a low flame until the coffee foams up madly in a boil. As soon as the foam comes up, remove from heat, divide the foam among the cups. Put pot back on flame, and bring coffee to boil twice more, each time dividing foam. Then pour each cup full to the brim.

As you've surmised, all the gounds (*mud* is a more descriptive word) go with the coffee into the cups, and sink to the bottom. Only about three-quarters or two-thirds of the cup is drunk. The dregs remain, and it is from them that you will take your readings.

18

DINNER FROM THE EAST

DOLMA
(Stuffed Grape Leaves)

FETA CHEESE & GREEK OLIVES

BAKED KIBBE
(with Pita and Onion Pilaf)

MINTED SALAD

BAKLAVA

TURKISH COFFEE

The nicest thing about this elaborate-looking (and exotically delicious) meal is that both the first course (or hors d'oeuvres) and the dessert come straight out of the store to you. The dolma can be bought in cans; the baklava is available at your local Middle Eastern bakery or restaurant; and the feta and Greek olives are available wherever there's a delicatessen or Middle Eastern grocery. As for the rest, "baked kibbe" translates "baked ground lamb" and is as easy as meat loaf. The not-at-all-complicated recipes follow:

BAKED KIBBE
1½ lbs. ground lamb (Buy lamb patties at the super-
    market, or have your butcher grind up some
    boneless lamb stew meat.)
¼ lb. pine nuts (available at Middle Eastern grocery
    or gourmet food shop)
2 medium-sized onions, chopped
1 medium-sized green pepper, chopped
1 egg
2 heaping tbsp. plain breadcrumbs
3 tbsp. ketchup
1 tsp. cinnamon (yes, cinnamon)
salt, pepper to taste
2 tbsp. olive oil

Combine all the ingredients except the olive oil; mix well with your own clean hands. Shape mixture into little pillow shapes. (You should end up with about twelve to sixteen of them.) Heat the olive oil in a heavy oven-proof skillet until it sizzles when you drop a bit of water into it; sauté the meat pillows gently, turning, until they're brown on all sides. (Don't crowd the pan; they'll have trouble browning.) Set them aside on a platter, while you make, in the same skillet:

THE SAUCE

Fat from frying the meat (about two tbsp.)
1 medium-sized onion, chopped
½ cup raisins
½ cup chopped parsley
1½ tsp. cinnamon
1 large (no. 10) can whole tomatoes
salt, pepper to taste
Small can tomato paste (optional)

Sauté the onion over medium heat until transparent; add the raisins, parsley (of which you should reserve 2 tablespoons), and cinnamon, and cook gently until the parsley is dark and the raisins are plumped. Add the *drained* tomatoes, cinnamon, and salt and pepper. (Save the tomato liquid to mix with half a cup of water and a bouillon cube for a late-night, low-calorie snack.) Break the tomatoes up with a spoon, and let cook gently until the sauce begins to thicken. (If you like a richer sauce, add 2 tablespoons tomato paste.)

Then, tuck the meat pillows into the sauce, filling the skillet, and place in a 375° oven for 20 to 30 minutes, until the meat is well done and the sauce is quite thick. Serve in the skillet or on a platter over rice pilaf, sprinkled with the reserved parsley. Serves four.

RICE PILAF

1 cup long-grain rice
1 medium-sized onion, chopped
3 tbsp. chopped parsley
½ cup currants
4 tbsp. olive oil (or melted butter)
2 cups boiling chicken broth

Heat chicken broth, keep over low flame until needed. Heat the olive oil in a saucepan over a low flame until quite hot, but not sizzly. Add the chopped onion and sauté gently until translucent; pour in the currants, and heat until they're plump. Add the rice, and toss in the pan with a large spoon, cooking gently until *it* turns translucent. As soon as it does, add *boiling* broth, pop a lid on it, and cook over *very* low flame for 20 minutes. Turn off heat and let rice sit, covered, for 15 minutes. Add the chopped parsley, stir once with a fork, and turn into a serving dish or onto a platter to receive the lamb.

MAKE-AHEAD MINTED SALAD

½ large head romaine lettuce
½ small head Boston lettuce
1 tbsp. dried mint, or 3 tbsp. fresh mint, chopped

THE DRESSING
6 tbsp. olive oil
1½ tbsp. fresh lemon juice
½ tsp. sugar
salt, pepper to taste

Mix the dressing in a screw-top bottle. If you're using dried mint, add to the dressing now. Refrigerate.

Then, using the Kate Woodbridge never-fail-salad-greens method, wash and dry the lettuce. Separate the lettuce leaves, and wash each one. Shake off loose water. Then, take a large and thirsty roll of paper towels and put a leaf or two of lettuce at the free end (only one layer, please). Roll the leaves in the towel. Add another leaf or two and repeat. Keep adding and rolling until you have a large roll of paper-towel-and-lettuce-leaves. Store in the refrigerator until needed, up to three days. (Honest!) When ready to use, unroll as much towel as you need lettuce, break into the bowl containing your dressing, and toss! If you're using fresh mint, toss with the salad *after* you've added the dressing. (The nicest thing about this method is that you can prepare one or two heads of lettuce and put them in the refrigerator to keep. You'll never again have that I'd-love-a-salad-for-dinner-but-I'm-too-bushed-to-wash-greens feeling again.)

Serving Suggestions

The dolma is good cold. Just chill the can, but open and put on a platter about 15 minutes before serving time. Pile them in a pyramid shape on a plate, pour two tablespoons of lemon juice over them, and decorate with round lemon slices or wedges.

Serve the feta on a cheese board surrounded with water biscuits or your favorite crackers, and accompanied by a bowl of the pungent, wrinkled Greek olives. All this can come to the serving table with drinks, or be offered as a first course.

The lamb and rice can be served separately, of course; if you're doing dinner buffet style, they're easier to take from the same platter, and look prettier that way, too. The *pita* should be warmed in the oven. Just tuck it in with the kibbe for the last five minutes or so.

Baklava is served straight out of the baker's box onto a dessert plate and is delicious that way—but if you want to fancy it up, heat some honey and pour a bit over each portion at the last minute. A small dessert fork is appropriate for eating this if you don't want to pick it up with your fingers.

Everything on this menu except the rice can be done the night before. For the lamb: Cook to the point where it goes into the oven; on the night, simply transfer from refrigerator to oven, and allow about five minutes more than given in the recipe. For the salad: Make the dressing and store in a bottle. Use Sister Kate's method with the lettuce, and store in the refrigerator until the party night, when you can proceed with the salad instructions given earlier. The balance is easy: Simply cook the rice, arrange the first course and dessert. Voila!

Preparing the Cup

When the coffee has been drunk almost to the dregs (which will cover the bottom of the cup), ask the subject to pick up the cup in his left hand and swirl it three times, clockwise. (The movement should be *vigorous*.) Then, still using his left hand, he should up-end the cup in the saucer and turn it slowly three times conterclockwise. Ask him to hand you the cup in its saucer with his right hand; you receive it with *your* right hand, and turn it up for the reading with your left.

As with the tea leaves, your examination of the dregs should be leisurely and serious; with coffee, hold the cup *extra* carefully, because there is a greater chance that the grounds will change in pattern if you jiggle them.

If there is more than one fortune to tell, you will of course read the cups one at a time. Perform the ritual carefully, keeping up one-to-one eye-contact with the subject as you read his cup and tell his fortune. If possible, move from subject to subject to create an intimate connection with each.

THE SYMBOLS AND
THEIR PLACEMENT IN THE CUP

As with tea-leaf reading, the shape of the cup's inside is an important background for the coffee grounds. The handle represents the sitter, his psychic center for the reading. It also represents geographical east—because the method originated in the East, and because Mohammedans in the Occident face east, toward Mecca, when they pray.

The symbols for coffee grounds are largely the same as for tea leaves, with some important exceptions and additions. The all-important dots of the tea-leaf pattern will be missing; instead, there will be a series of lines almost like the dune marks in sand, which are formed when the subject swirls the cup. The *direction* of these lines is very important to any fortune told with coffee grounds.

Watch them with the closest attention: Do they lead *toward* or *away from* the handle? If they tend toward it, fate favors the sitter; away from it, he is being sapped by life. Too, he may be destined to journey east if the lines are moving toward the handle; west, if away from the handle.

You'll also see hills and valleys formed by the grounds. They are read like the rim and bottom of the teacup. The hills represent the present or near-present; the valleys, the future.

Be sure to notice how the coffee grounds have mounted up the sides of the cup. If the mounting is *away from* the handle, the sitter will succeed in a public life; if the mounting is *toward* the handle, the subject will become more and more introspective, will find his life moving inward along some spiritual path. If there is no mounting of the sides, he can expect his life to be in balance, to continue evenly.

Whereas with tea leaves you depend upon individual leaves on a white ground to show you a series of symbols, be prepared to see a much more dense picture in the coffee cup.

Almost the entire bottom of the cup will be covered with the brown, powdery-fine residue. You'll see pictures both in the grounds themselves and in the white spaces made by the swirling of the cup. Both these sets of images—the negative and the positive—are important to the reading.

Although you will see just as many images in the coffee cup as you did in the teacup, the *over-all* pattern of the coffee grounds is much more significant. In fact, often with tea leaves it is necessary to connect the images by intuition; with coffee grounds, the symbols are likely to form a completely connected pattern. Just watch for it, and be prepared to interpret designs as they appear against the larger background. (You'll find a sample cup diagram below.)

The most clear sign here is the trail of coffee leading toward the handle. The sitter will turn inward, and his success will be spiritual or personal rather than public. It *will* be success—see star in bottom and crown at lower right?

READING THE SYMBOLS—
THE ART OF INTERPRETATION

Interpretation follows the same method for coffee grounds as for tea leaves; the difference is in the *style*, not in the technique. Remember, again, to go slowly into an interpretation, to gain the subject's confidence and co-operation, and to show both authority and modesty. But when reading coffee grounds, try also to *remove* yourself slightly from the subject—imply, ever so subtly, that you possess secrets that he cannot have. Without taking yourself too far away from the here-and-now, the domestic scene in which you are friend and hostess, suggest that there is another, more exotic world and that you have access to it. You will still invite the sitter's comment and response, but you must keep yourself more aloof from it. Rely upon the message in the cup, and enrapture the sitter with the seriousness in your eyes.

You'll find that the method itself will aid you in this different attitude. Because the over-all picture in the cup is so important, you can begin your reading by making a general—and perhaps somewhat mysterious— statement about the feeling-tone you get from the cup. For instance, you can draw quick conclusions from the amount of white space showing in the cup, the way the grounds have (or have not) mounted the sides, and the central image in the bottom of the cup. Say immediately, "I feel great good (or ill) fortune here," or "This subject is striving inward; let us see how he is going on," or "There is great worldly ambition in this cup. Let's see whether that is a good or a bad thing, and whether it will be successful ambition." A quick preliminary reading like this will give you a solid basis on which to build the rest of your fortune, and will provide just the right note of exotic distance that the method requires.

A NOTE ON THE
IRISH METHOD
WITH COFFEE GROUNDS

The Irish have a charming and easy method of fortune-telling with *regular* coffee grounds; it is used to tell "horary," or twenty-four-hour, fortunes. Make coffee by boiling water in an enamel pot and adding a tablespoon of coffee (drip grind) and one eggshell for every cup of water, plus one for the pot. Remove from the heat and let brew for five minutes. Take out the eggshell. Pour without straining.

Read the grounds exactly as you would for tea leaves, but using the handle of the cup as twenty-four o'clock (as in the military timetable: 100—1 A.M.; 1200—noon; 1300—1 P.M.; 2400—midnight). Read the sitter his fortune for the coming day, beginning with midnight to 3 A.M., and moving around the imaginary clock-face in three-hour clumps. Look for appropriate symbols in each area of the imaginary clock. This kind of fortune, of course, emphasizes small details: You might see, for instance, a delay in getting to work the next morning, a disagreement at the office, a surprise at the end of the day.

CEROMANCY
(WAX IMAGES)

Of all the methods of fortune telling we'll describe in this book, ceromancy is most mysterious in its origins. Practically all that we know is that divination by both candle wax and sealing wax are very important among Spanish-speaking peoples. The fortune-tellers of Spanish Harlem use candles to answer the questions of their clients, and to make wishes come true.

The Romans had a word for wax (cere), and "ceromancy," meaning divination by wax, has come down to us. But whether the Romans practiced ceromancy is another question. It is true that they did not have candles, but used oil lamps. (Wax was used chiefly for depilation, especially of men's bodies; it was the fashion among Roman men, and Greek men before them, to appear nude and hairless in the public baths and at sports.)

In medieval western Europe, wax had a double importance: Candles were the chief mode of lighting, and wax was used to seal important documents of state, signifying, by the impression made on the wax, the origin, authority, and confidentiality of the papers.

Probably wax was not used for divination before the invention of the wax candle and the use of wax as a seal of kings. For a substance to be considered a fit medium for fortune telling, it must have some *importance* to those who use it—either an occult significance, as with cards or magic numbers, or a more homely meaning. Candles were the chief source of light in Europe for hundreds of years; and even after they lost their practical usefulness, they remained an important part of religious rituals. Although the mark of the king's ring on an unbroken wax seal is no longer the stamp of true authority, many people still buy and use sealing wax to give their correspondence a touch of the personal and the confidential. These two ancient uses of wax make it a fitting and potent medium for divination; we'll discuss the use of both kinds of wax in making images that tell the future.

THE MYSTIC MOOD

Because ceromancy is chiefly a Spanish method, you'll perhaps want to evoke some of the somber excitement of the *fado* and the bull ring when you begin your reading of wax images.

Spanish women are traditionally pictured as dark, but remember that Castilian Spaniards are classically blond and blue-eyed, so that no matter what your coloring, you can dress the part. The Spanish look is, contrary to what you may think, almost *austere*: Black and white is a favorite color combination, and the hair is often, Katy Jurado style, pulled back severely from the forehead and done in a great chignon on the nape of the neck. Set large spit-curls in front of each ear, matching in size a great pair of hoop earrings. If you're dark, try a flamenco-ruffled black dress with a red rose between your breasts; blondes can get the same effect with white. Both should make-up with a true red lipstick, bold clear colors, and dark mascara. The result of both make-up and costume should be simple and dramatic.

One of the best ways to set a Spanish scene is to use the music of Spain—whether you like the classical guitar of Segovia or the flamenco music of Montoya, or are passionate about the high wail of the *fado*, you'll find that the rhythm will give you the mood.

Keep in mind that Spanish fortune-telling differs from that of other countries in its fatalism. *Que sera, sera* is more than just a song title—it's a pervasive cultural attitude. The Spanish do not expect to *control* the future by foretelling it; they are given to resignation, to placing themselves in the hands of the fates and shrugging gracefully at the whimsical turns of the wheel of fortune.

Equipment and Preparation

There are two basic variations of the wax-imagery method. One uses the wax direct from candles (they can be the ones you've lighted the table with for dinner); the other uses sealing wax from one of the wands you can buy in a stationery store. They are different only in preparation—reading is the same.

Candle Wax: Use a large black or red columnar candle, which you've let burn for at least an hour. (You'll need a good pool of wax gathered around the wick at the top.) You'll want a round, shallow dish of cold, but not iced, water, to drop the wax into. (Iced water will crack the wax as it sets.) Be sure that the dish is either white or a light color, so that the wax will show up nicely.

Sealing Wax: Buy a wand of sealing wax from a stationery store, and cut it in thirds. One third will melt down to a good amount for a fortune. Using a large serving spoon or a small ladle (preferably one you won't need for anything else—getting the wax off is murder!), the sitter melts the wax over a candle, then tips it all at once into the dish of water.

FORTUNE OF THREE

I t's fun, using either of the variations, to tell three fortunes for the same sitter. Use red, gold, and black wax: red for his sex or love life, gold to foretell his financial fortune, and black to see the length and general happiness of his life. If you use candles, let them burn, standing in a row, for the same length of time, then let the sitter tip them over into each of three separate dishes. If you use the sealing wax, melt the colored waxes over the candle and tip each quickly into separate dishes.

25

The Method

For both variations, make sure the sitter takes the wax and drops it himself into the dish, using his *left* hand. The reader holds his right hand in her left, so that their arms form an arc around the dish or dishes. As the wax falls into the water, it will form a kind of spreading puddle, which quickly sets in the cold water. The shape of this puddle tells the fortune. Watch carefully as the sitter drops the wax, saying softly, "Let the future . . . be present." The last two words should be spoken just as the wax hits the water.

Wait quietly until the wax sets. (If you're doing the Fortune of Three, repeat the process *exactly* for the other waxes.) Then, still holding the sitter's right hand in your left, look with him at the shapes formed by the wax, starting with the first color.

Since there will be only a single shape (even though it might be complex), your findings will be more limited than with tea leaves or coffee grounds. So you'll need all the help you can *get* from the sitter. Sometimes a generalized shape is perfectly visible (a heart, a cross, a house), but often the shape will be private, connected to the sitter's life. Question him closely about his associations with the shape. (The English witch Sybil Leek once found a map of the English Channel in her dish; the reader couldn't have known it, but Sybil's son was to sail the Channel later that month.) Of course, you will have looked over the glossary of symbols and the sample wax shapes given below, but do let your imagination—and the sitter's—run over the shape as well, to gain other insights. Don't try to see *too* much in one shape, especially if you're doing the Fortune of Three. Remember to associate to the subject of each color (money, sex and love, long life) and not to get sidetracked—or the wax is likely to fool you!

Special hints: As you'll notice in the list of symbols following, *broken* wax often *reverses* the meaning of a shape, or otherwise modifies it. Also be on the lookout for the *direction* in which the shape faces; for example, a tree or heart that is formed from the sitter's point of view, but looks upside down to you, refers to him; in a reversed position, it refers to someone else in his life. (This is a good time to get up and lean over his shoulder to examine the shape from his direction.)

26

SYMBOLS
IN CEROMANCY

Cross: *a religious experience;
difficulties and great danger to
overcome; if turned sideways to form an
X, it tells a seeker to keep moving
on—he'll find the answer. If the wax
breaks or cracks: a broken promise, lost
faith, or (but less likely) the difficulty
overcome*

Flag or Banner: *great undertaking
begun, and attachment to the
government or the armed services;
occasionally, though not often, bad
beginnings*

Flower: *great good luck in the
immediate future, especially in
connection with the family; a
pregnancy looked forward to; a new
affair, a marriage approaching; good
luck in all things*

Heart: *great concern with sex and love;
a sign of the most passionate nature, or
of a totally involving love affair or
marriage. If cracked or broken, a
tragically ended love affair; betrayal*

Square or Oblong: *a letter or parcel
coming; if cracked or broken, bad news*

Tree: *long life and health, a prosperous
time and flourishing days ahead*

Figure Eight or Hourglass: *the sign of
infinity, eternity; indicates fidelity,
steadfastness, loyalty through hard
times. Sometimes means death to come
for someone near*

Skull: *not necessarily a bad sign. Be
wary, the past is catching up with you*

Circle: *the nearer a perfect circle, the
more fulfilled the life. Not necessarily a
happy sign, but one of great
productivity. The sign for philosophers,
great executives, all those of industry
and determination in their work*

Triangle: *can mean a triangle in love
(not necessarily an unhappy one),
conflict in any area. Pay careful note to
whether it is equilateral or not: Where
are the long sides with relation to the
sitter? the apex? If perfect and
unbroken, can mean good luck and gifts
of money*

Bell: *news on the way*

Animal shapes: *see the tea-leaf glossary (pages 8-11) for meanings of these symbols*
Crown: *your efforts rewarded*
Building: *a significant move; perhaps a new job, a transfer to another city, or simply a new house or apartment. Cracked or broken: Reconsider any move*
Mountains: *high ambition; if the peaks are clear, successful; if the peaks are blunted, doubtful. Alternatively, may mean that there are hard times, great trials ahead, which may require enormous strength. Message does not reverse if cracked or broken—it intensifies*
Clouds: *beware trouble ahead. If cracked or broken, expect a silver lining that will soon brighten present troubles*

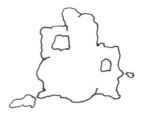

Other Methods of Using Wax

One of the most fascinating methods of wax divination is the Simple Question. Set nondripless lighted candle (beeswax is best) of any color in the middle of a table, out of drafts and directly in front of the sitter. He may ask one question, answerable only with "Yes" or "No." If, as the candle burns down, the wax drips more to his left side, the answer is "No." If it drips more to his right, the answer is "Yes." If it drips directly toward or away from him, the oracle refuses to answer—he must ask again some other time.

Some candles are specially produced to foretell—or affect—the future. They come in a variety of colors, and you burn them for several days to make your wish come true or to get a definite answer to a question. (See page 276 for where to buy.)

ORACLES, OMENS
AND OTHER RANDOM SIGNS

The true believer in divination does not assume that only the methods she designs or controls will give a reading of the future. The facts of nature and of our daily lives have always had a deep relationship to our present and future lives. Learning to read from the simple facts of life, from the signs of nature, from the movements of the world around you, is a part of prophecy as old as man and his curiosity about the world. It takes no special preparation, no equipment but your quick eyes and lively perceptions. The models for interpretation are as old as the hills and just as beautiful.

SIGNS IN FOOD AND DRINK

Of course, tea and coffee are both beverages. But as we said in the sections devoted to reading their dregs, both were exotic drinks originally, and a special set of rituals grew up around both the drinking and the readings. The importance of most foods is simpler, but closer to the bone—man cannot live by bread alone, but he certainly can't live at all without it. The food we prepare and eat is so important that many people from earliest times have claimed to be able to read the future from the signs left by food. Keep an eye out for some of the ones that follow—whether you're just looking for a good conversational gambit or are making a serious observation.

Fruit: 1/ An *apple* peeled in a single long spiral brings good luck; if the spiral is dropped on the ground—tossed lightly—it will spell out the initial of the peeler's true love. **2/** Wind an *apple* stem, reciting the alphabet with every turn. Whichever letter the stem breaks on is the initial of one's fated love. **3/** If a pregnant woman winds a *pear* stem, counting, she'll have a boy if it breaks on an even number, a girl if it breaks on an odd one. **4/** When eating an *orange*, think of a question as you peel it; then save the seeds. If the number is even, the answer is "Yes"; if odd, "No." **5/** To share a *pomegranate* brings good luck. (Recipe for a happy afternoon: one pomegranate, a bottle of good champagne, and two glasses.) **6/** Unripe *persimmons* foretell bad luck, a soured, a bitter life.

Wine: The precious liquid from the fermented grape has been used, ever since its invention, in religious rites and magical ceremonies of all kinds: Libations have been poured to the gods; great toasts have been drunk to honor the bride and groom, the newly born, good luck; and intoxication itself was once thought to be a way to communicate with deities and other great spirits. One of the most beautiful and classical rituals was inherited from the Greeks, and you can use it, too, either formally at dinner, or more casually at a picnic. After dinner, when the last of the Burgundy is at the bottom of each glass, toss a large white napkin, open, onto the floor, and invite your guest to throw, with a single motion of the wrist, the lees of the wine onto the napkin. The initial, numeral, or other symbol that the wine forms will suggest his fate. At a picnic, perform the same ritual with white or red wine thrown on the bare earth (or, at the beach, on the sand). In this case, both of you should throw the wine—your fates should intertwine somewhere if you've shared the same bottle.

Salt: Deeply important to man's survival, salt also gives savor to food. It has an especially great significance in the desert, where it is needed to keep men from dying of dehydration, and where it is scarcest. **1/** The Arabs considered that it was bad luck to ask an enemy to share your salt (eat a meal)—only true friends should have that honor. (Remember this next time you feel you have to "pay back" a dinner or lunch to someone whose motives you suspect.) **2/** To pass salt unconsciously from hand to hand (without setting the cellar or shaker down on the table) is to invite bad luck; to do so consciously is to cement a bond between the passer and the receiver. **3/** To salt someone else's meat at table makes you necessary to him in some way. **4/** And, of course, to spill salt is bad luck, omen of a coming quarrel—until you toss some over your right shoulder.

SIGNS IN NATURE

Animals: Bat: to see one in the daytime means a long journey; bad luck to see one at night, especially if it is heard to cry while flying. **Cat:** a very complicated omen. A faithful cat for a pet is a good sign, especially if it is black; if a cat suddenly leaves your house, it is a sign that death or other catastrophe will follow. A strange black cat crossing your path is bad luck; even worse if he visits your house without warning. Drive him away before he leaves of his own accord! **Dog:** coming to your house, means faithful friends, a favorable sign; to hear one howling at the moon is a prefiguration of death, though it gives no indication where death will strike. **Goat:** good luck. **Cow:** good luck if one comes into your garden gate or onto your lawn. **Hare:** bad luck, especially if it crosses your path. **Hedgehog:** a lucky omen, especially if he is facing in the opposite direction. **Horse:** a white horse seen by lovers is good luck; a piebald horse is good luck, unless seen tail first, when it may mean a friend's misfortune. **Mouse:** field mouse (white or brown) brings happiness, especially in love; grey means the threat of danger, a storm impending. **Pigs:** to see a male pig after marriage means bad luck; but to see a sow coming toward you is good luck, unless she turns away. **Rat:** running in front of you, means treacherous servants or business associates and losses through enemies; to see a white rat sitting up is good luck. **Sheep:** if seen in a flock, approaching, good luck; a lamb jumping means a happy birth is approaching. **Squirrel:** happiness is to be found through hard work. **Snake:** if it crosses your path, it means spiteful enemies and bad luck; you can reverse the luck by killing it.

Birds: Crow: a bad omen, especially if seen perching to the left. **Cuckoo:** heard, it foretells prosperity and a merry life, especially if the voice comes from your right. **Dove:** a happy sign, especially for engaged couples; a good omen for a new affair. **Gull:** settling on a ship, foretells a happy voyage; if a gull in flight touches anyone, it is a sign of sudden death approaching. **Hawk:** powerful enemies are watching. **Kingfisher:** scandal threatens. **Magpies:** one, bad luck; two, good luck; three, a wedding; four, a birth. **Nightingale:** lucky for lovers. **Owl:** always bad luck. Continued hooting near you means ill health; three long hoots are a sign of death. **Robin:** good luck, new beginnings. **Raven:** death to the aged; trouble generally. **Sparrow:** very good fortune, especially in early spring; if they build their nests under your eaves, good luck will follow. Disastrous to kill one. **Wren:** good luck, but very bad luck to harm or frighten it.

Insects: Ant: a nest near your home is a good sign, but avoid a bite—it means quarrels and strife. **Bee:** good luck if it is trapped in your room, but you must not catch it or the luck will change. **Cricket:** a universal sign of good luck, especially if heard clearly from the hearth or the center of the house. If they suddenly abandon a house, death and disaster follow. **Death-watch beetle:** an equally universal sign of bad luck, especially death. **Grasshopper:** in the house, some great friend or famous person will visit; elsewhere, a journey, good luck. **Ladybird:** betokens visitors; good luck to find one with seven spots on its back. **Spider:** a very complicated omen. Seen in the morning, it means grief, at noon anxiety; in the evening, financial loss. But to see the little red spider means good luck in money matters, and long-legged spiders bring good luck. A spider spinning a web means people are plotting. To kill one brings misfortune. **Wasp:** to be stung means danger through jealousy or envy.

THE TRAVELING
FORTUNE-TELLER

Using the signs above and a few more, long car trips can become adventures in prophecy. (It's even possible to enliven a Saturday morning trek on the Long Island Railroad.)

As the list above indicated, white horses are a good sign for lovers. There is a wish-spell to extend this omen: Count each white horse you see, "stamping" him by licking your right thumb, pressing it into your left palm, and then hitting the wet spot on the palm with your right fist. For a short journey, twelve horses will answer a question or grant a wish; for a long journey, you must find fifty. In the fall, look for loaded hay wagons and make a wish; the chant goes, "Hay, hay, bale of hay/Make a wish and look away." It's bad luck to look again; your wish won't come true. Scan the horizon every now and again: A forked, bare tree against the sky foretells a bad time in a quarrel; a fully rounded tree will bring harmony in the evening.

Cloud divination is dreamy, almost like walking in your sleep—perfect for lazy afternoons in the country or from the window of a car. (It's the perfect convertible pastime.) Pick a day when the sky is full of big, heavy cumulus clouds. (It doesn't matter whether it's sunny or grey, as long as the clouds are plentiful and visible.) Divide the sky into four quadrants—left front, right front, left rear, right rear. Ask your companion (the driver) to pick a quadrant, any quadrant, and ask a question of it. Then you must study the patterns the clouds make and see if they hold the answer to the question. The questions asked are often good indicators of what's in that man's mind, and the answers are usually to be found right there, hovering in the sky.

HOBO SIGNS

A traveling fortune-teller might also happen upon these *man-made* signs, chalked on trees or buildings by hoboes. See if you can spot them, and interpret them the way you would the random signs explained above.

Tell Pitiful Story

Doctor

Unsafe Place

Kind-hearted Woman

Wealth

31

Chapter Two

CARTOMANCY
PLAIN AND FANCY

PLAYING CARDS

Though "ordinary playing cards" are certainly used for playing various games, from bridge to strip poker, it's unfair to call them "ordinary." They are among the oldest and most mysterious tools for fortune-telling that we know. Their origins are as cloudy as those of the people who brought them to Europe—the gypsies. One version of the gypsies' history says that they came from Egypt up through Spain with the Moors, and thence north to wander over all of Europe; another claims that the gypsies came from India. In either case, they could have brought the cards with them—both the Indians and the Egyptians used cards. (The Indians used them as the gypsies did—for divination. They were religious objects, each suit named after an incarnation of the god Krishna.)

In any case, the fifty-two-card pack did not start its life as a parlor game, but as the medium for the serious business of prophecy. Unlike tea and coffee, cards had no primary purpose except fortune telling. For this reason, people often take the word of the cards far more seriously than they would a divination from some more familiar source. Use them with care—especially since they are very clear-cut and powerful in their messages. As you become familiar with their meanings, you will be able to see at a glance whether a particular layout is favorable—and if your client (the gypsy custom is to call the sitter the "client," even if the reading is private) is familiar with the cards, he'll be able to tell, too. Use tact and judgment; remember that death, financial loss, and disasters in one's sex life all are serious and frightening subjects. If you see a layout with a preponderance of spades, be careful what you say—you'll have to know pretty clearly what the client can take, whether you'll have to soften the blows. Even if fortune-telling is only a game to you, remember to take into account the superstitions of others!

THE MYSTIC MOOD

Cartomancy is the queen of the *gypsy* arts. But just how gypsy *you* want to go, of course, depends on how bold you feel, and how much the gypsy look suits your own particular style. The new bias-cut long skirts in different swatches of bright fabrics can be a clever substitute for the more conventional gypsy costume. Or you might opt for a bright peasant blouse and a gathered or ruffled skirt—and you *can* go all the way to a fringed shawl, a scarf tied over your forehead and knotted under your ear, huge hoop earrings, bangles, and ankle-strap shoes. But *do not* try a costume that feels to *you* like a parody. The seriousness of the effort to read the cards should be first in your mind; if it is, you will find soon enough that the cards themselves are powerful creators of mood.

A heavy (almost Eygptian) eye make-up is called for, though—and be sure that your colors are either very clear red, if you're dark, or smoky, if you're fair.

Let your look establish itself with the client. Don't leap from the first drink to a reading! Let the atmosphere, your costume, and the conversation have a while to work before you move toward the reading—even if the occasion has been planned in advance.

The card table, or whatever surface you'll lay the cards on, is all-important. Since the cards themselves are most vital to the atmosphere, they deserve a dramatic setting. Round or square, the table should be *about* card-table size. (Most dinette tables will work fine.)

If you can, buy a piece of billiard-table green felt large enough to cover the table, and fasten it underneath with thumb tacks, or cut it to fit the surface exactly and then paste it down with rubber cement. (It will come off easily later, and the rubber cement won't harm any surface.) The felt will make a clear background for the cards, and will keep them from slipping, as they might on a vinyl or wood surface. See to it that you have a clear light on the table, but leave your own face and that of the client in shadow, if possible. The ideal arrangement is a low light dropped from the ceiling over the table. Failing that, a long-necked high-intensity lamp set on the edge should do the trick beautifully.

You sit on one side of the table, the client on the other. Any observers or other clients waiting their turn—may sit at either side of you. Two or three readings at a sitting is about all that you should expect of yourself. Even when you're completely familiar with cards, the concentration needed to interpret a fairly simple layout can be tiring. Better to do a couple of *convincing* readings than a great many indifferent ones. Of course, in a more relaxed situation, you can go on longer (if, for instance, some of your guests want to learn fortune-telling with cards, or if you're just playing some of the lighter premonitory games we'll tell you about later). In every case, though, remember to treat the cards themselves with respect; it's a mistake to think that they are just the counters in a parlor game. They are, in truth, among the oldest surviving evidences of man's desire to read his fate.

THE PACK AND ITS INTERPRETATION

In all of the layouts for fortune-telling that we'll detail below, one element is most important—your familiarity with the fifty-two-card pack and the meanings *of each card*. For most fortunes, as you will see, the pack is reduced to thirty-two cards, so we'll concentrate on their meanings. But the whole pack is significant, and you need some awareness of its total significance.

The divisions of the pack are connected with *time*. The four suits represent the four seasons of the year; the twelve face cards, the months; the fifty-two cards, the weeks; the 365 spots on the cards, the days of the year.

The pattern set by the court cards (king, queen, jack) is that of the medieval court or nuclear family—an older man, a woman, and a young man or child. (The jack can also represent a young woman, but the queen is more likely to take *all* the women's roles.) Just as the medieval court was supposed to represent a microcosm, to show everyone how to live, so the court cards represent every type of person. The personality characteristics change with each suit. Though no one knows the origins of the symbols for the four suits, their meanings are now well established by tradition: The red suits are considered favorable, with hearts dominant; and the black suits are considered unlucky, with spades dominant.

Most layouts for serious fortune-telling use a thirty-two-card pack—all the cards with a value of seven or higher. (Ace counts high.) Separate them from the rest. This is the basic divinatory pack.

THE PRELIMINARIES
AND THEIR MEANINGS

Preliminary rites set the tone of a card-reading. The fortune doesn't begin with your reading of the final layout—it begins with the shuffle, the cut, and the information that you glean from those actions.

The Client Card: Before laying out any fortune, you'll have to decide which of the court cards (kings, queens, and jacks) represents the client. (As you'll see in the list following, the court cards represent the people in the client's life—and one of those people is *him*.) Each of the court cards shows a man, woman, or a young man, and the various suits also indicate age along with complexion and hair color. Here's a brief run-down: hearts—young, fair; clubs—young, dark; diamonds—older, fair; spades—older, dark. (The court cards have more meanings when they stand for others in the client's life, as you'll see later.) Select the king, queen, or jack from the appropriate suit to stand for the client. (Don't remove the card from the pack—just keep it in mind, so that you'll recognize it if it turns up in the layout.)

The Shuffle: Always ask the *client* to shuffle. He should go on shuffling until it seems to him that it is "time" to stop and lay out the cards. Never hurry him, because his shuffling may be the most telling part of the whole procedure.

The Cut: The client should cut the cards with his left hand, in the prescribed method for the layout. (We'll give you those methods along with the layout instructions later.) If a simple one-cut method is being used, you may want to read the cards on the bottom of the two packs thus formed: If both are in red suits, their combined numbers will be his lucky number for the day; if in black suits, especially spades, the number is unlucky, and should be avoided.

The Layout: After the shuffling and the cutting, you lay out the cards. Be sure to take the cards from the client with an air of serious reserve, and to lay them out carefully according to the pattern you're using. Never be casual or offhand with the cards—the client will feel foolish for having done his part of the ritual seriously. Respect the cards! is the first dictum of fortune-telling. There's a *chasm* between the way the cards are handled in, say, gin rummy, and the way they're handled in divination. Every movement has a meaning, every fall of every card is fraught. Never, for instance, let a card fall and just pick it up. If something—even something small—goes wrong, *start over*. You are dealing with your client's future, not just the pack of cards.

Some cards are important as they turn up in the preliminaries. The Nine of Hearts, for instance, is the "wish card." If it appears in the cut, it bodes good for the *whole* fortune to come—easing a bad fortune, assuring a good one. With any of the layouts we'll describe, try a Cut Surprise: Take a card from the *top* of one pile produced by the cut, and a card from the *bottom* of the other, and set them aside for a final reading to follow the entire fortune. Their judgment can improve a bad over-all fortune, or cast doubt on a good one.

On pages 40-58, we'll describe some basic methods of laying out the cards, and show you a sample and a reading for each. Remember these vital elements in all card fortunes: Pay careful attention to the preliminary steps, follow instructions exactly, and be *completely familiar with the meanings of the cards*. If you show doubt in interpreting the layout, the client can hardly be expected to believe his fortune. The best plan is to lay out the cards for your own fortune, or for that of a friend with whose life you're familiar, and refer each time to the list of meanings given below. After a few tries, you'll be sure of the meanings, and the layouts will be easy to read.

WHAT THE CARDS MEAN

THE SUITS AND THE INDIVIDUAL CARDS

 **The Sensual Suit:** It rules sex, love, friendship, family, and marriage; represents the emotions, especially the warm and positive ones. Court cards correspond to people with blond or auburn hair, or, in the case of old people, with white hair.

Ace: love, romantic and/or domestic happiness; good news; important developments at home

King: a good-hearted, generous man of strong affections, good-looking and fair-haired; given sometimes to rash judgments and occasional indiscretions

Queen: counterpart to the King, golden-haired and loving, domestic, prudent, faithful

Jack: not identified with any sex— sometimes taken as Eros; may be the best friend or lover of the client, or be read as a fair person's thoughts; not always trustworthy; must be read in context with cards on either side

Ten: card of good fortune; a good heart, happiness, the prospect of a happy love life and a large family; in some cases—happy surprises

Nine: the wish card; the fulfillment of dreams, plans, ambitions; a happy outcome

Eight: an invitation; the prospect of good food, congenial company, a convivial atmosphere; domestic happiness, or a pleasant journey

Seven: simple contentment in marriage or love; a friend who is affectionate but may prove fickle, depending on the context

 The Worldly Suit: It rules life outside the family, but rarely *public* situations; inheritances, gifts, money from unexpected sources. Court cards are blond-, auburn-, grey- or white-haired people.

Ace: a letter or message to be received; gift of a ring

King: a man of power and strength, blond or white-haired

Queen: a good-looking but perhaps malicious woman, who can injure through gossip and backbiting

Jack: a young man, possibly a messenger, or connected with the army or navy

Ten: large amounts of money through a change; a journey

Nine: news, probably about an unexpected sum of money from a hitherto unknown source—an unexpected inheritance, a new job

Eight: a loan repaid; a small present of money; a short, pleasant journey—in winter a ski trip, a picnic in summer

Seven: a present received by surprise, or, depending on the context, a small but hurtful bit of gossip or criticism

 The Ominous Suit: It rules death, misfortune, and treachery; enemies and scandal; suffering and loss. Spades can be eased by surrounding cards, but a layout consisting largely of spades should be taken very seriously. Court cards are people with dark hair.

Ace: intrigues, gossip, a possible court case; other legal matters; a proposition in love or business

King: a lawyer—perhaps of dubious reputation

Queen: a single woman, widow, or divorcee—sly, cunning, and subtle

Jack: an ingenious, devious, perhaps treacherous young man

Ten: news of death or illness; possibly a journey, not a happy one; imprisonment

Nine: failure in business, betrayal in love

Eight: persistent petty misfortune; threats of drastic action

Seven: quarrels that force a change in plans; bad or irrelevant advice

The Business Suit: It rules work and friendships outside the family; loyalties to a larger social circle; anxiety, betrayal, financial worry. Court cards indicate brown-haired people.

Ace: financial success; an advantageous marriage

King: a stranger or distant relative—friendly to your cause, helpful

Queen: a new woman in your life, dark and warm, perhaps a widow

Jack: a dark young man, affectionate and sincere

Ten: trouble in business

Nine: in connection with other cards, indicates "for sure"; if the other cards tell of no specific situation, may indicate a marriage with money

Eight: mild anxiety, perhaps connected with a dark young girl who is herself a source of joy and pleasure

Seven: a small delay or inconsequential worry; sometimes a small child, perhaps the heir to money

COMBINATIONS

Though each individual card has its meaning, affected by its suit, the most crucial element in telling any fortune is reading *combinations* of cards. Because every layout provides a *new* set of combinations, we can only provide you with the *major* ones. Look for the pairs, triplets, and quartets listed below. (Nobody can foresee exactly which ones, and in what kind or number, you'll find in any given layout. So be ready to put your imagination and intuition to work!)

Aces: 2/Change in life: a new job, a new house, a marriage, an affair. **3**/Flirtation or an insubstantial love affair; gullibility. **4**/Success.

Kings: 2/The portents are good, but walk carefully—you may be visited by an officer of the law. **3**/Success in business. **4**/Great success in everything.

Queens: 2/An inspiring friendship waits you, but beware—it could be threatened by gossip. **3**/A visit for a long stay; be on the alert for jealousy and slander. **4**/Scandal and treachery threaten.

Jacks: 2/Change of affections, caused perhaps by petty bickering.

3/Disharmony and bad feeling, especially in the family. Trouble in starting new projects. 4/Major quarrels, deep rifts in personal relationships. Sometimes leads to new and successful alliances.

Tens: 2/Change in the environment—your company will switch premises, you'll get a new landlord in the same building, an energy crisis will develop; occasionally, a small sum of money. 3/Financial problems, perhaps leading to litigation. 4/Good fortune, especially professionally.

Nines: 2/Change in your professional life, caused by external circumstances (a new boss, reorganization of the company?); can pro-duce either a small financial gain or obstacles to your goals. 3/Success too easily achieved; ennui threatens. 4/A happy surprise.

Eights: 2/Perhaps a journey, but not abroad; may be followed by quarrels and strife. 3/Family problems (or trouble with a roommate?) 4/Anxiety, frustration; a situation difficult to get out of.

Sevens: 2/A series of surprising and sudden developments in your personal life; you will have to change your plans; may include the appearance of an old enemy. 3/Pregnancy—or a new project about to take form. 4/Enemies are plotting.

COURT CARDS
HOW THEY
INDICATE RELATIONSHIPS

The court cards represent the people and personal relationships in the client's life, so pay special attention to them. When examining a layout for court cards, look first at the over-all picture: Which suits are most of the court cards in? Then look at the individual court cards. (See the meanings for suits and court cards in the lists on pages 37-39.)

Now, you'll want to put the meanings together into some sort of pattern, to give the client a picture of his personal-relationship fortune. The most useful point to remember is that the client has a special, positive connection with court cards in the same suit as his client card.

For instance, if a client's card is the Queen of Diamonds, a Jack of Spades in the fortune will have its conventional meaning: treachery and bad times. But if the client's *own* card is in spades, too—say, the Queen—the Jack of Spades might be a son, or a messenger with news about her life.

Court cards in the *opposite* suit from the client card are important, too. (Hearts are opposite to diamonds; spades opposite to clubs.) Opposites indicate a *negative* affinity. For instance, for the same woman whose client card is the Queen of Diamonds, a King of Diamonds suggests a love affair or marriage; a King of Hearts suggests a secret or difficult affair.

Look at the following sample fortune. (The client card is

the King of Diamonds). See how both the conventional meanings and the court-card—client-card connections are interwoven into a future:

INTERPRETATION: SAMPLE FORTUNE

The King of Diamonds (the client card) is in the *middle* of this layout—so the client is in the middle of an important life situation. To his left is the Queen of Diamonds (in his own suit—thus, a close relationship), showing a new or soon-to-develop love interest, possibly a marriage. To his right is the Queen of Spades, indicating difficulty. Perhaps the forces of convention are against his new affair. (The new mistress may be married, or a widow with children who will object to him.) Next to the Queen of Diamonds is the Jack of Hearts—a protégé, or a son, or even a younger lover. Since he's in the client's *opposite* sign, he will bode no good for the affair—will seem to be friendly but may undermine the interests of the client. On the other side is the Jack of Diamonds, in the *same* suit as the client. Friendly forces are operating! A son or a younger colleague at work may come to the aid of the client. He can count on help, and it may be decisive in overcoming the powers that work against his new happiness.

RELATIONSHIP FORTUNES

Sometimes the friends for whom you'll be telling fortunes will have a *particular* problem in mind, one that they'll want some insight into. And most often it will have to do with relationships: with lovers and spouses, bosses and co-workers, parents and other family members, friends and rivals. So you might want to start your fortune-telling practice by learning a simple, useful method for asking the cards what the future holds for someone's personal relationships.

Begin by taking the pack and separating all the court cards (kings, queens, jacks), thus forming a small pack of twelve cards. Now, select the client card. Keeping it in mind, replace it in the pack.

Hand the client the pack of twelve, and ask him to concentrate on the particular personal relationship(s) he wants the cards to speak about. Have him tell you the general nature of the problem: love, office staff, or whatever. Then ask him to shuffle the cards.

Now, have him select five cards and hand them to you. Lay them out from left to right.

Look for the client card in the layout. If it is not there, begin the process again from the shuffle. If the client card does not show up for three consecutive layouts, the cards wish to remain silent for the time.

If the client card is there, you can begin to read the fortune. Keep in mind the nature of the subject's problem. For the layout shown above, for instance, the interpretation given at the top of the page (under "Interpretation: Sample Fortune") refers to a romantic situation. But suppose the client has told you he is concerned about the troubles of an emotional nature in his *family*. Then you'll look for a slightly different reading. The Queen of Diamonds might be his sister, under the negative influence of the Jack of Spades (her husband or lover?) The Queen of Hearts and Jack of Diamonds would then indicate friendly forces outside and inside the family, working to bring peace.

THE FAN

After the client has thoroughly shuffled the cards, ask him to spread them face down on the table and select thirteen at random. He hands them to you with his *left* hand; you take them with your *right* hand, and then arrange them face up in a fan, from right to left.

Look first to see if the client card shows. If it is missing, look for a seven of the client's suit as a substitute. If you find *neither,* you must begin again, or accept the sign that the cards have chosen to be silent.

Now, beginning with the client card as number one, count five cards to the right. Read the fifth. Then, using the card you've just read as the first of the next five, count another five and read again. Continue this way until you've read all the cards. As you read, note the general layout and how it bodes: Which suits predominate? Are there pairs? triplets? quartets? How is the client card connected to other cards?

After you've read the individual cards, and formed a coherent idea of the fortune they represent, ask the client to deal five cards from the rest of the thirty-two-card pack, face down on the table. Spread these out below the fan, and read them in pairs, turning up first and fifth first, then second and fourth. Read the center card as the last, and perhaps determining, card in the fortune.

INTERPRETATION: SAMPLE FORTUNE

The client is a fair young man, good-looking and ambitious. His card is the King of Hearts.

As you begin your reading, notice the many clubs and diamonds (the fortune may be about business), the predominating red suits, and the single spade. (The fortune will be generally favorable.) The Queen of Hearts stands next to the client card—a strong sign of a powerful love interest, perhaps (considering those clubs) in a business connection.

Counting five from left to right, starting from the client card, the first card to be read is the Queen of Diamonds (opposite suit to his King of Hearts).

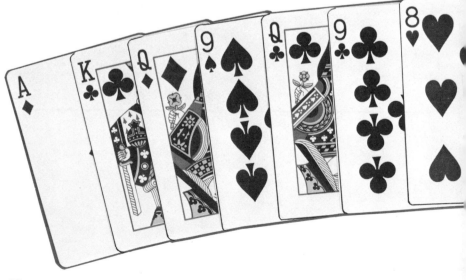

She is possibly his mistress, but may be jealous and shrewish. Counting five more, beginning with the Queen of Diamonds, you come to the Eight of Hearts, sign of conviviality and a new opportunity. An invitation will be issued, possibly a new acquaintance. (Remember that Queen of Hearts!)

Continuing, the Queen of Hearts comes up—and that must be the outcome of the party invitation. He can look forward to meeting a new woman.

Counting again, the King of Clubs is next. He represents a powerful man—a friend who is older, even a boss. Maybe the client met the new woman at the boss's house. In any case, there is reason to believe that the older man approves of the new connection.

The Nine of Clubs is next to be read, and it *rushes* things—it indicates a rich marriage. Perhaps the new woman is the boss's *daughter,* or even the man's *superior* at work. In any case, caution is advised. Next, the Ten of Clubs indicates trouble in business (is the new affair a little too hot to handle in the office situation?) but evidently, not enough trouble to prevent the offer of a *ring,* indicated by the next card, the Ace of Diamonds. (The Ace is generally a good harbinger, though often indicates an *arduous* time.)

The next card, Queen of Clubs, is a good omen for the long run—a warm and friendly older woman will be influential. Perhaps the boss's wife will intervene in favor of the new match, or a senior woman at the office will approve the client's work. (Don't forget clubs relate to business.) She must be encouraged; her advice must be sought . . . especially since the next card, the Jack of Hearts, indicates a *rival.* He may be a rival for advancement in the office, or for the affections of the new woman, or both. He could be treacherous, and should be watched. The older woman, who is near him, may be enlisted for aid. She may know him well, and is wise enough to know that he can't be trusted.

All is well for the moment, anyway—the Eight of Diamonds indicates a short pleasant journey (perhaps with the purpose of presenting the ring) and could represent the consummation of the affair.

The Nine of Spades suddenly appears—though not necessarily as a

threat to the *new* relationship. It could mean that the affair with the earlier and destructive Queen of Diamonds has been definitely ended. Nevertheless, look for clouds on the horizon. No spade should ever be taken lightly.

Even with the threat of the Nine of Spades, the Nine of Diamonds is the last card in the reading—and it indicates a new enterprise begun, almost certainly the affair (engagement?) that has been brewing in the earlier cards.

Now you are ready to ask the client to draw the five cards. Spread them in an auxiliary fan below the thirteen-card fan you've just read.

AUXILIARY FAN

There is real trouble on the horizon! After a fortune in which only one spade appeared, here's a five-card spread of *four* spades and a club. And two of the spades are court cards (personal relationships). The engagement foretold in the first fan is in for a hard testing, and no plans should be made for the immediate future.

The Eight of Clubs and the Seven of Spades (first and fifth) show that there will be at first only a mild anxiety, caused perhaps by a lovers' quarrel. (Perhaps the treacherous Jack of Hearts has succeeded in sowing discord.)

The Queen of Spades and the Eight of Spades (second and fourth) are a much more potent combination—an atmosphere of conventional disapproval threatens to undermine the new affair. Perhaps friends of the old lover (The Queen of Diamonds) are spreading rumors that threaten the careers of both lovers.

In the King of Spades (center) lies the ultimate warning—there may even be *legal* action. Great discretion is indicated, or the jobs of the lovers, and their whole future life together, may be threatened. However, because of the good signs in the first fan, the threats in the second fan may be overcome.

THIRTEEN
& FIVE

FIRST LAYOUT

Have the client shuffle the cards until he feels that he is ready to cut. He cuts the pack, and you take it from his left hand with your right.

Deal out six cards, face down; then lay a seventh aside. Return the first six to the bottom of the pack. Continue this process until you have laid aside twelve cards. Spread them out face up, left to right in the order in which you've drawn them. If the client card is not there, take it from the remainder of the pack and lay it to the right of the others. If it is there, take any card at random from the pack and lay *it* to the right. There are now thirteen cards in the layout. (See illustration at bottom of page.)

Starting with the client card (or random card) count off seven, and read the seventh. Then, starting with the card just read, count off another seven, and read the seventh. Continue reading every seventh card until you've read all thirteen.

SECOND LAYOUT

Now ask the client to shuffle the thirteen cards and cut them with his left hand. Deal the first five cards off the pack of thirteen—in a line, from left to right, face up. Place an additional card on each of the first four cards, so that both cards show clearly. Then place another card on each of the first two stacks of two, so that all three cards show. (See illustration.) Discard the remaining cards.

Each of the five piles of cards represents an element in the client's life. The first pile of three stands for the client himself—they describe him physically and emotionally. The second pile of three stands for his home environment, his house or apartment. The third pile (two cards) shows what is expected to happen. The fourth (two cards) shows what is *not* expected. The last card, standing alone, shows the true, and most surprising, moment in the future.

INTERPRETATION: SAMPLE FORTUNE

This sample fortune is for an attractive middle-aged man, fair or perhaps a little grey. His client card is the King of Diamonds. His thirteen looks like the one shown at the bottom of the page.

The Jack of Clubs (seventh from the client card) is probably a son or a favorite young protégé at work; his appearance here is favorable, leading to improvements or having a strong, affectionate influence in the client's life. The Seven of Clubs follows—money connected with a small child. Does the client pay alimony? Or it may be that he has (or wants) a family. He should beware of envying the young their youth.

The Nine of Spades indicates a bad time ahead in business or love; since the Jack of Clubs is likely to support him in business, perhaps he can look forward to a rough period in his love life. Ah, yes—the Queen of Hearts is next; since she's in his opposite sign, she may be a troublesome lover. But the Nine of Clubs follows—a marriage with someone rich enough not to eat up those alimony payments? But the Queen of Spades threatens—a divorcee (like an ex-wife?). He must have faith in his new love and put his trust in his friends.

Next, the Ten of Spades: The most relevant interpretation might be imprisonment (alimony jail?), though an unhappy journey might also be predicted.

The Ten of Hearts is the surprise card—a bright forecast. Since two tens have been read together, the surprising good news concerns a change—a better job, or more likely, a sudden marriage and a new house. The Ace of Diamonds follows—a ring has been given to seal the new happiness.

The Queen of Diamonds (in the client's own suit) reinforces the marriage prediction—all will be well, and perhaps *she* has a new and lucrative job! In any case, the Eight of Diamonds, next, indicates a short but happy journey (perhaps a weekend honeymoon), and the Ten of Clubs ratifies the impression of a change for the better.

So, the over-all picture is of a man who has had a couple of reverses on the job, but who, with the help of good and strong influences, meets a new woman and finds a surprising happiness with her. The appearance of the Jack, Nine, and Seven of Clubs indicates strong family feeling, not yet realized.

The same man's second layout—the five—is shown at the bottom of the next column:

Look it over to see what suit is dominant. Here, you'll find that clubs are supporting the Thirteen's forecast that the client has or *will* have a strong feeling for family.

Start with the *personal* stack (on the far left): The Jack of Clubs and the Queen of Clubs surround the Eight of Spades, indicating that the client's troubles are to be solved by reliance on others, and on the good instincts of his own heart.

In the second stack (home environment) the Queen of Spades indicates a malicious neighbor who gossips, perhaps hinting at his failure in business (the Ten of Clubs); but his own good sense and neighborliness prevails (the Ten of Hearts). Home will in the future be a more comfortable place.

In the third stack (the expected), the Eight of Diamonds and the Ace of Diamonds show promise of marriage to be given after a short trip.

The fourth pile is the unexpected—even *greater* happiness. The marriage will involve a good deal of money, and the proposal is accepted with great pleasure. There are no impediments.

The last card—the wish card—is the Seven of Clubs. It repeats the conclusion of the Thirteen: The client not only wants a happy marriage, but desires children and wants to leave them his fortune.

THE WHEEL OF FORTUNE

This is a favorite with clients, since the client card is the center, or hub, of the wheel. It is removed first from the deck of thirty-two cards, and laid face up in the center of the table.

The client shuffles the rest of the pack until he feels ready to cut. Then, using his left hand, he puts the pack face down on the table and cuts it twice to the left—forming three piles of cards. Ask him to turn each pile over (again using his left hand) to reveal the bottom cards. These are the three Indicators, which you'll read first separately, then in combination. They give general predictions for the client's future.

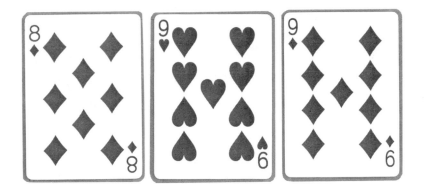

In this case, the client is a fair young woman, and her client card is the Queen of Hearts. Her first Indicator (reading from left to right), the Eight of Diamonds, usually means a short but happy journey. The Nine of Hearts (the wish card) foretells fulfillment of dreams; and the Nine of Diamonds, news or money.

The two nines together indicate a change in her *existing* professional situation, which will remain stable (a new boss or office, but not a change of job). All three Indicators together point to a state of flux in the client's life—ending in happiness (a new affair, possibly marriage, and a changing job situation that could result in more money).

Now that you've read the Indicators, lay out the Wheel. Using the client card (already face-up on the table) as the hub of the Wheel, take the remaining pack (don't reshuffle or add in the Indicator cards) and lay out eight cards face up in a circle around the client card—beginning directly above it and moving counterclockwise. (See illustration this page.) Then ask the client to reshuffle the remaining cards and, following the pattern started by you, use his right hand to lay out eight more cards, face down, outside the original eight; then a third set of eight.

Now, look at each column of three cards, beginning with the group above the client card (column 1 in the picture) and read it as a unit. Read each unit this way, moving counterclockwise. Then examine the *whole* Wheel for a summary of your findings.

Here is a reading for the sample Wheel.

Column 1 is super-favorable! The combination indicates a passionate affair with a wealthy man, a long, joyous journey.

Column 2 shows threats! A malicious woman (the Queen) may betray a confidence (the Nine). But a sweet, charming young man (Jack in the client's own suit) supports the client. (Look at her questioningly as you suggest: a younger brother? or a male friend?

Column 3 sees the intervention of a stronger male (King of Diamonds), whose relationship with the client is close but disagreeable (court card in opposite suit—remember?) He sends some money. (Is Daddy trying to bribe daughter to be good?)

Column 4 offers a warning. An invitation (Eight of Hearts) will lead to office trouble (clubs). Avoid advances from male colleagues!

Column 5 confirms earlier news: a "love nest" (Ace). But an older woman disapproves (Mom?) The Ten insures joy—but it will be a surprise!

Column 6 brings *more* trouble. Though the client has a strong friend in the King of Clubs, she's threatened by two spades—the Ace (serious difficulties) and the Seven (petty ones). But keep in mind the Ten of Hearts—and unexpected success.

Column 7 suggests further worries, but the affectionate and sincere Jack of Clubs indicates serious intentions on the part of her lover. The other two cards are less ominous than early spades—trouble dies down.

Column 8's Ten shows a flurry of problems, but the Queen helps and the Seven of Hearts assures contentment.

　　In summary: In spite of obstacles and possible trouble on the job, a happy affair will end well, and parental objections will subside. The client should be aware that she has many friends, and know she can rely on them!

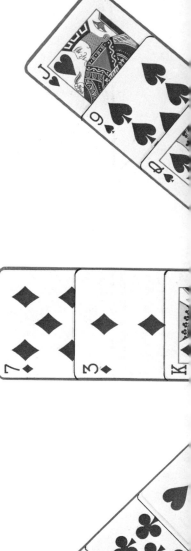

49

THE TWICE TWELVE

The Twice Twelve is not a difficult layout to read, and it is very rich. Its paired cards give interesting readings, and the number of cards used—(twenty-four out of thirty-two) shows the reader a great deal about the client's life.

After the client shuffles and cuts the pack with his left hand, lay out the cards in three rows of four cards each. (Move from left to right, and place each row under the previous one.)

Then ask the client to shuffle and cut the remaining cards. Lay twelve more out *on top of* the first cards, in the same order, to form pairs. (The bottom card in each pair should be visible, as in Solitaire.) See the picture below.

Now, locate the client card or seven of the client's suit. (If it's not in the layout, the cards wish to remain silent.) Note carefully the general look of the layout. Which suit is dominant? Which suit has more cards in the top layer? the bottom layer? Are there pairs, triplets, quartets? (In this layout, combinations count if they are touching, or if they are *on the same layer* next to each other (left, right, up or down. Diagonals do not count.)

Read each pair, taking care to note which card is on top. The covering card represents the *external* situation or influence; the card below is the underlying, but often more *powerful,* influence on the client. Be certain, as you go along, to take cues from your client—notice his reactions to your reading. Only he can *fully* identify the people and situations in the cards. Of

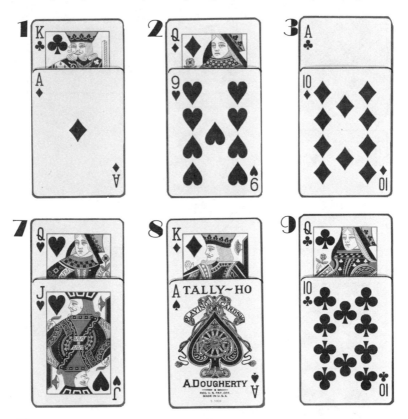

course, some cards refer to future events and meetings—which the client will not recognize because they're not yet in his life. But you'll only know that if you watch and listen to him. (You don't want to identify the kindly Queen of Clubs as a mysterious new friend when in fact she's his old Aunt Lillian!)

In the sample illustrated below, the client is a dark-haired young woman; her client card is the Queen of Clubs (lower left-hand corner, bottom card).

Pair 1 shows the Ace of Diamonds covering the King of Clubs. The client can expect a romantic message from a man who is a lover or a would-be one.

Pair 2 reveals the Nine of Hearts (the wish card), denoting good fortune, but it covers the Queen of Diamonds. The client should take care not to be so blinded by good fortune that she disregards danger signals. (The Queen of Diamonds is charming, but *not* always to be trusted. Since she is here next to the King of Clubs, she may be a rival.)

Pair 3 continues to promise good fortune: The Ace of Clubs (marriage with money) is covered by the Ten of Diamonds (a financial change for the better.)

Pair 4 becomes more *personal*. The Ace of Hearts covers the Eight of Hearts; a convivial evening leads to more permanent happiness and the setting up of a joint household, perhaps, with the lover from Pair 1.

Pair 5 points to happiness in the new situation. The Ten of Hearts is the card of general good fortune, and the Seven means domestic contentment.

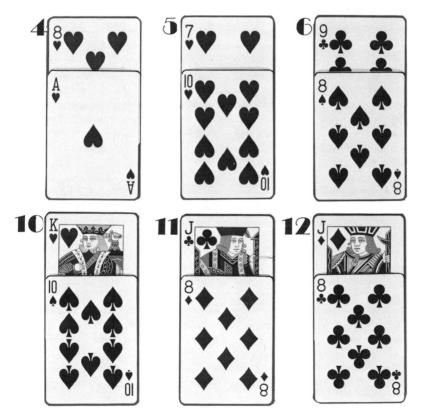

Pair 6 foretells a series of minor anxieties, but confirms the prediction of a marriage or alliance involving money (Nine of Clubs). The Eight of Spades is a card of petty troubles, and should not be taken too seriously. (The client shouldn't take her lover too much for granted when the first weeks of bliss wear off and small domestic quarrels arise.)

Pair 7 shows a possibility of real trouble. The Jack of Hearts covers the Queen of Hearts, and together they could mean anxiety involving tale-telling. The client should be certain of her loyalties, and *his*. Pair 2 showed the possible presence of less-than-friendly friends—perhaps a rival, or people who envy her good fortune and criticize her lover.

Pair 8 reveals the first serious threat in this young woman's future. It poses the possibility of malice, slander—even the necessity of a court battle to retrieve her reputation. The King of Diamonds is present, however, and as the underlying influence, he represents powerful help. He stands next to the Queen of Hearts in the previous square, and so may be able to convince her to remain friendly to the client.

Pair 9 indicates the source of the difficulty: The Ten of Clubs points to trouble at the office. It covers the client's card, and so seems very threatening to her, but she must remember that she is solidly grounded.

Pair 10 shows the King of Hearts, a clear reminder that her love will not desert her, no matter what. The Ten of Spades covering him means that there will be a death in his family—they must both be prepared for a hard time. The two tens side by side in Pairs 9 and 10 foretell a change—and because they are both black, the change will be for the worse.

Pair 11 is the sort of predictive moment that will test your tact. The client may not respond to her difficulties with fidelity and steadfastness. What is indicated here is a trip with a new man—a young and affectionate man, whom she has perhaps deceived about her relationships. The two Jacks (there is one coming up in Pair 12) indicate a change in affections. However, it is pretty clear from the threat of the Ace of Spades in Pair 8 that she should be holding steady at this time! No quickie trip with a new lover will solve the real problems that she faces, and you should warn her that this is no time to dally. Later, maybe, but not now!

Pair 12 is full of anxiety. The Eight of Clubs covers the Jack of Diamonds, who may be yet a third man, or may indicate that she will unwisely opt for the Jack of Clubs. (Remember, court cards don't always mean *people* unless they're in the client's own suit.) She'll face uncertainty and distress, due to her fickleness toward her first lover in their time of trouble.

To summarize: This will be a difficult and conflicted time for the client. She'll first find a promising, wealthy, affectionate lover, but will be beset by work problems, treacherous "friends," and her lover's family problems. But the Ace of Diamonds and the Ace and Ten of Hearts insure that she will ultimately have great happiness. For this reason, she must overcome her desire to find solace in more trivial love affairs—they will distract her from her real, and much more fortunate, fate. Advise her strongly to end her affairs quickly and keep her attention on her real problems. Her first love (who remains with her—the King of Hearts appears in a strong place, next to her client card and on the bottom layer) will be the most powerful in the long run.

FORECASTS

The methods we've described above predict the long run—months, or even the client's whole future life. Often the client and the reader, by concentrating together, can decide on a specific time-span for the fortune (two years, six months, or whatever they wish). In the case of daily and weekly forecasts, however, the layout itself is designed to refer only to a single and brief period of time. These methods should be used with some discretion, since the client is more likely to *remember* the fortune within that time-span—and maybe even *act* on it. (A forecast of treachery or a new love affair due next year may *interest* a client; but the same prediction for the coming *week* may cause a really susceptible person to become unpleasantly suspicious or depressed if the promise is not fulfilled.)

The Weekly Forecast uses only the meanings of the *suits* and the *numbers of spots on the cards*. It's a general outlook for the week, not a final statement. It's best used in conjunction with a larger and more detailed reading (just as the daily horoscope prediction is only meaningful in light of your detailed chart).

DAILY FORECAST

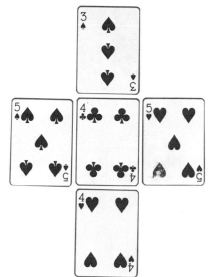

This method uses the cards *left out of* the thirty-two-card pack: the twos, threes, fours, fives, and sixes. (Obviously the client card will not appear since no court cards are used.) You'll find the meanings for these low cards on page 57. Because these cards have lower, less powerful numbers, they predict events that the client can control, incidents that are not crucial to his life. But that doesn't mean that the signs should be blithely ignored: Solid spades, for instance, advise the client to lay low for the day!

To lay out a Daily Forecast, ask the client to shuffle and cut the twenty low cards. Take the pack from him with your right hand, and lay out the top five cards in the pattern shown below (top card first; then left, center, right, and bottom).

The five cards stand for the divisions of a normal waking day. The top card is early morning; the left, late morning till noon; the center, early afternoon; the right, late afternoon to early evening; and the bottom, late evening.

The fortunes read from this layout tend to be more detailed and less dramatic than others; the assumption is that no extraordinary change in routine will happen, though an all-red or all-black layout would suggest an out-of-the-ordinary day!

Pairs, triplets, and quartets can also make the Daily Forecast a bit more lively. (But remember, they must be next to each other in *time*. For instance, the two fours and two fives in the layout shown do not count as pairs because they're separated by time.

This sample reading was for a man—madly attractive and verging on middle age. He's been a freelance copywriter for several years, and rarely knows what the day will bring. (It's a good idea to learn the basic daily pattern of the client before beginning.

The card in the early-morning spot, the Four of Hearts, means a brown-haired lady. Given the client's habits (he rarely rises before eleven), it's a good bet that she spent the night with him and will be there for breakfast. (So you can, at least, predict bliss for him on the evening *before* the day being forecast!) The Five of Hearts suggests that he's fond enough of the lady to keep her around for lunch, since the sensual suit is present through noon. But by early afternoon he's seeing a brunette (Four of Clubs) who is probably a creative director. (Remember, clubs mean business.) The early evening brings bad news or an accident (Five of Spades). Advise the client to take care going home, perhaps avoid that afternoon drink, since he's upset enough about the incident to lose some money through a careless act later on (Three of Spades). In all, the day begins just fine, and business gets transacted as usual—but the evening could be downright miserable! Late to rise and *early* to bed seems best!

WEEKLY FORECAST

This method uses the thirty-two-card pack. (A client card is unnecessary; the court cards are read for their basic meanings.) The client asks a question about the coming week. Then he shuffles until he feels the moment has come, and hands the cards to you. You spread them face down on the table. The client picks fifteen cards at random, and hands them to you one at a time. Lay them out in a row, face down, left to right, in the order drawn.

Now, turn up the first card and the last card. These, the first pair, represent morning (right hand) and evening (left hand) of the following day. The second pair (second from right and second from left) represent the morning and evening of the day after; and so on, through seven days. The central, fifteenth, card is the answer to whatever question about the coming week the client has asked.

MORNING

Now look at the sample below:

Day one is a good one: The Queen of Hearts in the morning and the Ace of Clubs in the evening add up to a very successful day personally and professionally.

Day two is less promising—there will be bad news in the morning, followed by conversation with a young friend later.

Day three shows the client getting an important message in the morning, followed by bad news of some kind at night.

Day four seems to point to a pattern—Diamonds and Spades again. The message of the morning cannot seem to ward off the bad times in the evening. The Ace of Spades is an ominous sign; the client should reconsider whatever plans he might have for this day.

Day five shows the pattern continuing, with the Ten of Hearts bringing good news in the morning, only to be followed by the Jack of Spades. This looks like a bad patch.

Day six suggests that his week is definitely looking up, for both halves of the day are represented by red suits. Toward evening, the client will be in very good spirits.

Day seven reverses the improvement: Both cards are black, and both are court cards. This would be an unpropitious day to begin anything—caution is the watchword.

The fifteenth card (at the center) answers any questions with a warning of vexation and anxiety. This card along with the reading for the seventh day, indicates that the week may be a bad one. Put off new affairs, job interviews, and redecorating the apartment! Stick close to home, and invite only close friends to visit.

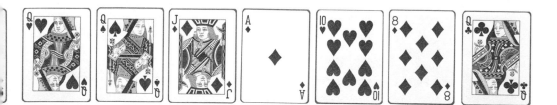

EVENING

SINGLE-QUESTION METHODS

Using the cards to answer a single question is an ancient, easy, and fascinating practice. It's much simpler than the larger layouts—though, of course, the information you can get from a single-question method is *limited.* Don't ask the cards a long series of questions; on or two per client is all they'll usually respond to with any accuracy. (The gypsies say that the cards get "tired" and they seem to be right!)

YES OR NO
To get a "Yes" or "No" to a question, have the client shuffle the thirty-two-card pack several times, stopping when he feels ready. Then have him cut the cards twice with his left hand, to make three piles. Look at the bottom cards. If the three cards that show are black, the answer is an emphatic "No." If two are black and one red, the "No" is less positive. If three cards are red, the answer is an emphatic "Yes." If only two are red, the "Yes" is a bit qualified.

THREE OF SEVEN
Have the client shuffle the thirty-two-card pack and cut it with his left hand. Lay out seven cards in a row from left to right, face down. Then turn up the first, fourth, and seventh cards and read them as a unit.

In the layout here, for instance, the Queen of Diamonds, Queen of Clubs, and Eight of Spades mean that a new and inspiring friendship may be vexed by small anxieties. (See the meanings of these cards in the list on pages 37-38.) Two cards in black suits imply a generally unfavorable outlook, and their position toward the right means that the future looks more cloudy than the present. (In layouts for the Three of Seven, time moves from left to right.)

LETTERS OF THE ALPHABET
Many questions can be answered by letters of the alphabet. ("What are the initials of my true love?") or by using the alphabet to represent a continuum of time or distance. ("Will I marry / move / find a new job soon?" The nearer the answering letter to the beginning of the alphabet, the nearer the heart's desire.)

You can use cards to answer such questions. Have the client draw a card from the full pack, and follow the key below. The card of the black suit means that the letter is, depending upon the context, either unlucky for the client or represents a dark person; red suits mean luck or a fair person.

KEY
TO THE SUITS
Two to Six

HEARTS
2 a blond young man
3 a white-haired, elderly man
4 a pale lady
5 love, affection, general well-being
6 change in affections

DIAMONDS
2 very good news, but not delivered in person: a telephone
    message, a letter, a telegram
3 errands, shopping, money spent
4 a bonus, pay for overtime or money
    from an unexpected source
5 a contract signed, a lease agreed to, or promise given
6 an important discovery; a lost article found

SPADES
2 a disappointment in personal plans
3 loss of money or valuables through carelessness;
    unexpected extra expense
4 expense incurred: emergency need for money
5 news of illness, or a minor accident
6 irritability, crossness; impatient restlessness

CLUBS
2 a dark young man
3 a dark elderly man
4 a brunette woman
5 a favorable business opportunity; a job offer
6 a trip that will prove favorable

A Ace of Hearts or Spades

B Two of Hearts or Spades

C Three of Hearts or Clubs

D Four of Hearts or Spades

E Five of Hearts or Spades

F Six of Hearts or Spades

G Seven of Hearts or Spades

H Eight of Hearts or Spades

I Nine of Hearts or Spades

J Ten of Hearts or Spades

K Jack of Hearts or Spades

L Queen of Hearts or Spades

M King of Hearts or Spades

N Ace of Diamonds or Clubs

O Two of Diamonds or Clubs

P Three of Diamonds or Clubs

Q Four of Diamonds or Clubs

R Five of Diamonds or Clubs

S Six of Diamonds or Clubs

T Seven of Diamonds or Clubs

U Eight of Diamonds or Clubs

V Nine of Diamonds or Clubs

W Ten of Diamonds or Clubs

X Jack of Diamonds or Clubs

Y Queen of Diamonds or Clubs

Z King of Diamonds or Clubs

THE
TAROT

The Tarot cards are magical. Almost anyone who has riffled through a pack has felt a thrill, a sense that the images come straight from the unconscious, from somewhere even deeper and richer than a single unconscious. The pictures are detailed and fascinating; are more cheerful than ominous; yet they suggest a world so much deeper than ours that even the lightest and most charming of them can be almost chilling. So don't casually use the Tarot for fortune-telling. Begin by reading a little of the history we'll tell you, and familiarize yourself thoroughly with the cards. They're likely to affect you as much as they do some of your subjects. (In fact, the Tarot and the "I Ching" are the favorite methods of fortune-tellers for seeing their own futures.)

ORIGINS OF THE TAROT

The Tarot is so mysterious in origin that at least a dozen books have been published about it, each with a different story of where the cards came from and what their symbols mean. We do know that they pre-date "ordinary" playing cards, which were probably based on the Tarot.

If you're interested in the mystical and religious origins of fortune-telling, the Tarot is indispensable. Its symbols are those of all the major Western and Middle Eastern religions. Various experts claim that those symbols were invented by the Hebrews as a secret language; or that they were known from ancient Egypt; or that the gypsies brought them from Asia; or that they are early Christian. The closest we can come to the truth is to agree with Edward Arthur Waite, the most popular modern commentator on the Tarot, who has said that its symbols satisfy the love of idols, and must be used, not for the messages they carry, but for the messages they call up in us.

The modern Tarot—the one we've illustrated here—is an English design derived from the French Tarot of Marseilles, which was used in the eighteenth century. But Waite, a nineteenth-century Englishman, popularized the Tarot in England and the United States.

Edward Arthur Waite was more a scholar and mystic than a fortune-teller. He wrote dozens of books on occult subjects, and considered his work on the Tarot to be of minor importance. He wanted to spread the word about what he called the "higher mystical disciplines," and felt that the Tarot was only a small part of magical lore. But as it turned out, his Tarot (he directed the work of Pamela Colman Smith, an American, in designing and drawing the cards shown here) and his book, "The Pictorial Key to the Tarot," were his most lastingly popular works.

In fact, the Tarot that Ms. Colman Smith designed is largely the invention of Edward Arthur Waite. He combined the symbols from the Marseilles Tarot, from a number of other packs of cards, and from the rich sources of his own research into occult sciences. The result is the mysterious and ancient Tarot, interpreted by a modern scholar, and executed by a woman who herself believed that all the dark and unknown world could be made light.

THE MYSTIC MOOD

The most vital approach to a mood for a Tarot reading is looking at the cards. Study them carefully, and consider what elements in them you identify with. Many have distinctive costumes that may feel right for you. The tunic-overtights of the Fool? the flowing Grecian robes of Strength? the formal dress of the High Priestess? the flowing earth mother gown of the Empress? Any of these might provide the inspiration for your look. (In some of the cards, the female figures are *nude*. That could be a possibility in intimate circumstances.)

Of course, you won't take the inspiration from the Tarot too literally; you'd look awfully *contrived* as a replica of the Knight of Swords! But do take seriously the *mood* that the cards give you. For instance, you might find that the headdresses of the women make you feel regal, and that might lead you to wear a jeweled headband, or a tall, elegant pile of curls. The timeless quality of the figures is a signal to look a bit noncontemporary. The pre-Raphaelite look may suit you—a flowing, mock-medieval style, with loose hair or a true pageboy or an austere Joan of Arc cut.

No matter what your basic coloring is, your make-up should *glow*, luminous and *healthy*. Your whole face should radiate, rosy and lit-from-within. Make-up can *help*, but the rest must come from your own serenity and good health. (See page 61 for a good pre-reading relaxation exercise.) Start with a pearly foundation, then add a clear blusher in your best shade. Use it not only on cheeks, but on chin and temples. Darken your eyebrows slightly, and use clear, light colors to shadow your eyes. They should look large and round—use a dark brown liner *under* the upper lashes (there *is* a little ridge there) as well as on the upper lid, thickening it slightly at the center. Be sure to use mascara on both upper and lower lashes, and superdarken lashes at the outer corners. Extend liner from the upper and lower lids just beyond the outer corners of the eyes, so that the lines meet—then fill in with a tiny dot of white; match the dot with another at the inside corner. That little trick will make your eyes look enormous and *very* round. Outline your lips, using a lipstick brush. Round the lips at the bow; don't make peaks. Use one of the luminescent powders—gold is best—over all.

As for the setting for all this magical beauty, your apartment should be as low-lit and rich-looking as possible. The single strong light, as for evenings with playing cards, should be lowered over the card table. Cover the surface with a black or dark blue piece of felt—green is too reminiscent of the poker table for the Tarot—and, if you have a flair for drawing, copy onto it in white or gold ink the four symbols of the suits: swords, cups, pentacles, and wands. (See the illustrations on pages 74-76.)

RELAX
FOR A
TAROT READING

Reading the Tarot is easiest when ·you're in a state of *relaxed concentration*—loose enough so you'll open up to all the suggestions of the cards and symbols, but alert enough to combine them into a coherent reading. Mere babbling from your unconscious depths, however free it is, won't be much help to your subject! On the other hand, if you're tense and overanxious, or dragged out from a work day, you're likely to let your attention wander, or close off the mood.

The following exercise—which takes about twelve minutes in all—helps you gain calm and intentness just before a reading (or, for that matter, before *any* event where you'll want to be both "up" and relaxed):

When you've showered, made up your face, and put on your underwear, lie down on the floor. (Use an exercise mat, beach towel or super-sized bath sheet, or the rug for softness.) Put the cards of the Major Arcana beside you.

Now, close your eyes and count backward from sixty, very slowly. When you reach zero, try to visualize it as a circle floating in the darkness. Let it become a smoke ring and disappear. Then let your right foot "sink" into the floor, thinking as you do this, "Heavy, heavier, heaviest...." *feel* that foot seem heavier and closer to the floor than the rest of your body. Now do the same with your left foot . . . then right knee, left knee, thighs, hips, stomach, ribs, each breast, each shoulder, upper arms, lower arms, wrist and hand, and then, finally, neck and head.

Now visualize the zero again, turning into a smoke ring and disappearing. As it whispers away, think of your eyes sinking into your head: "Heavy, heavier, heaviest. . . ." Breathe slowly and deeply.

After you're completely relaxed, open your eyes *slowly* and sit up carefully. Lean against the couch or a convenient wall, and spread the cards of the Major Arcana face down near you. Take any one of them, turn it face up, and look at it. Don't make too great a conscious effort to *scrutinize* it—just let your eyes rest on it steadily. After a few moments, see which of the symbols, or what part of the card, your eyes gravitate to. Then close your eyes and visualize that part of the card. . . . *Keep* it in your mind, visually, for about a minute. Don't try to squinch up concentration—just let your mind *rest* on the part of the card your eye has chosen. If your attention wanders, bring it gently back to the card. After a count of about sixty, open your eyes again, look at the card, put it back in the deck, and go slip into your dress, ready to read the cards.

THE PACK AND ITS MEANINGS

The Tarot, though unified by its rich and subtle symbols, is really *two* packs of cards, numbering seventy-eight in all. Fifty-six of these correspond almost exactly (there is one extra court card per suit) to our pack of regular playing cards; they are called the Minor Arcana. The other twenty-two are all face cards, titled and numbered from zero to twenty-one.

Though both the Minor and the Major Arcana are important in fortune-telling, the twenty-two cards of the *Major* Arcana make the Tarot unique. Each card has multiple meanings, and it would be impossible in a short paragraph to exhaust all the possible interpretations of the many symbols on each card. Use the graphic guide on pages 90-91, and the interpretations on pages 63-73, to help you read the cards. But the cards will seem different each time you look and for each subject whose fortune you tell. Don't be afraid to trust your own intuitions—the purpose of the cards is to evoke just those instincts and inklings. They are so suggestive that you are almost certain to supplement the "official" meanings with your own. Welcome such responses—they are why the Tarot was created!

As you will see, each card in the pack has two meanings: one for the card in its normal position, and the other for the card *reversed,* or upside down. So when you shuffle the pack, remember to shuffle both in the ordinary way and by turning some cards upside down and right side up several times. Don't assume that the meaning of a reversed card will necessarily be the *exact* opposite of its primary meanings. Sometimes reversal merely indicates a qualified or different meaning. The *full* significance of a card is a combination of normal and reversed meanings. Also, the Tarot cards can change in meaning depending on their position in an individual layout. Be careful not to take the meanings given here as absolute, and to read cards in the *context* of the whole layout and the sitter's personality.

A word of encouragement: Don't be intimidated by the many cards and their complex meanings. Even the most adept Tarot reader often consults his books (sometimes a great pile of scholarly tomes) to refresh his memory and seek all possible interpretations before settling on one. So with the Tarot, more than with any other method, feel free to consult this book.

THE MAJOR ARCANA

These twenty-two cards are the key to the power of the Tarot. Each is a potent force in itself: in combinations, they are believed not merely to tell the future but to *affect* it.

O The Fool: Waite describes this card as the "spirit in search of experience." It is so powerful a card it *can reverse and clarify all confusion in surrounding cards.* It shows a young man at the edge of a precipice, apparently unaware of his danger. One of its principal messages: *Trust in your fate; the fool who persists in his folly will become wise.* It also indicates that *a great life decision will be necessary.*

Reversed: vanity and carelessness.

I The Magician: He is the symbol of human mastery over all things both spiritual and worldly. (He points both to heaven and to earth.) Notice that the symbols of the four suits are on a table before him and that the horizontal figure eight, the sign for infinity, is above his head like a halo. He is master of all things, but without ambition, full of worldly wisdom but not of this world. *A sign of a high vocation; great self-confidence; diplomacy.*

Reversed: madness brought on by the subject's sorrow; arrogance, willfulness.

II The High Priestess: She sits be-tween two pillars—the positive and negative life forces. She represents *the eternal virgin* (the corresponding astrological sign is Virgo) *and the subconscious mind.* The veil behind her is decorated with pomegranates (for the female principle) and palms (for the male principle). *Duality, mystery, the unrevealed future.*

Reversed: accepting surface pleasures; physical vanity; coldness.

III The Empress: Seated in a garden, her scepter raised and her crown made of stars, the Empress is por-trayed as a mature, full-figured woman; she might almost be preg-nant. On her shield, which is heart-shaped, is the biological sym-bol for the female. She represents *the woman fulfilled by love, the fertile principle; that which is closest to the heart.* The sign for *good marriages; success in all undertakings, espe-cially creative ones; fertility.*

Reversed: inactivity, barren-ness, luxurious idleness; decadence.

IV The Emperor: The ram's-head throne indicates at once that the Emperor is the Empress's male counterpart. He holds the Egyptian Ankh— the Cross of Life—as a scepter, is more stern than compassionate. He represents *all that rules wisely; activity over inactivity; a kindly intelligence over unruly passion. May also represent harsh discipline over leniency.*

Reversed: confusion, immaturity, a foolish and rigid discipline.

V The Hierophant: This is the High Priest, the counterpart of the High Priestess. He sits between two pillars, dressed in the robes of a Prince of the Church. He is sometimes called the Pope. The Keys of St. Peter are at his feet, and two monks in priest's dress kneel at his feet. He signifies the *teachings of the traditional religions, a love of the conventional, a need for the outward signs of approval and conformity.*

Reversed: unorthodoxy, rebellion, gullibility, heresy.

THE LOVERS.　　　THE CHARIOT.

VI The Lovers: This is the card of *human love, but not only sexual love.* The man (Adam) looks at the woman (Eve); she looks at the angel above them. Eve is the means by which man will find the graceful and beautiful in life; Adam is *her* anchor to earth. *Beauty, harmony of the spiritual and the physical in love; the responsibility of the affections; the ability to make good choices and to love faithfully.*

Reversed: family difficulties, quarrels leading to divorce, children torn between parents; family interference in one's life.

VII The Chariot: Because of the commanding presence of this figure, a man in a chariot—*a symbol both of conquest and movement—this card means successful worldly ambition, triumph over adversity, and control of one's professional life.* It often means *the smaller triumphs of life: comforts found, journeys accomplished, money saved.*

Reversed: frivolous desires; vengeance; failure through laxity.

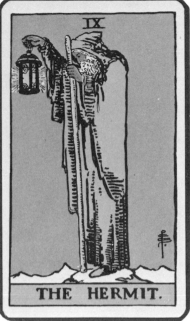

VIII Strength: One of the most beautiful cards, Strength is portrayed not as a man but as a *woman,* who with calm ease closes the gaping mouth of a lion. Like the Magician, she is haloed with the sign of infinity, but her confidence is in *the triumph of a calm and loving wisdom over hate, material power, and jealous lust.*

Reversed: physical arrogance; the abuse of power; greed.

IX The Hermit: Alone and reminiscent of the Greek philosopher lookng for the honest man, the Hermit holds a lantern with a six-pointed star, the symbol of attainable knowledge. Signifies *wisdom in solitude; a wise mentor who will appear; a journey.*

Reversed: the folly of false fellowship; trivial vices leading to emptiness; a refusal to accept maturity and the world as it is.

X The Wheel of Fortune: The letters of the Tarot appear on a wheel with the name of the Hebrew's God, Jahweh, surrounded by the Beasts of the Apocalypse, and supported by a jackal-headed Egyptian god. This card brings good luck to divination: *good fortune, bounty, and unexpected money.*

Reversed: reaping as you have sown; count on nothing in this earthly world.

XI Justice: The figure of Justice is worldly. She sits on a great throne, holds the scales of judgment in one hand and the double-edged blade of the law in the other. Her gaze is forthright, and she represents *the law of the world, the justice of society.* Contrast her with Strength (VIII), whose power needs no weapons. *The balance of intellectual judgment; legal matters such as lawsuits, divorces, will and contracts.* Corresponds to Libra in astrology.

Reversed: legal difficulties; prejudice and bias; severity and capriciousness. When found *near the Hanged Man (XII),* it means that mercy should temper justice and that spiritual truth should triumph over the letter of the law.

XII The Hanged Man: The only figure in the Tarot pack who possesses a real halo, he is suspended between heaven and earth by a leafy tree that grows and prospers. His hands are tied behind him; one leg is crossed behind the other. He is neither "hanged" in the sense of torture and death, nor merely suspended by his own will. He represents man's ambiguous position between the divine and the worldly. As his body is arranged, he forms many of the most important forms in occult science. His legs make a cross; his arms and head, a triangle; his whole body, a swastika or fylfot cross. Like the Fool (O), this card *changes any card it is near.* It symbolizes *surrender to a higher cause; self-sacrifice; a change in one's life; the possibility of a great awakening.*

Reversed: resistance to spiritual truth; ego trips; arrogance; false claims to spirituality.

XIII Death: A skeletal knight on a red-eyed horse rides down all the powers of the world—the crown of the king, the innocence of the child, the beauty of youth. He is welcomed only by the bishop. He carries the banner of the Rosy Cross— signifying a new and passionate spiritual life. The sun shines between two towers in the background. *Destruction—preceded or followed by a new life. A new consciousness—the death of the old self. A new understanding of desires; false desires spurned. Transformation and change, birth and renewal.* Remember that this card, while seemingly ominous, is never connected with actual death or its implications. Rather, it always means a spiritual rebirth.

Reversed: stagnation, inertia, fear of change.

TEMPERANCE.

THE DEVIL .

XIV Temperance: This powerful card teems with symbols and is full of the strength of both earth and sky. An angel, neither male nor female, pours the waters of life from one cup to another—his right foot in the water, his left on earth. On his head is the symbol of the sun; on his breast, the symbol of the Sacred Tarot, the triangle within the square. This is the card of *harmony between the sexes, androgyny.* As the man penetrates the woman and as she receives him, so the two cups join their liquors. The iris, growing on the bank, is both phallic symbol and vaginal emblem. *Successful combinations; good partnerships; life will flow on in spite of obstacles; the capacity to adapt, to co-ordinate, to modify and individualize.*

Reversed: unhealthy competition in business or sexual life; divisions in the family or in the personality; competing interests.

XV The Devil: Note the resemblance between this card and the Lovers (VI): In each, a man and a woman are aware of a greater power. But here the man and woman are chained by a demon. They each have tails: The woman's ends in a bunch of grapes, signifying enslaved fertility; the man's ends in a flame, representing captive intelligence. The pentagram on the devil's forehead is inverted, its point downward, indicating a reversal of normal values. *Bondage to matter; illness; violence and revolution; black magic, fear of spiritual life and the ecstasy of love.*

Reversed: a new and feared love; humility; convalescence; indecision.

THE TOWER.

THE STAR.

XVI The Tower, or the House of God: This is a difficult but very exciting card. The drops of light among the clouds are Hebrew *yods*, which represent the supernatural life force descending into the earthly life of man. Lightning strikes the tower, upsetting the crown (a symbol of earthly power): *Old forms break down, new ones are to come.* The tower is the Tower of Babel, the temple of false or overly strict doctrine. An *unforeseen but understandable catastrophe; revolution; violence followed by a new order; bankruptcy followed by a new way of life.*

Reversed: as above, but to a lesser degree: oppression, false imprisonment; unexpected freedom of the body or of the spirit.

XVII The Star: The mottoes of this card are, according to Waite, "Waters of Life Freely" and "Gifts of the Spirit." The naked female figure kneels with one foot in the water and the other on the land, pouring the water of life both into the pool before her and onto the land behind her. She is surrounded by great eight-pointed stars, symbols of hope. As the water may disappear in water, or soak into the earth, so may hope and inspiration disappear in human life. *A card of fleeting inspiration, hope, good health, happiness in the moment. Generosity, open-heartedness, and even-handedness.*

Reversed: ill-health, pessimism, fear of the future, stubborn doubt.

XVIII The Moon: *The force of the imagination, the power of the life force acting from earth to heaven; the card of evolution and earthly development.* The dog and wolf baying at the moon represent the tamed and the untamed forces of nature. The lobster climbing out of the pool of nature's resources is the earliest example of conscious life. The moon has a human face, and the *yods* flying down to earth represent heavenly influence on human evolution. *Intuition, dreams, the great collective memory of mankind. A return to the past, or a descent into one's deepest subconscious; secrecy; the perils of the unknown, the pains of necessary adaptation.*

Reversed: a great price will be paid for survival; peace will come, and great upheavals lived through at great cost; imagination must be abandoned so that life can go on.

XIX The Sun: *Joy unconfined.* A naked child is mounted on a white horse, crowned with flowers and a tall plume, riding before a wall with sunflowers over it. The sun shines serenely over all. *The simple and free life; vegetable nature (the sunflowers, the child's wreath) nourished by the sun, the universe; liberation; innocence justified; hard work rewarded with complete pleasure.*

Reversed: broken engagement; vigilance needed to protect happiness; contract revoked; plans spoiled, jobs lost, life unsettled or disrupted by chance.

XX Judgment: This card shows the Last Judgment—the dead rising at the sound of Gabriel's trumpet. *The rising of the true spirit in each one of us at the call of what we most desire.* Listen to your true desire, and you will be rewarded; *do not be deceived by anyone else's needs.*

Reversed: disillusionment; loss of worldly goods; fear of old age and death.

XXI The World: This is the card of *reconciliation.* Every element of the universe is blended into perfect harmony. *The unconflicted power of nature and heaven joined* is symbolized by a woman dancing with two wands; they are like the Magician's wand, but here the woman is unconfined by earth. The beasts of the Apocalypse surround her, swimming in the firmament. *Unexpected liberation and fulfillment; an inner awareness that comes suddenly and without warning. A great spiritual awakening and a final fullness. No further questions; all desires fulfilled; a life at ease.*

Reversed: a pulling in; fear of change; distrust of feelings and spiritual activity.

THE MINOR ARCANA

The fifty-six cards of the Minor Arcana are the direct ancestors of our modern fifty-two-card pack. Like modern playing cards, the Minor Arcana are divided into four suits: cups, swords, pentacles, and wands (which correspond respectively to hearts, spades, diamonds, and clubs). But there are fifty-*six* cards, instead of fifty-*two*, because each suit has an extra court card. (In the regular pack, the functions of the Tarot's knight and page are combined in the jack.)

As with the Major Arcana, each card of the Minor Arcana has a fortune-telling meaning in its upright and reversed positions. But while the Major Arcana predicts (as you'd expect) *major* trends for the future, the Minor Arcana gives details. Its cards also describe the sitter and his personal relationships.

Of course, if you're to become a true *adept* at reading the Tarot, you'll eventually want to study the images of the Minor Arcana and what they mean. But for a start, just familiarize yourself with the meanings of each suit and its court cards.

A final note: When you examine the cards of the Minor Arcana, you'll find that they're much simpler than those of the Major Arcana. Usually you'll see a dominant image, based on the card's number, rather than a wealth of images. So these simpler cards can help clarify the sometimes confusing richness of the Major Arcana.

Here are the meanings of the suits and their court cards, and a table of the meanings of pairs, triplets, and quartets.

CUPS: correspond to hearts in modern playing cards. Love, generosity, sensuality; the unconscious. The suit of goodness and passion. Suit of water, and the three water signs of the zodiac. Represents people of light brown hair, and hazel, grey, or blue eyes; even-tempered

Ace: fertility, love, joy. Spiritual nourishment, abundance from the earth. Good fortune crowned by a happy disposition and long life

Reversed: instability, madness, a reversal of the order of things

King: creative in the arts or sciences, probably a man in the professions (medicine, law, education) or at the executive level in business. Kindness, generosity, liberality, good sense. A friendly and sensible man who will befriend the sitter

Reversed: violent man of artistic temperament; treacherous, perhaps dishonest. Loss, scandal, injustice, betrayal

Queen: mature but youthful woman. The type of the True Love, destined to be a good wife and mother. Visionary, poetic, and imaginative. An active dreamer, idealistic. Love, happy marriage, the good life

Reversed: good woman, but sometimes perverse. May be a gossip, and treacherous. Dishonesty, bad temper

Knight: a highly intelligent and romantic young man. Might be the future lover of the sitter. Possibly a messenger; he may bring proposals in business or love, or an invitation

Page: a studious, thoughtful, and imaginative young man or woman, with a desire to serve mankind—he might serve the sitter in some way. News, a message; openness to spiritual and emotional experience; the birth of a child; in business, new methods proposed

PENTACLES: correspond to diamonds in modern playing cards. Material forces (in business, politics, the intrigues of personal life), and the power of magic and the emotions over material forces. The suit of apprenticeship and dedication to a craft; of trade, commerce, education. Stands for air and the three air signs of the zodiac. Represents people with black hair and black eyes, of melancholy or lethargic temperament

Ace: achievement of earthly happiness. Prosperity, ecstasy, fulfillment of ambition. The most favorable of all cards in the Minor Arcana

Reversed: corruption through luxury and decadence; the possible evils of riches; a share in an unexpected legacy.

King: usually a married man, highly intelligent and successful. May be a highly placed executive, or the head of his department in a university, or even its president. Bravery, reliability, success, mathematical genius

Reversed: perverse use of intelligence. Connections to gamblers, speculators, shady businessmen

Queen: a mature woman, creatively sensual. Tends to use her talents to make herself and her environment more attractive. She is intelligent, thoughtful, but not necessarily intellectual. Generosity, security, freedom from want

Reversed: unhealthy, dependence, neglected duties; paranoia, fear of failure, mistrust of those close to the sitter

Knight: a materialistic, methodical, not very exciting young man. Utility, patience, long and laborious toil; responsibility and good will. May represent the beginning or completion of a project or event

Reversed: stagnation, idleness, inertia. A careless young man

Page: a careful, hard-working young man or woman. May bring messages. Scholarship; respect for learning and authority; ease with elders; timidity and fear of the new.

Reversed: youthful dissipation, a wild life. Bad news. The sitter is surrounded by opponents.

SWORDS: correspond to spades in ordinary playing cards. The world or positive activity, both constructive and destructive. Quarrels, strife, war, domestic troubles; a quest, ambition, aggressiveness, force, courage. Symbolizes fire and the zodiacal fire signs. Signifies people with dark brown hair and brown eyes, with mercurial temperaments

Ace: the extreme in everything; enormous force in love and in hate. Conquest and activity; power triumphant. Fertility coming out of strife—plants growing after the plow has torn the earth

Reversed: the abuse of power; tyranny and rebellion

King: a man of great authority, one who may hold the power of life and death. A judge, a high police official, a military man; a wise man, a counselor to the mighty. The fruits of power: authority, government, the military, law, judgment

Reversed: a barbarian—cruel, unjust, and capricious. Beware of lawsuits.

Queen: a subtle, keen, quick-witted woman—temperamental and high-spirited. Widowhood, sterility, privation, sadness, separation

Reversed: a vain and narrow-minded woman, a prude. Intolerance, bigotry, petty cruelties

Knight: a dashing young man—skillful, strong, brave, dominant. In another century, he would have been a privateer; nowadays, he's likely to be a stunt man or a racing driver. Someone who may rush madly into one's life and sweep one off his (or her) feet. Skill, courage; defensiveness or aggression; conflict, destruction. Observe the context.

Reversed: sound without substance; extravagance; a braggart

Page: an active young man or woman, who hungers and thirsts after righteousness. Vigilance, attention, fastidiousness

Reversed: events unforeseen; a life unprepared; illness. An impostor will enter the sitter's life.

WANDS: correspond to clubs in orindary playing cards. Energy, growth, new enterprises. Travel; opportunities in love and business. Connected with the intellectual life, creation in the arts, and production in agriculture. An energetic suit, its energy may be constructive or destructive, depending on the context; suggests change, for the better or the worse. Represents the three zodiacal earth signs, and the earth itself. Stands for people with fair hair and blue eyes, of energetic, enterprising character

Ace: an enterprise beginning; the creation of a new business or invention. A birth; a new marriage or affair; the founding of a fortune; an inheritance

Reversed: False starts; doubt about a new enterprise

King: a man of maturity whose authority grows from his great energy and confidence. A countryman, usually married and with a large family, or one who wants a large family or is like a father to his friends and relatives. Honest, reliable; sometimes rises to unexpected emotional and spiritual heights—can be impassioned and noble in defense of a principle. Unexpected inheritance, nobility of character, a good marriage, a career in social service

Reversed: a severe and stiff-necked man, rigid and often cruel in the name of justice. Opposition, strife. Good advice that is hard to follow or unpalatable

Queen: an animated and fascinating woman, domestic and friendly. A lover of nature, she either has or wants a large family, and is deeply maternal in her feelings for her friends. Faithful to her friends and lovers (though not necessarily physically—she's also *generous*), she is deeply honest and offended by any double dealing or treachery. Success in enterprise; good crops; a large circle of friends

Reversed: an honest, loyal, but strict and intolerant woman; economical to a fault. Opposition, strife. Jealousy, deceit, treachery

Knight: a young man or woman of high spirits, who may unwittingly create conflict or rivalry. Not altogether trustworthy, but without malice. Departure, absence, flight; change of apartments, job, or even exile

Reversed: division and discord; a broken engagement or trouble in a marriage; a troubled love life

Page: an ingenuous young man, a faithful lover and charming friend. May be in uniform: the armed services, a postman, a messenger. May represent a boy or girl child, or a baby. Next to a man's card, means a favorable report

Reversed: bad news, indecision, possible betrayal of a confidence

PAIRS, TRIPLETS, QUARTETS

Here are these combinations: first in the upright position, then reversed. You must use your observation of the context and your imagination to determine the true reading if, for instance, a pair of kings appears, one reversed and one upright. In the case of a triplet, or a quartet, use the meaning for the position (upright or reversed) of the majority of the cards.

Upright

Aces: 2/ trickery; 3/ minor success; 4/ a lucky chance
Kings: 2/ good but trivial advice; 3/ a consultation; 4/ great honor
Queens: 2/ sincere friends; 3/ deception by women; 4/ violent arguments
Knights: 2/ intimacy; 3/ lively debate; 4/ serious undertakings
Pages: 2/ disquiet and annoyance; 3/ dispute; 4/ dangerous illness
Tens: 2/ change; 3/ a situation; 4/ condemnation
Nines: 2/ news received; 3/ success; 4/ a good friend
Eights: 2/ new knowledge; 3/ marriage; 4/ reversal of luck
Sevens: 2/ news; 3/ illness; 4/ intrigue
Sixes: 2/ irritability; 3/ success; 4/ abundance
Fives: 2/ vigils; 3/ determination; 4/ regularity

Fours: 2/ insomnia; 3/ the need for reflection; 4/ journey to take place soon
Threes: 2/ a calm and peaceful time; 3/ unity; 4/ progress
Twos: 2/ agreements; 3/ security; 4/ arguments

Reversed

Aces: 2/ enemies; 3/ debauchery; 4/ dishonor
Kings: 2/ projects; 3/ commerce; 4/ speed in a bright beginning
Queens: 2/ work and worry; 3/ gluttony, a new diet; 4/ bad company
Knights: 2/ gullibility; 3/ a confrontation; 4/ an alliance
Pages: 2/ society, conviviality; 3/ idleness; 4/ poverty
Tens: 2/ expectations justified; 3/ disappointment; 4/ a happening, event
Nines: 2/ small profit; 3/ imprudence; 4/ interest on a loan
Eights: 2/ misfortune; 3/ a spectacle, a performance; 4/ an error
Sevens: 2/ a man visits a prostitute; 3/ joy; 4/ quarrelers
Sixes: 2/ a comedown or a putdown; 3/ satisfaction; 4/ an emotional burden
Fives: 2/ an emotional reverse, a breakdown; 3/ hesitation; 4/ order, good housekeeping
Fours: 2/ a dispute; 3/ unease; 4/ walks in the country
Threes: 2/ safety; 3/ serenity; 4/ great success
Twos: 2/ mistrust; 3/ fear; 4/ reconciliation

SOME
SPECIAL
CARDS

As we've said, you won't need a *complete* account of the meanings of all cards in the Minor Arcana to begin reading the Tarot. (Later on, you can study the detailed lists that come with the cards we've recommended on page 167.) But some of the lower cards do have specific meanings, or meanings in relation to other cards, that are *especially* useful in fortune-telling:

CUPS

Seven/a fair-haired child, or new baby for fair parents;
a new idea, a firm resolve, a forward movement.
Reversed: if next to the three of Cups, success.
Five/a card of great good luck in love and money.
Reversed: Reunion with a friend or relative long absent or estranged.
Two/favorable to pleasure in sex and success in business.
Reversed: uncontrollable passion.

PENTACLES

Ten/a house or apartment.
Nine/"for certain"
(in relation to what is foretold by other cards).
Reversed: Vain hopes.

SWORDS

Ten/next to Ace and King,
imprisonment for a man, treacherous friends for a woman.
Nine/generally, a card of bad omen.
Reversed: reason to suspect someone of dubious reputation.
Five/an attack on the sitter.
Reversed: sorrow and mourning.
Four/a bad card; beware.
Reversed: with care, qualified success.
Three/the flight of a woman's lover

WANDS

Ten/if near a good card, contradictions and obstacles.
Nine/a card of bad omen.
Seven/a dark child; a baby for dark parents.
Four/unexpected good fortune.
Three/a very good card;
collaboration and co-operation will further an enterprise.

THE FRENCH TAROT

If you're a Francophile, you may want to do your Tarot layouts with one of the lovely French decks. The cards shown below are from a rare French Revolutionary pack designed around 1791. (You can buy a reproduction of this and other French packs; see page 277.) *La Grande Mère* is the Empress; *Le Grande Père*, the Emperor. (Compare to the ones on page 63.) They wear no crowns—the French were anti-royalty in Revolutionary times!

THE TAROT
ICEBREAKER

Unlike most icebreakers, this Tarot-based game is unlikely to have your guests rolling about the floor in uncontrollable laughter, or reacting with disgust as they face yet another bout with charades. The Tarot can *reveal* your guests to one another, but unlike *some* games based on the notion of self-revelation, it won't be embarrassing or cruel. But it *will* give insights into minds and emotions.

The group must be at least six, and any number up to twelve works fine. (Over that, the game gets cumbersome.) Here's how to play:

Materials/Tarot deck; pencils and paper

1/Remove the cards of the Major Arcana from the pack, and pass them around. Give everyone a chance to get familiar with all twenty-two. (If the group is small, you might want to use just twice the number of cards as guests if everyone is not already acquainted with the Tarot; so, for six people, pick twelve cards at random from the Major Arcana.)

2/Pair off guests. Deal each pair *one* card selected at random. Each pair is to examine their card together—but no talking! Allow three minutes or so.

3/Pass out pads of paper and pencils. Ask each guest to write a brief description of how he or she *feels* about the card, what emotions it evokes. *No one may describe a card in physical detail.* Pairs may *not* consult.

4/Ask each pair to read their two individual descriptions: Other guests must try to guess which card is being described. Questions may be asked, as long as they do not refer to the actual picture on the card. For instance, it's okay to ask: "Do you find the card sinister?" but *not* fair to ask, "Does the card show a queenly woman?" After all the cards have been guessed, everyone will know much more about the power of the Tarot—and about each other.

Scoring/If you want to keep score, give five points to whoever guesses a card first. High scorer wins.

Variation/Give everyone a look at the *same* card, again chosen at random from the Major Arcana. Each guest writes out his or her emotional response. Collect all slips, shuffle, and read aloud, one by one. Have each guest guess *who* wrote each description. Every accurate guess counts one point. (A group that has played this game several times may get sophisticated enough to attempt to *disguise* their own descriptions—which only adds to the psychological challenge!)

CLASSIC TAROT LAYOUTS

THE SITTER AND THE READER

With the Tarot more than with any other method of fortune-telling, you must be *in tune* with the sitter (the questioner, the seeker). The symbols of the Major Arcana are so potent that they are likely to affect him very strongly; you must be tactful, confident, and at ease with the cards. If a particular layout should somewhat catch you off guard, or even frighten you, observe the cards calmly. Your function is to watch and interpret, and to consider the *effect* of your interpretation on the sitter.

Try to know as much as possible about the sitter. In fact, we suggest that you begin reading the Tarot with intimate friends. As you've seen already from the meanings of the cards, the Tarot does more than simply predict someone's future finances, health, or emotional life. It's concerned with the deep unconscious, and you'll be reading and interpreting signs of your sitter's most intimate existence. We're not trying to scare you off! In fact, we urge you not to hang back—some of the most exciting times of your life may be waiting for you.

PRESENT

PAST UNCONSCIOUSNESS

THE GREAT

THE GREAT CRESCENT

Unlike most of the classic Tarot layouts, this one uses *only* the Major Arcana. So it is somewhat easier to read, although less detailed in its information. It is *not* used to answer specific questions, but to describe the general direction of the sitter's life, from the depths of his unconscious to the surface of his mind. For it, you need no client card, but the sitter must shuffle, cut, and lay out the cards himself. *You* will read them from his layout, and determine his deepest urges, his outward tendencies, and what he can expect in the future.

A tip: Since you're using only the Major Arcana, each card has great importance, and you may find yourself bogged down in individual cards, failing to catch an over-all pattern. One way to alert yourself to a pattern is to see which cards are side by side. The connections there will *tell* you something. (We'll show you how to do this putting-together in more detail in the sample layout coming up.)

The Method

First, ask the sitter to shuffle the twenty-two cards of the Major Arcana, being certain that he does so both ways: in the usual way, as for playing cards, and by turning the cards around so that some will be reversed, or upside down. He then cuts the cards once, and places a hand over each of the two piles. He picks up the piles, one in each hand, and places the left-hand pile on top of the right-hand one. Then he turns the whole pile face up in his left hand. With his left hand, he deals the cards from the bottom of the pack, placing them from left to right in a large semi-circle on the table. (See picture on pages 80-81.) When cards are all dealt out, you sit in his place to read them. He may sit beside you so that he can see the cards and how they are placed.

When you read the cards, remember that the left-most point of the crescent represents the deepest level of the unconscious mind; the top (between the eleventh and twelfth cards) represents awakening consciousness; and the right-hand point is the height of consciousness. Keep in mind,

AWAKENING CONSCIOUSNESS

FUTURE HIGH CONSCIOUSNESS

CRESCENT

too, that in general the left stands for the immediate past, the center for the present, and the right for the future. The last card dealt, at the extreme right, is the crucial one: It will signify what the sitter, in his most conscious and daring moment, will desire for his future, and how he will act on that desire. Your reading of the other twenty-one cards will be progress toward your interpretation of this last and most vital card.

Here is the reading for the Great Crescent on the next page. The sitter was a man in his thirties, a friend of the reader's—generally strong, but fearful of the future and of his deepest instincts. (This much the reader knew in advance.)

The reader noted immediately that Judgment and the Magician are the left-most cards, indicating a great unconscious upheaval and the power to deal with it confidently; on the right, just past the level of consciousness, are four important, spiritually vital cards, all reversed. There will clearly be a *conscious* obstacle to the unconscious awakening. A glance at the final card is enough to indicate a fair outcome: Strength, which indicates the great power of the feminine unconscious, stands at the doorway to the future. With these patterns noted, the reading of the individual cards can start.

The first card to be read is that at the left-most point of the Crescent—in this case, Judgment. It means a great upheaval in the unconscious, which is bound to find its way to the surface and become a major factor in the sitter's conscious life. Whether it will work for good or ill depends upon the remaining cards.

The next card is *more* than hopeful: It could determine the direction of the whole reading. The Magician, master over both the physical and the spiritual, the most serenely confident symbol in the Major Arcana, is deep in the sitter's unconscious. He almost *presides* over the great new change. He is a good omen—forecasting sanity, acceptance of the new experience, and a general movement toward a new life.

However, the next card—the Devil, reversed—indicates a deep uneasiness or indecision about this upheaval, and the card that follows, the Hierophant, makes it clear that the sitter tends to search for conventional explanations to veil from himself the implications of his new feelings. He prefers the safety of orthodoxy to the excitement of freedom. If the awakening is a sexual one, for instance, he may want to bolt toward a conventional and undemanding marriage rather than seek out a passionate affair that would let him explore his newly found sexual depths. The authoritarian Emperor reinforces this impression, making it clear that even unconsciously this sitter seeks power over himself.

However, the Star and Temperance, placed together and falling next in the Crescent, suggest that the sitter will be able to accept his new feelings. Temperance means harmony, and the sitter will probably be willing to consider his upheaval as a way toward growth and life, not a threat that needs censoring.

In fact, the set of six cards that begins with the Star and ends with the Empress indicates a powerful drive for a complete, full life. Justice and the Chariot are central in this set, flanked on one side (the left, or unconscious) by the Star and Temperance, and on the other (the right, or conscious), by the Hanged Man and the Empress. Justice and the Chariot mean ambition and a desire for worldly success; their appearance *together* indicates a generosity of spirit, too. (The sitter won't want to succeed at anyone else's expense.)

But the other four cards in this set strongly suggest a dedication to *emotional, sensual,* and even *spiritual* fulfillment. The sitter can overcome the indecision earlier suggested by the Devil reversed, and a strong worldly ambition will be added to his spiritual or sensual awakening. The Empress at the far right of these six indicates that happiness in love will be great. Note that she is separated from the Chariot and Justice by the Hanged Man—a card that always affects those next to it. In this layout, it repeats the prediction of an awakening, and suggests that the emphasis will be *spiritual* rather than sensual. (Perhaps the sitter has been more afraid of a love-commitment than of sexuality.)

The presence of the Hermit reversed at the center of the layout means that the sitter, at present, is frustrating the personal development heralded in the earlier (unconscious) part of the layout. Outwardly, he wants to stand pat, maintain the status quo. The three reversed cards that follow indicate a strong resistance to outward change and growth, a fear of what is to come: the Moon (avoidance of risk), the Sun (unsettled plans), the World (fear of success, change). All of these reversed cards are obstacles to a new direction in the sitter's life.

The Wheel of Fortune and the Tower come next. They indicate an unexpected change, resulting in good luck. In spite of the sitter's powerful resistance to the promptings of his deepest instincts, he will surprise himself by changing *anyway.* The influence of his deep but largely unrealized self-confidence (the Magician) will shows itself in a surprising willingness to succeed in spite of himself.

Nevertheless, the positive forces in his personality won't win out *easily.* The presence of both the Fool and Death reversed (a very powerful combination) indicates that he'll react against his confidence and success. He may doubt the evidence of his own feelings, doubt even the good luck that is prophesied by the Wheel of Fortune, and retreat to what he thinks is a safer position. It would seem that he'll find refuge in the enigmatic attitude of superiority represented by the next card, the High Priestess—who is not favorable here. She represents a willingness to wait life out, to accept duality without exploring it, to let good fortune come and go without taking advantage of it. This impression is confirmed by the reversed Lovers, who suggest a persistent disharmony. The sitter's true desire for success and enlightenment battles his outward wish to cling to a stagnant status quo.

The last card, Strength, shows a chance that vital unconscious forces will triumph. Strength can here be interpreted as a new *conscious* desire to overcome the reluctance and stubbornness of the past.

The conclusion from this reading is qualified but lively hope. If the sitter is willing to take the cue from Strength, his twenty-second card, and find a new direction for his conscious desires, he can live up to the enormous potential indicated in his earlier cards. Otherwise, the power of his own fear and pessimism can drag him down. He should concentrate with great force on the Strength card, which will provide him with optimism and a sense of his own potential.

THE CELTIC CROSS

For this method, you will need a client card. Pick it from the court cards in the Minor Arcana (see the list of characteristics on pages 74-76); lay it face up in the center of the table. Have the sitter shuffle the rest of the cards. (You'll use the whole pack, both Major and Munor Arcana.) Again, be sure the sitter shuffles both ways so some cards will be reversed. After the shuffling, ask him to cut the cards twice to the left—into three piles—with his left hand.

As he cuts, ask him to concentrate on the question he wants the cards to answer, and then to tell you what it is.

With *your* left hand, pick up the first pile of cards and begin laying them out according to the pattern shown here. Follow this ritual as you do so: Covering the client card, place the first card, saying as you do so, *"This covers him."* This card will indicate the general atmosphere surrounding the sitter or the issue he's asking about.

Covering those two cards, but at a right angle to them, the second card, saying *"This crosses him."* This card, which will be read as if it were upright, shows the nature of any obstacle to the sitter's desires.

The third card goes directly below the central cards, with the words,

THE
CELTIC
CROSS

"This is beneath him." It forms the lower arm of the cross, and indicates what past experience is relevant to the sitter's question.

The fourth card forms the left arm of the cross, and is laid down as you say, *"This is behind him."* It shows an influence in the recent past.

Lay the fifth card above the central cards. Say, *"This crowns him."* It forms the upper arm of the cross and denotes a possible future event.

The sixth card, forming the right arm of the cross, is laid down with the words, *"This is before him,"* and shows an event in the near future.

The next four cards go vertically at the right of the cross, from bottom to top, to form a vertical line (called the Scepter). As the seventh card is laid down, say, *"This is what he fears."* It will tell what the sitter fears most in the situation he's asking about. When the eighth card is laid down, second from the bottom, say, *"The opinion of his house."* This card will represent the feelings and thoughts of his close friends and family about the matter. As the ninth card is dealt, say, *"This is what he hopes,"* and as the tenth card is laid down, *"This is what will come."*

Interpreting this layout is fairly easy. You simply follow the instructions that you gave yourself as you laid out the cards. Begin by taking a look at the "outcome" card (top right) and deciding whether it seems like a clear answer

ACE of PENTACLES.

to the sitter's question. If the outcome card is vague or confusing, you might conclude that the cards have refused to answer—which is, after all, a *kind* of answer. If you feel that the outcome card is promising, go back to the beginning and read each card, beginning with the covering card.

Remember that each card affects every other—especially the crossing and covering cards. If the covering card is unfavorable, for instance, a crossing card that *looks* ominous will actually be promising, since it will combat the sinister force of the first card. (For instance, if the Devil crosses the Three of Swords—the flight of a woman's lover—the crossing card may suggest that a revolution will happen in her life as a result—and that could be *good*. It may even mean a revolution in the lover's affections, and his eventual return!)

As you read, pay close attention to cards from the Major Arcana. They will have the most influence. (For instance, if the House card is the Emperor, you can be sure that the influence of the sitter's family will be very great.) Next in power are the court cards; they indicate personal relationships that will affect the outcome. It is true, too, that the cards closest to the client card—those that cover or cross him—are important merely because of their close position.

THE TREE OF LIFE

This is the classic ancient method for reading life's full history. There are two versions of it: One is a good deal more elaborate and time-consuming than the other. We'll describe the simpler one in detail, then tell you how to modify and enlarge it when you're ready to graduate to the more complete method. Whichever you use, however, remember that the Tree of Life should only be read once a year for any sitter. It prophesies the meaning and direction of a whole *life*, and such a reading is unlikely to change in *less* than a year. (Some believers even feel that the cards get "angry" if they are used frivolously.)

The preliminaries are the same as for the Celtic Cross; the sitter shuffles the cards both ways, then cuts the pack twice to the left with his left hand, producing three piles. While doing this, he must concentrate on the whole of his life up to the present moment, and upon everything he desires and fears for the future, as if he were about to drown, with a lifetime flashing through his mind.

The cards are then handed to you, one pile at a time, from the sitter's left hand to yours. Lay them out according to the diagram on page 56. As you can see from the picture, the cards form three triangles: the top one with its apex up; the other two upside down.

The reader lays down the first three cards from the first pile; the second three from the second; the third three from the third pile. The tenth card is the base of the tree.

The first triangle (cards 1, 2, and 3) represents the spirit.

The second triangle (cards 4, 5, and 6) represents reason.

The third triangle (cards 7, 8, and 9) represents the emotions, the unconscious.

The tenth card represents the subject's physical body or earthly home.

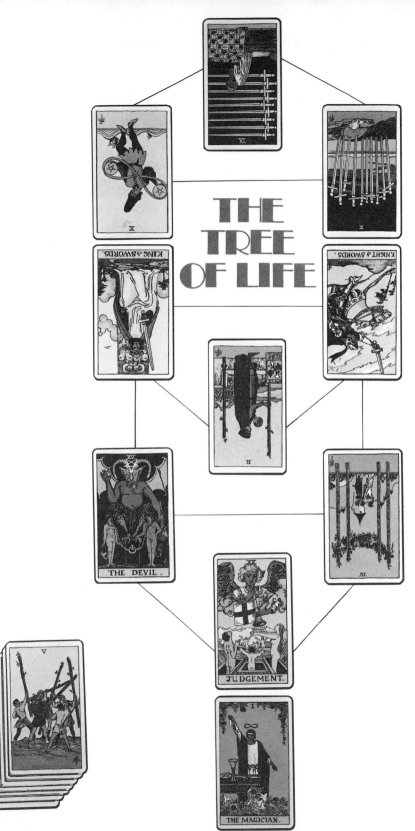

THE
TREE
OF LIFE

87

The individual cards have the following meanings:

1 the highest point of the subject's spiritual life
2 primal creative force; the father card
3 wellspring of life; the mother card
4 the virtues
5 intellectual or physical power; conquest
6 health and disposition
7 love, lust, marriage; the card of Venus
8 childbearing; the arts
9 the imagination—the source of dreams and creative power

After the tenth card is laid out, deal out seven cards face down; these are the qualifying pack called the Daath Pack. They will be read after the other cards are interpreted; they represent the unrealized dreams of the subject, and all the events in his life that are still in a state of development— his immediate future.

Notice that when you laid out the cards, you've made not only three triangles, but three *vertical rows* of cards. These vertical rows represent the Branches of the Tree of Life: the Branch of Discipline to the left, the Branch of Harmony in the center, and the Branch of Love to the right. These names are a guide to the reader. The cards in the left branch should be read with uncompromising vigor; in the center, with moderation; in the right, with love and compassion.

In the sample layout for the Tree of Life here, the reader will note at once that there are many swords in the layout; these foretell a good deal of strife and change in the life of the subject, who is a young man in his twenties.

The three cards in the upper triangle reveal deep conflict in the subject's spiritual life. The Nine and Ten of Swords reversed indicate that he feels suspicion and doubt in a situation that might lead to profit and power. (Perhaps this is some kind of ethical conflict, in his work life, for example.) The Two of Pentacles makes it clear that this conflict is deeply felt.

In the second triangle, further trouble is foretold. The subject will come under the domination (the Two of Wands reversed) of a cruel and unjust authority, the King of Swords reversed. (This is the father card—perhaps his *own* father?) He will have been unprepared for this blow, and will therefore take it hard and be unable to adjust to it.

In the third triangle, a quite remarkable state of affairs is shown by the Four of Wands reversed, the Devil, and Judgment. It is hard to know whether these cards indicate that the subject is going to succumb to the temptation of a great but evil power, or that he will, by great force of character, overcome his earlier difficulties and arrive at peace and harmony.

However, the presence of the Magician as the subject's earth card makes the latter interpretation of the third triangle more likely. The subject realizes his true desires (Judgment), and through enormous force, amounting to a revolution (the Devil), he manages to retain (or regain) his balance and benefit from the new.

In spite of the confused and distressed condition of the subject's spiritual and intellectual life, indicated by the cards in the first two triangles, it is clear from the powerful card in the earth position, the Magician, that he has the power to bring order out of chaos. At a time when he is in a state of deep conflict and under a terrible emotion strain because of the domination of a strong, cruel person, he has gained strength to respond to his own inner awakenings and turn them into a new form of harmony and peace.

88

Turn now to the Daath Pack to foretell the immediate future:

The Three of Pentacles: The subject has mastery of a trade to sustain him both physically and emotionally. (Perhaps he feels confident in his work, and this helps him through his ethical conflicts there.)

The Hierophant: Possibly he has a strong faith in one of the organized religions. In any case, he finds solace in a coherent philosophy.

The Emperor: This may be the subject's belief in authority, or a friend in power. It may indicate a way to counteract the terrible forces of the personal relationship described in the second triangle.

The Star: Again, the subject has great spiritual resources.

The Five of Wands: This means battle of life; it's another clue that the subject can't expect an easy way out of his conflict.

The Moon, reversed: The subject will weather the storms of the present; the peace he gains (as in the third triangle) will be a great cost, but this won't be his own fault.

Strength: This card is the companion of the subject's home card, the Magician. Clearly, he has enough strength to weather his difficulties, no matter how drastic they may seem.

This is a fortune of near-disaster averted—but *barely*—by the strong character of the subject. There is every indication that he will continue to be beset with difficulties, and that he will have to overcome enormous obstacles in order to feel secure. The many swords in his layout make it clear that his life is to be full of pain and strife, and there are no indications that material wealth will ease the way. On the other hand, he is well equipped to face adversity and overcome it; his spiritual resources are extraordinarily strong, and they will *have* to be—he'll need the power of the Devil just to keep from despairing.

There is an indication that through the great power of the Hierophant (perhaps his family, or an employer who believes in him), he will escape from the evil force in the second triangle. He may be able to change jobs, or leave his family (if his father is indeed represented by the reversed King of Swords); at any rate, that particular burden is likely to be a temporary one.

Also, the conflict in the first triangle, between a transitory advantage and a deep self-doubt, is likely to be resolved by the mastery of a craft indicated by the Three of Pentacles. By practicing his trade, the subject is likely to give up without regret the transitory profits of a perhaps shady way of life, and overcome shame and self-doubt through hard work.

In summary, the life we see in this layout is a difficult and painful one, but not without its rewards. Fortunately the subject has a number of tools that will allow him to salvage real happiness and peace from difficult situations: a serious craft, a deep self-confidence, and a powerful will combined with faith in both the social order and religion.

THE LARGER TREE

Once you're familiar with the reading of the Tree of Life and are certain you have mastered both the formation and the meanings of the Arcana, you might want to try the more detailed version of the Tree of Life, which is usually not recommended for beginners, and is *never* suggested for a more-than-once-in-five-years reading. In this method, seven cards, rather than a single card, are dealt in each of the ten places on the Tree. The Daath Pack contains eight cards. The layout is done three times—once for the past, once for the present, and once for the future.

As you can imagine, this is a *long* process, and quite arduous for the reader, who must often keep a written record of what each of the three layout records, and who must then read the three into a coherent fortune. It should be reserved for special occasions and special relationships, and should take up a whole evening, with both the reader and the subject at the highest possible pitch of concentration.

A PICTORIAL GLOSSARY
OF THE TAROT

The following list of symbols and signs found on the Tarot cards is partial. It is hard to imagine a *complete* list because the Tarot is almost an encyclopedia of occult symbols.

Although it's fascinating to research the symbols and signs, their power and significance are greater than any set meanings could suggest. Someone said of Pamela Colman-Smith, who drew these cards under the direction of Waite: "She *knew* that these things were true, and she *saw* them; . . . the one thing she lacked was an interest in the meaning of [them]." So don't worry if these limited meanings don't fascinate you as much as the possible ones they bring to mind—that's the whole *idea* of the Tarot.

CUP: one of the suits of the Tarot. Represents the Holy Grail—holder of the Holy Spirit and the Water of Life. Also a symbol of the female, oral, vaginal. Generosity, hospitality.

PENTACLE: one of the suits of the Tarot. The shape of the basic pattern in witchcraft, used to call up demons and other supernatural beings. A symbol of mastery of both spiritual and material worlds. Upside down: disturbance in the order of things. In the Major Arcana, found on XV, The Devil

SWORD: one of the suits of the Tarot. A symbol of force, worldly power, war and strife. Also a phallic symbol, complementing the cup. Found in the Major Arcana in the right hand of Justice, XI

WAND: one of the suits of the Tarot. Because it is growing leaves, reminiscent of the cross on which Christ was crucified, which was always portrayed as green in the Middle Ages. May be a staff to lean on, or a club to fight with. In the Major Arcana, the Hermit, IX, leans upon a wand *without* leaves—meaning he has given up the things of this world.

 SEPTENARY, OR SIGN OF THE SACRED BOOK OF THE TAROT: appears on the angel's gown on XIV, Temperance. Considered a sacred design because its two elements, the triangle and the square, combine to form seven parts (a magic number)

SIGN OF THE SUN: symbolizes brightness, steadfastness, the glowing power of life and eternity. Found on XIV, Temperance

WREATH: victory, praise, fertility that brings one honor. Found on VIII, Strength; III, The Empress; XXI, The World; Six of Wands, Two of Cups, Seven of Cups

MYSTIC ROSE: life in the face of death. The symbol of the Rosicrucians, who believe in reincarnation. Found on VIII, Death

GARLAND: fruitfulness, harvest, celebration. Appears on the One and Four of Wands

SUNFLOWER: symbol of the pure joy of the fruits and flowers of the earth. Located on XIX The Sun; and the Queen of Wands

LILY AND ROSE: the successful marriage of the earthly and the spiritual. Found on I, The Magician; and the Two of Wands

GRAPE ARBOR: man's mastery of nature to produce fruitfulness. On the Nine of Pentacles

POMEGRANATE: symbol of the fertile female; sign of many (seeds) in one (fruit). Found on II, The High Priestess

FLAMING TREE: enduring passion for truth and the true way to live. The fire of true understanding. On VI, The Lovers

 TREE OF THE KNOWLEDGE OF GOOD AND EVIL: temptation; threats to an earthly paradise; human frailty. On VI, The Lovers

DOVE: the Holy Spirit; the heavenly on earth. It also appears on the Ace of Cups.

RAM'S HEAD: symbol of masculine potency, leadership. Appears on IV, The Emperor

HOODED FALCON: man's mastery of nature. On the Nine of Pentacles

SPHINX: silent and mysterious power; ancient wisdom. Found on X, The Wheel of Fortune; VII, The Chariot

FOUR BEASTS OF THE APOCALYPSE: bull, lion, eagle, and man (or angel); symbols of the end of the world, the eternal truth. Also the wisdom of the prophets of the Old Testament, from Isaiah (where they first appear) to the Book of Revelation. Found on X, The Wheel of Fortune; XXI, The World

FISH: an early symbol of Christ. In the Tarot, represents the constant springing up of new ideas, evolutionary progress. It appears on the Page of Cups, King of Cups.

CROSSED KEYS: St. Peter's keys to the gates of heaven; the workings of worldly power in heavenly matters.

 On V, The Hierophant

CADUCEUS: a snake-wreathed staff, symbol of health and commitment to service of others. On the Two of Cups

TWO-HEADED WAND: mastery; the power to join the forces of heaven and earth. Found on I, The Magician; and XXI, The World

ANKH, OR CROSS OF LIFE: combines the masculine and feminine symbols; repels the powers of darkness. Found on IV, The Emperor

LANTERN: sign of the sincere search for truth. On IX, The Hermit

Orb of the World: in hand of the Emperor, IV, symbolizes complete rule over the physical world. On the Two of Wands, peaceful rule of man over nature

HEART: symbol of Venus and the unconscious. If pierced, represents a wounded imagination. If used as a shield, stands for the triumph of the unconscious and all feminine powers. Found on III, The Empress; and the Three of Swords

YODS: falling drops of light. A Hebrew word and image, meaning the descent of the spiritual from heaven to earth. Yods appear on XVI, The Tower; XVIII, The Moon; the Ace of Swords; and on the Ace of Cups

CHAPTER THREE
SPOTS
BEFORE YOUR EYES:

Baby needs a new pair of shoes! Come seven . . . come eleven . . . . The world's oldest established permanent floating crap game isn't the one run by Damon Runyon's Nicely-Nicely! Dice have been used for some three thousand years for fortune-telling—all over the world, and in ways that range from the frankly frivolous to the deeply serious.

No fortune-telling method is closer in spirit to the strange, superstitious world of the gambler than cleromancy—fortune-telling with dice and dominoes. After all, the gambler who talks to his dice as if they were naughty children, and lives for the next big "winning streak" the way some of us live for our work and our love affairs, is not just behaving that way on the off chance that he'll break even. He believes in a kind of magic. He has to—the odds against a given number turning up on the faces of a set of two dice are substantial; when, as is common in fortune-telling, three dice are used, the odds grow almost awesome (over two-hundred-to-one that a given number will turn up on any throw). All gamblers know this . . . and so they all believe not in odds, but in luck, their luck, their good fortune. They're not betting for money, but on their futures. They, too, are fortune-tellers, with only one client and an audience that can see them lose.

Of course, the gambler believes that he can change the future by talking to his dice, coaxing them to operate against the odds. The fortune-teller using dice or dominoes is merely trying to read the future, not change it—but she must beware of the temptation to wring out of the impersonal coldness of those little dotted cubes or rectangles a different number—and therefore a different reading—than the one that has come up. For this reason, it is considered the worst bad luck for one who throws the dice or shuffles the dominoes to use them to tell her own fortune.

Cleromancy and card-reading are far apart in emotional quality. The cards are varied in their messages, leave a good deal to the imagination and intuition of reader and sitter. But the dots (called "pips") on the dice and dominoes have no quality except number. There are no colored suits, no personalized court cards, no rich and fascinating symbolisms to weave into a narrative about the subject's past, present, future. There are only the odds. If you're optimistic, the best to hope for is that the fall of the dice or dominoes is affected by the conscious and unconscious wishes of the reader and subject.

Dice and dominoes are, therefore, much simpler to handle and interpret. But for some people, their mathematical finality seems cold, and creates an almost unbearable tension. The patterns are so maddeningly fixed, the odds so great against any particular outcome.

Using cleromancy to tell fortunes, you come very close to the origin of man's belief in magic: that we can change the unchangeable, triumph over fate, perhaps even escape death. Only numerology and astrology (one dealing with pure number, the other with the movements of the universe) are closer to the bare facts of life than the workings of cleromancy.

THE MYSTIC MOOD

Because cleromancy is so closely tied to the world of gambling, the atmosphere is bound to partake a little of the casino. But try to ease the tension and set up a situation that is as quiet and relaxed as possible.

There are two very different attitudes to cleromancy. The English witch Sybil Leek, who is certainly a show-woman in her chosen field, describes the throwing of the dice as a howling climax to an emotion-filled ritual. But other authorities prescribe that the dice be thrown or the dominoes shuffled in complete silence, broken only afterward for interpretation. Until you're familiar with the methods, we'd recommend the calmer atmosphere. (It takes a good deal of *panache* to rear back and shake the dice like a Saturday-night regular at the Sands!)

Although dice and dominoes share much of the same methodology, and are much alike physically (each single-faced, rectangular domino is marked like two faces of a die), the methods are entirely different *emotionally*. Dice are gambling paraphernalia, and are marked as perhaps slightly *wicked*, the tools of the gambler and the con man. Dominoes, in spite of their ancient and mysterious origins in China, are associated in this country with games that children and old men play in the park and in the doorways of cafés in European cities . . . charming, perhaps, but not very exotic. Keep the differences in mind when you're determining the evening's setting.

Another word of caution, which may sound a little *prudish:* Beware of offending some people by the use of dice. *Cards* used to be a moral issue (there are still fundamentalists who think of them as the devil's device to lead us to damnation), but they are by now largely considered a harmless way to while away a rainy Saturday afternoon . . . for those whose libidos are notably lethargic. But dice are usually seen in gambling's province—and some people are downright frightened by gambling, associating it with other and even more threatening forms of vice. (And there *is* such a thing as Gamblers' Anonymous—for compulsives who have sworn off and are trying to live straight lives. They don't disapprove of social gambling—or fortune-telling—any more than the alcoholic disapproves of drinking; but it would be downright tactless to include such a person in a fortune-telling session using gambler's paraphernalia.) The same rule applies here as in any other social situation—pick your people carefully, and *then* full steam ahead!

As for your own look, there are two ways to go, at least. The first is decorative, designed to make you a part of the black-and-white scheme introduced by the cubes and rectangles. You'd choose a black-and-white outfit, with a rather stark make-up and a generally quiet but quite dramatic bearing. (I have a friend who wears a black domino—a half-mask—decorated with white dots when she's manipulating the dominoes. Very effective—but a little spooky.) This look is copied, really, from the women dealers and croupiers in the casinos, both here and in Europe. All such women dress quietly and have a wonderfully businesslike air that's both slightly ominous and comforting. For you, that look can combine understated elegance with the exotic appeal of fortune-telling. A long black skirt in velvet or crepe with a perfectly tailored white silk blouse (or Liza Minelli's little-boy tuxedo with satin bow-tie), jet earrings, and sleek satin pumps can make you look so *together* that the fatalistic story of the fortune will hardly bobble *anyone's* psyche. Your Bacall-ish ease will give the occasion an air of the vulnerably hard-boiled, a little like the great gambling-house scenes in *The Big Sleep.*

Diversionary tactics can be just as charming. There you are, shaking the dice in their cup (or in your cupped hand), beautifully got up in pastel print chiffon pajamas, your hair in masses of carefully uncontrived curls, your face rosy and flushed. The more innocent and, well, a bit *flustered,* the better. *You* provide the antidote to the fear of the future, the dread that uncompromising numbers will deal a crushing blow. Use a glowy foundation, lots of translucent blusher, a pink lipstick, the longest and most *innocent* false eyelashes you can lay hands on. Don't, by any means, try to appear light-minded or unserious about the fortune-telling (if you weren't seriously interested in it, why would you do it?), but make your silence a bit like the solemnity of a child caught up in a particularly fascinating and quiet game, it adds deliciously to the atmosphere.

As for the setting—again, as for cards, the best background is a simple table (for cleromancy, it might be a little larger than card-table size) covered with *black* felt or with a *black* cloth. For the dice, you'll need a piece of chalk and a length of string to tie to it, to use as a compass for drawing a perfect circle on the felt; make the circle about nine or ten inches in diameter. (For one method, you'll also need a yardstick.) For dominoes, a plain black background is most effective—the white pips will show up almost magically against the black felt, while the domino itself "disappears." Light is important—again, a low lamp, almost at table level, is best; it should illuminate the table itself and very little beyond.

The materials for cleromancy are standard—even dime-store dominoes are dramatically beautiful, and black-and-white plastic dice are as effective as ebony-and-ivory ones. However, you might want to invest in a leather dice cup—the sound of the dice being shaken is curiously exciting to some people. (*You* may fancy yourself with the dice in your cupped hand. Make the decision according to your personal style.)

Do remember the first rule of fortune-telling: Be respectful of your tools. Don't treat dice or dominoes as if they were leftovers from a casual game you played one dull night in the country. If possible, take them from a special box—if you're using a dice cup, store the dice in it—not from the manufacturer's box they came in. A bright tin tea caddy or an old wooden collar box makes a good holder for dominoes; so does a small, lined jewel box. If you don't keep your dice in a cup, you might want to buy a soft suede or leather bag with a drawstring, in a bright color; the dice will look dramatic and interesting slipping out of their pouch into your hand or onto the black background of the tabletop. Make it a ritual, it adds to the mystique.

96

DICE

There are many variations on fortune-telling with dice, but two general rules apply: *Three* dice are used, and they must be thrown within a chalk circle. Some experts believe in the rule of silence, and some also have the notion that cool, calm weather is best for a throwing.

Not only the numbers rolled are meaningful. Dice that fall "away"—*outside* the circle—are part of the fortune-telling pattern, too. Here's what they mean:

One away: The two dice *inside* the circle are counted, and their meaning explained. But the future will not go as planned; bad times and quarrels are ahead.

Two away: A great breach of trust is in the offing; beware of taking any such trouble too seriously.

Three away (this may seem impossible, but it's been known to happen): The wish will be granted, but no good will come from it; a quick spate of good luck will be followed by trouble.

Rarely as it happens, it is good to know that if one die lands *on top* of another, extreme caution should be exercised in all ventures, romantic as well as professional.

The subject does not roll the dice—you do. He thinks of the wish he wants granted, or the question he wants answered. The simple throw into the circle relates only to a specific wish or question, and its outcome will be seen within nine days.

After the dice are thrown, count the spots on the top side of each die, and add them up. Each possible total has a meaning, and it is up to you to know what the number showing on the table means. The following numbers represent the possible totals on a throw of three dice:

Three: the lowest number possible; a favorable omen, foretelling unexpected good news

Four: disappointment, a sudden unpleasantness

Five: a new and exciting person to appear

Six: losses, but not without compensation

Seven: trouble in business; gossip causing sorrow

Eight: criticism from others that may affect your judgment; thoughtless action that may cause injustice

Nine: if there has been a quarrel, a reunion; if a courtship, expect a proposal; an affair in the offing, consummation. In general, success in love

Ten: news of a birth. General contentment domestically, and perhaps a promotion or advantageous change of job

Eleven: illness. Occasionally a parting, but not necessarily a permanent or long-lasting one

Twelve: an important message received; need for advice

Thirteen: grief and deep sorrow

Fourteen: a new friend, who will grow much closer and very dear to you

Fifteen: caution; temptation to act against your principles and (whether you know it at the time) your best interests

Sixteen: chance for a journey; if taken, pleasure and possible profit

Seventeen: a change in your plans suggested by a foreigner, or someone who has lived abroad; his suggestion should be accepted

Eighteen: the best of all omens; suggests good fortune, health, wealth, a rich marriage

Remember that with this simple method, the throw is everything. The single total is the prediction, and you must make the most of it. The more you know about the questioner, the better; if he's a complete stranger, you may have trouble connecting the prediction with his life. Remember, too, that the numbers foretell the *future* in all cases—they don't explain the past or present.

Do study the meanings of the eighteen possible numbers. While it is possible to consult a book on the Tarot and look properly wise about it, the meanings here are single and simple, and you'll merely seem uninformed if you scurry off to a printed source only to come up with a one- or two-word prediction. *Know the numbers and their meanings, and be prepared to relate them to the details you know about the questioner's life.*

THE DIVIDED CIRCLE
Once you've learned the numbers for the three dice and have practiced explaining their meanings as they fall, you're prepared to go on to a more complex, detailed method.

For this, you first draw the chalk circle, and then divide it into twelve sections, like the wedges of a pie. Number each wedge from one to twelve, moving counterclockwise, as shown below:

Each of these sections has a meaning:

First: next year's events

Second: money
Third: travel
Fourth: home and family
Fifth: current enterprises and plans
Sixth: health
Seventh: marriage; partnerships and contracts of all kinds
Eighth: death and inheritances
Ninth: the questioner's general state of mind at the time of the throw
Tenth: the questioner's work or profession
Eleventh: friends
Twelfth: enemies

Because each of the three dice can fall into a different section, you read the *individual* number on each die as well as an over-all reading for the total. The meanings for the numbers on individual dice are as follows:

One: success in matters concerning the sector into which the die has fallen
Two: success in all things
Four: bad luck
Five: good luck, likely to remain
Six: luck due to the actions of the questioner in the sector in which the number falls

Interpretation

So, you have three forecasts to work with: The total number shown on the dice; the number on each individual die; and the sectors into which each die falls. By reading each of these factors carefully and combining them judiciously, you should be able to give the questioner a fairly completely life reading. For instance, for the throw illustrated below, your reading might be something like this:

The dice have fallen into sections two, six, and seven, so immediate concerns in the future will be money, health, and marriage. The four in the second section indicates trouble in the offing—perhaps the loss of a job, or merely unexpected expenses. The three in section six suggests excellent health for the immediate future—money may cause trouble, but not illness. The one in section seven means that a current marriage will go well or that a contemplated one will be lasting and very happy.

The sum of the numbers on the dice is eight. The over-all comment, then, is that the questioner's judgment may be clouded by criticism. Because the only possible area where trouble seems likely is financial, he should be advised to take no hasty action in financial affairs: If he's contemplating buying or selling stock or real estate, he should wait a few weeks and not listen to friends who think he ought to follow their advice. If he is planning to change jobs, even at a higher salary, he should consider carefully. In any case, he should prepare himself for financial reverses, always remembering that both his love life and his health are likely to remain excellent.

DOMINOES

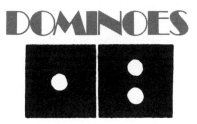

A domino is like two faces of a die set side by side on a rectangular tablet. Dominoes were invented by the Chinese, who wanted a calmer game, and preferred hand-moving dominoes to rolling dice.

There are twenty-eight dominoes in a set. The face of each domino is divided into two sections: some marked by dots numbering from one to six; some blank. Since there's a double blank, in dominoes it is possible literally to "draw a blank," which cannot happen with dice.

To read the dominoes, place all twenty-eight face down on a table and ask the questioner to shuffle them by moving them around at random. He then draws one domino. You read its meaning. It is returned and the dominoes reshuffled. A second is drawn and read; the dominoes are reshuffled and then a third is read. The reader then combines the three readings and considers what they tell for the questioner's future, or in what way they answer his question.

Here are the meanings of the dominoes:

Six/Six: success; money to come
Six/Five: a public occasion
Six/Four: an extended quarrel; a lawsuit unlikely to be successful
Six/Three: a short and happy journey (If a long journey is proposed, don't go by air—train or boat would be better.)
Six/Two: a useful gift; buying new clothes

Six/One: the basis of your troubles due to disappear
Six/Blank: caution with treacherous friends
Five/Five: a move to a new house or apartment
Five/Four: profit from speculation (Do not re-invest.)
Five/Three: a visitor
Five/Two: the birth of a child; a

long-awaited celebration
Five/One: a passionate love affair, ending unhappily
Five/Blank: sorrow, but not in your own life; a friend who will need comfort
Four/Four: a party whose host you don't know; a blind date
Four-Three: trouble at home, but due to pass
Four/Two: loss by theft; or a swindler to enter your life
Four/One: trouble through debts; possible privation
Four/Blank: reunion with an old friend, perhaps one who's been estranged

Three/Three: a rival in love; misery through jealousy
Three/Two: investments due to fail
Three/One: surprising news that will prove useful
Three/Blank: a young person, possibly a child; surprises
Two/Two: jealousy
Two/One: a desperate need will arise
Two/Blank: unavoidable trouble
One/One: a bold decision required (Do not hesitate.)
One/Blank: arrival of a stranger who has lived abroad, and may be of use
Blank/Blank: the worse of the omens; unhappiness, loss, disappointment

Sometimes, after a drawing and reshuffling, the same domino is redrawn. It confirms the first prediction, and is a sign that the prediction will come true in the very near future.

THE TWELVE POINTS

As with dice, the dominoes can be used for a more detailed and longer-range reading. For this, you'll need the divided chalk circle again.

The questioner shuffles the set on the table, and then with his left hand draws twelve dominoes, putting them in a row face *down*, again using his left hand. Then he turns each of them up, starting at the left and still using the left hand.

As he turns up the dominoes, he places them on the sections of the circle—the first in section one, the second in section two, and so on around the circle until all twelve dominoes are placed. Then you read the dominoes by the point system, as follows, relating each prediction to the section the domino is in:

Twelve points (6/6): a great good fortune

Eleven points (6/5): a parting

Ten points (6/4,5/5): complete change for the better; departure from routine

Nine points (6/3,5/4): pleasant prospects

Eight points (6/2,5/3,4/4): difficulties; reproach from unexpected sources

Seven points (6/1,5/2,4/3): personal and sexual problems that you will be blamed for

Six points (6/0,5/1,4/2,3/3): disaster, accompanied by financial loss

Five points (5/0,4/1,3/2): care needed in your domestic life

Four points (4/0,3/1,2/2): a bad time physically—not ill health, but perhaps a minor car accident; the need for a very strict diet!

Three points (3/0,2/1): surprising developments in the near future

Two points (2/0,1/1): unhappy surprises

One point (1/0): great difficulties and personal hardship

(0/0): great misfortune

4
Heavenly Sign: Saturn
Element: Earth
Color: Green

Chapter Four
PLAYING
THE NUMBERS:
FORECASTING WITH
NUMEROLOGY

Quick—pick a number from one to ten! Do the men you meet always seem to live at an address with the number twenty-two in it? Is there a number you think of as lucky for you—one you'd probably play if you went to the track and didn't know a thing about the merits of the horses? Numerologists believe that if you have these feelings, or a recurring sense that numbers are important to you in some way, you're unconsciously reflecting a universal truth: that the science of numbers can explain the sense of your current life and help to foretell your future.

The Greek philosopher Pythagoras supposedly founded numerology. He believed that all human history could be divided into cycles, and he measured those cycles with the numbers from one to nine. Modern numerology goes farther. It says that these numbers—plus the magical Master numbers, eleven and twenty-two—reflect the cycles of history and of individual lives. So numerology uses a series of formulas to reduce important data (names, dates, and so on) to these numbers. They also explain relationships between you and others—even give advice about specific situations. Will John be a good lover for me? Is changing jobs a good idea right now?

Of course, the person whose numbers mean most to you is . . . you. And since numerology (like all fortune-telling methods) takes practice, do your own "numeroscope" before you try anyone else's. Once you've done that, you can, with two pieces of elementary information, do the same for anyone—and not necessarily in his presence!

THE MYSTIC MOOD

Doing a numeroscope is like charting a horoscope: Not only does the subject not *need* to be there, it's really better if he's not. No ritual requires his absence—it's just that working out a numeroscope involves a series of calculations that are perfectly *riveting* to whoever's doing them, and a crashing *bore* to anyone who happens to be watching (sort of like watching a programmer prepare a bunch of those neatly punched cards for the computer—ho-hum).

So, gather the information from your subject, spend a fascinating evening working up the chart—and then *spring* the results. You can either do this verbally, and fairly casually—"By the way, I had a chance to work out your numbers the other night"—or you can turn the surprise into a little ceremony. I've a friend who makes special covers for her charts, with the subject's name and a numerological design on them. Inside, she puts a made-to-order fortune, showing the subject's numbers, what they portend for his future, what they say about his past and present. *She's* good at calligraphy, so she handwrites all her fortunes in an italic script—but there's no reason why you shouldn't type yours.

As for your look as mistress of the numbers, it's tempting to consider a futuristic approach—like the pale, extreme images in the film *THX 1138* . . . or even the plastic-cut-out Courrèges costumes of the early 1960's. (Maybe it seems a little soon to view Courrèges with nostalgia—but the look he created *is* the prettiest version of science-fiction cool.) Of course, a lot of us are still in love with *Star Trek's* Mr. Spock—and those uniforms worn by the lady lieutenant and her fellow-officers look awfully good if you have long legs. For you, these ideas might suggest crisp shorts and top, worn with tights and high boots; or bright full-length body-stocking with one of the new sleeveless tunics . . . all geometrics and clean lines, but *revealing*. (Characters in science fiction always seem to have advanced to the point where they display their bodies with efficient comfort.)

Numerology needn't be dressed for at all, of course—unless you believe that you need to convince someone of your ability to do all those computations. (They really aren't *that* complicated, but why let on?) One reason to do the calculations in private is that you can take as long as you want (even licking your pencil if that's how you work best) and then give a vague, blissed-out account, as if the numbers and what they mean had just, well, sort of *come* to you. However, an ancient-wisdom costume is all wrong for numerology. The science of numbers is too much a part of modern technology to make *that* convincing; and don't let yourself get *so* vague that you lose your sense of authority. That authority is the basis of fortune-telling; if you lose the special sense that *you* are the keeper of a magical, exciting knowledge, you've lost your audience, and all the fun evaporates.

Make-up? Well, believers think numerology is the most *natural* of the methods. Even though it's based on numbers, which smack of science and the coldness of twentieth-century technology, its idea is that the universe follows mathematical laws. So keep your make-up natural. Be bright-eyed and bright-haired, with a minimum of *obvious* aid. (In THX, the heroine had *no* reason to go that far in the pursuit of the Clean Look.) Wear near-translucent foundation and a blusher, and *pale* eyebrows. (Brunettes can use a brush-on lightener.) Clean, clean hair done as simply as your cut allows.

BASIC METHODS

Numerology is the easiest mode of fortune-telling to put into practice. You need only know your subject's birthdate (the *exact* one; as in astrology, there can be no fudging!) and name (the full name, plus whatever nicknames or married names or professional names have been tacked on since birth). *That's it.* With those facts, you can go straight to work, analyzing the subject's past, present, future—even letting him know how to soothe, pacify, and calm himself when his life seems a total muddle and his therapist is away during that miserable month-long August vacation.

Names

First, take a look at this chart:

1	2	3	4	5	6	7	8	9
A	B	C	D	E	F	G	H	I
J	K	L	M	N	O	P	Q	R
S	T	U	V	W	X	Y	Z	

Each letter of the alphabet corresponds to the number in whose column it appears. (In addition, the letter K represents the magical number 11, and the

V, 22—which we'll explain later. But for basic calculation purposes, the K is 2 and the V is 4, as on the chart. Watch for K's and V's in names, though—they indicate an old and highly developed soul.)

Let's take a practice name and work out its letter-count:

R E B E C C A   E L I Z A B E T H   S M I T H

Put the number equivalents of all vowels in the name (if there are Y's in the name, they count as vowels) on top and the consonant numbers on the bottom:

```
5 5    1  5 9  1  5              9
R E B E C C A   E L I Z A B E T H   S M I T H
9  2  33        3  8  2  28    14   28
```

Now, add all vowel numbers together. In our sample below, the total is 40; next add the digits in the total (4 + 0). Draw a *circle* around the final total—in this case, 4. It is the *Soul Number* for the name. The Soul Number indicates the subject's inmost desires—the deepest motivations behind everything he does.

```
5 5    1  5 9  1  5              9
R E B E C C A   E L I Z A B E T H   S M I T H
         = 40 = 4 + 0 = ④
```

Next add the *consonants'* number equivalents to find the *Impression Number*. This indicates the reaction other people have to the subject on first meeting. In the sample below, consonant digits total 55—which, when we add the two fives together, equals 10, or 1 + 0, for a total of 1. Draw a *box* around this 1 to indicate that it is this name's Impression Number

```
R E B E C C A   E L I Z A B E T H   S M I T H
9  2  33        3  8  2  28    14   28
         = 55 = 10 (1 + 0) =  [1]
```

We'll show you how to interpret these numbers in a minute.

Now, add the vowel total 4 (the Soul Number) to the consonant total 1 (the Impression Number) to determine the *Expression Number*. In our sample, this works out to 5. Enclose the Expression Number in a *triangle*.

```
5 5    1  5 9  1  5              9
R E B E C C A   E L I Z A B E T H   S M I T H
9  2    33      3  8  2  28  14  2 8
                    = 40 =  ④
                         =      △5
                    = 55 =  [1]
```

The Expression Number indicates the sum total of this person's abilities, tools, talents, and Karmic knacks—all the powers at her command.

About Nicknames, Professional Names, Married Names
The Expression Number is based on the name of the subject. It is very

106

important that the reader be given the complete full name of the subject . . . the name he was given, or saddled with, right after he was born. But what if the subject has acquired a nickname, a married name, a *nom de plume,* even changed his name legally? All these extra names are important, and should be considered . . . but only after the first name is counted, numbered, and interpreted. After that, do a separate reading for the other name or names, and see how the results match or contrast with those for the original name. Sometimes you'll find that the qualities of the assumed name have truly *replaced* the original ones. In that case, you are dealing with an exceptionally strong character, a person who can indeed make his own destiny.

Birthdate

The *Destiny Number* is derived from the subject's birthdate. To find it, you use the month, day, and year of your subject's birthday. Numbers for the months:

1	2	3	4	5	6	7	8	9
Jan.	Feb.	Mar.	Apr.	May	June	Jul.	Aug.	Sept.
Oct.	Nov.	Dec.						

For the day and year, use the simple number if it is under 10, or the added digits of the compound number. Take this sample:

January 31, 1940

January is 1; to get the day number, add 3 and 1, to get 4; for the year number, add $1 + 9 + 4 + 0$ to get 14, then add $1 + 4$ to get 5. When the three totals are added, you will get 10; add the 1 and the zero to get 1, which is this person's Destiny Number.

INTERPRETATION

The simplest way to define the two numbers—Destiny and Expression—is to compare their origins. The Expression Number is taken from the name—an outward identification. It tells how people view the subject, how he sees himself. It is truly expressive—of the subject, his life, his thoughts. His *consciousness* lies in his Expression Number (and therefore you'll read it first to learn about his character). But the Destiny Number is derived from his birthdate—one of the earliest, and certainly one of the most intimate, facts about him. It tells what is likely to happen to him, and what he is *likely to desire,* what is *beyond his will.* The Expression and Destiny numbers may not match; when they do, you're reading a *strong* character.

A Note About the Method

As you can see from the examples above, numerology reduces all numbers to the numerals 1 through 9, and to the Master numbers 11 and 22. No compound numbers, with the exception of the Master numbers, are used; they *must* be reduced to the numbers 1 through 9, or to 11 or 22. You just keep adding digits until you get one of these numbers.

The Master numbers are the only exceptions to this rule. The numbers 11 and 22 have been found by numerologists to have a wealth of cosmic vibrations—caused, according to some, by their suspension between good and evil, positive and negative. They are thought to be beyond the range of ordinary human experience, and thus unreducible. If a name or birthdate you're working on can be reduced to 11 or 22, you are dealing with someone who is extraordinary in this life and (according to the many numerologists who believe in reincarnation) in past lives as well. In the interpretative paragraphs that follow, we're included 11 and 22 as separate numbers, following the rest.

Interpreting Each Number

Each number has a myriad of interpretations—remember, numerology is a study of the whole of life and the universe—but we will concentrate here on the two that you will have found in your calculations: the Name or Expression Number, and the Birthdate or Destiny Number. Since each number has an Expression reading and a Destiny reading, you must combine the readings, usually for two different numbers, to arrive at a coherent fortune for your subject.

1
Heavenly Sign: The Sun
Element: Fire
Color: Red

Expression: The One character is strong, forceful, innovative; he's independent, but needs encouragement from lovers, husband, friends, boss. Not necessarily a fast starter—but once off and running, he's a *smash*, pioneering and original in thought, utterly individualistic. But he tends to arrogance, overconfidence, egotism. Ideas may come faster than they can be applied. The One personality can approach life with a certain coolness—he'll never have trouble finding new ideas or an abundance of energy.

There is great danger if One fights the rhythm of his powerful character. He might then fail, and fail badly. He is like his element sign, the Sun—he can burn a thousand years and never burn out, but if he represses his energies, there will be a *tremendous* explosion. He must work alone or in charge of *small* groups; the arts are a good outlet for his energies, and so are the sciences. Freelancing will be most congenial.

Destiny: A young and energetic soul, the person with a One Destiny Number can count on being a leader, a strong force in his own life and that of others—even if his Expression Number suggests otherwise. Beginnings will be very important—new jobs, new towns, new lovers and friends. A numerologist should inquire closely into the plans of a One: Does he expect to stay in his job forever? in some other kind of rut? If he hasn't made a new beginning recently, perhaps he should— his Destiny Number is pushing him.

A Double One (Expression and Destiny numbers *both* One) will be almost unstoppable, and must not ever run the risk of frustration. (A marriage of convenience, a sinecure in the family business, *any* confinement will drive him bananas!)

108

2
Heavenly Sign: The
Moon
Element: Water
Color: Orange

Expression: The Two personality is a *conductor* of energy, like water. He is a social being, functioning best in partnership, reveling in group activity, fickle in love only because of an attraction to so many. A *giver,* Two finds it hard to hold back, to turn energy and interest *inward.* The peacemaker of the numbers, Two will go a long way to avoid an argument. The desire for harmony may be a terrifying drawback, though—leading to humiliating self-abasement in order to pacify a touchy situation. The same tendency can bring on a lethargy and apathy that make Two's docility seem wishy-washy.

Twos are collectors and assimilators; they love to be surrounded by beloved, nostalgic objects, going into a hobby or favorite subject in *depth.* A Two is often the "quiet type" (that little girl at the third desk who turns out to have mastered High German and high karate on her lunch hours).

The Two personality may find the happiness that can only come to those who give themselves utterly to their passions, or the *unhappiness* that comes of giving to the *wrong* person at the *wrong* time. He may get stuck in a job or a love affair, and should be encouraged to examine his life: Is he *really* where he wants to be, or does he just feel comfortable because he's handling the situation so well? But beware of making these suggestions too obviously—Two can be hypersensitive, almost paranoiac, if he's afraid he's being misunderstood. His emotional dependence is something he's aware of, but it makes him nervous to be criticized—and that could be a problem for him. Point all this out *tactfully*—and he will be grateful.

Destiny: Those with a Two Destiny Number often need periods of gestation, rest, and long, quiet times alone to collect and assimilate the varied experience of their lives. The rhythms of music, dance, and poetry are great therapy for the Two Destiny person—they help soothe, and should always be in the environment, even if times are busy. If a dynamic One has a Two Destiny Number, for instance, it is a sure sign that the dynamism cannot be kept going without periods of easing off—long weekends at the shore or in the mountains, an afternoon at a quiet chamber-music concert, even a day at home with the stereo going and a good book. The quieter pulsations of sex are important to Two as well; they can provide a stable sense of harmony in a life that might—depending on the Expression Number—become too hectic.

3
Heavenly Sign: Venus
Element: Fire
Color: Yellow

Expression: Versatile and dynamic, Three is the extrovert and the entertainer, the salesman and the adapter. He's a lover of clothes, jewelry, and ornament, a *star* in any field he chooses. Because of his dynamism, Three is likely to be an entrepreneur, a mover-up and shaker-up on any corporate ladder, a voracious lover of all the goodies that status can bring.

Whatever Three is doing now, he must find a range of activity worthy of his dynamic powers. Otherwise, he will inevitably grow jaded, become a dilettante. Envy, conceit, and trendiness can take over—and *will* if Three has no consuming interest. Without a powerful life-style and some dedication, Three is doomed to frittering away his enormous potential.

Destiny: Threes can look forward to a happy and productive sex life—a period of prolonged happiness with another person. (There is little chance of lock-step monogamy here, but a strong possibility of lasting and faithful passions, even if for more than one person.) During the latter part of their adult years, Threes will enter a time of great interaction with others, personal recognition, fulfillment of social ambitions. Whatever the qualities of the Expression Number, a Three Destiny Number *guarantees* that they will eventually be recognized and rewarded.

4
Heavenly Sign: Saturn
Element: Earth
Color: Green

Expression: Four is a lover of order and precision, the ballast for others' free-floating lives. Deeply self-disciplined, he has no trouble balancing a checkbook or straightening out an entire company's accounts. He is always constructive, finding a *better* way before criticizing the status quo. While he never shrinks from hard physical labor, he's ingenious enough to avoid it.

Home-loving and patriotic, Four is passionate about ecology and the beauties of nature. He will develop his life around *practical* matters—as a super-organized housewife, a great stage-manager, a secretary whose skills never get rusty and whose files are always in order. Four is utterly trustworthy and loyal.

But Four may develop a bad self-image because of his occasional rigidity. If a situation is bad, he must learn to ride with it, not to expect his own self-discipline from others. He can look forward to success through diligence, but must be aware of envying those who seem more dynamic and forceful—and who often get the limelight. He tends to put down his great talent for pragmatic action—when in fact it's as important as dynamic creativity.

Four should try to find satisfaction in love and nature. There is land in his future, if he's lucky, and great success in his profession. He must also develop a *regular* life, with trustworthy friends and satisfactions he can count on. Otherwise, the negative side of his character is bound to develop, and he will become defensive, stubborn, and ill-tempered.

Destiny: People with a Four Destiny Number are in for heavy discipline, full practical *application* of their ideas—and they are likely to *succeed.* A Four who has been out of school for ten years, for instance, might be thinking of returning to get a graduate degree, or contemplating a change of jobs that would require a long training period. If this is the case, it's up to you to encourage the change! There's little likelihood here that the Four will turn into a dithering dilettante; his destiny leads toward practicality, positive results from effort. He's likely to move into the organizational aspects of business—office management, corporate structure.

5
Heavenly Sign: Mars
Element: Air
Color: Blue

Expression: The Five personality is free, changeable, attracted to everything, and tethered by nothing. A Five has an uncanny ability to diagnose trouble (friends tend to call *him* when their analysts aren't available), because he's intuitive, sophisticated, and an astute critic. Resourceful, active, an enormous lover of adventure, Five tends to run through friends and experiences—he's not *fickle,* but constantly on the move. He learns through *doing;* he's never a scholar, but often amazes the scholar by what he picks up in the course of conversation or by watching the background shots in a movie.

A period of great upheaval in Five's life is common every two years or so—there should be no particular worry about this. If he suddenly feels the Seven Year Itch, for instance, he should know that it is probably *just* because he's a Five. Overindulgence and recklessness are lifelong dangers, though; Five must learn that change is not always the *right* thing to do, and to pause and consider whether the proper moment has come. He may also be hyperactive sexually—and again, the question is not How much? but When? and Where?

Destiny: Someone with a Five Destiny Number is likely to "drop out" at *some* point in life—and if he hasn't already, maybe you should suggest it. He needs the freedom of the road—travel, new friends, new sexual experiences. If he's longed for these things and repressed the longing, maybe he's a super-industrious Four Expression, who just can't give himself change and adventure. So, if he's offered a job with his company's new branch in Uganda, or if the possibility of an exotic affair opens up, he should *lunge* for it—otherwise, he is likely to get a most embarrassing case of Unsatisfied Longing, the result of stifling a need that his basic character keeps telling him is unreasonable or selfish.

6
Heavenly Sign: Jupiter
Element: Earth and Air
Color: Indigo Blue

Expression: The planet Jupiter gives Six an enormously outgoing personality. Six can never have or give enough, but will always *try.* With the only number divisible by both odd (3) and even (2), a Six is balanced, responsible, poised between two points of view. So he's a great mediator, healer, seer-of-both-sides. He may also be a fine cook, even a professional one, because of his aptitude for combining all ingredients to produce a perfect mix. He shows great tenacity. ("No, I will not leave the office until the eighteenth letter is typed and I can see the bottom of the In box.") But this can lead him to be self-righteous, tyrannical in petty ways, and overly convinced of his own power to *know*. ("After all, I'm rational; I'm even more rational than *most people*.")

Sixes often use the notion of "responsibility" as an excuse to shrug off their true desires. (But is the world, your boss, your lover, *really* going to love you more if you fail to do your thing and do everyone else's instead?) At the other end of the danger scale is a tendency to social *irresponsibility*: never to read a paper, never to know what others care about, to look only inward to the circle of family and friends. A productive future for Six lies in *balance*, which shouldn't be so hard—that's what Sixes are good at.

Destiny: This Destiny Number may lead a dynamic and fluid life, but can look forward to a long time of consolidation, adjustment, responsibility, and completion. For instance, a fluid and extroverted Three Expression with a Six Destiny may flit along for years in the lime-light of his own personal celebrity (a Three Expression is always a Star to his friends) and then . . . pow!—he's hit with the realization that he yearns for *solid* achievement. Six Destiny can and *must* accomplish. The result may take many forms, but it will be the crowning event of his life: a book written, a career in acting finally established, an abandoned college degree completed—with honors! Also, Six will probably have a period of sexual experimentation in his life—even to the point of bisexuality. Because Six has a great sense of domesticity and harmony, and is unlikely to be shocked by his own desires for any sexual activity, he'll always undertake exploration naturally and without a sense of rebellion or distress. Often it's during the time of achievement and adjustment that Six comes out of the closet . . . and for women, this can often mean a realization that the Sexual Revolution has indeed taken place, that they are ready to enjoy it.

7
Heavenly Sign: Mercury
Element: Water
Color: Violet

Expression: Seven is the aristocrat of the numbers—the discriminating, intellectual, intuitive, needing a cushioned life to blossom in peace. Seven's mercurial intuition leads him on *searches;* there is a great air of mystery about a Seven, as if he could *be* a guru, not just *look* for one. He can be a mystical mathematician—can bridge the known and the unknown, the practical and the theoretical, the accepted and the unconventional. He's likely to do the most outrageous things as if they were everyday occurrences—and *get away with it*. Great personal fastidiousness, a sense of being "above it all," contribute to Seven's ability to get what he wants.

Seven needs a great deal of money and physical comfort to shut out the harsh world that would thwart his aristocratic intuition and intelligence. He

112

must be warned against his uncaring, unworldly attitude, which could *really* lead to poverty, or to more responsibility than his character can cope with. For a woman Seven, the best goal is marriage to a man who will give her the protection she needs; nowadays, marriage to just such a *woman* may be what the Seven *man* needs. All Sevens require a quiet atmosphere for work, and a job that will let them move *inward*. They have long periods of introspection—and should not confuse such times with melancholy, but should pay close attention to the insights that emerge then.

Destiny: Seven is the number for the sabbatical—the every-seven-years vacation that professors traditionally take. Recently a journalist came up with the idea of a sabbatical year for *every* working American, which sounds fine—and for the Seven Destiny, it's *essential*. He runs in cycles of seven years, and must have a year off at the end of a cycle. Of course, he may not be able to quit work and head for the Micronesian Islands to contemplate his life, but he should do what he can to make that year *different* from the others—change jobs, rearrange his sex life, begin study in an entirely different field than the one or ones he's been working in. (Often Seven is fated for a profession he never thought of—the only one in which he would automatically be granted a sabbatical. College teaching, anyone? Or the higher reaches of biological research?) In any case, the sabbatical will bridge the many different areas of his life: If he is highly practical, he will have a chance to explore the theoretical side of his nature; if he is always business-as-usual, he can take time out for play; if he's solitary, he can try a gregarious fling. Whatever the emphasis in his everyday life, he'll need time to connect with its opposite, complementary force.

8

Heavenly Sign: The Sun
Element: Earth
Color: Rose

Expression: Eight is the number of *control*. All the great business minds are partly affected by this number, which represents the highest form of worldly success and power. Eights have good judgment, organization skill, executive ability, and a great love for the material side of life. Disappointment can make Eight very bitter, and success can sometimes encourage the *worst* in his character—philistinism and greed. Almost all self-made successes are Eights: they seem to have an ability to push on without support from others.

Eight may *try* to convince himself that he is a lover of home, a defender of the faith, or a yearner for adventure in the far yonder. He's wrong—and if he acts on *anything* but his enormous ability to succeed in the world of business and commerce, he'll be wildly unhappy. Of course, he must *balance* his life, but that will be harder for him than for anyone else. He'll pay and pay and pay for his ambition. Advise him to give free rein to his ambition and ability, but to keep a benevolent eye on the rest of the world, and tell him to leave himself *just* enough time for refueling the fires with some rest-and-relaxation time!

Destiny: An Eight Destiny has great financial success in his future. Even if he is the visionary Eleven Expression, or the domestic and unambitious Six Expression, he'll find his efforts rewarded by money—and some power, too! Of course, he won't *refuse* the money—but he may, depending on his Expression Number, be confused by it. Power may be much more dangerous—some Expression numbers can't handle it. When an Eight Destiny shows up, study his Expression Number warily. For instance, for the disciplined, sometimes stubborn and intolerant Four Expression, Eight Destiny could turn him into a petty tyrant. As for Double Eights, beware the combination—often greed and ruthlessness take over, the pursuit of money and power becomes and end in itself, and the Double Eight risks ruining his life and the lives of those he loves.

9

Heavenly Sign: All the
Planets
Element: Fire
Color: Black and
White

Expression: Like white, Nine is all colors in the spectrum; like black, Nine soaks up all colors, and can, if he chooses, destroy them. Nine tends to great extremes—not always holding them in balance, but vacillating wildly, first one way, then another. He'll be trusting and pessimistic; generous and selfish; powerful and wasted. Nine needs *control*—some way to find the middle, include *all* the elements without destroying his own personality. Nines should remember above all that they need stabilizing influences—in work, love, in every activity. Otherwise they fly off on tangents. A passionate but secure love affair, a steady but exciting job—without these, Nine will grow bitter and exhausted, full of life but not knowing what to do with it.

Nine needs to plan! He should focus his actions on a goal—not veer off in all directions. Activity is his chief value (idleness can literally drive him mad), but he should watch his activity, to keep it from being *frenetic*. A course in a foreign language is fine—but not *four* courses. Take French—and then fly to France to try it out; read in French; see movies in the original language. Make a pattern for progress.

Destiny: The future of a Nine holds certain success. The haul might be long, full of reverses, dry places, and difficult times, but Nine can be sure that his life's work will come to real fruition . . . and that he will experience no frustration of his desires *in the long run*. Advise patience: Completion and fulfillment may *feel* constantly elusive. Fortunately, success may come at the end of a life *cycle* rather than at the end of an entire life. Often Nine will have a series of successes, with periods of struggle and difficulty in between. Nine may even have a series of *careers* in his future, each of which will end in success. (One Nine woman started out as a secretary in publishing, rose to be executive secretary to the editor-in-chief, then gave that up to start at the bottom in computer programming. When she'd mastered that and gone on to analysis and design, she decided to find out more about the human side of things, and ended up with an advanced degree in clinical psychology. She's now a practicing therapist.)

Master Numbers

Whereas the Expression Number usually controls the basic personality, and the Destiny Number the future, an Eleven or Twenty-Two in either Expression or Destiny always takes over. Watch for these magical Master numbers, and realize that they are dominant factors in a life. If your subject has a Master Number for just one of his numbers (Expression or Destiny), its power will always modify the other number. Always give the Master Number interpretation prominence in a numerological reading.

11
Heavenly Sign: Neptune
Element: Air
Color: Silver

Expression: This is the number of pure genius, untainted by earthly thoughts. It's the number of saints, great sinners, visionaries, the heights of fame. Its personality is dual—without conflict between light and dark, good and evil, male and female. The Eleven needs a practical purpose, because his character is so totally caught up by the spirit that he tends to pursue rainbows and dreams.

An Eleven man has the deepest sympathies with women, understands them as if he *were* a woman. An Eleven woman can think and feel from a man's point of view without effort—and is never threatened by her *own* masculine component. Elevens are avant garde; they love the passionately new, the shifting image on the silver screen of films.

An Eleven must focus this remarkable set of qualities and that's hard to do. He must not get discouraged by what seems to be lack of appreciation. Disappointment can lead him to extravagant evil, delusions of grandeur and egocentricity, to dissipation and degradation. But such a loss will be the world's; Eleven's amazing qualities will be unaffected.

Destiny Eleven's future holds the most idealistic and spiritual fulfillment of his life-goals. It doesn't matter what his Expression Number is—the power of the magical Master Number is so great that he's almost as its *mercy* (though that's not the feeling he will experience). With the Eleven power *in him,* he will only know that he gravitates to the most demanding and spiritual areas of life—sometimes *despite* the other forces of his character. For example, a highly *practical* Four Expression can, with an Eleven Destiny, become an ascetic mathematician, interested only in the purest forms of numerical thought, the rarefied study that leads to entirely new concepts.

Anyone with an Eleven Destiny should be encouraged in his idealism, *never* discouraged. The only danger to point out is that his power may be translated into fanaticism, delusions of grandeur, or the frittering away of energy.

Heavenly Sign: Uranus
Element: Water
Color: Gold

Expression: Twenty-two represents the power of practical idealism—magic at its most positive and beneficial. Twenty-two succeeds at the highest levels of finance, education, science, culture. He may be a philanthropist, or a gifted politician who can turn a depressed urban area into a replica of classical Greece.

But when his power deteriorates, its effects are much more dangerous than Eleven's decadence. Because Twenty-two is so *practical,* his drives can become greed, hatred, and black magic at their worst, destroying not only himself but all that he touches. Not many of us know a true Twenty-two (other forces operate in most of us)—but to know one is to see the full human potential, for good or evil.

Twenty-two's future is in his own hands. A fortune-teller can understand, advise, and hope, but Twenty-two will control.

Destiny: The Destiny Number Twenty-two is the most powerful universal force of them all. It perfectly combines the idealistic and the practical. A Twenty-two is motivated to lead a life of enormous value, no matter what his Expression Number may be. But beware: If a Twenty-two is *thwarted,* he can let loose great forces of evil in the world. His Destiny Number—if perverted—is also the number for black witchcraft and evil.

EXPRESSION NUMBERS OF CELEBRITIES

Test your own understanding of numerology by seeing how well you think the personalities of the following celebrities fit their Expression Numbers. (*Real* names are given in parentheses.)

1
Diana Ross
Bob Dylan (Robert Zimmerman)
Mike Nichols (Michael Igor Peschowsky)
Marlon Brando

2/11
Elizabeth Taylor (Elizabeth Frances Taylor)
Coco Chanel (Gabrielle Chanel)
Joan Baez
Hugh Marston Hefner
Gloria Laura Morgan Vanderbilt

3
Barbara Streisand (Barbara Joan Streisand)
Bette Davis (Ruth Elizabeth Davis)
Frank Sinatra (Francis Albert Sinatra)

Ava Gardner (Lucy Johnson)
Paul Newman
Gloria Steinem
Janis Joplin

4/22

Jacqueline Onassis (Jacqueline Lee Bouvier)
Vida Blue
Leontyne Price (Mary Leontine Price)
Joe William Namath
James Taylor
Audrey Hepburn (Audrey Hepburn-Rustin)
Elaine May

5

Roman Polanski
Yves St. Laurent (Henri Donat Mathieu)
Julie Andrews (Julia Elizabeth Wells)
James Baldwin
Richard Avedon

6

George Harrison
Lauren Bacall (Betty Joan Perske)
Warren Beatty (Beaty)
Federico Fellini
Howard Robard Hughes

7

Mick Jagger (Michael Philip Jagger)
Ringo Starr (Richard Starkey)
Ralph Nader
Norman Mailer

8

Elvis Aron Presley
John Wayne (Marion Michael Morrison)
Rock Hudson (Roy Scherer)
Kurt Vonnegut, Jr.
Judy Garland
Richard Burton (Richard Jenkins)

9

Greta Garbo (Greta Louisa Gustafsson)
François Truffaut
Zsa Zsa Gabor (Sari Gabor)
Shirley MacLaine (Shirley MacLean Beaty)
Cary Grant (Archibald Alexander Leach)

HOW TO FIND COMPATIBILITY: NUMEROLOGY AND THE ELEMENTS

As you've seen from the interpretations of the numbers, each number connects to one of the four elements: fire, air, earth, and water. Each number is part of a *trinity* grouped under these elements. (One number, six, appears twice.)

By checking the charts below, you can discover which numbers are likely to be compatible (and *how*)—and which are *not* likely to mix well. So, if you want to know whether a new man will suit you, whether you'd work well on a project with a friend, or just what number-personalities are likely to mesh *best* with yours, find the elements of the numbers and then see how these elements go together!

The Fire Trinity
(Inspirational Qualities)

1/Individual creative energy
3/Self-expression through inspiring *others*
9/Friendship and compassion

The Air Trinity
(Intellectual Qualities)

5/Learning through experience
6/Taking responsibility at home or in society
11/*Visionary* interest in spiritual truths

The Earth Trinity
(Practical Qualities)
4/Self-fulfillment through hard work and concentration
6/Material responsibility for relatives, friends,
the extended family
8/Large-scale organization; industrial production

The Water Trinity
(Emotional Qualities)

2/Private emotions and feelings
7/Connecting personal emotions to the outside world
22/Using emotions to help all humanity

The following table of elements shows how they conflict and harmonize. It will tell you which people are most likely to be attracted to one another, and *how*. (You can also use the chart in making an individual numeroscope, to see in what ways the Destiny and Expression numbers of the subject go together.)

Fire
with fire: powerful, but often leads to excess
with air: harmonious
with earth: restrictive
with water: productive, but frequently explosive

Air
with fire: harmonious
with air: powerful, but often unstable
with earth: conflicting, too many restrictions
with water: adaptable and harmonious

Earth
with fire: restrictive
with air: conflicting
with earth: practical, fruitful, but can be heavy and unimaginative
with water: harmonious, joyous in a "down-to-earth" way

Water
with fire: productive, but can explode
with air: adaptable, but elusive
with earth: harmonious, easy movements
with water: sympathetic, but over-subtle, mercurial, dangerous

Chapter Five

THE I CHING
AND OTHER
MAGICAL TEXTS

Are you one of those linear types who believes something must be true if you see it in print? Does information seem more convincing to you in "The New York Times" or "Newsweek" than it does on the eleven o'clock news on radio or TV? Then your special brand of fortune-telling may be the wisdom book, or magical text.

Telling the future from passages chosen at random from a book is based on two assumptions; the power of words, especially written words; and the idea that a single book can be comprehensive enough to cover all human situations.

This method of fortune-telling is not universal. Most magical and religious rites were based on secrets—arcane knowledge that could only be passed verbally from one magician or priest to another. To write the secrets would have created the danger that an outsider might discover them. The oracles (priestesses) at Delphi in ancient Greece, for instance, were initiated in their teens by the oracles before them. After that ritual, they never left Delphi, and were not allowed to write anything down or to be alone with a non-priestess.

But two very literate peoples were the exceptions to this general rule: in the West, the Jews, whose religion is founded on the Torah, a document that is more holy to them than any other single object in the world; and in the East, the Chinese, who developed not merely one written language, but a double handful of them.

So great was the Chinese faith in the written word that they devised a book, the I Ching, which they believed could answer all the questions of life. It was first developed around 2000 B.C., and later was added to by Confucius and other Chinese philosophers.

Certain Western secret and occult societies have also had books like the "I Ching"—sources of wisdom and prophecy—but theirs were usually tied to belief in an orthodox religion: Judaism and the Old Testament; Christian Science and the works of Mary Baker Eddy; and darker books like the "Grimoires" of the Middle Ages (which gave magic spells and incantations in detail) and the Cabala, a numerological study of the Old Testament. But of all the books of wisdom, only the "I Ching" was designed for fortune-telling and gives rules for using it to reach prophetic conclusions about individual lives and problems.

THE I CHING:
THE BOOK OF CHANGES

The Master said: The Changes, what do they do? The Changes disclose things, complete affairs, and encompass all ways on earth—this and nothing else. . . . The holy sages used them to penetrate all wills on earth and to determine all fields of action on earth, and to settle all doubts on earth.
          —The Great Commentary on the *I Ching*, attributed to Confucius

Since Confucius, who lived in the sixth century B.C., was commenting on an *I Ching* that was already fully formed and in use as an oracle, it boggles the mind a little to consider just how *old* the greatest of all wisdom books must be. The translator and Orientalist Richard Wilhelm, who was responsible for introducing the West to the intricate beauties of the *I Ching,* places its authorship at the beginning of the Chou Dynasty (around 2000 B.C.), which means that its wisdom has been available and in use for nearly four thousand years.

The *I Ching* is different from the methods we've talked about in earlier chapters, because it depends on a *written* code and *written* interpretations. The user throws three coins (or fifty yarrow stalks—we'll get to the details later), and the results of the throw send him to the book to find a diagram, which is then interpreted by a series of written explanations and commentaries. These writings, which form the major part of the book, are poetic as well as prophetic. And many poets—usually those who believe that poetry is a visionary art, a way to see one's present and future through the eyes of an artist—find it a superior source book. The *I Ching* grew out of one of the world's oldest and most sophisticated cultures, and embodies an entire philosophy. To predict the future with the *I Ching* is not merely to see farther and live more wisely, but to absorb and act on a way of thinking quite alien to our Western mentality.

Perhaps the most pronounced feature of Western thought is the idea of cause and effect. We believe, almost instinctively, that everything has a cause, and that once we determine the cause of an event, we are more in *control.* And we think of "fate" as the operation of mechanical chance. (If a two-ton rockslide comes thundering down a hill at your shiny new Vega, the inevitable effect, you assume, will be a pile of rocks on the road and a ruined heap of metal underneath.)

The Chinese don't *deny* cause and effect—they just say, reasonably and with the patience born of a few millenia of meditation on life, *Look at specifics.* Every rockslide is different. Remember learning that all snowflakes are hexagonal? Well, each snowflake is also unique. The Chinese, and the *I Ching,* are more interested in the *individual* case than in generalities. Their assumptions about fortune-telling reflect this interest.

One of those assumptions is that the moment of the fortune-telling is actually *part* of the entire situation that the *I Ching* comments on. That moment—as you throw the coins or yarrow stalks and consult the book for a reading—helps determine the outcome, and can change events as well as predict them. That may sound fuzzy and metaphysical, but once you start using the *I Ching*, you'll begin to sense that the fortune you obtain applies very specifically to the moment in which you sat down to consult this book of wisdom. The *I Ching* has an uncanny knack for answering you in words that point very directly to the precise way in which you're fooling yourself or overlooking important facts at that particular time. It talks to your *immediate* state of mind—your attitude toward the situation you've asked about, and towards the *I Ching* itself.

THE MYSTIC MOOD

Because your state of mind is so important when you consult the *I Ching*, you'll want to pay special attention to setting the scene. Aim for an atmosphere of serenity, where concentration can be totally immersed in the *I Ching* itself. Oriental peoples know how to do this beautifully—with simple, deliberate touches of beauty in their surroundings. A single flower—a camellia or gardenia—floating in a crystal or glass bowl will bring a sense of peace to any room. A packet of Origami papers (available at most crafts and stationery stores, as well as Oriental import shops—see page 279) can be spread out in a fan shape and weighted with a glass *objet* for a dramatic point of focus on a coffee table.

The *I Ching* materials themselves will also be factors in establishing a serene mood. The most ancient and honored method of choosing a part of the book for consultation is by throwing fifty yarrow stalks, which are bit like thick dried weeds. Aside from the difficulty of *finding* fifty yarrow stalks (they are available in stores in some Chinese communities in larger cities, but if you live in a small midwestern town, you'd have to make a fast trip to your local marshland to gather them), I can testify that the method of using them is excruciatingly tedious. It isn't nearly as *difficult* as some accounts claim, but it seems to go on forever. It involves holding bunches of the stalks between all the fingers of your left hand, which is like manipulating multiple sets of chopsticks in the wrong hand. Besides, exactly the same information can be obtained with coins, so I recommend *them*. (If you're *determined* to use yarrow stalks, your *I Ching* edition will tell how.)

Chinese coins are most authentic. They have a square hole in the center, a beautiful greenish patina, and are inscribed with Chinese symbols. You can get them at any coin dealer, or at an Oriental specialty store. (See page 279.) You'll need three of them. Of course, ordinary modern U.S. coins will do (quarters or pennies or even Kennedy half-dollars), and so will francs or *anything* with heads and tails. But the Chinese ones are so lovely and inexpensive that I'm sure you'll want to use them; one girl I know wears hers on a silk cord around her neck.

It is feasible to throw the coins on a coffee or card table, and to note the results on a small pad in your lap. But the mood is best established by sitting on the floor—especially if you have a thick, smooth-pile rug. You'll have plenty of room to throw the coins, and won't have to chase them as they go rolling off a tabletop. Besides, a close, low-lying circle establishes intimacy and concentration. An old and valued friend of mine, who knows a lot about people's instinctive reactions to the occult, uses a large, patterned silk scarf to throw the coins on. It's visually beautiful, makes a fine background for the coins, and dramatically focuses attention on the throw.

You'll also need, of course, one of the many editions of the *I Ching*. (See page 279.) Whichever you choose, keep it at hand during the reading.

124

Because the *I Ching* is a *literary* source, a book of magical writings, you aren't expected to know its contents by heart.

Don't use an old pencil stub and office memo pad stamped FROM THE DESK OF for working the *I Ching*. The materials you use should have some of the dignity of the method itself. My friend with the silk scarf owns an edition of the *I Ching* with a beautiful yellow binding (the Bollingen Edition—see page 279), and he buys yellow paper specially for readings.

Now, there is your *own* look to consider. For some reason—maybe the Great Détente between East and West—we are experiencing a renaissance of interest in what the 1920's called the *mode chinoise*. Actually, the renaissance isn't all that new. Vidal Sassoon has been using Oriental models for years (that gorgeous heavy black hair is perfect for his cuts), and the high-necked, side-slit Dragon Lady dress has always had its advocates among girls with great legs and absolutely no stomachs! But today we're coming into an interest in the truly *contemporary* Chinese look.

Mao-style quilted cotton work suits, though, aren't quite appropriate for a ritual that pre-dates the revolution by a few thousand years. You want a look that suggests ancient wisdom and, at the same time, suits your modern-day self. One of the great costumes from the 1920's *chinoise* revival is the pyjama—and it's especially geared for individuality. It's similar to a lot of outfits you may already own, and wearing it won't make you look as if you're experiencing culture shock. Most Oriental specialty shops (see page 279-280) and the lingerie and at-home departments of your local stores carry lots of versions of the authentic-looking Chinese pyjama in cotton, rayon, silk—printed with lotuses and birds and geometrics in a dazzling range of colors. Wear one of these, perhaps with soft, embroidered slippers to match.

About make-up: *Don't* try to imitate the Oriental face—unless, of course, you happen to have one already. You can create the effect without theatrically copying the reality.

Those wonderfully slanted Oriental eyes are not *really* slanted at all, and the trick required to make yours look that way is entirely different from what you'd suspect. Consider the charm of the ideal Oriental face: It doesn't depend for its beauty upon contour—peaks and hollows—but on smoothness. So the first move when making up your eyes is to do the one thing you'd *never* do normally: Blank out the *whole* eyelid, from upper eyelashes to eyebrows, with a lightener like Erace. If your eyebrows are very dark or heavy, use soap over them to tame and lighten. Then, simply ignore that whole eyelid area. That's right. *Ignore.* No shadow, no Garbo-ish contouring. Now, starting a bit outward from the inner corner of the eye, use liner (light brown or brown unless you're *very* dark—then black) to make a crescent-shaped line on the upper lid. It should be heavier in the center, narrowing toward inside and outside corners. At the outside corner, extend the line a bit beyond and *down*. Under the eye, paint a subtle line that extends to meet the upper one. This slightly drooping-at-the-corner effect will achieve *subtly* the slanted-eye look.

Keep mascara gentle; use on upper lashes only. Brows require a sharp pencil and feather strokes; their contours should follow the curve of the bone above your eye. The ideal brow does not interrupt the line of the forehead; a high, clear forehead is much admired in all Oriental cultures.

There! These eyes should *peep* out of the mask of the face. That mask is not one to hide behind, but a smooth background for the eyes' expressiveness. Use the lightest (in color and texture) foundation your complexion can take, and (if you can get it) rice powder on top. Since the Oriental ideal is a slightly *round* face, put blusher forward on the flesh of the cheeks, rather than under the bones where it would create hollows.

As for your hair—again, there's no reason to imitate the Oriental version. And who could? (It's so beautiful in its own right, and so tacky when faked.) But try to catch the *spirit* of Oriental hair styles, which are either perfectly simple (like the banged bob) or perfectly elaborate (piled high off the forehead, lacquered to ebony-smoothness, decked out with flowers and hair ornaments.) Whichever you choose, remember that the idea is to look glowingly well-kept and quietly unflustered . . . as if you were *born* in your clothes and your face was *made* that way.

The most important element of the Chinese look is not costume or make-up, but the aura of serenity and calm that you project. A sense of *ease*, of event following event effortlessly, is a must. Practice the graceful use of your hands, stillness of your eyes, position of your head. Aim for a temple-like effect of tranquility. The Oriental woman has been trained to keep her hands still and *down*—resting in her lap, on her knees, or on her man's hand or arm—always poised, like a butterfly on a flower. Her head is still—it turns *quietly* from one object of attention to another, inclines gently to listen. Movements are deliberate.

Try watching a tea ceremony. (It's Japanese, not Chinese, but the atmosphere is the one we're talking about.) Cities with large Japanese populations have museums or universities that occasionally demonstrate this beautiful ritual, and it will teach you a lot about the quality of movement that will make your Oriental look convincing. While you certainly won't want to *imitate* a tea ceremony, you might try presenting a tea-and-spirits tray for an *I Ching* evening. (See below.)

Of course, no one would suggest that you change your personality and become a tradition-bound, submissive flower. You're a modern girl, and shouldn't *dream* of reverting to a time when women bowed and murmured "My lord" to men. But remember: An atmosphere of calm makes the *I Ching* ritual most effective. Don't play your new Band record or stage a frenetic back-to-the-kitchen-for-more-drinks routine. Organize—yourself, the evening. Then relax.

Sweet Tastes and High Spirits

The Chinese have long had a reputation in Asia as hard drinkers and hearty eaters—but the Chinese idea of everything from a snack to a banquet is based on *variety*. They like little tastes of many distinct flavors (as you no doubt know from experiences with "two from Column A and two from Column B.")

You can, of course, *cook* Chinese for guests at your *I Ching* reading (there's a list of reliable cookbooks on page 280); but when you want to concentrate totally on the fortune-telling session, you may have little time or energy to spare in the kitchen. So try small trays of various "little tastes" (as the Chinese call snacks), along with a variety of drink-tastes, too.

Sweet Tastes
chilled Mandarin oranges (available canned)
chilled lichees (white, globular, luscious—
     also come canned)

skinned, toasted almonds (from can or jar)
dry-roasted cashews
candied violets
preserved kumquats
red and green candied cherries
jujubes (date-like, red-skinned fruits; you can find in
    an Oriental food store under the name *hung-tsou)*
small, fresh fruits that can be eaten by hand
    (strawberries, grapes, cherries—but don't serve
    fresh and candied cherries together)
candied ginger
candied orange peel
sweet-and-sour pineapple and green peppers (pick up at your
    local Chinese restaurant, then reheat at home)
fortune cookies (also from Chinese restaurant; try
    removing the printed fortunes with a tweeezer,
    then inserting your own hand-lettered ones—
    cleverly worded to apply to your guests)
(Note: Most of these foods can be found at any large supermarket. If you have trouble, try a gourmet shop, Oriental food store, or the mail order sources listed on pages 279-280.)

High Spirits
chilled Japanese plum or honey wine
chilled dry sherry
icy aquavit or Russian vodka
sweet and dry vermouths, chilled, with twist of
    lemon peel
Cognac or Calvados (the latter is Norman apple brandy)
candied ginger
Grand Marnier
chilled Sauternes
green or yellow Chartreuse

Serving: Place foods in small bowls. (The Japanese rice bowls, found in the shops listed on pages 279-280, in different patterns make a pleasant varied showing.) Put groups of several bowls on small trays (like the *papier-mâché* ones found in Oriental gift shops). Then pass the trays, letting guests try something from each. Don't worry about plates for guests; if a food is hard to handle, or sticky, put a small glass filled with toothpicks on the tray beside it. Of course, you won't serve all these foods at once; select a combination that seems to please your eye and palate.

    Serve a selection of the spirits, in small liqueur glasses. You'll notice that all the drinks suggested are rather unusual—several are sweet, others almost tasteless. You might want to include the vodka or aquavit no matter what else you serve, because they clear the palate well between other tastes.

    Leave lots of time for guests to experiment with the tastes. Don't allow the food and drink to be taken for granted, but make a small ceremony of passing and pouring.

HOW THE I CHING WORKS:
THE TRIGRAMS AND HEXAGRAMS

The I Ching's wisdom is based on the idea that there are two complementary forces in the universe: the negative and positive; or the female and the male; or, as you may have heard them called, the yin and the yang. These forces are always in tension, melting into each other, creating constant fluctuations and change in human lives, and in nature. Everything is always subject to that change—an idea that is reflected in the I Ching's title, which means the Book of Changes.

These two forces are represented diagramatically by two horizontal lines—one broken, one straight.

The broken line symbolizes the female (yin) principle: receptive, yielding, dark, earth-bound rather than spiritual. The straight line symbolizes the male (yang) principle: active, thrusting, light-giving, and spiritually creative.

(These meanings often raise problems for women using the I Ching. It is best not to take the designations "female" and "male" literally. Nowadays, we live in a completely different culture from that of ancient China, in which women are no longer bound to be passive and men aggressive. Apply the figurative meanings of the I Ching lines to situations for both sexes. And when you find the text of the book referring to "the superior man," remember that it may also be referring to the superior woman—you. Don't let the book's superficial sexism blind you to its truths. Just be aware that when it talks of "male" or "female," it means the qualities traditionally associated with those sexes.)

Now, originally these two lines—broken and straight—were used as the simplest kind of oracle. Broken meant "No" and straight meant "Yes." Yarrow stalks were thrown to obtain a numerical value that keyed the seeker to one line or the other. But the subtle Chinese soon wanted more from an oracle than that. So they developed a more complicated method. The broken and straight lines were arranged into eight groups of three lines each, called trigrams. These were supposed to represent universal situations or ideas suggested by the arrangements of the lines. (See below for pictures of these eight trigrams and their meanings.)

The trigrams were intriguingly suggestive, but not various enough to apply to every situation. So they were combined in all possible ways to produce the hexagrams—groups of six lines each. (There are sixty-four in all.) Each hexagram was given a name, and ultimately a number of Chinese sages, including Confucius, explained their significance. These commentaries came to be the final court of appeal in judging all human conflicts. (Any I Ching edition shows them all with their meanings.)

THE TRIGRAMS AND THEIR MEANINGS

These eight three-line symbols combine the yin (broken) and yang (straight) lines in all possible combinations. They represent the constantly changing, interweaving states of being that the Chinese saw as *basic*. Each has certain meanings and represents a certain function in the family. Look at them not as definite, fixed symbols, but as a group in which each symbol is always changing into another.

Name	Attribute	Image	Family Relationship
The Creative	strong, active	heaven	father

▬▬▬▬▬▬▬▬

▬▬▬▬▬▬▬▬

▬▬▬▬▬▬▬▬

three solid lines

Name	Attribute	Image	Family Relationship
The Receptive	devoted, yielding	earth	mother

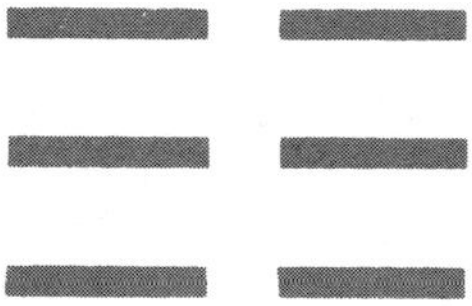

▬▬▬ ▬▬▬

▬▬▬ ▬▬▬

▬▬▬ ▬▬▬

three broken lines

The Arousing	inciting motion	thunder	first son

▬▬▬ ▬▬▬

▬▬▬ ▬▬▬

▬▬▬▬▬▬▬▬

like an open bowl

Keeping Still   resting   mountain   third
                                                           son

like an upside-
down bowl

The Abysmal   dangerous   water   second
                                                        son

solid in the middle

The Clinging   light-   fire   second
                      giving   daughter

open in the middle

The Joyous   joyful   lake   third
                                                   daughter

open at the top

130

| The Gentle | penetrat-
ing | wind,
wood | first
daughter |

▬▬▬▬▬▬▬▬▬

▬▬▬▬▬▬▬▬▬

▬▬▬   ▬▬▬

open at the bottom

Before using the *I Ching*, take a look at the illustrations of the trigrams and hexagrams. Try to get a feel for the way in which the simple devices of broken and straight lines are combined to suggest the qualities of female and male, dark and light, rain and thunder, earth and sky, and so on. There's no need to "learn" them, but let their style sink in until you have a good sense of the Chinese attitude that all things are based on the mingling of two opposites. Now you're ready to learn how to *form* a hexagram that will answer a question about your life.

Using the Oracle

The hexagram is the means through which the *I Ching* speaks. To obtain a hexagram as an answer to your question, you must use a *random* method so that the workings of fate can become part of the event. That is why coins are thrown. (We assume you *are* using coins, as we suggest, and not yarrow stalks—though the principle is the same.) The coins fall *as if by chance,* but actually the throw is determined by the moment in which you throw them; and the resulting hexagram will guide you, on the basis of that moment, about what will happen and how you should respond.

The first step, then, is to assemble your materials (coins, *I Ching,* pad of paper, and pen or pencil) and then ask your question while holding the coins in your hand. (If you are doing a reading for someone else, tell him to *silently* ask his question.) Concentrate hard. The question may be as specific or as general as you wish. But remember that the *I Ching* is an *advisor* as well as a fortune-teller. You are going to learn not only what will *happen* in a certain situation, but what you must *do* that will be both good and advantageous to you. Think of the *I Ching* as a guide and mentor, a wise person who is advising you.

Building the Hexagram

Now, throw all coins at once onto the floor or table. (If you're reading for someone else, he must throw his own coins.) The first throw will give you the

131

first (bottom) line of the hexagram; succeeding lines are built on five more throws of all three coins at once.

Now obviously, with three coins, you have four possible combinations per throw: three heads; three tails; two heads and one tail; or two tails and one head. Heads has a value of 3; tails, 2. (With Chinese coins, the most heavily inscribed side is heads.) Add up the total numerical value of the throw. An odd-number total gives you a straight line; an even-number total gives you a broken line:

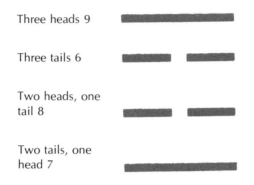

Three heads 9

Three tails 6

Two heads, one tail 8

Two tails, one head 7

Build your hexagram by throwing all three coins six times, and (starting at the bottom) marking down the line obtained on each throw. (If you're reading for someone else, you may write down the hexagram for him.) Here's a sample hexagram, obtained by throwing 9, 7, 7, 6, 8, and 9:

last throw (9)

throw 5 (8)

throw 4 (6)

throw 3 (7)

throw 2 (7)

first throw (9)

You must also notice whether any lines are formed because you throw a 6 or a 9. These lines have supercharged energy and are called moving or changing lines. They will radically affect your reading. So, as you throw a 6 or 9, mark that number down next to the line you draw:

9

6

9

READING AND INTERPRETING
THE HEXAGRAM

Now comes the part that you simply *must not* let spook you. Remember, the *I Ching* was written some four thousand years ago. Its references are often to emperors and imperial favors, the difficulties of survival in a stratified society ruled by networks of tradition and class. Its statements about princes and servants, deer-hunting and oxcarts, won't seem—at first—relevant to equal-opportunity urban America in the twentieth century! At this point—you must have faith. We promise that the reading you obtain *will* apply to the situation you've asked about. All you need do is read carefully, using your imagination and insight to see how its words apply to a contemporary life. Consider all the successful seekers who have gone before you and are *devoted* to the *I Ching*.

One of the surest ways to banish your fear of the Great Flounder when confronted by the oracle for each hexagram is to be *completely familiar* with the *form* of the book—with how it works. It's a relief to know you don't have to memorize a thing, although you should know the value of the coins so that you can build the hexagram. (You can even consult the book for *those*, if you feel shaky.) The book is a tool for divination; you must simply learn to *use* it as you would a typewriter or an electric mixer.

The first thing to know is where to find the hexagram you've drawn. There is a table in all the *I Ching* books, giving each of the sixty-four hexagrams, their names and numbers, and the pages on which you'll find their interpretations. Once you've found yours, turn to the page given. There, you'll find the Chinese character for the hexagram, which you can conveniently ignore (it's nice to know you can ignore something, right?) and its number and name. The name is made up of the names for the two trigrams that form the hexagram (pages 128-131), which are, of course, sometimes identical. Then there is a picture of the hexagram itself, with its two parts (the *trigram* above and the *trigram below*) named beside it. In most books, the translator then comments on the form of the hexagram and what it means.

After the hexagram and its description comes a series of comments (translated from the Chinese) headed "The Judgment." This is the *moral* part of the oracle; it indicates whether the action about to be taken (or the event being thought of) will bring good or evil, is advantageous or disadvantageous. It allows you to prepare for the best or the worst, and sorts out the possible consequences of having thrown this hexagram. These lines are followed by modern commentary; until you're capable of interpreting the lines for yourself, the commentary is *hugely* helpful.

After the Judgment comes another series of sayings headed "The Image." These describe the picture of the situation—a picture, remember, not of a static object or situation, but of a shifting moment. This is perhaps the chief thing to keep in mind at this stage: The *I Ching* and its sayings are *not* designed to describe one single future event, or only to recommend a course of action in one situation. The image must be interpreted as moving *in* the *moment it is read*, just as a fire changes and consumes itself as you watch it.

After you've taken in the meanings of the Judgment and the Image and jotted down whatever seems to be pertinent (not everything is—consider the question and the questioner), go back to your own drawing of the hexagram and see which, if any, of your lines was formed from a throw of 9 or 6. If none were, then you must be content with the reading of the Judgment and the

Image; you can assume that the situation is soon to be resolved, or is simpler than you supposed. If, however, you have 9's or 6's in any of the lines, you must read the interpretations of those lines that follow the Image section. Each 6 or 9 line will be interpreted. Pick the ones that apply from your own throw. For instance, in the example above, you would read the lines for "Nine at the beginning" (the bottom line), "Six in the fourth place" (fourth from the bottom), and "Nine at the top" (the top line). Jot down the relevant meanings of these lines.

Now comes the part that makes the Book of Changes just that—a book based on the notion that the whole of the universe and all of man's affairs are constantly changing, opposites shifting to opposites, one situation turning into another. If you have had 6's or 9's in your hexagram, it is assumed by the *I Ching* that because of their strength they will tend toward their opposites with greater force than the weaker lines . . . a little bit like a very strong man who is not reluctant to express his feminine side, or a woman who *knows* her strength and is unafraid of being thought masculine. So, to reflect this change and uncover its meaning in the current situation, you will *reverse* the moving lines in your original hexagram, and draw a second one.

For example, the hexagram we drew above went like this:

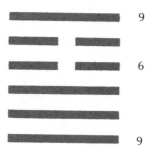

So, the moving lines are 9 in the first place, 6 in the fourth place, and 9 at the top. When the moving lines are reversed, here is what you'll get:

Voila! An entirely different picture. Now begin again at the beginning—look up this second hexagram in the table or index, then find its Judgment and Image. Read them and write down what seems appropriate (or what will *become* appropriate in the light of the reading you made of the first hexagram).

With all this information, you'll have a wealth of material to consider and weigh. If you are reading the *I Ching* for someone else, you may ask him to tell you his question and then present the fortune to him verbally (as you learned to do with other fortunes); or simply point out to him the sections in the book that apply to his hexagram, and let him read and interpret for himself.

A Sample Hexagram, Its Circumstances, and Its Reading

Since using the oracle can seem daunting, you'll perhaps be reassured to see how a perfectly ordinary (but painful) situation was handled by the *I Ching*. A woman threw the coins for herself to determine how to act when her lover, to whom she's been clinging unhappily for some time, took an additional mistress, threatening her with replacement and the accusation that *she'd* made *him* unhappy. The first mistress wanted to know whether to go on seeing him, and what the outcome would be if she did. Here is the hexagram she threw:

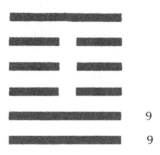

9

9

Looking up the hexagram in the index, she discovered that it was Number 41, *Decrease;* the upper trigram is *Keeping still; mountain;* the lower trigram is *The Joyous; lake.* The title of the hexagram convinced her that she had thrown true and was being answered accordingly. Certainly her life had decreased; she was threatened both by loss and the withdrawal of love.

The Judgment for Hexagram 41 reads:

> DECREASE combined with sincerity
> Brings about supreme good fortune
> Without blame.
> One may be persevering in this.
> It furthers one to undertake something.
> How is this to be carried out?
> One may use two small bowls for the
> sacrifice.

Reading this, she felt that the whole of it applied to her situation except the last two lines, which seemed rather mysterious. She was being told very clearly that the new love was not a complete threat, even though it meant she would have less of her lover's time and attention. "Sincerity" could apply either to her lover and his feelings for her, or to her desire to continue the relationship. In any case, "One may be persevering in this" indicated clearly that she need not abandon the field; in fact, the next line is a signal to her to take the initiative, not to succumb passively to a painful situation, not to acquiesce to being hurt. But the last two lines were a puzzle; she wanted to know what to do, but they didn't seem to say. On she went to the commen-

135

tary on the Judgment, which informed her that the "small bowls" for the sacrifice meant that one need not have every attribute in order to be considered worthy. It would seem she needn't worry about competing with a possibly more desirable rival; she should count on *herself,* following her own instincts and believing that what he loved in her in the first place would *still* be loved. So she went on to the Image:

> At the foot of the mountain, the lake:
> The image of DECREASE.
> Thus the superior man controls his anger
> And restrains his instincts.

Clearly this was an indication of the spirit in which she must act—without rancor, with restraint. The mountain, which means the higher aspects of the soul (or of a relationship), will only be strengthened if the lake (her unrestrained, clinging passion) evaporates and is *decreased.* Here is a new and applicable meaning for the name of the hexagram: Her lover's affection may have *decreased* or been displaced, but by *decreasing* her independence she still has a chance to enjoy him and perhaps to win him back entirely.

Now she went on to read the two *moving* lines, the 9 at the beginning, and the 9 in the second place. For 9 at the beginning, she found:

> Going quickly when one's tasks are
> finished is without blame.
> But one must reflect on how much one
> may decrease others.

For 9 in the second place she found:

> Perseverance furthers.
> To undertake something brings misfortune.
> Without decreasing oneself,
> One is able to bring increase to others.

Though these readings seemed a bit contradictory, she concluded, after reading the commentary, that her "undertaking" must be made quietly and quickly. Without making her lover feel that she was possessive, she must not *decrease* him by appearing indifferent to the new situation. The repetition of "Perseverance furthers" was encouraging, but the next line was disturbing until she read in the commentary that it could mean that she must not *throw herself away.* In other words, she must not decrease *herself* . . . her undertaking to keep her lover must not hurt her.

The last step was to reverse the two strong lines, achieving a new hexagram to complete the reading:

This hexagram proved to be Number 23, *Splitting Apart.* The upper trigram is *Keeping still; mountain;* the lower, *The receptive; earth.* This was rather an ominous sign; perhaps the first hexagram's invitation to perseverance and action wouldn't help after all. The Judgment reads:

> SPLITTING APART. It does not further one
> To go anywhere.

The commentary explained that the "inferior people"—for that she read "the rival"—are in danger of destroying the good situation, represented by the strong and creative straight line at the top of the hexagram. The Image reads:

> The mountain rests on the earth;
> The image of SPLITTING APART.
> Thus those above can ensure their position
> Only by giving to those below.

This hexagram suggests that splitting apart in this case is bad, a threat to what is good in the world, and so a danger to this woman and her affair. Clearly she must not rush into hostile or irresponsible action; she must, even when it ran against the grain, bide her time and hope for a good outcome.

My friend didn't exactly have a marvelous time ahead, but she found a fairly detailed answer to her question, and a set of principles for action. She was reassured that *she* was not in the wrong, and that until the *real* splitting came, she should act with resolution and restraint. Finally, she was told to bide her time in hope and generosity.

Of course, not all throws will yield this clear an answer to a question, and some will be *more* specific. You must prepare yourself for infinite variations and be authoritative in your interpretations. Spend some time practicing throws and looking up hexagrams, and take recurrent looks at the table of trigrams, which is full of clues. As you experiment, you'll find that the enormous amount of information in the *I Ching* makes it almost impossible to throw a bad fortune—unless, of course, you trifle with it. Even if you're just practicing, maintain a serious attitude. Try to ask real questions about real situations. While I was working out some of the examples for this book, I threw the same hexagram twice in a row. This seemed extraordinary to me, since I wasn't really trying for *anything*. I told a friend, who responded with a touch of scorn: "Oh, that often happens if you're not serious. It's just the *I Ching* telling you to stop fooling around."

OTHER MAGICAL TEXTS

Any book that has a powerful meaning for you can be used for fortune-telling. In fact, a book that has a special significance can often seem more prophetic than the *I Ching*. You might, for example, pick a favorite book of poetry to use (with the techniques explained below); poet Allen Ginsberg says that poets are the great prophets of our time and must be listened to if we're to know our real futures. In this chapter, I'll tell you how to use *any* book to tell fortunes, and will give you sample readings from some books that are used by people I know to answer questions about their lives and the lives of their friends.

THE METHOD

Do pick a book that is likely to contain wise advice and evocative sayings, one that is meaningful to you (or to the person whose fortune will be told). *The Guinness Book of World Records* or *Ten Ways to Better Posture-Control* won't quite provide a range of passages that apply to profound life-situations (unless you're a true believer in the idea that *any* random words have some meaning!) The best readings are obtained from books of poetry, novels that you have a special feeling for, and works with a religious or mystical tone (though I know one young man who regularly consults *Bartlett's Familiar Quotations* with what he claims is great success!)

The method you use should be invariable. (Rituals that change always lose their potency.) First, simply take the book—always the same edition— and lay it on the table, closed and facing you. Ask it your question. *Concentrate.* Then open the book entirely at random. (Try not to *choose* a place; just let your fingers pick up the pages instinctively.) When the book is open, select a page—again, as instinctively as possible; you shouldn't be aware of making a conscious *choice* between right or left—and then run your finger down it from top to bottom, stopping when it feels "right" to you. Don't read the words until your finger has stopped! After you've done this a few times, you'll be surprised at how certain you are when to stop your finger; there is a kind of automatic *catch* in your mind that tells you when. Remember: The words are finding *you*—you're not *looking* for them.

Once you're stopped your finger, carefully read the line or lines that your finger rests on. See if the words apply to your life or the life of the questioner. Sometimes, the book will simply refuse to answer. (If, for instance, you come across a verse that reads, "This is not the time for the making of the sacrifice," you can be pretty sure that the time—or maybe the *book*—was wrong for a question.) If the words seem rich and interesting to you, though, then consider all the meanings they might have. You are on your own here: Unlike the *I Ching,* most books of poetry have no commentaries to help you with interpretation. You'll have to count on your own intuition, your knowledge of the person involved and his or her situation.

In addition to asking the book a question, try using a reading as a guide to your life for the next twenty-four hours, just as you would use a good horoscope.

THE MYSTIC MOOD

If you're drawn to this method at all, you have probably already set the stage just by furnishing your apartment. That is, you're probably a reader, and have shelves of books to choose a text from. You can pick one that fits the personality of the questioner, or his mood—or if you're reading for your *own* life, you might just select a book at random and see what it has to say.

Once you've chosen your text, isolate the book on an uncluttered surface so that it looks *impressive.* Have a good light nearby, so that the words will be *visible* once you've found them.

This method should not be surrounded with hokey "atmosphere"; it is a simple (almost *deceptively* simple) technique, which can become as exciting as word association games: What will it say? Why? What does it mean? When reading for another person, show your own authority always: Look carefully at the words, and decide then and there whether they apply to the situation. If not, simply say, "The book will not speak," and go on to

138

something else. If you decide the words *do* apply, explain carefully the reasons why, and the interpretation. As you practice, you'll become remarkably adept at seeing the hidden meanings in odd lines and verses.

THE OLD TESTAMENT

Many of us were raised on the Old Testament in one way or another. We were given Bible verses to learn in school, or we had a relative who quoted the Scriptures to make a point or point a moral. But a lot of us grew away from the Bible as we matured, and at least one very wise man, the poet Philip Whalen, thinks that's a bad idea. He says that to throw the coins for the *I Ching* and, as well, to read a verse chosen at random from the Bible each day will give you a sense of ease and direction. After all, the two books are complementary: While we're unfamiliar with the language of the *I Ching*, it offers definite answers to questions; the Old Testament is in a language most of us know, and it can comfort even when the quotation isn't specific.

Because the Old Testament is really a *series* of books, it offers a great variety of styles and messages. And there's almost nothing that one would want to know about life that the Old Testament doesn't cover *somewhere*. Use, by all means, a King James Version (rather than one of the relentlessly "modernized" editions that substitute the word "dime" for "drachma" and so on). The rich, archaic-sounding language will yield more subtle, interesting readings.

Here are some actual readings that were done by people we know— questions asked, and answers courtesy of the Old Testament:

Should I go all out for a promotion by telling the boss it's now or never—or stay quietly in my present job? "And he did that which was right in the sight of the Lord, and walked in the ways of David his father, and inclined neither to the right hand, nor to the left."—2 Chronicles, 34:2. It's pretty clear that the questioner is advised to hold quietly to the present position. The phrase about "to the right hand, nor to the left" seems to counsel moderation and a waiting game.

Should I hold my tongue about the really bad time that deceptively nice guy gave me? Or should I let the world know that he's a bad hat? "Let there be none to extend mercy unto him; neither let there be any to favor his fatherless children." That's surprising! It seems he's even worse than you thought. The reading certainly doesn't seem to call for any great restraint.

Will I have a good day? "Mountains and all hills; fruitful trees and all cedars:"—Psalms 148:9. Well! Mountains may suggest challenges, but with all those fruitful trees, it can't very well be a *bad* day.

Can I trust a friend? "Do they not err that devise evil? but mercy and truth shall be to them that devise good."—Proverbs 14:22. Hm. Absolutely ambivalent. You're being told to wait and see; there isn't enough information for a judgment.

Have I happiness in store for my life? "For every battle of the warrior is with confused noise and garments rolled in blood: but this shall be with burning and fuel of fire." Isaiah 9:5. Oops. Well, it may not be an *unhappy* life, but it looks like it will be eventful and full of stress. You'll probably have to fight for your rights. Don't be a shrinking violet, or you'll lose out!

Should I move, or stay put? "Depart ye, depart ye, go ye out from thence, touch no unclean thing; go ye out of the midst of her; be ye clean, that bear the vessels of the Lord."—Isaiah 52:11. Wow! Not only should you move if you're planning to, but maybe you should plan to if you haven't already. Your present situation might not be good for you—there's a sense of *urgency* in that verse.

Should I take the trip I'm planning, or stay home for my vacation? "And Babylon shall become heaps, a dwelling place for dragons, an astonishment, and an hissing, without an inhabitant."—Jeremiah 51:37. Assuming Babylon represents your destination, maybe you'd better cancel those plane reservations; of course, if you live in New York, which has always been *called* Babylon, maybe the text is a sure sign that you ought to have reservations on the next flight.

Daily Readings

Readings can be obtained without asking a question—as a way of guiding yourself for the immediate future. Be very careful to clear your mind completely before finding the verse: Don't think of a question or of a specific situation in your life, but simply let your fingers move down the page, prepared to use the text as a guide to the situations that come up in the next twenty-four hours. Remember the verse, or write it down, and see if it applies. Some examples (again, from actual cases), with possible interpretations, should give you a feeling for how the method works:

"For thus saith the Lord: Like as I have brought all this great evil upon this people, so will I bring upon them all the good that I have promised them."—Jeremiah 33:42. Things are likely to look up; or, if things go badly, they'll come right before long.

"Thus were the visions of mine head in my bed: I saw, and behold a tree in the midst of the earth, and the height thereof was great."–Daniel 4:10. You're in for a period of great creative fertility. Don't ignore the promptings of your imagination. For instance, if you have a sudden urge to take Japanese cooking lessons or open a toy boutique, don't shrug it off as a whim. You're being told pretty clearly to follow your instincts, and that they're fruitful.

"And the vine said unto them, should I leave my wine, which cheereth God and man, and go to be promoted over the trees?"—Judges 9:13. Either you've been overambitious, and not appreciative enough of your own gifts, or you are a truly modest person who has abundant fruits for your friends and lovers. You're content to give the "wine" of your life to others. In any case, a very benevolent verse, sure to do you good.

"Thou has given me the necks of mine enemies, that I might destroy them that hate me."—2 Samuel 22:41. This would imply that you can get away with practically anything at the moment—you'll not be bested in love or work, and you'll probably get that promotion that you have such a nasty rival for. But beware of that vindictive tone—sometimes such prophecies have a tendency to backfire into other people's revenge against *you.*

"And the foundation was of costly stones, even great stones, stones of cubits, and stones of eight cubits"—I Kings 7:10. This looks pretty mysterious, but has a nice *solid* sound. It seems that the basis for your life is strong. Even if you fail in details, or have trouble in the short run, your "foundation" is firm, and you'll come through with flying colors.

"And they said, This is blood: the kings are surely slain, and they have smitten one another: not therefore, Moab, to the spoil."—2 Kings, 3:23. Another mysterious verse, but one that seems to say, Beware! There is dirty work afoot somewhere—perhaps not in your life, but in the larger world. It may be saying, too: Take advantage of a situation in which others will be hurt.

140

"And thou shalt make it a perfume, a confection after the art of the apothecary, tempered together, pure and holy"—Exodus 30:35. Your life will be full of harmony in the near future; you can make for yourself and those you love a sweet-smelling bower, a happy home, a good love.

Get the idea? Interpretation isn't all difficult, and the Old Testament has hundreds of thousands of verses that you'll be able to apply to life and love. Don't be afraid to interpret *liberally* what you read—otherwise, you might never find out what that "foundation" means, or just what the "vine" is doing there in your life. Be bold about seeing the symbolism in what you read; you are, after all, translating into modern terms a book written many years before the birth of Christ—and that takes a good deal of imagination.

SPECIFIC TEXTS FOR SPECIFIC SUBJECTS

The Old Testament is an all-purpose text full of information on every subject under the sun. It covers nearly every human situation—just like the *I Ching,* though less systematically.

But sometimes you will want to know about a specific subject, or will want an answer with a special tone or quality. Then go through your shelves for books that you think will apply, and use one of them to answer your immediate query.

One of my favorites is the poems of Sappho, because the subject— love—is one I've often got on my mind. Sappho lived in Greece (in about the sixth century B.C.), and she wrote almost entirely about love. She was married, but legend says that she had affairs with both men and women. Her poems are passionate and unsentimental. If you are thinking about love, have a question about love, or just want a comment for your general guidance, open the book and point a finger. You'll almost always come up with words to ruminate over, and they'll give you a place to move from.

A friend of mine, convinced that a love affair had not only ended, but ended badly, was comforted when her finger landed on this little verse from Sappho:

You may forget but

Let me tell you
this: someone in
some future time
will think of us

She says that she suddenly knew that no love is lost, and that her memories were better than she had ever supposed—rich, full, and well worth the pain the affair had cost her.

Or, again, I was asked one day if a young woman should pursue a seemingly indifferent young man. The answer came like magic:

I said, Sappho

Enough! Why
try to move
a hard heart?

Of course, answers are rarely *this* specific and to the point. But when they are, it's downright mysterious—and very convincing.

Less direct, but just as interesting, was the answer to a question about whether a new love affair was a good idea:

With his venom

Irresistible
and bittersweet

that loosener
of limbs, Love

reptile-like
strikes me down

There is no obvious answer here. The lines seem to be merely a *description* of falling in love. But consider the words and the images they create: "venom," "bittersweet," "reptile-like," "strikes." The mood indicates that the affair will be beautiful but doomed to end in sorrow. There is reason to beware, not to fully trust the man or his affection. But perhaps the experience will be worth the cost. The word "irresistible" seems to point to an emotion that's bigger than two people.

Sometimes Sappho is less than passionate and committed; she can be downright cynical. Here's her version of "Diamonds Are a Girl's Best Friend":

Say what you please

Gold is God's child;
neither worms nor
moths eat gold; it
is much stronger
than a man's heart

How's that for advice to provide for your old age by hard work and good luck, and not to count too much on a "man's heart"?

These examples will give you some idea of Sappho's range: She has only one subject, but she covers it exhaustively and without fear. What she wrote was set down long ago, but has lost none of its freshness or appropriateness. You can find in her lines almost any situation that confronts the lovers of today, an answer to any sexual dilemma.

Of course, Sappho isn't the only book to consult for special situations. Your imagination and curiosity will lead you to others; when telling fortunes for friends, be sure to ask them about books that they might want to read from. Everyone has a favorite: the poems of Leonard Cohen, the works of Kahlil Gibran, the sweet and enigmatic *The Little Prince*. The method is the same for each—a careful randomness in opening, tracking with finger, and stopping when the feel is right. Do not assume that the book will *always* give an answer, but be prepared to judge whether the line or verse applies. Accept the book's judgment, and interpret it, if it speaks, with authority.

142

Chapter Six

DREAMS
UNCONSCIOUS
FORTUNES

All fortune-telling is based on the notion that you can marshal unknown powers to predict the future and plan advantageous courses of action. All methods assume that the unconscious minds of the reader and subject are communicating and that both are in touch with the forces of destiny. But only one method looks into the unconscious: the dream.

The first famous dreamer was also an interpreter of dreams. The biblical Joseph, hated by his brothers for being his father's favorite, was sold into slavery. He then turned his gift for dream interpretation into an advantage that brought his people, the Jews, into favor with their masters the Egyptians. Joseph's brothers hated him yet the more for his dreams, and for his words. . . . "And they said one to another, Behold, this dreamer cometh." Later, Joseph was to interpret Pharaoh's dream and save the land of Egypt from famine and plague.

It is true that gifted dreamers and interpreters of dreams have often been misunderstood and feared. It is a little frightening to realize that someone can look into your unconscious and knows what lurks there. It is true, too, that you can't be a good interpreter unless you pay close attention to your own dreams and try to understand them. We often unconsciously (there's that word again!) distort the content of our dreams in order to avoid their real meaning. After all, there are a lot of things we'd just rather not know. But, on the other hand, we are closest to the sources of our own dreams, and can often spot meanings that would be unfathomable to others. So, start by using dream interpretation to tell your own fortune—then go on to others.

Because dream divination has been going on for so many thousands of years, there are dozens of systems. The most famous in our culture, the one that nearly overturned the scientific and medical worlds nearly a hundred years ago, is that of Sigmund Freud, whose revolutionary "The Interpretation of Dreams" gave back to the dream what the mechanistic, scientific thought of the nineteenth century had taken away: deep meaning, relevance to man's deepest wishes and needs, his future and his past.

Most scientists in the nineteenth century explained dreams as the result of some minor physical disturbance—indigestion, an uncomfortable bed, a passing desire to urinate. No one saw any need to examine a dream's content. To do so was thought to be a superstitious practice indulged in by the unscientific and the ignorant. Then Freud concluded (largely from a courageous examination of his own dreams) that dreams have a deep psychological meaning. They are the most honest expressions of our desires, and by examining them we can know why we are who we are, and what we can expect to accomplish, seek, find.

Although there have been many revisions of Freud's original system of dream interpretation, no one now claims that dreams are fugitive and unnecessary elements in the life of the brain. In fact, the latest research has concluded that the brain (not just the psyche, the unconscious, or any of those vague and unphysical areas) needs to dream, that dreaming is probably a great factor in keeping us sane. So, instead of moving away from ancient beliefs in dream divination, we in the twentieth century have come back to it—using a new and exciting method, and exploring deep into the dream to find what it means, what it foretells.

In this chapter, we'll explain two different methods you can use to interpret dreams and foretell the future with them. The first is the newest. It is based on Freud's system, and can be used in divination in the way that any deep psychological insight can be used to foretell the future. The more you know about a person, the more easily you can tell what he'll do, want, need, feel. The second technique is the ancient, arbitrary, and charming system used by gypsies, Victorian ladies, and other diviners through the centuries. It is thoroughly unscientific (although some claim that the Freudian system and those that have followed it aren't exactly models of scientific method, either) and very authoritarian. It takes dreams just as seriously as Freud did, and that's about all it has in common with him.

THE MYSTIC MOOD

For the interpretation of dreams, we'd suggest one of two approaches, each based on a famous dreamer. Wear a Coat of Many Colors (in honor of Joseph)—perhaps a caftan in multicolored stripes. Or float through the room like a dream-vision in a long white gown—straight out of that old dreamer Poe's terrifying and immortal work.

With the Coat of Many Colors, try a head-wrap to match the caftan, or perhaps do your hair in two braids woven with ribbons in the colors of the costume. Leave your feet bare. Eyes should appear almost *unnaturally* bright—use a shiny eyeshadow on upper lid and under the eyes. After mascara, brush Vaseline on your lashes to make them shiny, and on your eyebrows as well. Lips should be emphatically red, cheeks a little *feverish*. (Keep hair off the forehead to show all these effects.)

145

As for that Poe's heroine look, you'll want to be *pale:* a dream walking, a vision from the underworld. Your white gown should have *almost* the look of a nightgown (and not *quite* the look of a shroud, though Poe would have been crazy about *that*), and should flow down over your bare feet as if you'd forgotten that you had other clothes or ever wore shoes. Hair must be loose and flowing, with a light wave. (If it's short, use a fall.) Make-up is a little tricky, because you must tread the line between dreamlike (which is pretty) and ghostly (which is *creepy*). Use a pale, pale foundation (though not drastically lighter than your natural coloring), and sweep it right over eyes and eyebrows. Use a mauve, brown, or taupe eyeshadow under the eyes, mauve shadow on lids. Keep brows as faint as possible, and use just a touch of blusher (suggesting the fever of disturbing visions). Lips must be very pale—not *chalky,* but natural, perhaps slightly glossed. You might use a mauve lip liner very subtly (but you really *do* want to avoid the Vampira look). Wear no jewelry, except for an opal or two if you have them—you must seem as virginal as possible.

As for the setting, you know that the interpretation and divination of dreams begins with telling dreams as *stories,* which they are—stories the unconscious has made up and told to the conscious mind. So the best atmosphere is the same as that for story-telling: everyone in a circle, preferably sitting on the floor on soft pillows or rug, perhaps even holding hands, with each subject in turn telling the story of his dream or dreams. (Some dreamers are very prolific.) Keep lights dim enough to encourage intimacy. And do remember that this *is* one of the most sensitive areas of fortune-telling. Dreams are part of people's most intimate lives—and even when they don't *know* it, they are revealing their deepest secrets when they tell their dreams. Be tactful in your interpretations, and tread lightly where you sense painful or difficult ground. It isn't wise to blurt out something like, "Oh, well, that's obviously a dream about your unconscious wish to sleep with your father" to a woman whose husband is thirty years her senior, even though that probably says a lot about her past, present, *and* future. Gently, gently.

HOW TO LISTEN TO DREAMS

There is a special technique for eliciting the stories of dreams and for drawing from them the symbolism that is inherent in each one. First, remember that the dreamer *is* his dream. Everything in the dream comes from the dreamer's mind—from his impressions of the day just past, from his deepest responses to his waking life, from the recesses of his memory. In the dream, the characters can be other people—friends, family, strangers briefly glimpsed—or they can be lightly or heavily veiled versions of the dreamer himself. Sometimes a dreamer will dream about several versions of himself—one he approves of, for instance, and one he hates; or one he remembers as his child self, and one he thinks of as his adult self. Listen for all the clues to just *who* is *who* in the dream. Also listen for clues about the locale. You may ask some questions: "Who (where) do you think this was? Did you recognize the person (place)?"

Sometimes a dream will seem incomplete—and you might want to use a fascinating technique that some psychotherapists use to augment patients' dream material: Ask the dreamer to *finish* the incomplete dream, making up the "ending" as he goes along. After all, it was *his* dream—maybe his unconscious will direct him to tell you how it came out, or how he *wanted* it to come out.

146

The most important thing to note in a dream is the *feeling* it evokes in the dreamer—and the feeling it evokes in *you*. Some of the worst nightmares seem, on the surface, to be quite ordinary tales—but the feeling-state of the dreamer is one of *terror,* and there must be a reason for it. Listen for the feeling, not the overt facts.

Then consider the over-all story, if there is one. Some dreamers are very narrative—they dream in technicolor, with pan shots, zoom shots, and close-ups. As you listen to the story, jot down the *objects* that the dreamer mentions, and the people that he reacts to most strongly in the dream. Not everything is equally important; you must judge how much weight the dreamer places on each incident or object or person, and make careful note of which seem most important.

The plotless dreamer—the one who dreams in disconnected images or in single flashes of vision—is often easier to follow in his symbolism. He probably doesn't have so much to hide from himself. He dreams to visualize the important symbols of his unconscious life, and they will be right there, very close to the surface. Take down the images as they come.

After the dreamer has recounted his dream, and you've asked him to elaborate on it in any way he wants to, ask him what *he* thinks the dream is about, and how it made him *feel.* (Often you'll *know* how he felt from the way he told the dream—but if there's a discrepancy, it could be important.) Ask him if there are any elements from his conscious life that he recognizes in the dream—memories from the day before the dream or the far-distant past, people that he knows or has known, places he's familiar with. Once you have all this information—the dream itself, the dreamer's associations to it, and your own notes on symbols and narrative—you can begin to string all the beads of knowledge to make an interpretation that will reveal what the dreamer wants and what he is likely to get—what his future will be.

THE PSYCHOLOGICAL METHOD

The two forms of dream interpretation differ in their attitudes toward the future. Modern psychologists from Freud to the present day believe that dreams can foretell our futures by revealing our *deepest* wishes. What we want most, we are likely to pursue most diligently and therefore find. The older methods (which we'll explain later) are all strictly divinatory, maintaining that dreams are always prophetic and always foretell the *immediate* future of the dreamer.

Of the two methods, the first is by far the most personal and delicate. Almost everyone knows a smattering of psychological symbolism by now, and it *can* be dangerous. (People have been known to scare themselves into believing they're neurotic or completely crazy by having dreams that seemed "abnormal.") So go gently with this method, and apply the symbols with tact.

Psychology is a science, if not a very *exact* one. But the two major modern interpreters of dreams—Sigmund Freud and Carl Jung—did not entirely agree. Freud believed that the purpose of all dreams is to fulfill desires that seem unacceptable to our conscious minds. (For instance, repressed sexuality may emerge in highly sexual dreams.) Freud's rebellious disciple Jung decided that the repressed-wish theory was too limiting. He was convinced that dreams are built of many more universal components. And he insisted that these common dream-ideas don't merely show up in a certain culture at a certain time, but occur throughout the world and throughout history.

Jung believed that the themes of dream-visions are the same as the themes of religion and art. He theorized that all people share a *collective unconscious*. Even when we're not communicating with one another at all, and believe communication would be *impossible* (are you aware of any recent conversations with a New Guinea chieftain or a handmaiden of Cleopatra?), Jung would say that our deepest unconscious images—the ones that come out in dreams—are drawn from an unconscious reservoir available to all human beings.

Until recently, it would have been hard to find any reputable M.D. who agreed with either Freud *or* Jung. Physicians were skeptical—after all, dreams do seem fugitive, wispy, open to almost any interpretation. Freudians harp on sex as if we still lived in the Victorian age . . . Jungians sound more like mystics than scientists . . . and besides, who cares what happens during *sleep*? Well, scientists finally posed that question seriously: Why do we need sleep? They began running volunteer subjects into research laboratories at all hours to doze off (if possible) with electrodes attached to their heads. And guess what? It just may be that our eight hours every night (or six hours, or whatever—individual requirements vary) are important because, as one New York City experimental psychologist says, "the brain needs to sleep."

Sleep researchers have found that there is a specific time, perfectly measurable, when you're in *deepest* slumber and most likely to be having your most detailed, fully unconscious dreams. When sleepers are awakened as they are sliding into this state, they feel the next day as if they hadn't slept at all, even if they've had *more* than their usual amount of sleep. But if they're allowed to experience deep sleep and *then* awakened, they're completely refreshed, even if the total sleep-time has been much less than usual.

These findings forced the researchers to re-examine the old theories and develop tests to study new ones. Today, while no one is sure that Freud or his followers were absolutely right, it *is* clear that dreams can't be ignored anymore. Now, both sleep researchers and psychotherapists seem open to *more* interpretations of dreams; and all over the country reliable scientists are carefully keeping logs in which they jot down their *own* dreams for later analysis.

Much of this activity, of course, is geared to science and therapy: People want to know more about dreams in order to understand the workings of the brain and in order to help those who are disturbed. But, for many, dreams have always held another kind of fascination: From them, we can interpret ourselves *and* the important people in our lives, and that's a way to get insights into the *future*. (In fact, sometimes a dream will reveal clues about a relationship that your conscious mind doesn't want to *face*. Hints like that can quite literally *predict* events and help you prepare to face them.) So the pyschological approach to dreams is not *just* a way to understand your basic character or childhood traumas. It can be a tool for fortune-telling—one of the most accurate available.

HOW DREAMS WORK

In order to analyze the meaning of a dream—and therefore predict the future from it—you'll need to know a little of what goes on in a dreamer's mind. Although we may not know precisely *why* people construct their dreams the way they do, we're relatively certain that most do it the same way. Here are some common mechanisms that will help you see the *processes* at work in any dream:

Distortion & Displacement: Don't take anything in a dream at its face value. A dream may *seem* narrative, for instance, containing long sequences that sound like the plot of an Agatha Christie . . . but on closer inspection, you'll find that each event refers to the same feeling. That is, the episodes aren't part of a *time sequence*, but a *feeling* sequence. This is an example of *distortion*, a disguise used by the subconscious to conceal the true wish.

   Displacement is another dodge, often easier to spot. It substitutes one person or event for another. A girl will say, "I met that perishing old Mr. Hodgins the other night in a dream—he stopped me as I was on the way back from lunch and wasted half an hour of a precious afternoon. I remembered that he's Dad's best friend, and I couldn't understand what the old man sees in him." Well, *that's* pretty obvious, especially if the dreamer is having trouble breaking away from her father or is in any way anxious about her relationship with him. The real threat to the "precious afternoon" *isn't* Hodgins. The dreamer's unconscious can't come out all the way and declare that dear old dad is (at very best) an impediment to his daughter's life. So the unconscious replaces Dad with his best friend, for whom negative feelings aren't taboo.

   Remember, displacement can be *very* thorough. A dream full of furious activity may *really* be a wish for the opposite—peace, or even death. Any person in a dream may be either the dreamer or someone else the dreamer knows. People can dream of themselves as someone of the opposite sex, of a different age—all these are ways of disguising "unacceptable" information about oneself. Look for significant details that will give away the dreamer's true self and wishes.

Condensation: Dreams are very economical. They often compress several events or people or wishes into one. Sometimes a single dream-incident conveys *all* the dreamer's conflicting emotions about a subject. So, when you're analyzing a dream, consider every possibility. When that very statuesque friend of yours dreams about the Statue of Liberty awkwardly moving through a crowd of normal-sized people, the statue may stand for the dreamer's feeling of being ungainly and obtrusive in her super-tallness, as well as her desire to achieve "liberty" from those problems by acting "above it all." Let your imagination play with the dream's elements. (And do encourage the dreamer to help out with as many associations as possible!)

   Try turning dreams upside down to find what is compressed into the "story." If a dream is full of sunlight, look for darkness. A young art student was in the midst of her first really serious affair (having *real* orgasms for the first time) when she had a quite lovely dream: She was standing in the middle of a small but beautiful stream, with trees growing lush and tall on both sides. She had her skirt pulled up around her waist and was lowering herself into the water as it rushed past, then raising herself again. The sensation of the water on her labia was erotic; she woke feeling sexually aroused. She talked for a long time about the dream, about how good it felt to be out in the open and almost naked, enjoying her body . . . and then she said, "I felt so clean; that I was washed clean." Then we looked at each other in dismay. The "lovely" dream wasn't exactly based on complete acceptance of her body and its sexuality. She wanted to be "clean"—and that meant washing away the evidence of her affair. There were *two* feelings in the dream: She was experiencing her body pleasurably, and she was "cleansing" it of sex . . . reconciling her pleasure and her guilt. The process of condensation often lets the dreamer do that.

Symbolization: We all know that dreams are full of symbols. And we have some idea (as you'll see later) of what certain symbols mean for *most* people. But dream symbols can't simply be decoded, like the words of a foreign language. They differ for every person, and take on new meanings with every change in an individual's life.

You'll want to know how to interpret symbols so that they aren't merely mechanical contrivances that falsify the individual dream. The first step is to *know your subject* as well as possible, and get him, or her, to tell you as much as possible in the course of talking about a dream. A cautionary tale: A close friend of mine, whom I'd known since grade school, had been having great career-decision trouble in graduate school, which I attributed to a conflict with his father—a raving success in at least two fields and contemplating a new one at sixty. One night my friend had a remarkable dream. Two snakes were coiled around what looked like a broomstick held in a man's hand; they were intertwined with each other, but the heads were fighting furiously. I launched immediately into a long analysis of his relationship with his father, how their fates were entwined but unhappy, and how he must let go of that broomstick to be a real man, when he turned around and said, "But damn it, I thought you *knew*—I decided to go to medical school last week, and already my dream has me holding the caduceus!" Which shut *me* up. I should have known that the double-snaked staff had a *special* symbolism for him and couldn't be seen as simply a sign of phallic conflict with his father (though I was probably right that the furious snakes didn't bode well for his self-confidence in his career choice).

DREAM SYMBOLS

Anything can have symbolic value for a particular dreamer, but there are some common categories of symbols that do turn up in most dreams. As you might expect, the family and sex are two of the most-often-dreamed-about subjects; and you should be alert to the many disguises they can wear in dreams.

The Family: Even for the most independent adults, our families still represent our origins, our most long-standing fears and wishes. The man who coolly claims never to *think* about his folks ("Oh, yeah, I heard from them last month. They're fine") still has, racing around in his unconscious, a whole set of emotions about them—and about all the substitutes for them he's found since childhood. So be on the lookout for family figures in dreams:

The Father: Often appears in the dream as a king, master, chairman of the board, president of a company, teacher, doctor, father of someone else, Pope, God, or some other representative of authority. Psychiatrists find that the father also appears as the Sun.

The mother: She may be disguised as a queen, an empress, a woman teacher, a nurse, the mother of someone else, a servant, a housekeeper, God's mother—or by such symbols as a closed building, a city, an island, the dreamer's childhood house, a fountain.

The sister: She may be a nurse (called "sister" in England) or a nun (also

150

called "sister," and sexually taboo like the *real* sister), someone else's sister, or a young girl the sister's age.

The brother: He could appear as a fraternity "brother," someone else's brother, a clergyman (who may call his parishioners "brothers and sisters"), or a young black man (who also speaks of "brothers and sisters").

Sex: This, of course, is where all the fuss about modern dream analysis got started. Freud began his study of dreams to get at hidden sexual feelings in patients, and for years it was thought that there was no *other* material in dreams. No one takes that attitude today—dreams are clearly so large a part of the mind's and body's functions that they cannot be considered the province of one drive (no matter *how* important that drive is!) But sex is still a strongly distorted (if not repressed) drive, so it is a crucial element in dreams.

In general, remember that all desires in dreams *may* be sexual, but that all desires in dreams tend to get equal emphasis. So you'll have to look closely at hunger, thirst, itches of various kinds, to know which desire they represent—themselves or sex. Closer to the mark, *all* bodily orifices are sexual in dreams. Mouth, ears, eyes, nose openings, anus, urethra, and navel are all equally powerful, and stand for the sexual organs as surely as if they *were* those organs. Of course, that's only the beginning—there is an enormous range of symbols that represent both the male and the female sex organs.

THE MALE: *Inanimate objects:* umbrella (which, opening, represents the erection), necktie, sail, flagpole, key, fishing pole, fountain pen, pencil, brush, any weapon (gun, sword, arrow), syringe, tail, rope. *Persons:* all those obvious male names like John, Dick, Henry; my friend, little man; a burglar, soldier, dwarf; a child, especially a mischievous one. *Animals:* snake, rat, squirrel, mouse, horse, bull, a bird (especially if diving). *Fruits and vegetables:* all the elongated kinds. *Plants:* especially signify erections, what with all that stalking and flowering and growing. *Other parts of the body:* any part that sticks out, like a finger, nose (there is a long and famous passage in the novel *Tristram Shandy* where the word *nose* is substituted over and over again for the word *penis*—but that was before the heavy hand of Queen Victoria got laid on English literature), hair, arm, tooth, breast. *Numbers:* most often 1, because of its shape; and 3, because it represents the triple formation of the male genitals—two testicles and a penis. *Monuments:* These often suggest memories, and Jung claimed that the memories are of the time when there were no phallic repressions, but on the contrary phallus *worship*—when the phallus was considered man's link with immortality. Obelisks, tombstones, totem poles, often have this significance.

Note, too that *castration* may be represented in a dream when a phallic symbol is destroyed; when the dreamer loses an arm or leg or is blinded; when he fights with another man and is frightened by the encounter. If such dreams are very mild, or less frightening than exciting, probably they refer to loss of virginity instead of castration. *Emission* dreams are most common in adolescence, but all men have them from time to time. Their symbols are invariable: Speeding cars (just where *was* sexual symbolism before the invention of the internal combustion engine?), exploding bombs, fireworks, fountain, hurricane, volcano.

THE FEMALE: *Inanimate objects:* bag, pocket, wound, nest, cavern, ring, target, front door, room, window, pot, pool, cage, drawer, house. *Persons:* a little girl, a girl friend, a servant, any common female name. *Animals:* kitten or cat, oyster. *Fruits and vegetables:* peach, pear (which combines both phallic and uterine symbols), cabbage. *Plants and flowers:* uncurling leaves, rose, lotus, the heart of any flower. *Other parts of the body:* mouth, ear, navel; orifices in general; an opening and closing hand.

Menstruation may be symbolized by bathing; seeing the color red; dramatizing in the dream any of the old popular expressions for menstruation ("falling off the roof," etc.) Another special female attribute: *Breasts* appear as mountains, apples and other fruits, a well, a fountain, a balcony, any protrusion from a smooth-sided object.

FOR BOTH SEXES: *Masturbation* can be represented by squeezing fruits, shaving, swimming, riding a bike or in a car, or any rhythmic activity.

There is no evading the fact that the entries above for "Male" are more detailed than those for "Female." The reasons are simple—and infuriating! Until quite recently, it was assumed that most women thought of themselves as "not men"—a negative attitude—especially in their dreams. Psychologists assumed that we were either resigned to our "deficiencies" or were seething masses of penis-envy and overcompensating power-drives. Only recently have women been able to tell their dreams to male and female therapists who listen for what is unique and not a mere shadow of a man's psychic life. So be sure to count on your own intuition and experience in interpreting dreams for yourself and female friends. Keeping a detailed dreambook of your own can help. (For instance, what are your *personal* symbols for masturbation in dreams? They may be universal!)

Intercourse: The possible symbols here are as varied as the sex act itself can be. A dream may follow the whole progress of a sexual encounter—from the moment eyes meet right to the time of orgasm—or can leave out almost everything. Sometimes intercourse is represented by any act of *contact:* a walk with a friend, dancing, writing a letter, eating a meal. Any of the social activities that can, in real life, *lead* to sex (like a party) can also express the act itself. Any scene of increasing excitement or mounting tension is symbolic of sex. (That's why some good dreams seem like scenes from a movie; they're directed to reach a climax!)

Men and women dream of the sex act differently, of course; and again, there is more agreement on what symbols men use: plowing, bowling, riding, shooting. Erections may be dreamed of as rising or flying. Women, alas, often still dream of being wounded, soiled, broken, of losing objects, of things canceled or used. But they, too, may dream of flying, dancing wildly, and all the other symbols of joyful abandon!

Abstractions: This group of dream-symbols is not as potent as the family or sex—but it can be important, especially in the dreams of someone who is highly intellectual or concerned every day with *ideas* (a professor, political activist, laywer, and so on). In these dreams, he or she may act out conflicts about work or beliefs, and such dreams can be tough to analyze—so we've given them some special attention here.

Ideas don't have the fireworks quality of gut emotions about parents or sex, so the way they're symbolized in dreams is likely to be subtle. Know your dreamer! A dream about a strong black man may mean one thing for a timid young girl, and quite another for a former civil-rights worker.

Often, too, a dream about an abstraction will contain many *components* of a complex idea—without any obvious connective threads. For instance, a deeply idealistic teacher at Columbia University during the student rebellion of 1968, deeply in sympathy with the goals of the students and convinced that their actions were right, dreamed that he was caught in one of the buildings during the police raids. Suddenly, instead of being a teacher, he was a policeman in blue, hitting students. Then he was on the grass of the campus, sitting under a tree talking to the students, who were small children and furry animals. He stroked them and gathered them to him, and they purred. In real life, the teacher believed that the students *should* rebel; but he believed, too, that they were young, inexperienced, and should be subject to discipline. He could not quite live up to his conviction that they should make their own decisions, have a say in the running of the school. So, in his dreams, he was, first, himself (a teacher) sharing the students' position (trapped in the building); next, a policeman; then a sort of shepherd of docile students. The three guises put together form a complicated abstract notion of justice and rebellion: Youth must be served, but also disciplined; one must sympathize with students in their desire for freedom, but not become one of them. Conflict is clear in the dream, but the three elements do form a coherent idea.

Abstractions in dreams are not always situations. Sometimes they're *people.* Wisdom may be an old man or woman; ambition may be the president of the company reaching out to shake hands; and so on. Often, dreams cloak abstract ideas that are *painful* for the dreamer to think about: One girl dreamed that her brother came home from college with presents for the whole family, but could only stay an hour or two. "Then he got up, smiled at us all, and left," she said. Her brother had died five years before, in his sophomore year.

These general notes on some common groups of dream symbols should serve as a guide to deciphering most dreams. But dreams are usually full to bursting with all *sorts* of specific symbols that may not immediately strike you as transparent. So, on pages 153-173, you'll find a glossary (in alphabetical order) of the most common dream symbols and what they often mean. Put these together according to the mechanisms explained above— and, with the dreamer's help, you'll find that dreams are not so mysterious after all.

PSYCHOLOGICAL DREAM GLOSSARY

Abandonment: If left alone (perhaps by parents seen dimly—if at all—in the distance), you're uncertain of your identity. Can you handle that problem, or is it complicated by lack of confidence? If a *lover* abandons you, perhaps the dream signifies distrust, or a feeling you're not good enough. All abandonment dreams reflect a low self-image, and perhaps even a wish to *prove* you're worthless.

Abortion: Are you sure about your birth-control method? The dream could be a warning. It may also mean that you want to reject (abort) childish (get it?) hangups.

Accident: If *you're* involved in it, maybe an impending trip is the source of worry. You don't really want to go . . . or your unconscious is telling you the driver is unstable. The accident might symbolize a quarrel or clash you've had—or want to provoke.

Ace: If you're drawing an ace, you feel confident. An "ace up your sleeve" or "ace in the hole" has sexual meaning: You know you're a good lover, mean to prove it. Don't be shocked if the opponent in a dream card-game is somebody you think is sexually "forbidden."

Agency: You're being tested or challenged. Maybe you're unhappy at work, but insecure about making a change. If only someone would take over, make the decision, "place" you. Perhaps you wish an agent would arrange your love life.

Airplane: Is it just crouching on the runway? You feel tied down, can't "get off the ground." Does it fly away without you? (See Abandonment.) Planes can also indicate "high-flying" ambitions, drives, ideas. As for the sexual connotations, isn't taking off truly *orgasmic?* (If the 747 doesn't *budge,* maybe you feel your sexuality is earthbound, too.) *Piloting* a plane means you feel in charge.

Airport: This is a place where transients gather . . . so you're about to make a change. If your destination is obscure, you've acknowledged the need for change but are still brooding about it. Since an airport (or railroad station) is a "taking-off place," it may symbolize childhood, especially if you've just begun therapy or a finding-yourself process. Now reverse the idea: An airport is an *arrival* place, too. Have you just landed and no one's there to meet you? Are you insecure about a lover? Or do you fear that therapy or some other form of change may remove old habits and scenes, leaving you with . . . *nothing?*

Alley: Skulking around dark alleys means you're moving around among secret fears and guilts. Dark alleys can also represent your mind, with its threatening array of thoughts and ideas that dismay or disgust you.

Animal: Vague, generalized animal forms—often *groups* of them—according to Jung represent the self, your own instinctive nature, its ability to relate to the outside world. So a nightmare about a pack of horrid little animals may indicate confusion about yourself or other people. If you dream of horrid little *dead* animals, the episode (though unpretty) is an encouraging sign that you've outgrown the need for your "pack" of defenses.

Apron: Could this innocent garb be a *sexual* cover-up? If it resembles one that Mother used to wear, maybe you haven't rejected her sexual attitudes.

Arm: One that's clearly a "right arm" symbolizes best friend, reliable comrade. If the arm floats disembodied, or threatens with gestures, it might be the "long arm of the law." Is this a warning dream about some minor offense—unpaid parking tickets, about-to-expire license?

Athlete: A dream about a famous athlete might *really* be about your *own* dynamic force. Are you grappling with unusual pressures?

Atomic bomb: This horror-and-devastation symbol has replaced, for our generation, older religious fantasies of hell. Even if fears of the Bomb haunt you in real life, *dreaming* about is imminent approach indicated *personal* threats or fears. According to some psychologists, the Bomb may be part of you—a self-destructive drive that's potentially explosive; uncontrollable impulses.

Baby: Even though you're holding it very sweetly, it may be *you!* Have you been feeling sorry for yourself lately? You want to be babied. An obstreperous, noisy, crying tot may represent a younger brother or sister you're hostile toward, or contemptuous of. Or the infant could be a childish lover or friend. Examine your *reaction;* those emotions can be a clue to real attitudes about playing mother-child roles with another adult.

Bad guys: A prominent person you hate (politician or famous movie villain) is the contemporary dream-equivalent of the devil. Perhaps the baddie is Hitler, or somebody else who symbolized threat and fear to you in childhood. He could be your father in disguise. Examine your real feelings. Are you as trusting and comfortable with your father (other men friends) as you think? The bad guy could also be a rigid, threatening aspect of *you.*

Baking: "Nothing says lovin' like something from the oven. . . ." Dreams of baking bread indicate a desire to please. Freudians would have it that *oven* equals *womb* and baking equals a desire for a child. Since baking is essentially a *creative* act, perhaps the dream means your creative abilities are being frustrated in real life. If you *burn* the goods, and accompanying emotions are anxiety or fear, maybe you're involved in a creative project that overwhelms you . . . or consistently believe that nothing you do works.

Bank: This may be a word-game dream: You're "banking on" (hoping for) something. Are you cool, in charge? You have new confidence in your ability to get somewhere. If you're warm and happy, you've got a new lover, feel "treasured." But if you're afraid, the dream may represent a problem with authority.

Bar: Even "swinging singles" bars symbolize a need for the company of people—but since these folks are strangers, you preserve anonymity. Some interpretations say that dreaming of bars shows a desire to get to the "bottle"—the baby one that Mommy fed you with.

Bathroom: Scrubbing yourself? Searching vainly for a bathroom in the house? Maybe you're guilty about "dirty" behavior, so in your dream you desperately try to "clean up." (See Elimination and Toilet.)

Beach: Maybe you feel "beached," desolate. However, a sunny dream of standing on a beach may be similar to optimistic "taking off" dreams: You're about to *plunge* in. If the dream-you longs to drift out to sea, you're uncertain, beset by "What's the use?" doubts. A *beach party* dream, populated with sociable types, indicates a desire to come *out* of yourself, strip away restraints.

Beard: A *woman* growing one (in a dream, of course) maybe *still* thinks manhood is better than femininity. A beard on another person who lacks one in real life may mean you unconsciously think he (or she) is *hiding* something.

Beating: Frequent dreams of being beaten *or* doing the beating (or whipping or whatever) aren't necessarily sexual. They usually show a firm unconscious conviction that you're bad, dirty. If you were spanked or hit much as a child, that "I'm naughty" conviction was reinforced. The beatings also may have been sexually titillating. (Never mind *how* you touch me, just *touch* me!) Whether you take the active or passive role in the dream, both aspects are *you:* one still digging the beating, sort of, and the other taking revenge by *doing* it.

Bed: Seeing someone's bed *empty* may reveal fear of that person's death or disappearance. Seeing your *own* bed empty may indicate an unconscious wish to "die," escape all pressures. Dreams of being in bed with someone you don't necessarily want to make love to *may* mean simply a strange desire to know him or her *better.*

Belts: Dreams of buying belts indicate you're trying to pull yourself together, and not in the fashion sense. If you were ever *hit* with Daddy's garrison belt or Mommy's St. Laurent, the dream may indicate guilt over some action or impulse— you're threatening yourself with restraint or possible punishment.

Bird: Our feathered friends are *classic* dream symbols of release and liberation—similar to the airplane taking flight. A flying bird or flock of birds is considered very important because it shows willingness to let go of past hangups and leave the parental "nest." If you dream of being *attacked* or *pursued* by birds (assuming you haven't been watching the Hitchcock movie or *Suddenly Last Summer),* you're still engaged in big conflicts. Part of you *wants* to be free (the birds battling); part of you is afraid to let go (fear of the birds).

Blood: A woman's dream of lying in a pool of blood may be a "reminder" her period has arrived. That's all. Blood, however, *does* symbolize wounding, and not necessarily the physical kind. Someone may have hurt your feelings. If another person is bleeding, have you unconsciously realized you hurt his or her feelings? There's also the possibility you're angry at that person; the dream lets you act out feelings of violence.

Breast: Kissing or stroking breasts, even those of a contemporary, probably refers to the warmth and security you wish your mother had given you.

Brush: It may symbolize pubic hair—depends on what you're doing with it. Are you cleaning it? You *still* think sex is a trifle dirty. Perhaps you're using a clothes brush on somebody's coat, brushing someone "out of your hair." Careful, though—the unwanted may be a hangup rather than a person.

Camera: Taking someone *else's* picture shows undercover sexual interest. If you're taking your *own,* and it comes out distorted and horrible, deep down *inside* you're bad. Is someone else taking your picture? You wish to be noticed, turn that person on by revealing yourself.

Car: Your own car symbolizes energy, drive. If the dream car is lost, you've been feeling tacky and listless lately, haven't accomplished as much as you should. If the car has been stolen, perhaps you feel taken advantage of. Is it a lover's car, suddenly new and shiny in the dream? Secretly you wish the lover had more staying power in bed.

Cave: The cave generally sym-bolizes Mother, or some quality she represents (security, protection, restriction, or confinement). How do you *feel* in that cave? Comfy? Maybe you want to be taken care of. Panicky, lost? Are you struggling to get out from under maternally inspired hangups? Or do you have an older female relative or employer who exerts a strong but possibly suffocating influence on you?

Champagne: Like *any* lovely drink, champagne usually refers to Mother. Offering it to someone else means a desire to "mother" them.

Coat: We "coat" walls with paint to *cover* them, cover ourselves with coats. So a dream coat may be donned to protect you against the "chilling" truth. If you dream your lover is coming and you can't find your coat (or discover suddenly it's too small), perhaps you've been "putting on." If the lover always wears a coat, then unconsciously you know he's been "covering up."

Crying: Usually dream crying is just what you think it is: real sadness about something. But what? Is the cause a substitute or disguise for a real-life upset? In the dream you're crying over a pet that died years ago. Have you repressed a current unhappiness because you think adults shouldn't cry? Some experts think dream crying can be elaborate but *phony* display of the "proper" response to something you're *secretly* deliriously *happy* about.

Date: Dreamers prone to word-game dreams may dream of eating dates or date-nut bread, meaning you tend to overpower most people you *date.* The devouring may also refer to some oral sexual act that you long for or fear. Dates may also be calendar ones. Could this be a warning dream, reminding you of a blocked or forgotten appointment?

Deer: Isn't a deer or fawn usually *shy?* Perhaps the dream reflects a

156

timidity you haven't fully vanquished. If the poor deer's being *hunted,* the hunter may be you, attempting to conquer deerlike qualities, and be brave and tough.

Desert: You feel deserted—not necessarily by another person, but by customary good humor, ideas, or feelings. You could also just be very thirsty.

Diamond: Unless your background was extraordinary, you've been conditioned to associate diamonds with romance. So a dream diamond symbolizes marriage and/or a secure love situation. Losing a diamond (or engagement ring) indicates unconscious lack of confidence in a current romantic situation. If the diamond is *stolen,* you doubt your ability to hang onto a lover.

Disaster: Dreaming that you're part of a *massive* scene of destruction or despair, like being in a refugee camp in India, may indicate a potent social conscience, especially if you're politically involved. Or, for other reasons, you may identify with victims of a disaster currently in the headlines. During the Second World War, many American Jews dreamed of internment in Nazi concentration camps; middle-class blacks sometimes dream they're slaves on antebellum plantations. Sometimes these dreams reflect guilts: "Who am *I* to be unhappy? I've never *really* suffered." Frequently, though, the dream expresses extreme anxiety about your *own* real-life situation. So you *project* yourself into a situation *guaranteed* to evoke sympathy.

Disfigurement: Looking into a mirror, you see your face horribly pocked or twisted, or that your hair has fallen out. Tremendous past guilts are lurking, demanding to be faced. If you're in therapy, a fixation may be on the verge of revelation. A simpler interpretation applies to people who've always been conscious of their looks: fear of losing

beauty or youth, as if there were nothing *else* to rely on!

Disorientation: A typical dream for many: Arriving home from work, you find your apartment is *gone!* Or you're a child again, coming home from school; home has been replaced by a market; no one recognizes you. Some theorists say disorientation dreams refer to insecurity. If home isn't *there,* your parents probably disappointed you a lot. If it's your *own* pad that's vanished, you aren't utterly certain of your ability to handle life.

Doctor: This symbol of *helpful* authority means you wish to be taken care of. A dream conflict with a doctor could symbolize a battle—with your weaker, perhaps self-limiting, self fighting with the part that really *wants* to shape up, take charge, and *move.* Doctors can also be dream symbols for Father, as they often are fatherly types in reality.

Dog: If a dog is being mistreated, maybe you feel you're a *dog,* and have had some unfair breaks. Dogs are also guardians—to the gates of hell, or, in our terms, to the unconscious. A barking dog is a dream device hiding some fear you don't want disclosed. More word games: If a dog follows you, it's a stand-in for someone who has been "dogging" your every action (a hanger-on friend? a snoopy co-worker?) Dog dreams also could be warnings. Unconsciously you know someone's *after* you, your job, your lover.

Doll: You're back in childhood. Is the doll broken? You feel a touch of self-pity. Did *you* break the doll? You're trying to shed infantile hangups. Dolls can also be stand-ins for your own children, if you have them, but more often than not symbolize yourself as a child.

Door: Opening a door or series of doors implies opportunity. Your unconscious supports you in those good feelings about a new lover or job. Freudians claim that if you dream of going in *back* doors, your sexuality may be anally oriented. Such dreams may also indicate feelings of getting short shrift in life, always being asked to use the "servants' entrance." Closed doors echo frustration, sexual and otherwise.

Douching: Possibly a displacement mechanism is at work. Vaginas and mouths are interchangeable dream symbols, so perhaps you're not guilty about a current or recent scene, but about something you really shouldn't have *said!*

Driving: If you're the driver, the dream indicates a wish to take charge of the trip, determine the destination. You're ready to make *decisions.* If your wheelmanship is swift and commanding, you have a new sense of direction, feel positive about a decision. Are you lost, driving through rain or snow? You're uncertain of abilities to *cope.* Perhaps you're driving wildly, speeding. Then unconsciously you lust to break away from controls, disciplines, responsibilities. If you're being driven, someone else has charge of what happens to you—or so you really *feel.* Who? Father, analyst, lover, boss? (The dream "driver" may be a stand-in, remember.) Do you have a trapped sensation? Maybe you're longing to "drive" yourself . . . make your own decisions for a change. Or do you feel relaxed? Then you have achieved confidence and trust in your authority figure.

Drowning: "In a sea of troubles. . . " is one interpretation. Too much pressure, too many problems, overwhelm you. Usually, though, drowning-dreams have an eerie calm about them, reflecting wishes to return to fetal security and comfort. More *frantic* dreams of going under also relate—less appealingly—to Mother. Has she smothered you with love (phone calls, care packages)?

Drugs: Whether you're smoking, swallowing, or shooting up, the dream act can reflect an actual drug-taking experience—particularly if you're coming down from a trip, or trying to stop using. However, if you have little or no experience with drugs, dreaming about them may represent a desire to escape reality, possibly through death. (You've *heard* drugs can kill, and unconsciously wanting to use them is much easier than actually contemplating suicide.) Shots and oral consumption of drugs can have sexual implications; getting high may be a substitute for a transporting sexual climax.

Dyeing: If you misread that as "dying," you're already on the trail! A word-game dream like dyeing your mother's hair is a clever cover-up—not just for the gray, love, but for far more unattractive things you'd like to do to her. Dyeing your *own* hair doesn't necessarily mean you'd like to do those same things to yourself. It may simply indicate a desire to "kill" some of your less appealing characteristics. Hair is a sex symbol, and the color change may symbolize a wish to hide or revise sexual drives or impulses.

Ear: Ears, like other orifices, get awfully confused with vaginas in dreams. A woman's dreams of deafness can mean she's unconsciously tuned out to intercourse. Or they might simply be telling you you're afraid of hearing bad news.

Earring: Freudians would have it that since ears stand for female sexual organs, putting *on* earrings implies a yearning to add to that basic equipment. A penis maybe? *Other* sexual interpretations: Are you longing for more sexual attention? Putting on the earrings yourself might signify masturbation. Earrings inserted into pierced ears suggest in-

158

tercourse. Losing an earring may mean you've been frustrated lately.

Eating: Food usually stands for love. If you dream of a banquet where tables creak under too *much* food, some nearby loving soul may be too possessive. Starving, or seeing a full plate whisked from before you, means you're hungry for love.

Egg: The egg is a female symbol. It's not only sexual, but stands for idealized purity, shelter, perfection of form—qualities classically attributed to women. So a woman's dream of eating delicious eggs means she likes herself. A sickening meal of eggs, on the other hand, can mean she unconsciously resents her sex. A dream of cracked or broken eggs, or a slapstick scene of being pelted with them, may be symbolic of an encounter that humiliated the woman involved (you?)

Election: People are voting; one of the candidates is you. Unconsciously you've sensed an impending *choice* involving you. The faceless "voters" in the dream are disguises for a lover or an employer. This dream may also express sibling rivalry; brothers and/or sisters were *candidates* for parental affection. Another theory holds that you're a candidate for *self*-approval: Elements of your own personality are vying against each other.

Elevator or Escalator: No tricks here. If the elevator's going up, you feel things are "looking up." If it's going down, you're "let down," "down and out." The elevator's stalled? Well, you aren't getting *anywhere!*

Elimination: Unattractive though they may be, these dreams usually are *not* what they seem. Elimination often symbolizes other activities you think are unclean or repugnant (sex? work?) If you're in psychotherapy, you may disguise it as elimination in your dream, because unconsciously you believe it's a disgusting experience or a cleansing one.

Employer: Actually, a dream of your employer is very likely a disguise dream about another "boss." Dear old Mr. Osgood may stand in for Daddy or he may represent another part of you.

Eye: If you were brought up in a religious family, or have read much mythology, a disembodied eye watching you in a dream symbolizes the Evil Eye, or Eye of God. In other words, you are, if only in your unconscious, concerned about right and wrong in the most primitive sense. Most "watching-eye" dreams are more like nightmares. These dreams mean you're guilty, want to be caught and *punished.* Other eye dreams concern blindness. If you're blind, you feel unable to understand someone close to you ("blinded" by love to their faults?), or you can't "see your way clear" to a decision. If someone *else* is blind, you sense that person doesn't understand you, or is blind to *your* faults.

Fabric: Search-for-identity dreams often show you wrapping up in swatches or cloaklike lengths of fabric. Look for clues in the *kind* of fabric and your associations to it.

Fire: Dreaming of a fire in your room suggests a raging, flaming passion that's frightening. Your sexual tensions have "gone up in flames." Dream fires may symbolize other impulses, too: jealousy, ambition, any all-*consuming* emotion. Fire dreams may also be simple warnings: You left a towel on the floor in front of the electric heater.

Fish: Fish are usually phallic symbols. However, you might be having a word-game dream: Are you "fishing" for information? Does somebody you'd *like* to trust seem sort of "fishy"?

Flower: Beautiful flora usually represent your own youth and looks. If you're cutting flowers, or trampling on them, look into self-destructive tendencies. Is somebody *bringing* you flowers? They may represent a new, lovely you, a fresh "lease on life." However, flowers (like colors) have strong associations for many people. So think about what *kind* of flowers appear in the dream. Filling your sister's room with white stock and lilies is touching—until you realize those flowers are seen mostly at funerals. A glorious bouquet of cornflowers from your lover is divine! But wait—aren't they also called bachelor's buttons?

Fox: If you dream of a fox hunt, the fox is probably you. Has somebody been trying to out-*fox* you? A fox or fox fur can also symbolize the clever or wily elements of the self.

Gallery: Visiting an art gallery or museum probably indicates a wish to explore your past and unconscious. Take a close look at what's on exhibit. A museum can represent old ideas and principles passed on from grandparents; you're finally viewing them objectively, evaluating them.

Garbage: Are you wading through disgusting muck? You feel guilty, "dirty," about an action or thought.

Ghosts, Ghouls, Goblins: Perhaps you're fearful of an odd new creative urge that's been "haunting" you, or some "ghost of an idea" (quitting your job, starting a new kind of life). If you're religious, or have religious associations to certain symbols, ghosts or ghouls may represent dead people or their ideas. Goblins may be similar to other little dream creatures (see Animal); they may symbolize what you consider your worst, most evil instincts.

Gift: *Wrapped* presents from someone symbolize concern that the giver is *hiding* true emotions. If *you* always bring the dream presents (or *forget* them, or don't quite get them

wrapped in time), you're terribly anxious to be accepted. In childhood the impression sank in that *whatever* you did was not *enough*; that somehow you were inadequate.

Glass: A glass, goblet, or sheet of glass (see also Window) represents someone or something you "see through." Depending upon the specific symbol, it may be an element of yourself that's "coming clear." As with all symbols, be sure to run through your associations. What does "glass" mean to you essentially? Clearness? Fragility?

Glasses: You usually wear glasses, lose them in the dream. Well, if you can't *see*, you won't have to face that problematic person or situation. Suppose you dream of wearing glasses, but don't in real life: Your unconscious could be telling you to take a better look, open your eyes to the truth. Do your dream glasses break? Illusions are shattered. If someone important to you, say your father, has always worn a certain style of glasses, and now *you're* sporting them in the dream, maybe you strongly identify with him.

Glove: Suddenly you wouldn't *dream* of appearing without your gloves. Are you ashamed of some *handi*work, or guilty about a nasty act performed with your hands? On the other hand (hmmm . . .), gloves can cover up creative, artistic drives and abilities—which you refuse to acknowledge because all those raised expectations would mean you'd actually have to *work!* Much depends on the *style* of the gloves you dream about.

Gold: Dreams where you're given something golden show your need to be more loved, appreciated. "Golden hands" is a term for super capability, creativity; so if you dream of being spray-painted gilt or donning golden gloves, you may have unrealized ambitions. *Giving* a gift of gold—even just a piece of candy wrapped in gold foil—indicates unconscious awareness that you should be showing someone more affection. Could the recipient be your mother? Most of us are unconsciously guilty (*gilt*-y?) about not loving Mother enough.

Graduation: You're moving from one phase to another, into new awareness, consciousness. Are you watching a graduation . . . rather unhappily? You feel left out; friends are succeeding while your life has stagnated. Maybe *part* of you wants to move, but part of you doesn't.

Grandparents: They may represent themselves, or symbolize old, comfortable, security-making values. Often you'll dream of an especially loved grandparent when loneliness strikes; they tend to be more comforting figures than parents, with whom we're likely to have more electric, ambivalent relationships. An especially vivid dream of a *dead* grandparent—so real you'd almost swear he or she really visited you—commonly indicates strong unconscious longing for the undemanding, uncritical, unquestioning love that is the grandparent's forte. Could be, too, that the grandparent possessed qualities you'd like to emulate, "bring back to life" . . . possibly because he or she was so admired by your parents? Did they love that grandparent more than you think they love *you*?

Group: If groups or crowds recur in your dreams, they show secretiveness, the desire to be "alone in a crowd." Groups also enable your dream mechanism to conveniently disguise disturbing people or ideas. Another sort of interpretation (from a school that likes to see every dream element as its opposite) says that dreaming of crowds means dreaming of *no one*; you're isolated, have always felt abandoned. This theory makes sense when you consider that vague groups or crowds don't pro-

vide much love or security, can even *reinforce* feelings of alienation.

Gynecologist: Sexy dreams about him are normal for girls. Apparently nonsexy ones (having him over for dinner?) are just cleaned-up versions that *still* concern sexual feelings. However, since doctors are frequently father symbols, consider the implications in that. Maybe the two interpretations *combine* in your case: You suffer from a sexual hang-up, unconsciously wish for some authoritative, fatherly advice.

Hair: Brushing your hair is usually a disguise for masturbation, unless it's somebody else's hair. (See Brush.) If your hair falls out in the dream, you're worried about losing your attractiveness or youth. If you suddenly develop lots *more* hair, lush and long, you've been working on improving sexual confidence and security.

Hand: Your hand may symbolize creative ability. Or sexual significance may be the case, especially if you dream your hands are dirty or bloody—signs of repressed sexual impulses your conscious might find revolting.

Hat: If you're trying it on, you're testing new images, ideas. Since hats are considered female symbols, think about the *style*. Now, what do you *do* with the dream hat? Keep it on? Throw it away? A hat may also symbolize covering up, hanging back, trying not to lose control. ("Hold onto your hat!") If you dream of wearing a hat while making love, perhaps you unconsciously fear ultimate sexual abandonment.

Hero or Heroine: He or she may be a mythological figure, movie star, or someone like Robert Kennedy or Malcolm X who seems to embody a heroic ideal. In your dream, the hero represents your own strength, power and will to achieve—your positive aspects.

161

Horse: It's the power, sexual drive, or forceful aspect of your self. Maybe that part of you "stampedes," while other (more "responsible") traits get "carried away."

Hospital: Unless you've been ill recently, or work in a hospital, this building represents the "house" your unconscious lives in. You'd like to get your head into better shape, with some professional help. If you dream another person is hospitalized, you don't necessarily wish illness upon them; maybe you just think they need help.

House: Chateau, cottage, or high-rise apartment, a house is rarely just "in" your dream; it's *crucial*. It represents the dwelling your unconscious "lives" in, your entire psychic set. The condition of the house, your feelings about it, are accurate evidence of how *together* you are. Is it familiar or strange? A castle or hovel? Under construction or in ruins? Those are clues to your *psychic* condition.

Incest: Most incestuous wishes are disguised even before they're allowed to filter into dreams. But sometimes they do sneak through quite overtly, in which case a Freudian would say the dream is exactly what it seems: a desire to make it with brother, father, or whomever. Other interpretations hold that you simply wish to be closer, know him or her better, be more loved. Remember, just as sex can be symbolized by other activities-for-two (dancing, hugging, swimming together), nonsexual aspects of love can be symbolized by sex. Yet another possibility: the relative is a stand-in for a lover.

Injection: That dream of getting or giving a flu shot *could* symbolize intercourse. An injection may also represent shooting with a gun. A Freudian would trace *that* to sex, too, but isn't violence pervasive enough today so that the shot could scare you, elicit unconscious terrors of death? We've seen people we admire cut cown by bullets, and they (see Hero) usually stand for our own value. So maybe you're dreaming out the fear that your best impulses will be cut short before they're fulfilled. Do you favor word-play dreams? Perhaps you're wary of being "shot down," "warning" yourself because of an unconscious sense that somebody is out to give you a hard time. To find out *who*, examine your associations to whoever administers the shot.

Insect: Like other crawlies generally considered horrid, insects are symbols of "dirty" unconscious thoughts. Does someone take on an insectlike appearance in your dream? Assuming you haven't been reading Kafka's "Metamorphosis," you probably feel the person is "bugging" you, and want to squash him underfoot. Dwellers in old Manhattan apartments and other locales likely to harbor the domestic roach may have quite realistic dreams of insect invasions. Interpretation depends on your personal situation: The dream might be a warning that you're supposed to be home next day to let in the exterminator, or a symbolic picture of your "house" (psyche) becoming infested with naughty ideas.

Isolation: See Group; people who dream of groups often experience isolation anxieties. But in some dreams, you're stranded, *alone;* you try to call for help but no voice emerges. Unconsciously (or knowingly) you're insecure, don't feel able to "reach" people. If you've experienced the common dream of being the last human left in the world, you believe people don't "relate" to you. In interpreting all such dreams, you may discover that a supposed inferiority· complex is actually the reverse: you are *so* ex-

162

traordinary, who *could* comprehend you, even if he wanted to?

Jail: Being jailed may represent feelings of stagnation at work or in your sex life. Everything closes in on you, like a trap. Jail could also mean a wish for control, better discipline. The jailer takes over, orders your life—the way others did in childhood, when you didn't have to make the decisions. If you feel you've made some *wrong* choices lately, being held in custody protects you from making further mistakes—and gets in a little effective guilt satisfying *punishment,* too.

Jewelry: If you *give* jewelry to someone, perhaps you want him or her to think *you're* a "jewel." Suppose the gift is given to you: What is it? A choker? Unconsciously, you fear the giver wants to suffocate or hurt you. Bracelet? Perhaps it bears an interesting resemblance to a handcuff. A ring usually means marriage—or maybe you'd settle for a "ring" on the phone. Losing jewelry that a lover gave you may mean you fear (or desire) loss of that person. A lost stone from the setting of your dream jewelry symbolizes a person, maybe a friend you've lost over an argument. The person *could* be *you*—the valuable part of you, "lost" because you've done something to decrease your value.

Judge: A judge may also symbolize Father, or another authority (boss? dominating lover?) If you come up before an entire *tribunal,* how do you react to the judge or judges? Who seems to be right—you or them? Do you feel unjustly accused? Think why you might feel guilty.

Kissing: This rather innocent activity can symbolize sexier involvement. If you kiss someone repulsive, perhaps unconsciously some sexual impulse seems loathsome, or your lover has made you feel bad, dirty, (maybe by criticizing, or making you self-conscious in bed). Remember, too, that kissing can symbolize love in general—so kissing someone improbable might mean you love whatever he or she represents.

Lamb: Remember, animals represent aspects of the self. What does a lamb mean to you? Innocence? Mindless docility? Being led to slaughter? Your unconscious would like to see a little more independence, please. Or have you been feeling "sheepish"?

Laughing: You're giggling, and the scene happens to be your father's funeral. Before assuming you hate your father, remember that laughter is frequently a dream disguise for crying (and vice versa).

Leaves: Are they falling autumnally? Perhaps you (the tree) are shedding old ideas, hopes, fears; trees *often* represent the solid, firmly "rooted" strengths of the self. A flowering tree (or springtime one with baby green leaves) may symbolize new chances, new love, "turning over a new leaf."

Leaving, being left behind: Recurring dreams of being left alone signal rejection anxieties, feeling you've failed or won't quite "make it." It might be that your unconscious life plan intends to thwart the high expectations that others (especially parents) have of you. Massively disappointing them gives you *power.* You fail (by lagging behind in life), so you make *them* feel like failures, too—after all, they raised you!

If you dream of leaving others behind, a similar interpretation may apply. You don't complete relationships, stick with projects; you're ambivalent about that life plan. Perhaps what you really want to abandon is failure itself—but you don't know how.

Leg: A dream of losing one or both legs indicates the fear of losing determination, freedom. Haven't got a leg to stand on? You suspect people don't believe or trust you, want to be taken more seriously. Such dreams may also reflect a morbid terror of losing your physical attractiveness. Dreaming that you suddenly can't walk represents an unconscious feeling of being trapped, paralyzed (perhaps sexually).

License: Any license, but especially one to drive, symbolizes independence, freedom of will. A judge taking away your license may mean that Daddy's ideas about what you should or shouldn't do still have— even unconsciously—a lot of clout.

Lion: He represents your power, courage, strength. Is the lion attacking some authority figure (like the judge who took your license away)? Unconsciously, you're getting together a personal set of values, feel ready to take charge of your own life. There *is* a Cowardly Lion who might crop up in dreamland: If he's wearing long curls and sulking in a corner, perhaps you've been operating on two out of a possible *twenty* cylinders.

Lover: Does your lover turn into a total stranger in your arms? He or she is still emotionally a "stranger" whom you don't quite understand.

Dreams about your current lover may well be favorites; they're a possible way to spend more time together. However, lover dreams are *not* necessarily the most important or revelatory dreams in your repertoire, so don't fix on them and neglect other less *overtly* interesting ones. A dream that appears utterly unrelated to "real life" may tell you *more* directly and specifically about your love relationships.

Machine: To dream that a typewriter, computer, photocopier, or other machine you routinely work with turns into a giant or living creature shows you feel overwhelmed by work. A broken machine may symbolize *you*—feeling short-circuited, bogged down, "broken"-hearted, in need of some repair work. A dream of fixing a machine may represent the "mechanical" sexual experience of masturbation; or sex has lately seemed "mechanical," you'd like it to "work" better. Intricate mechanisms may also stand for the male sexual equipment.

Masturbation: Vividly erotic masturbation dreams are common, and can give real sexual release. These dreams may also reflect stubborn independence, fear of asking for help and advice, reluctance to put yourself in another's *hands*.

Merry-go-round: You've been going around in circles recently? That's if you're *on* the merry-go-round. Merely watching *others* whirl means you feel everyone around you is a little *crazed—you're* the only one with any stability. Or perhaps you feel left out of the competition for the gold ring. Try to recall childhood associations to merry-go-rounds: Were you always dizzy? Afraid? Excited? Happy? Something that's happening to you *now* brings back those old emotions.

Milk: Drinking it is wanting to be mothered. Giving it to another means wanting to mother them.

Mirror: According to Jung, seeing yourself in a mirror symbolizes insight into the *real* you. Your unconscious can show you hidden depths. How do you see yourself in the dream mirror? Objectively? Or is the mirror fogged, darkened, broken? You probably don't want to look too closely. Maybe the reflection is terrifying, like a scarred face. (They could be emotional scars.) Or perhaps your face is all wrinkled? (Have you wasted *time*?) Does the reflection wear a ghoulish mask? (You've been beastly to someone.) In some mirror dreams, you know the reflection *is* you, but it *looks* like a friend. (You *wish* to be them, or have been copying their qualities.) Or instead of *your* reflection, you see one of the whole family, or a group of ghostly images. (You're still searching for an identity.)

Money: It usually symbolizes love or sex, so if you're spending a lot in a dream, you probably want to get into "circulation." Hoarding money can have a special Freudian interpretation: You've always been overly retentive, from the time you didn't want to to be toilet-trained to today's *Darling*-like behavior—you don't want to let *anyone* go, not even a former lover you've no longer any use for. If, in a dream, you have to pay for something and can't fork over, perhaps you feel sexually inadequate or unable to love enough. If *you're* paid a sum—and suddenly it disappears or turns into dust—you feel "short-changed."

Moon: Dreams of going there—or to any point in outer space—represent far-reaching goals. If you get there, you have unsuspected self-confidence. If not, what's the reason in the dream? You tried to fly on your own? (Maybe those ambitions are unrealistic.) Trouble struck the spaceship? (Underlying fears of lacking the basic equipment hang you up.) If you get there and are all *alone,* see Isolation. Dreaming that you *want* the moon means you think you're entitled to *more* in life.

Mouth: It usually symbolizes the female sexual organ. If you're being gagged, or a hand is clapped over your mouth, you're dreaming about sexual repressions.

Movie star: (See Hero, too.) Dream celebs usually symbolize aspects of ourselves. What qualities do you associate with the star? What sort of character does he or she usually play? Suppose you dream Lucille Ball is prancing around your bedroom, creating madness and confusion. Maybe *you* (unconsciously)

use jokes as a defense against potential pain. The movie star might also be a lover (or other intimate).

Musician: If music plays an important role in your life, a dream about musicians or being a musician may simply reflect conscious experiences and wishes—so look more deeply into the dream. But if shy little you, who doesn't even own a decent stereo, suddenly stars in a dream as a lead rock singer, that's probably a sign you'd like to express yourself more openly.

Nausea: A dream in which you throw up—or simply weave about in a seasick state—may be a reaction to a *previous* dream that "brought up" a repressed impulse, or almost did. Nausea and its unpleasant consequences may also symbolize certain guilts or problems you don't want to "keep down" anymore. Do you long to get rid of something or somebody? Are you behaving or being treated in a way that "makes you sick"?

Neighbor: A dream character who lives "next door" or "nearby" but doesn't mean much to you in real life probably symbolizes someone who really *does* matter—a lover or close relative.

News: You pick up a newspaper and read about your own arrest or death. *Reading* about these events, however, adds the implication that—even in dreams—you're inclined to be *detached,* to intellectualize instead of feel. Seeing yourself in the paper, on TV, may also indicate an unconscious wish to "make news," be important, noticed, appreciated. The amorphous "public" that finds out about you in the dream may represent a *specific* person you long to reach, or some aspect of your self. Your unconscious is giving "news" about the *real* you.

Nun: You may appear as a nun—meaning you'd like to be thought super-good and self-sacrificing, maybe even virginal. If you dream of your mother wearing a nun's garb, a Freudian might figure out that you wish *she* were a virgin—in which case she wouldn't have slept with your father (so perhaps *you* could have had him).

Oral sex: If you're the recipient in the dream, but *not* in real life, you wish this act were part of your lover's repertoire—and also desire the ultimate intimacy and acceptance it implies. Your unconscious may be nudging you to be wary: Just how total is this lover's commitment? If roles are reversed—*you* play the active part, but don't ordinarily—the dream may be an unconscious questioning of *your* commitment.

If oral sex is an activity you *do* enjoy, the dream in which a lover makes love to you may express a disguised feeling of inability to express yourself. Maybe you want to be "babied" a little, or something about the lover reminds you of your mother. (Work that one out yourself, O.K.?) From here, it's only logical to proceed to . . .

Orgasm: You may have *real* orgasms while dreaming about them; but many people also wake up to find the urge still throbbing—turned on but incomplete. Dream orgasms may begin with a latent physical longing you've repressed or stolidly ignored; it pushes itself up from the unconscious and emerges to make you have a sexy dream. Some interpreters, however, believe that an erotic dream may create the physical sensation. Either way, the effect is the same.

Some orgasm dreams are disturbing—if the dream contains violence or sexual activity repellent to your conscious. Perhaps you've dreamed the same scene before—but this time the orgasm awakens you, and you "catch" the dream

clearly, are forced to deal with troubling emotions. If you accept the fact that nothing "horrid" or "outrageous" is *original* with you, that countless people have the same unconscious wishes, you should feel better.

Painting: Your unconscious has created a picture for you to discover. Is it a self-portrait? (See Mirror.) By presenting you with a painting rather than a real scene, your unconscious removes the information from reality, giving you an illustration of some impulse you don't even want to act out *unconsciously*. Is it a Pollack-like abstraction? Maybe you're unclear about a project or goal; or, if abstract expressionism is your favorite style, perhaps you've been expressing *yourself* lately. Now, perhaps you are doing the actual painting in your dream. The question is, how? With firm, sure strokes? Tentative dribbles? Angry stabs with the palette knife?

Let's not overlook the lowlier art of painting a house or room. Are you covering up dirty old walls with rapid, anxious swirls? See House—perhaps you want to hide some recent discovery about your *self*. Do you have a tendency to gloss over upsetting matters? Have you been hiding serious flaws in a relationship? On the other hand, a blissful, carefully done paint job may indicate improvements in *you*, refurbishing worn-out ideas.

Party: (See Group.) Giving dream parties indicates a fear of loneliness, a compulsion to give or buy attention. (Do you also act like this in *life*?) Parties are also celebrations, usually; so if you're wistful at one, unconsciously you wish to accomplish a feat worth celebrating. Are you searching for someone at a party? Maybe the absentee is you, the talented, worthwhile person who *should* be there but isn't. Consider, too, the possibility of a wedding reception—with no bride and groom. Is it a festival funeral—*sans* corpse? You resent someone so deeply that your unconscious won't even allow him (or her) a part in the dream. Or it's a dance—where you stand and watch on the sidelines. Remember that dancing symbolizes lovemaking. In bed you tend to "watch," remain too tense to get fully involved.

Pear: Like other globular fruits, this one is generally a breast symbol. But word games are also possible: *Pear* equals *pair*. Did you dream of a pear tree? It's *you*, always of *two* minds about decisions. A pear might also represent a friend with a dual astrological sign—Gemini, Pisces. Rotten pears (pairs)? If you gobble pears, maybe you're angry at your *par*ents. Always try these verbal tricks with dream elements that seem totally irrelevant.

Penis: Possibly it doesn't represent anything other than itself. But it could also symbolize abstractions: drive, force, thrust, power—and not necessarily in a sexual context.

Pig: (See Animal.) Now, what associations do you have with pigs? If you're Jewish, even the dearest little porker could symbolize something forbidden, unclean. A politically left-of-center dreamer might associate pigs with authority—father, boss . . . or police. This might be a warning dream if you've been up to something you shouldn't and fear getting caught.

Planting: Digging in the ground probably stands for doing your dream homework, getting deep into your unconscious. You're planting seeds? That *could* be a sexual wish coming true—but just as likely may symbolize the hope that good luck will "spring up." Planting and gardening dreams will often occur when you're particularly introspective, looking into your roots, getting

fertile ideas.

Police: Also authority figures, they could be your parents or your self in a reproving mood. Or perhaps the nice young officer in blue symbolizes "*copping* out," guilt, repression. If you dream a policeman guards the door to your bedroom, submerged sexual trauma or urges may be indicated.

Pregnancy: (See also Abortion.) The dream could be a warning about a girl's birth-control method. But consider: "Pregnant" also means "full of," "meaningful." So a dream that a friend is pregnant may merely point out some quality of hers that is important to you; the old unconscious is telling you to pay attention to her. If *you're* pregnant in the dream, perhaps you've begun to feel full of life—or just *wish* you could feel that way.

Prostitute: Complete with stereotyped trimmings—frizzy red wig, kohl-rimmed eyes, dangling earrings, chewing gum—she usually represents the *bad* in you. If you dream of being paid to make love, you could feel degraded in your sex or work life. But because money usually symbolizes *love*, the dream might be much more tender.

Quake: If you live in California, an earthquake dream may reflect real fears. But usually quake dreams symbolize *emotional* shakiness. Maybe your world is unsteady; at any moment your job, love affair, or psyche may simply *crumble*.

Quarrel: Know your antagonist! The conflict may be symbolic—with your unconscious. Hassling with the police may go back to a battle you had with your father—you'd *thought* tensions were resolved, but he's been acting strange with you lately, and your unconscious has sensed the signs of uneasy truce. Or Daddy may be a stand-in for another authority, like your boss. A dream fight may mean you wish to take a stand but *can't*. Finally, a verbal or ideological "contest" may represent a *physical* one; fighting is one of those takes-two-to-tango activities that often symbolizes sexual intercourse.

Rape: You may have rape *fantasies* as an occasional erotic *frisson*; but when the *unconscious* gets into the act and you *dream* of rape, maybe you really do *equate* sex with force. Dream rape can also symbolize *any* force or pressure, not just *sexual* assault. The rapist could also be anybody who's trying to probe your feelings, pressure you. If *you're* the rapist, you want to take what you want by force.

Rat: What can you say nice about a rat? There's probably no such thing as a pleasant rat dream. This rodent symbolizes creepy feelings about sex; grubby, mean, shifty thoughts and guilts in the unconscious. Maybe the dream means you feel poor and shabby, hated and trapped, or exploited like a laboratory rat.

Relative: He or she may symbolize some family *trait*—perhaps one you've inherited but don't *want,* or admire but fear you can't live up to. Relatives may also appear as stand-ins for moral judgment, social convention. A dead relative in a *seemingly* set-in-the-present dream may be a tip-off: The dream *really* concerns a childhood conflict. (Try thinking back over the last few occasions when you saw the relative alive . . . you may find a clue to current troubles.)

Road: Freudians like to view a road as the birth canal. But a specific road or street from the past may symbolize a crisis or decision that upset you when you lived near that road or regularly traveled it; your unconscious wants to remind you of that time. An unfamiliar road symbolizes new ways of thinking or behaving, a new job or romance. How do you feel about this road? Are you walking slowly, looking behind you as if someone is following: Maybe you've not broken cleanly with past guilts, unfinished business. Are you speeding along on a motorcycle? *This* time you mean to take charge, go ahead confidently . . . or *want* to. If you're lost, and the road is full of ruts, holes, old tires—life seems hopeless!

Rock: According to Jung, a rock or stone is the symbol for a lasting self, the part of you that won't break or crumble. A rock could also mean you're as stubborn as one. But more often it represents solidity (the Rock of Gibraltar), your unconscious knowledge that you can rely on yourself. These days allowance probably needs to be made for word plays on "stone": If you dream of being "stoned" (with rocks), maybe what you *truly* wish is to turn on and opt out.

Scale: For a Libra, scales may symbolize the self. If you're getting weighed, perhaps a decision needs to be weighed. Or you know you're too fat, but won't admit it—because if you *did,* some measure of action like a *diet* would be required! Now try some word games. You're *scaling* the heights (facing a challenge). There's a weight around your neck (like a problem "weighing you down"). The blindfolded lady holding the scales of justice may be *you,* "blinded" by love into making a bad decision.

Sewing: Are you sewing something up? A dear little purse, perhaps? Such receptacles (along with sleeves, socks, pockets) symbolize vaginas. If you're sewing a doll, consider voodoo; who does the doll look like? Sewing also represents mending, repair—of a neglected situation or person you'd like to help.

Shopping: (See also Money.) Shopping may involve buying a disguise for aspects of yourself that are wearing thin in their *old* costumes, are in danger of coming out of hiding. Perhaps you're desperately searching for a way to avoid revealing an unpleasant truth or facing a problem—a way you'd like to be viewed by others. What's your *image* in the dream?

Silence: A curiously *total* absence of sound is often an important element in dreams of being alone. (See Isolation.) Freudians believe such dreams reflect back-to-the-womb wishes. (See also Drowning.) They might also represent a real experience from the past, like going under anesthesia.

You may dream a variation: Despite the total silence, you can hear yourself think. Maybe you long for a retreat from pressures and conflicts. Another common silence dream is the one where you *try* to call out, but you're mute; you may awaken in terror, feel that even in *reality* you can't scream (and maybe even attempt a little cry just to break the spell!) Do you rely heavily on verbal communication? Are you convinced that denied the gifts of speech and wit, you'd go unnoticed? This doubt may accompany insecurities about your physical attractiveness, about being liked for *you* rather than for your gossipy stories, inside information, "connections." For that matter, who *are* you, anyway? Perhaps your unconscious put you in a silent place to force you to go deep inside yourself.

Skating, skiing: In the silent, snowy world, you long to express yourself directly, powerfully, quickly, to glide over troubles as smoothly as if you were wearing skis or skates. In *real* life, you get bogged down every time so much as a *pebble* lies in your path. If you dream of an admired friend skating or skiing, she may be you in disguise, fulfilling your

wishes. Dreams of *sportif* skill often show anxiety about *sexual* satisfaction (which also demands attention—it just doesn't happen!)

Snake: This fellow is your common, garden (of Eden) variety phallic symbol. But snakes do have *other* characteristics. Suppose you dream of several giant warriors wearing loincloths, which they abruptly pull aside, revealing hideously toothy, grinning snakes where their penises should be. At first glance, you think this dream means you're frantically scared of men. But wait!—snakes also symbolize wisdom and healing powers. (Remember the caduceus—the medical symbol, a staff entwined with two snakes?) Perhaps these warriors are *you*, realizing that your serious ambitions have "teeth," beginning to develop a healthy respect for your own powers and drives. This positive discovery may be presented in such a scary way because you're quite terrified of your ambitions; they'll mean shedding old "skins" (snakes do that), habits and neuroses you've been comfortable with, roles other people like to see you in.

Suitcase: Like a purse, bag, box, refrigerator, or any receptacle, a suitcase—even a matched set of Vuitton—often symbolizes female sexuality. But a suitcase may also represent *psychic* "baggage," the hangups you travel with. Missing a plane because your luggage has disappeared into the bowels of Kennedy airport may mean your problems hold you back from getting on with life. Examine the objects you pack into those dream suitcases.

Teacher: He or she is a stand-in for authority—usually a parent, perhaps an employer or older lover. A teacher may also symbolize a *feeling* like guilt, fear, approval.

Whatever you're tearing up must be troublesome, something

to get rid of. It may represent the person it belongs to. (You?) Have you been self-destructive, or are you angry at yourself? Feeling all "torn up"? Seeing your own clothes torn, muddy, bloody, and so forth may mean that unconsciously you feel humiliated. Perhaps the dream is a warning that some action of yours may lead to a pride-wrecking conclusion. Tearing *does* also have sexual connotations—perhaps it relates to a childhood experience that was painful.

Telephone: If there's such a thing as the contemporary collective unconscious, it must harbor the symbol of the ominously ringing phone. You know the nightmare: The telephone, larger than life, screams into the surrounding silence. You pick up the receiver. No one answers. Or you hear terrifying breathing, or a hideous dial tone. This dream is partly a cliche we've picked up from *Sorry, Wrong Number* and other mystery movies . . . but it also reflects an unconscious fear of isolation. (See Isolation dreams.) Is a dependent person troubling you, making you feel guilty? Do you struggle to express yourself and never quite feel successful? (See Silence.) Trying to dial a number, getting only a busy signal or out-of-order recording, may mean that you don't think people give you a chance. (Your lover is avoiding a long talk.) This can also be a general frustration dream. (You've been looking for a new job, apartment, lover, or "way out" of a bad situation; life itself seems "out of order.")

Tennis: Like skating and skiing in dreams, this active sport shows a desire to perform with ease; but because tennis is directly competitive, even combative, it may represent sexual hostility.

Tiger: This beast always symbolizes the strong, aggressive you.

A common dream: You need to go to the bathroom, search through the strangest places, discover the most *peculiar* assortment of johns. Maybe lots of them fill a big room, which turns out to be a stage; or row upon row of them are out of order, or dirty, or suddenly seem to be in the center of a cocktail party. Sometimes in these dreams you decide to use one of the unsuitable toilets, but afterward feel as though you haven't—so the search must continue, usually until you awaken and dash to your own bathroom. (This is the most common example of dreams in which elements of reality—like physical urges—are incorporated into the dream story; the unconscious will do *anything* to keep you from waking up in the middle of a good rousing dream!) The dream also indicates that you're fairly fastidious, like privacy—in *everything*, not just bathroom activities. How *disturbing* the dream is may indicate just how far you carry these tendencies in real life.

According to Freudians, toilets can also symbolize female sex organs (the "receptacle" idea). One more possibility to consider: Since a toilet is where you put what is "gotten rid of," it may represent a place to discard hangups, conflicts.

Tying: Being tied up (or *down*) may symbolize your feelings about life right now. Who's tying the knots? That person may be a clue to the conflict or relationship that's causing the most trouble. If it's an aspect of yourself, guess who is your own worst enemy. Are you *enjoying* the process, finding it erotic? Think about masochism (not necessarily the sexual variety); maybe you want to play the dependent role. Or you feel frustrated, held down against your will.

If you're tying someone else, unconsciously you realize you're putting pressure on others, or are aware that your lover feels "tied down" by your clinging. The dream

170

could also express a wish for closer *ties* (word play) with some person in your life.

Underwear: Dreams of dirty underwear (see Tearing) show fears about "bad" thoughts or actions. Dreams of going without underwear show anxiety about your ability to project warmth, the *real* you: "There's nothing beneath that facade."

Undressing: If you're taking off *infinite* layers of clothing, you're looking for your true self. Undressing before the House of Representatives or some other unlikely place means you want to be more open—unless the scene deeply frightens or intimidates you. If another person is removing your clothing, he or she (or you) is trying to know you better. The same is true for reversed roles: Undressing anybody doesn't mean you lust to bed them down; the stripping away of clothing can symbolize a move toward emotional intimacy, even if the dream is erotic.

Vacation: Before you take one, you may have dreams or nightmares about it, because you're anxious about change, the unknown. Some may be warnings: You lost your luggage, a reminder to take out travel insurance or put tags on your suitcases. Perhaps you dream that the lush vacation spot is hostile, inhabited solely by Urdu-speaking natives. That's simple anxiety about not being able to communicate, relate to new people and places.

Veil: You're in flowing black, mourning rather dramatically—for yourself, most likely. A black veil may also symbolize covering up a death wish: Someone you dislike dies, so you veil your true feelings.

Victim: Victims *do* get lots of attention without having to exercise too much ingenuity or effort (though *always* being victimized does take serious thought and application, as perhaps you've discovered!) Dreams that cast you in this sort of role generally indicate a longing for sympathy. You want to be rescued, most likely from reality. If you see someone else being victimized, and play rescuer, you want power over that person.

Voice: Many people dream disembodied messages, like the announcer's voice-over in a commercial, sometimes commenting on the dream. Frequently male, these voices may represent *any* part of you, giving a reaction to the dream. Suppose the dream shows a wedding, and as your mother appears, a voice intones, "And this is Mrs. James Robinson, the only mistake Mr. James Robinson ever made." A part of you (one you'd prefer not to acknowledge as *you*) has evaluated your mother "objectively."

Wandering: Foggy, vague, wandering dreams may be Antonioni-like scenes in which the limbo of your unconscious hasn't focused on a particular plot. Sometimes they roll directly into more specific looking-for-a-room, searching-for-a-lover, or bathroom dreams. Often they reflect *actual* anxiety—about losing a loved one—or yourself.

Watch: Any dream timepiece that ticks or looms gigantic and surreal shows you're pressured about time. Maybe you're on a deadline, or must make a decision *soon*. Or you feel *generally* oppressed by a sense of "time running out"—you want to stop, think, do what *you* want, but your time is not your own. If the clocks or watches are stopped or broken, time stands still—you're bored, trapped, depressed. A huge watch weighs down your fragile wrist . . . time hangs heavy on your hands. Dreams of chronic lateness indicate anxiety, and may also reflect a tendency to be *obsessed* with punctuality, run *yourself* down.

Water: Dreams of floating, swimming, diving (and see also Drowning) usually hearken back to a longing for prebirth security, the serenity of the womb. You may have a dream like this if you've been driving yourself too hard. But a plunge at a pool party may symbolize a wish for *more* action; you want to "get into the swim." Diving through waves may show an unconscious need for greater challenge; you need to "dive in." Swimming with your lover usually symbolizes sexual intercourse, perhaps a desire for it to proceed more rhythmically, easily, or with more placid affection and less bone-breaking passion. Floods indicate you feel swamped and submerged (especially if what's flooded is your house). Possibly the *cause* of the emotion is your mother, or childhood hangups.

Wedding: Unmarried people with no *immediate* plans to marry probably dream about weddings because they want one. A horror-trip of a dream wedding, of course, would mean the reverse. Even if the wedding doesn't *appear* to be yours, the bride or groom could be a standin; the way *you* feel about weddings, you won't show up at your own even in a *dream*! Suppose the bride and groom are your parents: Maybe you'd only submit to a wedding to make *them* happy. Or perhaps you want them to start anew, relate to each other better. Your lover is marrying another? Is the person a "better" version of you?

Wig: (See Hat.) It must might be a power symbol, like a halo or crown; that's if you feel *superior* in the dream. More often, a wig is a *cover-up*, a superficial role. Your wig falls off in public? You fear "flipping your wig," showing your real self, replete with worries, insecurities—or maybe the *security* that would mean greater demands on you.

Window: Shuttered, closed, or dusty windows symbolize your inability to see *out*, get a view or perspective on your life. (House is *you*, remember.) Broken windows with rotting sills and a dreary view beyond indicate pessimism about what's around you. Open, airy views of wide landscapes show optimism, a sense you're free to get out and go, develop insights and a point of view. Examine that view. Do rocky crags jut menacingly against the horizon? Life looks hard, you've been working away with no end in sight. A desert at least means you can *see* where you're going, but what a *bleak* panorama! If the window opens on your childhood garden, the past is on your mind; you want to learn what *started* you on this journey. If you look out a window, discover you're forty stories up, and feel scared of tumbling down, you fear that you are losing control.

Wings: Having wings shows a longing for power, magical problem-solving abilities. Or perhaps you want to *prove* you're an angel. A winged horse is usually your own supercharged powers, drives.

If the winged dream-character carries *wicked* connotations, appears shadowy, veiled, or dark, it may symbolize fear of death or abject failure. Suppose the winged horse is gray, and limps through a dense fog. You feel completely rejected lately; maybe you've been sick, are afraid you'll never have energy again. The sound of beating wings, or a vague sense that huge wings hover nearby, symbolizes anxiety. Do the sounds resemble your own wild heartbeats? You want to escape from something, but feel like a trapped bird; your spirit is caged. Winged angels may indicate valid fears for a sick relative, or a loved one you haven't heard from.

X-rated movie: To dream of being filmed while making love probably

172

shows a healthy unconscious fantasy life. *Some* interpreters believe that exhibitionist dreams reveal one or more of the following problems: narcissism, inability to *personalize* sex (get emotionally involved with the partner), insecurity (you need an appreciative audience to convince you of your desirability), and unhealthy power-drives (you relish turning on those passive customers by your commanding erotic performance). More *contemporary* interpreters disagree, say these dreams provide *fine* releases for natural curiosity and fantasy.

Don't be alarmed if some quite improbable characters appear in the dream. Perhaps you want some nonsexual *attention* from them. If you're directing the film, who's the star?

X-ray: This miracle of technology can see right *inside* you—and isn't *that* scary! (Especially if you want to *hide* something.) Dreams in which you're afraid of the x-ray machine that's trained on you may symbolize fear of psychotherapy, if that's been on your mind. If you're sure that therapy hasn't been a concern for you (not even an unconscious feeling you need it?), perhaps some *lay* person has shown alarming insight.

Zodiac: If you're familiar with your astrological sign, you may dream about it as a stand-in for you. A Gemini might dream of twins; a Sagittarius, about an archery champion. The symbol represents the qualities you feel most strongly identify your astrological sign. In an Aries dream, for instance, the ram would stand for the part of you that's ambitious, headstrong, extravagant, a bit of a dilettante. You can dream about other people in zodiacal guise, too; maybe your Pisces lover is represented by a fish, or *two* fishes.

Zoo: Visiting a zoo often symbolizes a trip around your entire unconscious world; you peer at every animal (aspect of yourself). How do you react to each one? (See also Animal, Lion, and Tiger.) Certain creatures *can* represent more general ideas: Snakes may symbolize evil; eagles, war or death. Even these associations, though, have some connections with your unconscious.

HOW TO SHAPE A FORTUNE FROM A DREAM

Using a dream to predict the future is a highly reliable method, because it's based on information that the dreamer already *knows*—even though the facts are inaccessible to him, buried in his unconscious. Your role is to extract that information from the dream, and then to use it as the basis for a forecast.

Perhaps just *because* fortunes told from dreams are likely to be accurate, you may encounter much more resistance to them from the dreamer. People who go to gypsy card-readers or who throw the *I Ching* have an easy out when the results are unpleasant: "Oh, it's nothing but superstition anyway!" But a *dream* comes from the subject's very own psyche; and if he doesn't like your interpretation, he may get quite adamant about insisting that it is false. You're in a delicate position: telling the dreamer things he's been hiding from himself—and maybe would like to *keep* buried.

Resistance is often a sure sign that your interpretation is on the right track—but it's not a flag telling you to persist! You'll have to judge on the spot—with tact and consideration—whether to press (gently!) or move on to another symbol or interpretation. (If a dreamer is violently opposed to the idea that she dreamed of dissatisfaction with her lover, she's not in any emotional state to profit from the prediction that she'll need to be more *inclusive* in her relationships.)

A dreamer who is less blocked will be an easier subject—but not all *that* easy! You never know whether a wish expressed in a dream is one that the dreamer can *admit* to feeling. Sometimes a strong unconscious wish is so consciously repugnant that you'll be able to predict, easily, that it's the one thing the dreamer will *never* do in waking life. (A girl who dreams of killing her lover or abandoning her baby brother on a desert island may never *act* on such wishes!) *Use* the dreamer's resistance in shaping your prediction: Look for both the dream-wish and the fears that oppose it. Which is the stronger? How is the dreamer's personality built to cope with the conflict? Is he more likely to admit the wish, and get what he wants no matter *what*? Or is he more likely to cling to his fear, and modify his basic wishes? Your *personal* knowledge of the dreamer can tell you which.

Another hint: Keep a dream book of your own beside your bed—handy for nighttime and wake-up notes. The process of recording and seeing patterns in your *own* dreams will help you acquire sensitivity to the dreams of *others*. Practice predicting your own future from your dreams, too!

Fortune-telling with dreams, then, is simply projecting the dreamer's personality and unconscious desires into the future. The dream will give you strong clues about what he wants and what keeps him from getting it; so will his reactions as you proceed to explain, symbol by symbol, what is going on in the dream. Be definite, but keep a sharp ear tuned to his responses.

Here's a sample: A man dreams that he is in the woods (though he's not all that crazy about the country) in a clearing, and feels very expectant. There seems to be a rustling all around him . . . and then a great stallion comes crashing through the trees, ridden by a beautiful woman. The horse comes to a sudden halt, and the dreamer feels an uncontrollable urge to climb aboard. The woman smiles broadly, but she does not beckon him. He mounts the horse, and he and the woman ride off together. He awakens feeling released. What you *might* know about this dreamer is that he has had homosexual experience, or at least thought along those lines. What the dream seems to make clear, though, is that he is changing his orientation—or at the very least, losing his fear of women. The horse is a strong masculine symbol, but he ends up riding it, not abused and inferior on the ground; and he rides it *with* her—she does not beckon him or threaten him. At the end, they are both in control. You could predict from this dream a happy but perhaps quite unconventional relationship with a woman—a truly liberated affair.

As you can see, projecting dream information into the future isn't so difficult. After all, the unconscious is *powerful*, and often knows what you will do—long before *you (consciously)* find out.

THE TRADITIONAL METHOD

The only trouble with interesting new methods is that they tend to eclipse interesting *old* methods. Freud, long considered a quack by the medical profession, has become an orthodox authority on dreams. But psychology is older than Freud, and dream interpretation for fortune-telling is as old as any form of magic practiced by man. Every culture has its own traditional interpretations of dream symbols. (It is odd, and significant, that *no* culture takes the images and stories in dreams at face value; people have always believed that there is more to dreams than their surface content.)

Traditional dream divination depends not on analysis of the specific dream and dreamer, but on meanings assigned *arbitrarily* to symbols in the

174

dream. This may sound woefully unscientific compared to the talk of *conscious* and *unconscious* in modern psychology; but it is close to Jung's notion of archetypes. An archetype is a dream-symbol available to everyone; it has the same meaning for every dreamer. Jung believed that these archetypes are deeply lodged in our unconscious; but the gypsies and the old wise women of Europe and Asia claim access, by tradition, to the collective unconscious, and say they can interpret its symbols. To a lot of people, this doesn't sound any more far-fetched than the idea that there *is* a collective unconscious, or what we can repress desires into dreams.

Most of the traditional divinatory meanings of dream-imagery were censored by the timid Victorians. But originally, interpretations were as bloody and sexy as the unpurified versions of Grimm's fairy tales. You can find some of these untampered-with dream interpretations in old ballads, full of dead sailors whose dreams foretell their deaths and the sinking of their ships; and even in legends about Saints:

> *They told her how, upon St. Agnes' Eve,*
> *Young virgins might have visions of delight*
> *And soft adorings from their loves receive*
> *Upon the honeyed middle of the night,*
> *If ceremonies due they did aright;*
> *As, supperless to bed they must retire*
> *And couch supine their beauties lily white;*
> *Nor look behind, nor sideways, but require*
> *Of heaven with upward eyes for all that they*
>   *desire. . . .*

> *She sighed for Agnes' dreams the sweetest of the*
>   *year.*

That's part of John Keats's poem "St. Agnes' Eve," about a young man who takes advantage of a legend to carry off his lady on the one night when she *wouldn't* be frightened to see him appear suddenly in her room!

Before the invention of the telegraph, there were few ways to get news of loved ones who were away and in danger. It must have been very tempting to believe that dreams could bring you news of someone who was otherwise completely out of touch. And in all times, it has been assumed that dreams can create powerful connections between people. "I dreamed of you the other night" has always been a statement of intimacy (real or *desired*). In the great ballad "The Wife of Usher's Well," when the old woman hears that her sons are dead, she then wishes them alive again in a dream that is hair-raisingly real.

The nineteenth century seems to have been fascinated by dreams that foretold disasters. Since then, almost every great catastrophe of modern times has been predicted by a dream (usually reported after the fact). The *Titanic* disaster was supposedly foreseen by numbers of dreamers, as was the burning of the Hindenberg; and *The National Enquirer* informs us almost weekly that virtually no one of prominence can die without some forecast in a dream.

Such dreams suggest a connection between dreams and the visions of those who consider themselves prophets—clairvoyants and seers like Edgar Cayce and Jeanne Dixon. They have visions that are *like* dreams, but occur in the waking state, are much clearer than dreams, and much more to the point. (Jeanne Dixon doesn't waste vision-time on minor anxieties like where the can-opener has gotten to or whether that party dress is all right.) But a dream—like a clairvoyant's vision—gives ordinary, nonvisionary people a way to glimpse another world, to see the future, to command a higher knowledge than they do in waking life.

So even when you're interpreting dreams with the traditional, arbitrary, nonscientific method, remember you're not just playing a game.

LISTENING AND INTERPRETATION

Ask in advance whether there is a special question that the subject wants answered. Find out whether he had that question on his mind *before* the dream; if so, the dream is more likely to answer it lucidly.

It also helps to know if a dream has *recurred*. That automatically gives it more importance. Some fortune-tellers believe that events in a dream are likely to occur in real life exactly as many times as the *dream* recurs; or that the event in the dream grows closer and closer to happening the oftener the dream is dreamed.

Some dreams, too, simply cry out with import—they shake the dreamer, impress the fortune-teller, and should *never* be ignored. Sometimes these dreams don't seem to have much narrative force, but are full of terror or a sense of something impending. Pay careful attention to every detail. There was one story, well documented in several turn-of-the-century books about psychic phenomena, of a young man in England who dreamed that he was out on a boating party with his girl and a crowd of other young people. They pulled up to the river bank for a picnic. When they had finished, he couldn't find his girl. There was no sense of panic in the dream; everyone laughed and said that she must have gone down the path for a walk. They all rowed off, including the young man, saying that she would turn up later back at the dock. In the dream the young man wasn't worried, just annoyed, but he woke up feeling gloomy and uneasy. The dream had been full of pleasant weather, good company, and fine times—but the feeling remained that something was wrong. A day or two later, he *did* go with friends on a boating party, and when he couldn't find his girl, it developed that she had tripped on a root and drowned in quite shallow water a few feet from her friends. A fortune-teller would say that the young man could not *bear* to know what his dream prophesied—and so he only *felt* gloomy, without being able to really spot the reason. All such dreams should be carefully analyzed; that is *your* responsibility!

Finally, as we've pointed out earlier in this chapter, the main problem with dreams—no matter which method of interpretation you use—is that they're so *rich* in symbols and images that it's hard to know where to focus. With this traditional method (as with the psychological one), rely on the subject for clues. Ask what he feels is important in the dream—and notice what he wants to *avoid*. Make a list of the images in the dream, and then refer to the Traditional Dream Glossary (pages 178-183) or to one of the more complete ones recommended on page 281. Then concentrate—on working out a coherent fortune, fitting the symbols and their meanings into a logical pattern that meshes with what you know of the dreamer *personally*.

THE DREAM CYCLE

One of the most ancient theories about the origins and power of dreams is that they are examples of the cyclical working of the Moon on man's fate. Certainly some people report greater dream activity during the full Moon, or in the dark of the Moon, and women are known to dream very actively during menstruation and ovulation (which is, of course, another instance of theories overlapping—psychologists would say that the greater sexual awareness of these times leads to greater dream activity).

A well-developed tradition says that certain days of the month foretell automatically the fate of the fortune told in the dream. A bad dream dreamed on certain days is neutralized; a good dream, intensified; certain times bring bad dreams or bad results, no matter what other forces are at work. A table of these days can be found opposite, showing generally what dreams signify on each day of the month. Of course, there can be *personal* variations. You might want to look up the Destiny Number of your subject in this book's numerology chapter (pages 103-119). Dreams on days with that number may have more predictive force.

The cyclical nature of dreams is a strong reason for keeping *track* of them—in the crucial dream-book. Both for yourself and for your subjects, only a regular and recorded acquaintance with dreams can help you learn how they predict the future. Any *one* dream may be fugitive, incoherent, and indecisive. A dream book will let you see whether dreams recur, *when* they recur, what over-all patterns of symbolism mark an individual's dreams.

For instance, a dreamer may never have a *whole* dream that recurs—but his father, or a father figure, may appear again and again. Or he may have a dream that produces the same emotional impact at the same time each month. Or a woman may dream the same sort of dream (about a body of water, for instance, or about empty streets) at the full Moon or at menstruation time. All these patterns are important, and will remain completely unknown if dreams are taken as units rather than as part of a larger dream *life*.

The idea of a dream life is what dream interpreters and fortune-tellers mean when they talk about the *higher self, the other self,* or the *shadow* or *alter ego.* Dreams happen in a world of their own. It is unfair to take them as isolated signs, no matter how important. Look for the larger picture—a secret dream life and its connection to the dreamer's wakino life. In the interaction between the two, you'll find the future.

DREAM DAYS AND WHAT THEY MEAN
(listed by day of the month)

1/Good; dream will counteract a bad prophecy.
2/Dream will not come true.
3/Events foretold by the dream will not work out well for the dreamer.
4/Excellent; don't let bad dreams worry you.
5/Any good fortune foretold will reserve itself.
6/Keep dreams secret, except from a fortune-teller.
7/Dreamed-of desires will be fulfilled.
8/Beware—a tricky day!
9/Dreamed-of desires will be granted.
10/Happiness will win out . . . eventually.
11/Dream's effect will be felt in four days.
12/Hard times ahead!
13/Dream will come true.
14/Happiness will be postponed.

15/Dream will come true in thirty days.
16/Dreamed-of wish will be productive.
17/Tell dreams to no one—not *even* a fortune-teller—for thirty days.
18/Treacherous friends will turn on the dreamer.
19/Worldly affairs will bring happiness.
20/Dream will come true in four days.
21/Trust no one.
22/Dreamed-of desires will be fulfilled.
23/Dream will suddenly seem clear in three days.
24/Much happiness!
25/Dream will come true after nine days.
26/Unexpected help is on the way.
27/Good news!
28/Dreamed-of desire will be fulfilled.
29/Money is in the offing.
30/Good news is due in the morning.
31/Prepare for the worst!

TRADITIONAL DREAM GLOSSARY

These traditional dream symbols are more *arbitrary* than the psychological ones. But you'll find that there are some fascinating coincidences. Not-so-mysteriously, the ancient seers who first developed these traditional meanings *did* base their insights on rudimentary—if unconscious—psychological understanding of the human psyche. They were, in their magical way, *primitive* psychologists!

Accident: If *you're* the victim: great success. If *another* is the victim; beware of false friends.

Adultery: Temptation . . . you *resist;* and that's a lucky omen. If you succumb: Troubles will follow, failure and treachery await you.

Advertisement: If you dream of *reading* the ads in *The New Yorker,* you'll get favorable news—probably from a distance. If you place a want ad in the dream; you will find yourself in difficulties from which others will have to extricate you.

Amputation: Of an arm or leg—it's a certain warning of the death of some near, dear person, or of loss by sudden separation.

Anger: To dream of your own means you have powerful enemies.

Animals: Domestic ones (cats, pups, etc.) mean the happy return of absent friends, peaceful domestic life, and reconciliation of quarrels. Wild beasts mean secret enemies—beware!

Ants: You'll move to a large, populous city where you will have a numerous family of boys! If you're industrious, the dream also means you'll get rich. If in love, you will have a speedy marriage and good fortune.

Auction: Generally unfavorable. If you're *bidding* in the dream, expect to lose something in reality. Just looking? You may still meet misfortune. If you pass up a dream auction, you will attain within a few years everything you want.

Bachelor: A young one means that you will be deceived, especially if you are a woman; but *you* must be candid and generous anyway. If the bachelor is old, bad luck is coming.

Bacon: Oddly, a symbol of sorrow. To eat it denotes sadness; to see it, the death of a friend, and the parting forever from a lover.

Baldness: A sign of approaching sickness. For a young woman to

178

dream that her lover is bald means that he will never marry her. For her to dream that *she* is bald implies that she will die unmarried and poor.

Bankruptcy: You are about to undertake something that will be disastrous for you and earn the disapproval of all your friends. Take advice!

Bathing: If the water is clear and transparent, you will be lucky; if muddy and dirty, bad luck!

Beans: If eaten in the dream, they foretell sickness; if seen growing, a quarrel with those you love best.

Beard: A long beard in a man's dream means good fortune, especially in business and marriage. For a woman to dream of a man's beard is unlucky: If she is married or has a lover, she will lose him. If a *young* woman dreams of a man's beard, she is ready to be married, and *will* be quickly! For a woman to dream she *has* a beard is a *very* lucky omen.

Bells: A speedy marriage; good news on the way.

Birth: For a married woman—maybe she's pregnant. For an unmarried woman—her lover approaches, and she may lose her virginity.

Bleeding: If an unsuccessful attempt is made to stop it, bad luck—maybe a long and dangerous illness.

Bones: You'll get rich bit by bit. Human bones mean an inheritance on the death of a rich old man.

Breaking: Evil and ill luck to the dreamer. If you break an arm or a leg, sickness is foretold. If you break furniture, you'll fail in business. Breaking a window means danger from fire. (A warning dream?) Breaking a mirror means the death of your nearest friend or relative. If dishes break, you'll be robbed by your cleaning woman.

Bride, bridesmaid, or bridegroom: To dream of any of these is unlucky, foretelling grief, disappointment, a funeral.

Bridge: To cross *over* one is a good omen; to pass *under* means you will never feel at ease. An obstruction on the bridge foretells sickness, but not necessarily serious. If a bridge breaks down under you, sudden death will follow.

Burden: If you're bowed down under a heavy load, you'll have to support someone else, financially or emotionally. If you find the load unbearable, there will be many freeloaders; but if you *can* bear the load, you will be rewarded for your kindness.

Business: An unknown friend wishes to be your partner.

Butchers: An injury may occur to the dreamer. To see meat being cut up means that your friends will be executed.

Buttons: Many bright buttons— good fortune, an orderly life; rusty buttons—loss of fortune; covered ones—sadness. If a man dreams he's lost all the buttons on his clothes, he'll soon die.

Cage: Letting birds out of the cage means a speedy marriage, or a business success.

Castle: A legacy is on the way! But to depart from a castle means desertion by friends. A castle besieged: lawsuits or overdue bills.

Cats: Your lover is deceiving you; or you are being betrayed in some other way.

Chains: Sorrow and affliction. If you're encumbered with chains, a legal matter will not go your way. To wear a chain means enslavement to passion.

Cherries: Disappointments in life; a troublesome, annoying love affair.

Children: A sign of success in all undertakings. If a child dies, your lover will leave you for someone else. Ragged and dirty children: A friend will ask you to do something you disapprove of.

Church: A quarrel may ruin you, or you will lose out in business.

Climbing: Up a tree? Success! Up a steep hill or high mountain? Many difficulties—if you reach the top, you can expect success eventually.

Clothes: A new wardrobe means you'll have a visitor. Old clothes: sickness.

Clouds: White clouds signify prosperity; clouds mounting high from earth mean voyages, the return of the absent, and revealing of secrets; red clouds are a bad omen; dark and obscure clouds mean anger in the near future.

Coffee: Very favorable! You'll have a great social success.

Cold: To dream of being cold means poverty, misfortune, unrequited love.

Cooking: The wedding of a friend; unexpected success.

Corns: To dream that you have corns on your feet means success in proportion to the number of corns.

Crocodile: Misfortunes at sea, or on a trip.

Crutches: To walk on crutches in a dream is a very bad omen in general.

Cucumber: Recovery of the sick; a love affair; you're loved from afar.

Cuckoo: To hear the cuckoo means you'll be betrayed in love.

Cucumbers: Recovery of the sick. Or the dreamer will soon fall in love. Or a pleasant voyage to the traveler, and a new love in a distant place.

Dancing: Joyful news from a long absent friend; an unexpected legacy; a particularly good lover.

Darkness: A very bad omen! Moving out of the darkness into the light means trouble resolved.

Deafness: A false friend is advising you to do an evil or disadvantageous deed.

Death: A wedding! If you've been at home a long time, it signifies a change of life, perhaps a trip abroad. If you see another person dead, you will be ill-used by friends.

Dirt: Sickness and dishonor. If you fall into the dirt, you will be betrayed.

Disaster: At sea, you'll be crossed in love; a rail accident means you'll quarrel with your lover.

Divorce: Your partner is false.

Dog: If one bites you, your best friend will become your bitterest enemy; if he only barks, you'll quarrel with your friend.

Dolphin: A beautiful animal, but invariably a bad omen: death to the sick, loss of love to the young, bad luck in business. Though it would not be wise to travel after dreaming of dolphins, it would be a good idea to change address and to find another job.

Dragon: A symbol of enormous change, for better or worse. Note the exact circumstances of the dream for other clues.

Drowning: Losses in business, even bankruptcy.

Drunkenness: A forewarning of what is as yet wholly unknown. You may meet a man who is to become your lover, or change jobs and move up the ladder in a wholly new and unexpected way. For a man, it means that he is loved by a woman he is not at present thinking of, and that she will prove a terrific mistress.

Ear: To dream of having fair and well-shaped ears means fame and fortune to come; deformed ears mean the contrary. To clean the ears means good news from some source.

Eating: If the dreamer is eating, it means disunion among the family, losses in business, storms and shipwrecks.

Eclipse: Of the sun, the death of an older male relative—a father, uncle, or grandfather. A man will bring you trouble. To a pregnant woman, it is a sign that her child will be famous and a joy to her. An eclipse of the moon means the death of a mother, aunt, or grandmother, or sorrow through a woman.

Execution: To dream of a hanging, a firing squad, or an electrocution means that you'll be sought after for relief by people in great need.

Face: A swollen face shows that you will amass wealth; if you are in love, your lover will come into money and share it with you.

Fall: From a high place, a tumble from current status.

Fat: To grow fat in a dream implies that you are about to be very ill.

Feet: To wash your feet in a river or fountain signifies trouble, perhaps even rape; if someone is scratching your feet, it means loss by flattery.

Finger: To cut a finger and see it bleed is a very good omen; if you do not bleed, bad luck. To lose your fingers means loss of whatever is dearest to you.

Fire: A mixed but interesting sign. In the long run, happiness and long life; in the short run, a fierce tantrum over a trivial matter.

Flowers: Gathering them—expect to succeed in all enterprises. If, however, they wither in your hands, your business will not prosper, or your lover will die.

Flying: Unattainable aspirations should be abandoned.

Friend: To see a friend dead means sudden joyous news.

Fruit: A mixed omen, differing with the circumstances of the dream. *Miscellaneous fruit in large quantities:* prosperity, success in love, happiness in general. *Pears:* great wealth through marriage. *Peaches:* sickness and deceit in love. *Pineapples:* an invitation. *Plums:* a voyage, especially abroad. *Figs:* wealth from afar; a happy old age. *Cherries:* false love, an unhappy marriage. *Grapes:* riches and honor, and a great rise in social status.

Funeral: A dream burial means a speedy marriage, or a trip together for lovers. Money and property may come to you from a relative on your mother's side.

Game: Playing one? You'll have an uncertain job future and be fickle in love.

Garlic: If you are *eating* garlic, it signifies a discovery of hidden secrets, perhaps an infidelity; but to dream garlic is in the house is good luck.

Glove: If you lose your right-hand glove, a husband or wife will die. Losing both gloves indicates failure and bankruptcy.

Hair: If a man dreams his hair is long, he is being deceived by a woman. To dream of a bald woman means famine, poverty, and sickness. But a bald *man* is a good omen.

Head: Ever dream your head is *larger* than usual? More dignity will come to you! To dream of having one's head cut off means great loss; to cut another's head off means revenge. To dream of washing your head is to be delivered from danger.

Heart: Your *own* means trouble in love. If you see *another's* heart, trust your instincts about the person. Bleeding hearts mean trouble.

Honey: Either to see it or to eat it is a very fortunate omen—long life and prosperity through hard but rewarding work.

Horns: If the dreamer is wearing horns, it means he will succeed and have great power. To see another wearing horns means he is riding for a fall.

Ice: A favorable omen—it shows that one's lover is kind and sweet. To slide on the ice means a *faux pas.*

Ink: A sign that you'll be involved in some disgraceful business venture, if the ink is black. If it is red, you have good news coming.

Island: To be on a desert island implies the death of a lover; but if the island is fertile and pleasant, you will lose your present lover and find a *better* one.

Jewelry: You are on the way to great good fortune.

Journey: A great change—whether for better or worse, time will tell.

Keys: Favorable if you are self-employed.

King: Hard times, an obsession with a more powerful person.

Kiss: A bad omen, implying deceit in love, false friendship.

Knives: Lawsuits, general failure in life, bad-tempered lover, or a bitchy spouse.

Lease: To rent a house or apartment in a dream means great success will come.

Legs: An itchy leg means profitless anxiety. If the dreamer has a wooden leg, good changes to bad, and bad to worse.

Lemon: Contention in the family, worry over disobedient children.

Lettuce: You're incompetent—get organized!

Lips: To dream of having red, healthy lips means that friends will enjoy good health and long life.

Lobster: A new love affair with a generous, affectionate lover; if the dish is spicy, the lover will be unpredictable but warm-hearted.

Love: If you dream of being in love, you are feeling cold and unreceptive. To dream of another loving you is a bad sign for your sex life.

Machinery: A machine-shop or factory is a good omen; it shows that industry will be rewarded by success and happiness.

Madness: To dream that you are mentally disturbed, or in company with the mad, is a good omen. You may have trouble at the outset of your career, but you will end successfully.

Meat: Loss and damage if you dream of eating the meat you had for supper that night.

Medicine: A passionate, faithful lover.

Metals: Gold—sorrow and sickness; silver—deceit and disappointment in love; copper—accidents and loss in traveling; iron—marriage to a widow or widower, and wealth through hard work; lead—death of a lover or close friend.

Milk: A good omen. To dream of drinking it shows you're industrious and sensible.

Mushroom: To dream of gathering them means that you love more than you are loved. To eat them signifies an unpleasant incident about to happen.

Nakedness: To see a naked man—fear and terror; a woman—honor and joy if she is pretty, shame if she is old or deformed.

Newspaper: For a young woman, it signifies a proposal to come; for a married person, it means family trouble.

Old Man: For a woman to dream of an old man means she will succeed on her own, or by the aid of a small legacy.

Old Woman: For a man to dream that he courts an old woman and is successful means that he will be successful in everything.

Oyster: After many years of labor, the dreamer will succeed; marriage after a long courtship.

Paper-hanging: A newly papered wall in a friend's house means he or she will be sad; such a wall in your own house means a death. If you are the paper-hanger, you will be early widowed.

Pearl: A good omen: You will succeed through your own efforts—beyond your wildest dreams.

Plant: If it grows before your eyes—like Jack's beanstalk—whatever is due will come quickly.

Being in the audience means good luck.

Quicksand: Many dangers that are your own fault.

Rain: Favorable to lovers; fidelity and affection are sure to follow.

Rose: A completely favorable omen, it foretells happiness, long life, a good marriage, and success in business.

Running: To dream that you are running to avoid danger means that you will be falsely accused of wrongdoing.

School: To dream that you're back at school and haven't done your homework means you're about to get involved in something you don't understand.

Shaving: A bad omen—the dreamer may be stripped of all that is important to him.

Shoes: If a young woman dreams she has a new pair of shoes, her lover will try to seduce her. For a businessman, shoes mean prosperity.

Singing: It's unfavorable to dream you're an opera star. To hear others singing is a good omen for *them*.

Snake: Many dangers, a false lover. To kill a snake means you are to overcome trouble.

Statue: If a bronze statue is moving, you'll find wealth and fame.

Student: To dream of being a student means that you will get needed help.

Tambourine: If you're beating it vigorously, a calamity will befall a good friend.

Teapot: New friendships.

Tooth: If it comes out of your mouth while you're eating, you will be very sick, or have trouble and misfortune. Getting a new tooth means that you'll find a new lover, or that you are pregnant.

Toothache: The loss of a lover.

Thirst: This means ambition. If you drink water, you will succeed; if you take wine, you will fail; impure water, and you will fall into disgrace. If you quench *another's* thirst, you will be the *bestower* of success.

Umbrella: Lost? You'll get a fancy present from someone you admire. To borrow an umbrella signifies bad luck. To walk under an umbrella with a lover means great trouble, but fidelity will solve problems.

Valentine: To receive one is a portent of illness for the dreamer; to send one means that a dear friend will be ill.

Vegetable: You will be puzzled and troubled by the behavior of a close companion.

Volcano: If you're in jail or some other "imprisonment," you'll get out soon. If not, peace and contentment.

Vomiting: For a rich dreamer, loss; for a poor one, increase.

Wedding: Especially for those in love, very bad luck.

Weeping: Joy will come.

Whale: The dreamer will become a great person, and live to an old age.

Wig: For a person with a full head of hair to dream of wearing a wig means that he or she will be called into court.

Wind: To dream of it blowing hard means that you will soon be called away in a hurry to another part of the country.

Window: Sitting at a window and looking out at people passing means that you will be vexed by lies about you, especially from one who was once a friend.

Wine: If you're poor, to dream of drinking wine indicates sudden loss.

Witchcraft: Going to a fortune-teller, witch or voodoo doctor signifies bad luck.

Wrestling: A serious accusation will be brought against the dreamer, who will need all his agility to disprove it.

Wrinkles: To dream of oneself grown old is an indication of an early death.

Yacht: Many ups and downs in a current love affair; but success and a contented marriage will result.

Chapter Seven

THE
OUIJA BOARD
AND
AUTOMATIC
WRITING

The Ouija Board is a form of automatic writing. It was patented and sold and became immensely popular during the craze for the occult that swept England and America during the twenties (along with mah-jongg, the Charleston, and lipstick). And it has never entirely lost its hold on the imaginations of people who like to believe that they can get in touch with what's "over there," or who want to foretell the future.

Like the "I Ching," the Ouija Board and automatic writing use the written word. But with the "I Ching" the text is already there, and all you do is find the right portion of it to interpret. With the Ouija Board and automatic writing, the forces of the future and of the occult guide the hand of the seeker—so you are the writer of the prophecy as well as its interpreter. This participation gives these methods an extra dimension—which invariably leaves you with a spooky feeling of being on your own. The messages received through the Ouija Board and the hand of the automatic writer come direct from another world—and can be most direct. Prepare yourself for some effects that aren't available with other methods, and that have kept the Ouija Board popular for over seventy or more years.

THE OUIJA BOARD

The Ouija Board was "invented" in 1904. Those quotes mean its maker took one of the oldest methods of fortune-telling and spirit-contact and turned it into a manufactured parlor game that would solve the problem of paraphernalia. For years, people had been using tabletops to write the letters of the alphabet on, and glasses, bits of wood, or flat stones to move around (at their wills or the spirits') to spell out messages from the spirit world.

The Ouija Board was (and still is) a piece of beaverboard with a shiny surface; printed on it are the letters of the alphabet, the numbers from one to ten, the words *Yes*, *No*, and *Good-bye*. It comes with a *planchette*–a small piece of wood shaped somewhat like a heart; it has felt-tipped legs, and a pointer that indicates the letter or number or word finally selected. An individual or a group of from two to six can use it to communicate with the occult world, or to foretell the future. Its messages are mysterious or fun or informative, depending on *your* attitude.

Long before the Ouija Board reached *game* status (Parker Brothers of Salem, Massachusetts, make it in this country, and have been doing so for over fifty years), it was seriously used for divination by spiritualists and mediums who were not in the parlor-game class at all. Madame Helena Blavatsky, a Russian medium who was the center of a spiritualist circle in Europe in the late nineteenth and early twentieth centuries, used it, and so did Edward Arthur Waite (of Tarot fame) and W. B. Yeats, both disciples of Blavatsky.

The Ouija has several advantages for students of the occult and for those interested in a clear message about the future. For one thing, you can't *misinterpret* its words. If you concentrate on a question, it will almost certainly be answered—in black and white; or, at any rate, the refusal to answer will be just as definite. Also, it is easy to know just what is going on with the Ouija. If there's a group using it, each seeker has his hand on the planchette, and can *feel* it move. It is hard to fake a move, and very easy to feel someone trying to take "control."

Of course, the forces that move the planchette are very complicated. Each seeker has his own unconscious reasons for helping it move one way or the other. But be *prepared:* Everyone who has ever seriously asked questions of the Ouija says that the planchette moves *as if of its own accord.* It *does* seem to move without the volition of the seekers, giving a "Yes" or a "No," spelling out names and places and whole sentences. Just as you can feel someone's attempt to control it, you can also sense when the seeker is impatient or the planchette *refuses* to move—because when it *does,* the sensation is unmistakable. It just goes where *it* wants to, and no one is aware of pushing or of being able to stop it.

Of course, there are numerous explanations for this phenomenon, and they've all been rehashed by everyone who thinks of Ouija as a mere parlor game: social hysteria, subliminal physical signals, the charisma of the leader. All those explanations are plausible. But once you experience the unique movement of the planchette and take it seriously, none of those reasons will quite do.

THE MYSTIC MOOD

The Ouija Board is part of a special time in history. It rose to popularity in the twenties and was one of the symbols of the Lost Generation trying to find itself. Perhaps you should take advantage of the feverish decadence of that period to give your own experiments with fortune-telling by Ouija a special atmosphere.

Your props can be magnificent. Try using a round table with a fringed silk shawl over it, and an art deco bridge lamp (or contemporary copy of one). Whatever other lights you have should be *low.* Keep in mind that you're working with a commercial version of an ancient method. The attitude you want to encourage is a little like the first responses to the talking movie—it's not quite serious, but too exciting not to make a part of one's life. The surroundings should be *almost* "camp"—eclectic, suggestive of innocent sin. Throw an animal skin (fake, we hope—or an unendangered species like sheepskin) over the couch; hang a beaded curtain (they're available now by the yard in a nice jangly plastic); play that low dreamy cocktail music with a tinsely overtone that made every girl think she was Gatsby's Daisy.

If the long-hipped, bugle-bead-fringed look isn't for you, try the great at-home costume of the twenties—the kimono. It's very colorful, a bit Sadie-Thompsonish, and awfully seductive. French girls are wearing them a lot lately, along with real Egyptian henna for the hair—to keep in period. Another possibility: printed chiffon pajamas that drip with hothouse elegance. Your make-up should suggest innocence-gone-wrong: baby-wide eyes, smudged with shadow and spikily lashed, bee-stung lips, an over-heated pallor (pale foundation, powder, and rouge in circles on the flesh of the cheek, rather than under the bone).

But don't turn yourself into a total flapper. Remember, you're using a fortune-telling method that has its origins in ancient forms of divination. It deserves to be taken seriously, at least while you're using it. You'll want to carefully consider your subject's questions and help him interpret the answers as if you know what you're doing—or what the spirit forces are doing. So keep in mind that the flapper was also a serious lady undertaking the business of liberating herself and the rest of the world from Victorian mores and morals. And when, after a little fluttering and a *certain* amount of cynical lip-curl, you do get down to the business of poising your hands over the planchette, give it your full attention—and give *him* a chance to see the real girl beneath the spitcurl and the headache band and the big Mia Farrow eyes.

THE METHOD

You *can* use the Ouija Board alone or with up to six people. But for fortune-telling, we recommend *two* people as ideal. Adapt the instructions below for all-alone practice (don't tamper idly with the board, though; ask it *real* questions) or for a high-spirited group that suddenly decides to commune with the ghost of W. C. Fields. The technique is always the same—and everyone must keep one hand on the planchette.

For two: You and your subject sit side by side at the table, with the planchette between you on the Ouija Board. Each of you puts a hand, or both hands, on one side of the planchette, fingers touching it lightly. *Do not bring any weight to bear*—just let fingers rest lightly.

Then gaze into each other's eyes. The seeker states the question he wants answered. You repeat it. Then both wait for the planchette to respond. It is best to begin with simple questions, those that can be answered by "Yes" and "No," so that you'll have a chance to feel how the thing works. *Don't be in a hurry.* It can take up to ten minutes for the planchette to begin to move, and during that time you must lose concentration. If you do, the planchette will have no response. (This is one reason to make sure the question is really *important* to the seeker. It's hard to hold your concentration if all you want to know is whether the weather will clear for the picnic next week. . . . Real *issues* about one's life are the only questions to ask.)

When the planchette *does* move, be careful not to anticipate it. Sometimes it will start toward the *No*, then change its "mind" and move toward *Yes,* only to head back to *No* again. Let the piece move as it wants—don't decide *for* it, only to have it balk in the middle of the board.

Sometimes you may feel that the *best* way to find out about the future is from someone now *in* it. Mediums often try to find a spirit who will answer questions through the Ouija Board. The best way is to ask if there is someone who will speak to the questioner; if the planchette says "Yes," ask what the name is. (It will be spelled out by the planchette moving from letter to letter.) Then put your questions, *unless* the spirit *volunteers* information.

Sometimes you'll be surprised at the amount of time and energy the Ouija gives and takes; other times, it will suddenly dip toward the *Good-bye* at the bottom of the board and that will be that for the session. *Don't fight it.* There are those who are convinced that you can make an enemy of the Ouija Board, and never again have it work for you. Co-operate with its urges, and follow where it leads.

When you come to the point of asking more complicated questions, try to frame them well. For instance, if the seeker is worried about a decision he must make, have him ask: "In what month can I expect this problem to be solved?'' Then, if he gets an answer to that one, ''What must I do to aid in the solution?'' Or, ''Have I done everything I can do to bring it to a good outcome?'' If the answer is ''No'': ''What must I do?'' If the Ouija goes silent, change the subject; you can come back to the original problem at some other session.

Because there are numbers on the board, you can ask all manner of questions about dates—*when* (as well as where) things should or should not be done. Make the questions clear, and accept the answers implicitly. The Ouija does not take doubt at all well. *No scoffing!*

Variations on the Ouija

If the idea of what looks very like a board game seems too childish to you, you can devise your own version of the Ouija with a table top and a simple glass tumbler. Many people prefer this approach because they believe that making the materials puts them into much closer touch with the hidden forces that guide their hands on the planchette.

If you're using a dark-surfaced table, use white chalk for marking a board; on a white table, colored chalk. Wood takes the chalk marks fine (and they wipe off). On Formica, washable felt-tipped pens do well. Whether the table is square or round makes no difference. Write the letters of the alphabet around its edge, giving each equal space; add numbers from one to ten, the words ''Yes'' and ''No,'' and the word ''Good-bye.'' (Space these out in the center of the table.) Instead of a planchette, use a glass (*not* plastic) tumbler. Turn it upside down, and rest two fingers of your hand on the bottom. Then proceed as you would with the Ouija Board.

The version you use is up to you—it's really a matter of style. If the kitsch of the commercial board is a quality you like, or can rise above, don't hesitate to buy one. But you may feel that a board you've made with your hands will have greater authority in the eyes of your subjects. Remember, it's not the paraphernalia but the *spirit forces* that count; and *you* have access to those forces.

AUTOMATIC WRITING

When the poet W. B. Yeats had been married three days, his new wife said that she would like to try automatic writing, which was one of the many occult practices Yeats and his friends had been indulging in for years. (Yeats was an enthusiastic spiritualist who belonged to the mystic circles led by Waite and Madame Blavatsky, and to the Rosicrucians; he finally founded a mystical system of his own, which he describes in somewhat confusing detail in his book *A Vision*.) Mrs. Yeats later said that she became interested in automatic writing to ''keep her husband.'' And certainly she chose the right tactic when she took up automatic writing. Yeats came to believe his wife was a natural medium, and took copious notes from the messages she received while writing ''out of herself''; there is even some evidence that he developed ideas for two of his one-act plays from his wife's automatic writings.

Even if you're not doing automatic writing to hold a Nobel-Prize-winning poet, the method has its fascinations. It is an attempt to plumb the depths of the subconscious *directly*. It is freer than the Ouija Board, allowing you to ''receive'' messages from the occult world in whole sentences, long paragraphs, or short telegraphic bursts. In fact, the form of the communication has no limits except your own inhibitions. Usually, the fortune-teller (*you*) does the automatic writing while concentrating on the subject and his questions. That takes a special blend of intense concentration and totally *relaxed* openness.

Of course, automatic writing takes practice (like all the other methods we've talked about), and also it takes a rather special kind of *confidence*. Not just anybody can write to order, without the hitches and panics that overtake *some* of us when we're asked to do so much as compose a note of thanks to that nice man who made our stay in Santa Fe so memorable. But for those with an ordinary writing block, automatic writing is often easiest.

In most kinds of writing, we try for a conscious effect, and are all too ready to *judge* our efforts according to our own—or someone else's—expectations. But with automatic writing, the process is exactly the opposite. You don't aim for *any* effect. You don't know what the result will be until you get it—and the most spontaneous effort gives the best result. For some people, writing with no aim and no inhibitions is *much* harder than drafting a Ph.D. thesis! They prefer to be in perfect control, thank you, and certainly don't want to let their hand write something unguarded—especially if that something turns out to be *revealing,* maybe even *embarrassing*.

So, beware: Some fortune-tellers and some subjects are just not prepared for the revelations of automatic writing, may be put off by the freedom of the method, no matter what it does or doesn't reveal. *You* may be one of those people, in fact—but of course, you can still learn and use the method, providing that you know a potential *subject* or two who would be interested. If you wish, let a responsive subject do his own writing, and be the interpreter. However, I think you're probably adventurous enough to try your *own* automatic writing—even if the practice is private, and your self-revelations kept private.

THE MYSTIC MOOD
The major difference between the Ouija Board and automatic writing is that the latter is much more *personal*. The Ouija Board, after all, uses *gear,* and is limited in what it can say (often by the reticence of the spirit who is talking through the board). It necessarily concentrates on the *mechanics* of receiving the message, rather than the message itself. That can, of course, be an advantage—it takes some of the psychological burden off you—but it is not nearly as *dramatic* as automatic writing, where the spotlight is unswervingly on the fortune-teller who writes and interprets. So to use this method—whether you write *and* interpret, or merely the latter—you'll have to establish a strong sense of *credibility*.

You must appear calm and competent, but prepared to relax completely and let your mind rove about, ready to pick up clues from your subconscious and that of your subject. If *he* is doing the writing, you must provide an atmosphere of collected and easy imperturbability. The atmosphere must be rather like the kind people needed in the sixties when they began to make serious personal experiments with drugs—a guide was needed, one who had been there, and who could help out with any rough spots, but who believed thoroughly in the project and was convinced that it was worthwhile, whatever the risks. And there *are* elements of risk in every fortune-telling situation; the more personal the method, the more reassurance the subject needs. So be certain that the method is congenial to you, practice enough so that you're really familiar with it, and then set the stage so that the subject immediately feels your familiarity and assurance.

Since there will be periods when you'll be sitting quietly with eyes half-shut, take special care with your make-up, hair, and general grooming. There is nothing like an extended period in repose to give someone a chance to see every little thing that's wrong. (How often have you counted on your *animation* to bring off an effect?) This is no time for high coloring or new and bizarre effects—you want to look very much like yourself, only better, quieter. This might just be the time to do a complete make-up and then take a self-portrait with your handy Polaroid, eyes shut, face grave. You may find the result a little *funereal,* but you'll get a pretty good idea of what you will look like to someone watching you in the act of automatic writing for a longish stretch.

The important thing about this careful image is subtlety. Your foundation is blended smoothly—no telltale cut-off points, blotches of highlighter or blusher. Eyes must be downright *perfect.* With your lids down, your whole made-up eye will be under scrutiny! Also: If you've given up powder for the shiny look, now is the time for a brief return to the subtle matte finish. Your face should glow in the soft light, but never *gleam.*

About your hair: Don't go in for a style that requires you to rush off and maintain it at regular intervals. Unless you have a terrific permanent or naturally curly hair, find a style that's soft, falls naturally, and is likely to hold up for an entire evening. (No one can be expected to concentrate on your fascinating performance as an automatic writer if they are riveted by the two slowly-but-surely-dropping sausage curls over each ear.) If you've ever thought of trying the serene and smooth Brontë look—hair parted in the middle and drawn back into a smooth chignon at the nape of the neck—this would be the time for it. Or, if you have a good smooth fall, wear it hanging straight from the crown with your own hair pulled smoothly back under it. Of course, if you have a neat Afro or a smooth little neo-Jean-Seberg, you are already set!

As for what you wear, choose that for its staying power, too. Avoid a short skirt that might ride up in mid-phrase and send your nonwriting hand creeping down to tug at it. Also steer clear of clothes that look too *sportif;* automatic writing is sedentary, and the mood will be disrupted if you sit nearly immobile in jeans, sneakers, fringed vest. If you do wear pants, make them part of a ladylike and flowing pants suit, with floppy legs and a wispy Indian top. Other alternatives: a long skirt, caftan, or ankle-length t-shirt. (If the latter, be sure you have the figure for it—the automatic writer can't be bothered to worry about holding her tummy in.) If you have pretty feet, now's the time to go barefoot.

Your hands are, of course, extremely important—they will be the center of attention as you write. Perfect that manicure, keep nail polish—if any—subdued. Don't be-ring your hands too obviously. Plain gold and silver rings are fine, but avoid flashing jewels or over-large stones. You're not trying to *hypnotize* the subject with your rings!

Before you begin, be certain that you're perfectly comfortable, and that your subject is at ease. (If he is doing the writing, and you are observing and interpreting, ask him where he'd like to sit, and share with him the relaxation exercise on page 61—omitting the Tarot cards). The lights should be low, but not *soporific* (it would be embarrassing if your subject went to sleep while you're writing away like mad), and during the writing all other activities should cease. No smoking, no eating, perhaps an occasional sip from a drink. There should be general attention to the matter in hand; with a method as trickily personal as this one, you need lots of help in the way of intense concentration and *no* distractions. Insist on it.

RELAXATION AND MATERIALS

The assumption underlying automatic writing is that the key to our futures and to our personalities lies in our subconscious, and can be beckoned to the surface by writing, without plan or design, in a state as near as possible to a half-trance. In this state of complete relaxation, the hand becomes an extension of the mind; the mind opens to its own secrets, impressions received from the outside world, and the consciousness of others.

There are two absolute *prerequisites* to successful automatic writing: a near-perfect state of relaxation, and materials that will make the best use of that relaxed state. Of course, the first requirement is the hardest to get—but there are some techniques to help. Both you and your subject (no matter which of you will do the writing itself) should both do the exercise given on page 61, to reduce tension and encourage a feeling of physical well-being. If anyone else is to be present, they should either participate in the exercise too, or come in later after it's over.

This is one method where spiritualist talk about good and bad "vibrations" makes perfect sense. No one who is prepared to scoff, or make the occasion a laughing matter, should be let in on it. Whether or not you are a true believer and expect to receive extraordinary information from your foray into automatic writing, the one thing that *will* squash all possibilities of an interesting result is a crowd of gigglers or (worse yet) interrupters. Guests in the wrong mood will run roughshod over the occasion. So choose your people carefully—ahead of time. While you're writing, you won't have the energy or time to fix someone with a gimlet eye and *dare* them to scoff.

Now, the next question is choosing your *materials*. Assuming that you're going to work in longhand (although it's possible to use a typewriter, and we'll describe that method in due course), you should probably *not* work at a table, but in a chair or on a couch, using a lap-board. (The Ouija Board turned upside-down will do, or a cutting board from the kitchen.) The paper should be in loose sheets—you will not, if you're writing fluently, have the time or inclination to tear sheets off a pad, and such an action would break the receptive flow of the writing. Paper should be white, so that even fugitive or pale marks will show up. Pick a size that you're used to. Some writers like a large board with sketch-pad-size sheets, which solves the problem of changing the paper. But if you're not used to writing on paper that large, it might slow you down rather than speed the flow. Experiment with large sizes; you might find yourself coming automatically back to regular typing paper. Be certain the paper is smooth and of fairly solid quality—a good typing bond will do nicely. Don't get erasable paper—it will smudge and crinkle, and is generally a mess when the time comes for interpreting the words.

The writing instrument is *crucial*. It is the extension of your hand, which, for the moment, an extension of your unconscious mind. Your instrument must write with perfect fluency, not skip or stick or do any of those maddening things that can make even perfectly *ordinary* writing a trial. A new felt-tipped pen, fine pointed, is an ideal instrument—but make sure it *is* new, because the older ones sometimes begin to skip or to develop the "pales" and don't produce entirely legible results. Avoid ball-point pens—they have a tendency to skip at the best of times, and don't work at all unless you hold them upright. (And you may find yourself unconsciously sinking into all *sorts* of positions while writing fluently.) Some writers swear by a regular fountain pen—but make sure it's one you've owned for years and are familiar with. Pencils? Yellow number-one pencils are soft and give a dark result, but you'll need lots, all well-sharpened in advance and kept ready to hand in a container. (You can't afford to break the flow because your pencil's getting dull or has suddenly broken.) Use several instruments in practice until you've found the one that suits you best, and then stick with it. If your subject is the writer, and it is his first time, he may need several tries with several instruments before he finds the one that will give the best results.

Now, assume *you* are the writer. (If someone else is, guide him before he begins, suggesting some of the tips below.) Sit comfortably to begin with, and be sure that your writing arm has something to rest against—the arm of the chair, your own lap, or the board or table. (Whatever the interferences, physical fatigue and discomfort shouldn't be among them.) Use a largish pile of paper—you don't want to chance running out at a particularly interesting time—and be sure that you have both your good reliable writing instrument *and* a substitute ready at hand. Be certain that the lighting, the temperature of the room, and the mood of the moment feel *right* to *you*. To test your feelings about this, just settle yourself for the task, then rest your hands on the surface of the first sheet of paper and close your eyes. If everything feels amenable, you are ready to begin. If not, simply ask for a recess and do more relaxation exercises, or have a drink, and then try again. Perhaps you just weren't fated to write that evening—and to know *that* is a lot better than to get involved with a tedious and unsuccessful session.

Of course, practice sessions are different. Mood or no mood, it's often better to go on with the writing if you're practicing. A lot of people can produce the mood by the act of writing itself, and have had some of their best sessions in the course of practice.

THE METHOD

The goal in automatic writing is to make the words that appear on the paper correspond as nearly as possible to the state of the writer's unconscious mind. To to this, you'll have to forget a good deal that you've been taught about the act of ordinary writing—penmanship, spelling, punctuation, sentence and paragraph structure. *Everything* must be subordinated to the process of getting down what comes *first* to your mind as you write. Remember, you're not committed to producing a story or nicely turned anecdote for the guests, and certainly not for your subject, whose interest lies in what your unconscious (or his own if he's the writer) has to tell him about his character and his future.

Once you're ready, begin by writing the first things that come into your head—even if that's just a list of the people in the room, the date (or a date—if it's other than the current one, it might be significant), or a sentence describing whatever your eyes last rested on. Once begun, *don't let your hand stop.* It is important at this point to make a small but conscious effort to continue, to let the *activity* go on, no matter *what* is (or isn't) happening in your conscious mind. This can feel a little foolish, since you'll probably begin by writing something like:

I can't imagine why im going on with this
it feels as if nothing at all will happen
the whole room seems to me distant and I
cant imagine what the point is.

That doesn't seem a very promising beginning, but here's what's happening: You are *clearing the way* for the deeper levels of your consciousness to get through. The Transcendental Meditation people have a diagram describing this process as it happens during the recitation of the mantra that each of its members is given to meditate on. TM initiates are instructed to ignore, but *not suppress,* all trivial and foreign thoughts; not to expect themselves to go immediately into some sort of trance state, but to let *all* thoughts simply occur and *pass by.* That is what *you* must do as you write: And as you go on, the trivial thoughts will pass, and the deeper ones will begin to come to you. At an even later stage, you won't be aware of thinking or even feeling *anything.* Impressions will be directly transferred from your unconscious to the paper via your hand. You'll hardly be aware that you *are* writing—certainly not of *what* you're writing. *That* is the state to aim for. In it, the best revelations about your own life and that of your subject are likely to come through. (*Don't* stop to turn sheets of paper neatly or make a careful pile. Toss them on the floor or table.)

This process is sure to take some time: Don't expect anything much of consequence in under thirty minutes. Don't try to hurry the process. It is necessarily slow and must move according to your mood. Never actually *clock* yourself—you shouldn't be distracted by the thought of a timer. But on the other hand, don't push yourself to the point where the writing has become just a *chore.* If you're tired, stop—the fatigue itself may be a sign that the productivity of the session has come to an end. Some writers, however, do experience a second-wind phenomenon—they feel bored or tired and, after a minute or two of pressing on, they find that the flow begins again.

A feeling of loose fluidity is what you're after. When you begin to feel that you're writing with no trouble at all, not bothering to think of what goes down on the paper, *don't let anything stop you.* What you are into is very like what the mediums call a trance; and they say flatly that it is *dangerous* to interrupt one. You will not, of course, be in a *real* trance, and there's no personal danger involved at all. But danger could strike the fortune-telling project if you're interrupted at this point. You'll want to go on from here for as long as your hand and the mood holds out, because if you're ever going to get a solid message about the future, it will be at this time.

One of the best ways to induce this sense of fluidity is to cloud your vision just slightly, so you can concentrate fully on the *processes* of writing, and not on either *what* you're writing or on anything in your immediate environment. (It won't help to keep picking up on something visually, like the pattern of a tie, and repeat descriptions of it *ad infinitun.*) Let your eyes half close, as if you were going to cat-nap; the lids will feel heavy. Your vision should rest in the middle distance, *not* on what you're writing, *not* on the movements of anyone in the room or any particular object. It is often helpful to unfocus your eyes while looking at a glowing lampshade or the gleam of a cocktail glass—a spot of *light* rather than an object. Often you won't be able to induce this soft focus until you've written a sentence or two. The act of writing will *help;* then the process of unfocusing will generate more writing. It's a phsyically co-operative venture.

It is important not to concentrate in any way on the actual *content* of the writing. (*That* process comes later—with interpretation.) If you find yourself repeating a word or phrase, try to think yourself *gently* away from the repetition; but if it goes on, let it—you may discover afterward that the phrase *and* its repetition is most significant. But if the repetition goes on for so long that you feel uneasy, it's a signal to stop writing.

The moment to stop writing is a difficult one to fix. Most experienced automatic writers insist that they just *know* when to quit. Mediums who use this method to get in touch with the spirit world feel that it is not *they* who decide to stop, but the spirits who are writing through them. You'll have to make the decision in terms of your own feelings and how they fall—fatigue, restless repetition, a sense of malaise or boredom, all are perfectly good signals. Sometimes you'll find that you are suddenly *compelled* to look at what you've written—and that is often the clearest signal of all to stop and do just that. Experiment with this, as with other aspects of the method. You'll soon know what your own rhythm is, and how long you will be able to write with good results.

Interpretation
The shock of seeing the product of your first try at automatic writing may be considerable—especially if you're one of those people who pride themselves on fine penmanship, solid style, and accuracy. What you'll see is a loosely-put-together string of words, without punctuation and often with no seeming exterior structure at all. Don't be dismayed—that appearance is a sure sign that you have begun to master the technique. The more "together" the writing looks, the more likely that you were merely writing, and not *automatically* writing.

First, read everything over very quickly, looking for references to your subject—direct or indirect. Make notes or underline the obvious references. Then go back again, this time looking for significant dates, names, or secondary references—events, objects, or ideas that might have some bearing on your subject's life. Don't assume that any of these references will be coherent—you're unlikely to find a *whole sentence* of any great relevance. Don't expect, for instance, that you'll find a reference that runs, "The subject should keep away from dark women and is in danger of missing out on his long-awaited vacation to Tortuga." In fact, if you do, you can bet that you've got a playful unconscious; its heavy humor is probably to be discouraged. Instead, you're likely to find, in the midst of what looks suspiciously like gibberish, a name or two and a series of vague references to objects or events that you must connect to form some relevant account of your subject's life and future.

If the subject *himself* has been doing the writing, you have both a more and less difficult job. You can be sure that everything he's written *is* relevant to him, just because *he's* been doing the writing. On the other hand, you are less familiar with his style than you are with your own; and chances are, he is less used to the process of automatic writing, and so will have produced a less interesting or less revealing reading. It's your job to find out what is truly *automatic* in his sample, and to discover from him what clues are likely to be relevant. As with all methods, know as much about him in advance as possible. (Constant references to "mother," for instance, may be a solid sign of the Old Oedipus at work, or could refer to a nickname or even to half of a well-known obscene expression.) Don't take anything for granted.

Once you're fairly sure that you've garnered all you can from the sample, and have made notes if you need to, see if you can match what you've found with incidents and wishes in your subject's life. Don't confine yourself to the obvious. Maybe the images in the writing are profound ones that don't apply *merely* to this subject. For instance, references to mountains, caves, and universal images (see the chapter on dreams—pages 143-183) should all be carefully noted. The word "mountain" can mean a hundred different things—you must find out which interpretation fits. Ask how he feels about them: Is he afraid of heights? Fascinated by the conquest of Everest?

Remember, too, that you must assume a *future* significance to the information in the sample. You wrote with the thought that what you produced would be affected by the future life of the subject. Have faith in that thought, interpret the results accordingly.

Here's a sample: The automatic writing of Sabina, who was doing her *own* fortune, and the interpretation that she made:

> Plants in the window at night not as interesting
> as in the daytime so sunlight just plants plain a
> little homely taken care of but do they deserve it
> do they deserve that kind of attention the avocado
> is okay but the dieffenbachia is too big for its own
> good and really ugly. Black night outside window
> open curtains not at all friendly should close
> blinds at least Robert always does that later but I
> feel jealous of him sometimes all the domestic
> tasks are his because he likes them better
> really he is better at them too, full of faith
> in the domestic the regular I have less concern
> for it certainly less faith in it as if I thrived
> on the uncertainties or expected someone to take
> care of the certainties for me Small apt living not
> like houses No real outside only a sense of other
> apts and something huge The World? But not as
> big as it feels in the country other lives pressing in
> domestic routines keep out the night give us an
> illusion of whatever security we have Do we know
> any more about ourselves than we did before? The
> country can't teach us anything But can we teach
> ourselves?

Robert was a lover Sabina had been living with, in *his* apartment, for several months; she had been thinking of leaving the city to live in her house in the country—but she didn't want to live *alone,* and wasn't at all certain that she wanted to live *anywhere* but with Robert.

Sabina's interpretation: The plants, the references to Robert's care of them and to his domestic concerns, made it clear that she enjoys being taken care of but isn't certain that she deserves it. And Sabina is jealous that Robert is living in his *own* house while she is just camping out. Sabina thought that she'd be better at taking care of her *own* things, her *own* plants. Though attracted to the nature of the country, and frightened of the crowdedness of the city, her security seems to lie with Robert now, rather than with a move to the country, which feels like a threat. Sabina predicted for herself that she wouldn't take off for the country in the near future, but would stay put until she felt more stable and certain of herself.

This is, of course, a fairly short sample: It was made in less than twenty minutes, in longhand. The writing was fairly slow, and the mood was ruminative. But it shows a goodly number of the common characteristics of automatic writing: beginning with an object (the plants) and the eye has happened to fix on; moving on to other objects and ideas suggested by the first; and then the trip inward, to concerns about the interior life of the subject. The concerns here are fairly limited, because the subject was doing her *own* writing and interpretation, and because she was alone at the time of the writing, with no one present to suggest *their* consciousness. Notice here there *is* punctuation, but that it is irregular, and that there is at least one interesting capitalization: The W in "World" is capped, which indicates that Sabina is in awe of a world greater than her own small circle; she may have a sort of infantile notion of the Great World.

Remember, when interpreting, that because you are *not* consciously trying to be *correct* in punctuation and capitalization and grammar, variations may have a great deal of meaning. For instance, if you find that you have consistently capitalized "Father," or that you lower-case a proper name over and over, you might consider what those words mean and why they've been chosen for emphasis or purposeful de-emphasis.

Variations:
The Typewriter

Automatic writing on the typewriter is not new; but it is, of course, not nearly as venerable as the longhand method. For some people, it is much the preferable way, because they write more fluently when they are typing. (Most of us have learned to compose on the typewriter in school and at work, and a lot of us earn our livings partly by typing.) Because most people who *do* type well use the touch system, it is often easier to set up an interior-oriented situation at the typewriter than with a pen. Most people need to be at least *partially* aware of the paper and where they're writing on it, but the touch-typist can close his eyes and take off without worrying about what will come out. The better a typist he is, the more likely he is to produce terrific automatic copy. But this is no method for the hunt-and-peck typist. He is usually far too concerned with the *mechanics* to do good automatic writing; better let him stick to the traditional instrument.

Mechanically, there are fewer problems with automatic typing than with pen and paper, but one logistical matter has to be taken care of in advance: The writer *cannot* change the paper in the typewriter, and even if he waits with his eyes closed while someone else does it, he will lose the impetus of his flow. The answer is to make a long roll of paper to feed into the typewriter. Just rubber-cement or tape a series of twenty sheets or so together to make a long scroll. Insert one end into the typewriter, and go on for as long as the roll lasts. (Twenty sheets is usually well beyond the capacity of most writers, at least at one sitting.) Some Beat Generation writers used this method to produce, not fortunes, but novels—Jack Kerouac is said to have written *On the Road* on a single roll of rubber-cemented paper.

The possibility of using the typewriter for automatic writing points up an interesting contrast that you'd do well to remember when you're working on interpretation: In graphology, the study of handwriting, the *manner* of the writing is more important than the content. Often graphologists would rather see a typical sample of the subject's hand than one in which he had some emotional investment. In automatic writing, the *message* is all-important.

Even if the writer doesn't look at what he's writing and produces a result wholly unlike his ordinary hand, or uses a typewriter that has no personal character at all, the result can be very telling—because the writing itself is only a *medium*. The mind of the writer is the crucial factor in automatic writing.

Chapter Eight

READING THE BODY

THE SENSUAL METHODS

These methods of telling the future are the most physically direct—and the sexiest. They assume that our bodies tell the stories of our lives—and that by examining the body's parts (as well as extensions of those parts, like handwriting), you can tell anyone's future. In this chapter, I'll discuss methods that use purely physical evidence: palmistry, phrenology (reading the skull's shape and conformations), and graphology (handwriting analysis). In the following chapter, you'll see how psychics can combine a total-body reading with nonphysical perceptions to discover the present and future of a client.

All humans are physically different. (There is no head exactly like yours; your palm print is unique; banks use your signature to identify you among their thousands of customers because only your hand can produce it.) But we're also the same. (Certainly no human head could be mistaken for any other object; hands are enough alike so that when two of them clasp, they fit; and our handwritings are similar enough so that we can usually read each other's pretty easily.) The sensual methods of fortune-telling use both the differences and the likenesses to make predictions. For instance, all people with a certain hand shape share basic character traits; but differences in finger size, lines on the palm, and the subject's reactions to the fortune teller as she takes his hand in hers—all combine to create a unique set of attributes.)

These methods are more nearly scientific than any other. Experts in each field believe they are serious practitioners of a rational discipline. Some have convinced the world that they are serious—or at least uncannily accurate in their conclusions. One certainty: We are all imprinted with the double genetic stamp of our parents. The genes we have at birth do remain a constant. So any study that reasons from these basic physical characteristics, with a long history of startling accuracy, is extremely likely to tell us who we are, and who we are going to be.

THE MYSTIC MOOD

Your approach to these *physical* methods should be, naturally, unabashedly sensual. In fact, they can appear slightly foolish unless you have some confidence in your own body and its powers. Make it clear—through your posture, clothing, attitude towards the subject, and environment—that you know the *power* of touch . . . and of these fortune-telling methods based on touch. You know the aura that indicates a girl is sure she's alluring, in tune with and in control of her body? Now you have a double reason to project it. The methods themselves need your sensuous confidence to be effective. You will, after all, be *touching* your subject quite a bit during the proceedings—even if your aim is innocently divinatory—and you don't want to unconsciously convey to him a sense of nervousness or embarrassment.

Of course, you're not out to *seduce* the subject—or are you? In any case, seduction is a little different from a session in palmistry, phrenology, or graphology. But the two have *some* common ground. First, you need to generate a feeling of physical ease and security in the subject—otherwise he'll feel violated or just *shy,* no matter how gently you take his hand or hold his head. *Trust* is crucial! And the best way to establish it is to create a subliminal bond between the two of you by being warm yet tactful.

You'll be quite directly physical in these methods of fortune-telling, but if you convey your own vulnerability and feminity, the subject will feel the session is *personal,* and will relax, too. Don't *overwhelm* him with earth-mother caresses. But on the other hand, be sure not to appear "above it all" like a seer or medium who acts superior to the subject and the general run of humanity.

Think of your roles as rather like that of a lightning rod—you're the conductor of liberating physical knowledge. There's a fine line to tread—moving between confidence as a fortune-teller and vulnerability as a person—but with these methods, you'll find the try rewarding.

Wear your sexiest and most intimate dress. That doesn't necessarily mean the most *revealing.* You don't want to frighten the subject by looking rapacious—he may be skittish *enough* at the thought of letting you stroke his temples or palm. Think of yourself not as a vampy witch, but as an initiate in mysteries that would be a little frightening . . . *if* you were not so soft and reassuring.

So: ruffles around a lowish neckline, perhaps, or heaps of softly draped knit jersey that clings but doesn't look sprayed on. Evening pajamas are wonderful if they're very feminine—in a soft flower print, with a low, button-up front. Wear almost-formal shoes (like satin sandals) for reassurance, and your hair not-quite-down, to project a confidence that if you *did* decide to be wanton, you'd be welcomed.

Make-up should be all-out, unabashedly designed to please. Put great emphasis on your natural coloring, carefully heightened, and on the eyes, which should glow with pleasure and brightness (gleamer on lids, in a warm shade like bronze or peach). Perfume is important—use it at the pulse points and between your breasts, and spray all over with the cologne version. (You'll be *close* to the subject.) If your dress is low-cut, use blusher on your breasts—the frosted kind.

Hands are most important of all, since they'll be touching him often, and he'll be watching them as you manipulate his palm and fingers. Do a total manicure, with lots of softeners for cuticles and tons of hand cream afterward. *Perfume* your hands, and stroke a bit of blusher onto the palms. (*Babies'* hands are always rosy!)

Jewelry should be unjangly but opulent-looking: a magnificent brooch between your breasts; long earrings. Don't hide any part of your body that you can reveal *un-self-consciously,* and don't leave unadorned any part you can enhance without fussiness. When you're all dressed, *forget* the way you look. Reach way down to your complete trust that you and your body can generate tremendous excitement. Confidence!

As for the setting, aim for a subdued but faintly *thrilling* mood. Avoid overly languorous effects like incense or velvet throws. The sort of physical confidence you want is full of energy and power—so don't make the lights too dim or play sleepy music. Instead, use lots of low lamps, and a softly pulsing rhythm. Put pillows on the sofa—which will be the arena of action, a place to be *close* to your subject.

These are such intimate methods that they're best confined to one subject at a time. They are not designed for groups, but are best suited to an intimacy *à deux*.

This is the perfect time to make an entire *evening* of fortune-telling. Serve drinks and dinner (grand and satisfying—see below for a sensualist's menu, with recipes and serving suggestions). Dinner should be face-to-face, across a small table so you'll end up looking into each other's eyes. Don't make this evening a week-night (unless you and your subject are both joblessly fancy-free). Take all evening—and perhaps well into the morning—to work the kind of magic these methods are famous for. Give yourself time, and don't be surprised if you succeed triumphantly in more ways than one!

Sensuality is always a pleasure, but not all sensuality is automatically sexy. It takes a certain happy calculation to insure that one great experience of the senses connects to the others, and that they all connect to suggest that greatest experience of all—sex.

Eating is a favorite activity for almost everyone, but for some it is a sadly *solitary* activity, not necessarily a time for the communication that leads to other, and greater, pleasures. You can serve a meal that emphasizes the communication between you, the warmth of touch and the excitement of seeing, as well as the satisfaction of the palate.

The great eating scene in the movie *Tom Jones* is bawdy and earthy— he and his new inamorata are hugely hungry, and they're satisfying one appetite in full knowledge that they're about to rush pell-mell down the hall to satisfy another. What the dinner here attempts to do is much more subtle: It will explore and titillate *all* the senses, combining them in the experience of the meal and suggesting an even more intense combination. This is not a subtlety that denies what it's doing—you must be frankly sensual, or you'll seem half *ashamed*. The subtlety lies in a commitment to *all* the senses when only one is *obviously* involved.

The menu that follows is founded on a number of assumptions that I've found true over a long and varied career of serving dinners to men. They're not all *invariably* true—sometimes you can reverse them and get much the same effect—but they *are* all worth exploring.

202

THE SENSUAL DINNER

OYSTERS
on the Half Shell
or
HOT ARTICHOKES
with Lemon Butter

STUFFED CHICKEN BREASTS

ASPARAGUS HOLLANDAISE

WILD RICE

RAW SPINACH SALAD
with Mandarin Oranges

CHAMPAGNE

MOCHA PARFAIT
or
FRESH PEARS AND APPLES
with Rolled Champagne Cookies

CAFÉ FILTRE

COGNAC

First of all, whether or not any foods are true *physical* aphrodisiacs, there are certainly foods with that reputation, and the *idea* of serving them is almost as good as the reputed physical reaction. That's why oysters are offered here.

Second, food that is handled, taken by the fingers to the mouth, especially in luscious bits, becomes doubly sensual because it combines touch with taste. You and your companion will be sharing a sensation, each touching the warm artichoke, pulling away the leaves one by one, dipping them into the lemon butter, carrying them to your mouths.

And that kind of sharing isn't the only kind involved here—each course should be served from a dish on the table, not put on plates in the kitchen, because there is a kind of magic in eating from a common dish. The Arabs eat a whole lamb from a single huge dish—they sit around it, sing as they eat, and tell stories. If you are intimate enough with your dinner guest, you might try a variation on this—use only *one* butter dish for the artichokes, so that you will both be dipping your leaves in the same dish.

Formality titillates. Not so great a formality that it produces stiffness, but just enough so that there's a tiny, exciting tension between the earthy, sensual appetites being satisfied and the slightly stylized grace of the dinner. Also, formality allows you to feast the eye in every way—you can be at your prettiest, the table can be lavishly decorated and the candles numerous enough to be both romantic and illuminating.

Expensive is sexy. That may sound slightly overworldly—because, after all, better a dinner of herbs with the beloved than a whole ox where there is *no* love, right? But after all, people like to believe that they're worth a good deal in time, trouble, *and* money—and the elegant simplicity of oysters on the half shell, the lavishness of your use of butter and eggs and good wine, and your willingness to spend time and money on a fine array of courses spells *caring*. Of course, no one doubts for a moment that eventually he will give up dinner at the Four Seasons to share a bowl of good homemade soup with *you*, but meanwhile *give* a little.

Sweet is sexy. *Especially* for men. By now, most women are horrified enough by the thoroughly unsexy business of overeating so that richness and sweetness are a bit tainted by the specter of five pounds gained (and the subsequent suffering to lose it). But for a good number of men, sweetness brings back all of the great memories of childhood—the first ice cream cone, the pies mother used to make, the boyish raids on the icebox for cake-and-ice-cream. What is smooth, rich, sweet, and goes down easy is an unalloyed pleasure. But for those of you whose meal will *really* be ruined by a madly sweet dessert, I've included an alternative—luscious pears and apples, the peeling of which is almost as good a sensual ploy as the sweetness of a chocolate-mocha parfait.

Let the courses be numerous and small. Every taste of food should be presented as important, part of a ritual that makes each moment you have together important. Also, food looks much prettier, more appetizing, if each dish can stand alone. The pauses between courses are crucial—they give you a chance to look into his eyes, to brush the back of his head with your fingers as you go out to the kitchen, to let him see you handle plates and glasses and food with expert ease and grace. Not an opportunity to be missed!

Music is the food of love. Let there be music throughout dinner—but not of music so loud that it drowns out your voices. Avoid vocal music for this reason, and stick to something soft and a bit stately. (The tinkly piano that some people call "dinner music" shouldn't be allowed within miles of any sensual meal.)

RECIPES

For the oysters, you need no recipe—just ask your fishstore man to open the oysters for you, and serve them six to a plate with a lemon wedge on the side. *Don't* use a ketchup-based cocktail sauce if you can possibly avoid it. The elegant sexiness of the oyster shouldn't be obscured by *anything*; if you don't own oyster forks, borrow some—any other implement is a bit awkward.

Artichokes with Lemon Butter
Use one large, firm, fresh artichoke apiece. Cut off the stem very close to the body of the vegetable, so that it will sit up straight on the plate. Boil a large pot of water, adding a teaspoon of salt. Plunge the artichokes into the water, and boil vigorously for twenty minutes, or until a leaf pulls away easily.

The lemon butter is just as simple: Melt ¼ lb. (a stick) of sweet butter in a small pan; add lemon juice to taste (about half a lemon for most people) and a half teaspoon of salt.

Serve the artichokes on salad plates, with small dishes of the butter on the side. Make sure that you have small forks ready as well, for cutting up the artichoke bottom, that succulent secret the leaves hide.

204

Stuffed Chicken Breasts

2 large chicken breasts, unsplit, boned, and skinned
    (Your butcher will do all this.)
2 slices prosciutto or salty Virginia ham
1 cup ricotta cheese
2 tbsp. Parmesan cheese
2 tbsp. parsley
½ tsp. salt
1 egg, beaten
flour for dredging
butter for sautéeing

Lay the chicken breasts out, skin side down, and pound to flatten them. Lay the prosciutto or ham on top of each. Make the stuffing by combining the ricotta, the Parmesan, and the parsley and salt in a bowl. Spread half of the stuffing on each chicken breast, and fold the breast over, tucking its ends under and fastening it closed with toothpicks. Dip each breast in the egg, then dredge in flour. Sauté in butter over a medium flame until golden. Cook over low heat, about ten minutes on each side. Remove from the pan to a warmed platter. Add more butter to the pan; let it brown lightly, then pour over the chicken breasts. Serve on or with:

Wild Rice

If you are so horrified by the price of unalleviated wild rice that you can't quite bring yourself to use it, use half-and-half with white—but you'll have to cook each separately. Follow package directions, but add a teaspoon of butter for each cup of water you use for boiling. Make about 2½ cups.

Asparagus Hollandaise

Cut the woody stems off the asparagus—just the bottom inch or so. Then, using a potato peeler, peel the outer skin away from the stalk, to within about an inch of the tip. Then either plunge asparagus into boiling water in a skillet (the water should just cover the vegetable) or put on a rack over boiling water. If you're boiling them, they should be done in about five minutes; if you're steaming them, eight minutes.

The sauce:

1 stick of butter (¼ lb.)	juice of ½ lemon
3 egg yolks	salt to taste

In a double boiler or in a stainless steel bowl over boiling water, melt about one-fourth of the stick of butter. Then beat it well. Add the first egg yolk, and continue beating until the yolk and the butter are well mixed and the color is pale. Then add the next fourth of the stick of butter, in tiny pats, beating constantly. Continue, alternating egg yolks and pats of butter, and beating constantly, until the butter and yolks are all used and the mixture begins to thicken. It should be about the consistency of whipped cream, but a bit heavier. Remove from the boiling water as soon as it's thickened, and add the salt and lemon juice. Set aside in a warm, but not hot, place until serving time. Serve the asparagus and the sauce separately—ladle the sauce over the asparagus at table.

    Note: If you plan to serve the artichokes as a first course, skip the asparagus—the flavors are too much alike. You can add to the sensuality of the meal by eating your asparagus in the wholly approved English style, and inviting your guest to do likewise: Pick up each one by its stem, dredge it around in the sauce a bit, and then put it in your mouth tip first, right down to wherever you think it will be tender. Bite it off!

Spinach Salad with Mandarin Oranges
½ lb. spinach
1 can mandarin orange slices
1 tbsp. honey
1½ tbsp. lemon juice
¼ tsp. cayenne pepper
salt to taste

Wash the spinach carefully, removing all woody stems. Dry on paper towels. (See pages 20-21.) Mix the dressing: Whip with a fork the honey, lemon juice, cayenne, and salt, and toss in a bowl with the spinach. Arrange the drained oranges on the surface of the spinach.

Serve on glass plates.

Mocha Parfait
1 pint Haagen Daaz coffee ice cream
1 small can Hershey's chocolate syrup
1 oz. Baker's unsweetened chocolate
2 oz. creme de cacao
4 oz. heavy cream
chocolate shavings (½ oz. Baker's unsweetened
        chocolate, grated)

Heat the chocolate syrup in a small saucepan; add the unsweetened chocolate, broken up or grated; when it is melted, add the creme de cacao, and let bubble for a few moments. Remove from heat and let cool.

Whip the cream until thick and spoonable, preferably using an electric mixer; sweeten if you like, using sugar to taste.

Heat the sauce until just warm, and pour some in the bottom of glass dishes or parfait glasses; spoon in Haagen Daaz coffee ice cream. Add another layer of the sauce, another of the ice cream, and a final layer of sauce. Top with whipped cream, and sprinkle with chocolate shavings. Serve immediately with the Pepperidge Farm rolled champagne cookies.

The Wine
Choose (or let your wine-and-spirits man help you choose) a really good champagne to drink throughout the meal. It should be a Brut (the driest there is), French, and of an old and respected name. You may not be able to afford a vintage year, but if the name is good enough—Taittinger, Bollinger, Moet & Chandon—it will be a deep pleasure, from the first course to dessert. Serve it icy cold, in tulip glasses (borrow a couple, or splurge and buy them for the occasion). If you don't have a wine bucket, you can borrow or rent one—but have one there, near the table, keeping your splendid wine cold. You'll need at least two bottles.

The Coffee
Café filtre is simply the French version of espresso—and for it, all you need is whatever method you can get together most easily for good drip coffee: your

own drip pot, a filter pot like a Chemex or a Melita, or the most authentic version, the tiny tin pots that most restaurant supply houses sell and that make a strong pot of filtered coffee for two. Whatever you use, boil the water briskly, use a full heaping tablespoon of espresso-roast coffee (Medaglia D'Oro, Progresso, Café Bustelo) per demitasse cup, and then flood the pot with the boiling water. Serve immediately—if you reheat, you're in danger of *boiling* the coffee, the only real sin.

The Cognac
Again, ask your wine-and-spirits man. I'd recommend Bisquit, Courvoisier, or Remy Martin. If you would like to serve another liqueur or two that would be in taste with the dinner you've served, you might choose Grand Marnier (which will echo the mandarin oranges in the salad) or crème de cacao, which will follow the flavor of the dessert.

One of the pleasures of champagne as the only wine is that you can go on drinking it afterward without breaking the precious continuity of the occasion—whether it's just champagne in the living room, or the more potent French Seventy-Fives (three parts champagne to one part cognac).

PALMISTRY

Palmistry is really a combination of two different studies, which are always combined to produce a complete analysis of the hand. *Chirognomy* is analysis of the shape of the hand; *chiromancy*, analysis of the lines of the palm. The first tells the subject's emotional and psychological makeup; the second is used to tell the future.

Probably the ancient Hindus *first* read palms to understand character and predict the future. But the method was widespread in ancient times, known by philosophers before the time of Aristotle. The most famous *modern* palmist was Count Louis Hamon, who took the professional name Cheiro (and gave the two palmistry methods their present names). He published half a dozen books on the subject, and persuaded numbers of famous people—including the writer Mark Twain—to give him their hand prints for analysis. In fact, he perfected the method of taking hand prints to study at leisure; since his readings were often long and complicated, he could not take as much time with each subject in person as he needed. (You'll find instructions for taking hand prints on page 220.)

Cheiro was a poet as well as a palmist, and very bold in his predictions and analyses of character. He pioneered in the reading of children's palms, since he believed that the major lines on the palm are formed—and the life laid out in them—before the person is one year old.

Although chirognomy and chiromancy are two different studies (some experts accept one and think the other is bunk), they are usually treated as parts of a whole. Of course, when you do readings, you can emphasize whichever area of the art you do best, or like best, or more clearly applies to the subject's questions about himself. (If he wants to know, "Am I naturally creative?" you'll look at his hand *shape* for an answer. If he asks, "Will I marry before I'm thirty?" you'll analyze the *lines*.)

Remember, though, predicting the *future* from the lines of the hand (or from any part of the body) can be a delicate business. The subject's hand, unlike a card layout or coin throw, will be with him forever, and suggestion is *powerful.* If there's any doubt in your mind as to how your subject will take a prediction, stick to simple character analysis. Use your best judgment . . . and be *gentle.*

FIRST STEP: Taking the Hand

You're sitting together on the sofa and (I hope) enjoying the afterglow of dinner and conversation. But even for the most *willing* subject, the moment when you first take his hand in yours can be awkward and spoil the confidence you need to go on. Begin by asking him to simply hold out his right hand, palm down and then palm up. Examine it with authority (but not touching yet). Say something *positive* about the hand shape, skin texture, gracefulness of the fingers, or whatever strikes you as attractive. (One girl who always seems to have ink-stained fingers and broken nails—she types a lot—has been in love with a man for years because he said she has "capable-looking" hands. For some reason, that hit her as exactly the quality she desires, and she'd rather have heard that honest comment than some gobbledegook about "artistic fingers" or "lily-white softness.") Of course, if the subject has magnificent hands, by all means gush—though beware of telling men they have lovely, graceful hands if they seem at all uncertain about their masculinity.

Now, look into the subject's eyes and *tell him* exactly what you are going to do. ("First, I'm going to look at the over-all shape of your hand to see what basic type it is.") Then take his hand in your own two, firmly but gently. Try to feel objective—you're not "holding hands," you're holding a hand. Don't *encase* it—let it rest lightly on your slightly cupped palms.

The subject's reaction may give you some psychological clues that you can throw into the character analysis for good measure. If his hand is tense or tends to pull away from yours, you don't have to be Freud to discern that he is somewhat uncomfortable about physical contact, may be emotionally reticent. If he jokes nervously about the quasi-sexual nature of the contact, he probably comes on stronger with people than he really feels. Give yourself time to absorb his general reactions—a few *non*chirognomic insights can bolster your reading, give you confidence that you'll have *something* valid to say in the interpretation. Smile reassuringly if the subject seems nervous—a *pat* on the hand might be a friendly gesture to ease tension—and then proceed to the actual reading.

Note: If the subject is a girlfriend, ask her to remove her nail polish, if she's wearing any. (Provide her with cotton, remover, and hand lotion.)

SHAPE: The Seven Major Types

1. The Elemental Hand has short, thick fingers which look all-of-a-piece (rather than delicately jointed like a marionette's). The thumb is very broad, tends to turn outward from the palm. This is the hand of the physical worker, builder, handler of raw materials. Slow but sure, and very conservative, the elemental personality likes traditional surroundings, where he can feel secure. He'll sneer distrustfully at anything "new-fangled," like women's liberation or free mass transportation. He trusts nothing except what he can see and touch. A materialist from lack of imagination, he may scoff at fortune-telling, "arty" ideas. He's not an intellectual, but has a powerful personality, strong character.

2. The Aggressive Hand widens like a spade across the finger-span. (The shape is called "spatulate"—think of a pancake turner.) Fingers are flat; joints are even and unpronounced. The personality that usually goes with this hand is like the Elemental in that both have a great capacity for endurance in a struggle; but there the resemblance ends. The Spatulate is shrewd, ambitious, self-centered, and highly intelligent. He has the energy to do what he wants—and he wants a *lot*. He'll have dynamic career ideas—and an efficient master plan for achieving them. Largely unemotional, he'll let nothing and no one stand in the way of his climb.

3. The Artistic Hand is the most controversial: Many palmists feel that *no* hand should be called "artistic," since art can be produced by so many personality types. Nevertheless, this hand, traditionally associated with artists, is extremely pliable, with an almost delicate thumb and a medium-sized palm. Variations on this hand make it a hard one to spot: It may be quite large, but don't let size fool you if it's the basic shape described above; it may differ by being larger and, as well, longer and more trim. These two larger versions of the type usually indicate a great love of luxury as well as art; their owners may not be content to paint or write, but may seek wealth in order to collect antiques and indulge themselves in satin sheets.

4. The Practical Hand is square in shape. The palm is deeply hollowed; the joints of the fingers are strong and well-developed. The owner of this hand is a believer in authority—will base his convictions and actions on the wisdom of orthodox religion, his parents, or an admired boss. He'll be useful in the world, perhaps in some service occupation like medicine or politics. He's a getter-ahead, but in a sane way—never a tyrant or a fool.

5. The Philosophical Hand might be mistaken for a workman's: It has a large palm, large thumb, knotty finger joints, and squarish finger ends. But it is quite flexible, as if ready to take on any task. The owner of this hand will subordinate his whole life to reason, and so is often unconventional in a perfectly logical sort of way (like the professor who always wears two raincoats because one might get drenched, or the girl who *seems* eccentric until you discover that her oddities are part of some ingenious time-saving plan she devised). This *bristly* sort of person is not open to easy friendships, but makes lifelong commitments, both intellectually and emotionally.

6. The Idealistic Hand is the most classically beautiful of the types, tapering from a long, narrow palm to even narrower fingers, which are noticeably varied in length—with a very long ring finger. Just as the idealist is often hard to pin down (he may *seem* to be the most practical person you know), so this lovely hand may appear on someone who is otherwise chunky and clunky; but it can be the most striking feature of a totally graceful person. In any case, the *personality* is likely to match the hand—to love beauty, honesty, and nobility; to want fine surroundings (really *good* furniture, loving and generous friends). The owners of Idealistic hands are utterly un-at-home with compromise, tilt at windmills all their lives.

7. The Mixed Hand is the one most often found. If you're familiar with the other six, you'll be able to spot the basic characteristics of each when they appear in a Mixed Hand, and combine them into a personality reading. Notice especially which *palm* shape the Mixed Hand has—it will be the strongest element in the combination.

After determining this basic hand-shape and its characteristics, you may—if you feel very much the *novice* at palmistry—take a few notes so that you'll have the information at your fingertips when you give the subject his interpretation. Or, if you feel more certain, interpret to him as you go along. ("Ah, this seems to be a mixed hand. See, your palm is very square, which means you're probably quite *practical* . . . but your fingers are long and tapering, which means idealism. Maybe you have trouble reconciling these two sides of yourself?") If you don't think you can carry off this moment-to-moment interpretation, by all means do take notes; but don't jot something down every few seconds. Examine the basic hand shape, then take your notes; then proceed to the next phase (finger details) and takes notes on *that;* then, if you're also going to do a predictive analysis, examine the lines on the palm and note *their* meaning. Then give your subject his entire interpretation at the end of the full reading.

FINGERS and Other Structural Details

After studying the over-all shape of the hand, you can add to your character analysis by looking for smaller details. Keep the subject's hand in yours, and gently touch or stroke each part as you examine it for significance.

Note: In the explanations below, I refer to "long" and "short" fingers. This means long or short in relation to the other fingers and to the length of the palm.

1. The Thumb: This gives you a clue to the subject's inner energies; it represents the vital forces that propel our natures. The larger the thumb, the more driving and powerful the character.

If the thumb's top segment (the section above the joint, holding the thumbnail) is *large* and *broad*, the subject has staying power and a strong ego. A *narrow* top segment, slightly pointed, indicates wasted energies and a weak ego.

A *thick* second segment is a good sign, though it is considered best for the personality as a whole if the two segments are similar in width. A too-broad second segment indicates stubbornness and a foolish amount of caution. A very *narrow* second segment means the subject is emotional, flighty, and weak-willed.

Notice also the different *lengths* of the two thumb segments. If the top one is noticeably longer, the subject will be more impulsive than rational; if the second is longer, he'll be more logical and head-ruled.

A thumb set *low* on the hand, down toward the wrist, indicates suppressed energy.

2. The Index Finger: Often called the Finger of Jupiter, it shows how much pride, enthusiasm, and desire for power the subject has. (If you know your astrology, you'll remember that Jupiter rules these qualities.) A *long* index finger indicates great craving for power, strong ambition. But these won't necessarily lead to success unless the *thumb* is also energetic (large and broad).

A *short* index finger suggests a tendency to shrink from challenges and responsibilities—though this quality may be counterbalanced by a powerful thumb. If the rest of the hand is sensitive or artistic, the person will be shy almost to the point of paranoia, and perhaps a repressed artist.

A *straight* index finger shows that the person is a keen observer. (Great scientists and investigative reporters often have noticeably straight index fingers.3

A *curved* index finger (bent toward the middle finger) shows acquisitiveness, a tendency toward miserliness, a general distrust of others.

210

3. The Middle Finger: Called the Finger of Saturn (the planet that, in astrology, rules such temperamental factors as patience and responsibility), this finger is considered the chief indicator of over-all personality.

A *long* middle finger indicates an over-intellectual and maybe even *rigid* approach to life. The subject may feel helpless or locked-in under stress, and will not adapt well to new situations or people.

If *medium-length,* this finger shows balance, an ability to handle emotional crises with equilibrium.

A *short* middle finger suggests impulsiveness, a tendency to rush important decisions and relationships.

If this finger is *heavy* and *dominating,* the subject will be serious to the point of brooding and depression.

Look at the second segment of the finger: If it's *heavier* than the others, the owner may be an earthy, country-life type (or at least cultivate an apartment roof garden).

4. The Fourth Finger: This is also called the Finger of Apollo. The god Apollo was always honored at weddings in ancient Greece, which explains why this finger is also called the ring finger and traditionally wears the wedding ring. Apollo was also the patron of the oracles at Delphi, and was believed to give them access to higher truths through their ecstatic worship of him; he was often prayed to by musicians, as well, and is frequently shown holding a lyre. All these qualities make it clear why this finger rules the emotional nature of the subject. If it is proportionally balanced with the other fingers (not drastically longer or shorter), the subject is emotionally secure—neither excessively outgoing nor overly inward.

A *short* ring finger indicates trouble adjusting to other people's feelings and the demands of the world in general. (Emotionally disturbed people often have this sign.)

A *long* ring finger can mean a tendency to introversion, a great self-preoccupation—not necessarily a bad sign, but tending toward withdrawal from emotional fuss.

5. The Little Finger: The Finger of Mercury (ruler of communication) is important especially in the way it relates to the fourth finger. If it tends to *separate* from the fourth finger (examine the subject's hand while it is relaxed, resting on a pillow, or on your own arm or hand), it indicates difficulty in forming emotional relationships, emotional isolation, trouble in expressing one's own feelings. The subject may tend to stand apart and be pointlessly critical of others.

If the top segment of this finger is relatively *long,* it means great verbal facility.

A *twisted* little finger may mean that the owner is given to lies—white ones or big black ones.

6. The Nails: In general, the *shorter* and *broader* the nail, the sturdier the character and physique.

Short-nailed people also tend to be shorter-tempered than others, more critical of the world around them.

Long-nailed people are dreamers—idealistic, often unaware of the true nature of practical reality. They are artistic and easy-going, and likely to make their short-nailed friends impatient.

The most difficult character occurs in people whose nails are *broader* than they are long. They tend to be pugnacious, meddlesome.

Look at nail color, too: *Red* nails (*naturally* that way, not enameled with Jungle Blood polish) indicate a fierce temper. Very *pale* ones mean a selfish nature (or anemia!) *Large half-moons* (the white area at the base) indicate a generous-hearted, emotionally robust person.

THE MOUNTS

These raised areas are on the *palm*, directly beneath each finger—but reading them is considered part of chirognomy, the study of the hand's basic shape. On some people, the mounts may be nearly invisible; on others, true *mountains*! (To see them clearly, have the subject relax his hand slightly, allowing the fingers to curl a *bit* toward the palm.) In general, the better-developed the mount, the more strongly it indicates the basic characteristics connected with it. The mounts and their locations are shown in the drawing on page 213. Here are the meanings:

The Mount of Venus (at the base of the thumb): This large bump, extending from thumb almost to wrist, covers one of the largest and most important blood vessels in the hand. If it's high and well developed, it indicates robust health, a powerful sex drive. A small, low mount indicates poor health, tepid desires. Its size also shows the subject's capacity for affection, sympathy; his desire to please; love of beauty, color, melody in music.

The Mount of Jupiter (at the base of the index finger): This is an indicator of ambition, pride, enthusiasm, and desire for power.

The Mount of Saturn (at the base of the middle finger): It's the key to love of solitude, a quietness of spirit, prudence, earnestness in work. The more prominent it is, the more likely will the subject be to study serious matters like philosophy, appreciate sacred and classical music.

The Mount of Apollo (at the base of the ring finger): Well developed, it is a sign of involvement with beauty (though not necessarily as a professional artist); a desire for harmony and noble thoughts rather than petty scrabbling; a passion for painting, literature, and all works of the imagination.

The Mount of Mercury (at the base of the little finger): This formation represents love of change, travel, excitement; a clever wit, quick thinking. This mount is a *secondary* formation. That means you interpret it in light of the others. If the rest of the hand is good, the qualities listed here can be seen as positive ones; if the rest of the hand is bad, the subject's Mercurial qualities may be expressed negatively (as caustic sarcasm, verbal combativeness, excessive desire for novelty and thrills).

The Mounts of Mars: There are two formations with this name. The first is below the Mount of Jupiter, lying above the Mount of Venus. It relates to active, physical courage, the "martial" spirit. If it's large, it shows a fighting disposition.

The second Mount of Mars is below the Mount of Mercury, opposite the first one. It denotes *inner* courage—self-control, spiritual strength, resistance against evil and temptation.

The Mount of Luna: Lying directly opposite the Mount of Venus, this formation shows the subject's degree of refinement, imagination, idealism. A very poetic, dreamy personality will probably have a very plump Mount of Luna.

Relationship of the Mounts: If two mounts lean toward each other, or blend into each other, the qualities will combine. For instance, if Saturn is blended with Jupiter, it will give a somber cast to the Jupiterian enthusiasm and ambition. The subject may tend to work in isolation, like the over-earnest

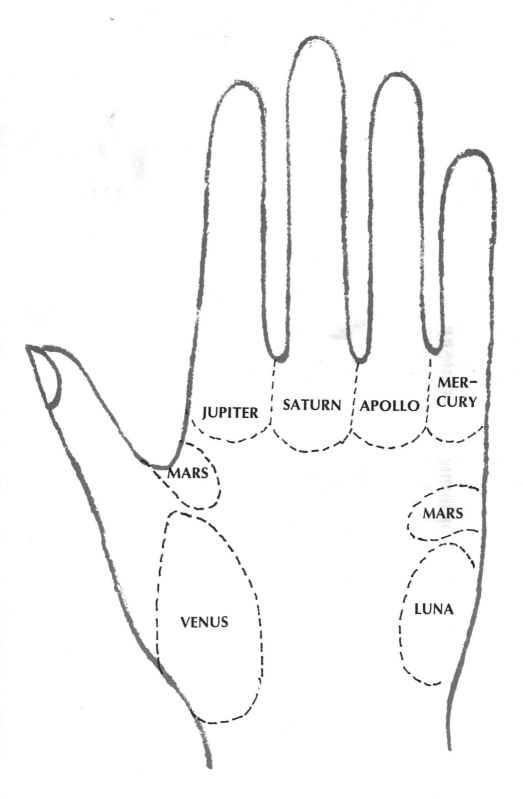

executive who never leaves his corporate tower for a social life. It would not be surprising if Ralph Nader had this combination.

THE LINES OF THE PALM
Six main lines cross the palm and are studied in chiromancy. (See the diagram on page 215). In combination, they determine the fate of the subject. They should be studied *after* the basic hand-shape has been mastered—that is, after you know the essential personality of the subject.

Remember that the *lines* of the palm must be studied according to the right- or left-handedness of the subject. Study the lines on the dominant hand.

You'll need to *manipulate* the hand a bit more than you did when examining over-all shape. Sometimes the lines are not clearly marked when the hand is lying relaxed and open. Note that the line or lines are vague, but then—in order to see where they go—take the hand in yours and very gently curl its fingers so the hand is slightly *cupped.* You'll see all the lines suddenly deepen as the fleshy parts of the palm press together. Now, examine each major line in turn, and look for the signs described below.

Note: Small breaks and chains in a basic line indicate troubles and upheavals in whatever area of life that line rules.

1. The Life Line: Though it is theoretically possible to measure the exact duration of a person's life by studying the length of the Life Line, the most *important* factor is the basic condition of the line. A strong, solid line with few breaks or chains means long life and good health. A Life Line crossed many times by other lines, or dramatically broken in several places, signifies ill health and discomfort. Sharp, clear breaks indicate surgery and recovery, or severe illness and convalescence.

A delicately pink Life Line is a good one—implying an emotionally stable life. A red line shows a strong, impulsive nature. A *heavy* red line indicates brutality and coarseness. A faintly blue line means a passionate nature, many love affairs; darker blue, a tempestuous emotional life.

2. The Head Line: This line often begins joined to the Life Line (starting on the side of the palm below the index finger and above the Mount of Venus). If Life and Head lines are separated at the beginning, the subject will be careless about his own safety. A clear and fairly straight Head Line indicates a well-developed will, strength of mind. If the line veers down toward the Mount of Luna, the subject will be an imaginative thinker. (An exaggerated veering right *onto* the Mount of Luna indicates an interest in the occult.) If it moves up toward the Mount of Mercury, the subject will be a calculator of some type—either a schemer or a mathematician—with his head dominating his passions. If the line moves up toward the Mount of Apollo, the subject will use his intellect to acquire money.

3. The Heart Line: This line begins below the Mount of Mercury and swoops across the palm horizontally, usually curving upward toward the fingers. A short Heart Line (stopping short of the middle finger) indicates a fickle person; a long line (moving well over toward the index finger or even all the way across the palm) means great devotion to one or more people. The more curved the line is, the sexier the subject.

If the Heart Line forks around or near the Mount of Jupiter (under the index finger), the subject will be emotionally balanced and can handle several love affairs in his life—or even at the same time—without superficial-

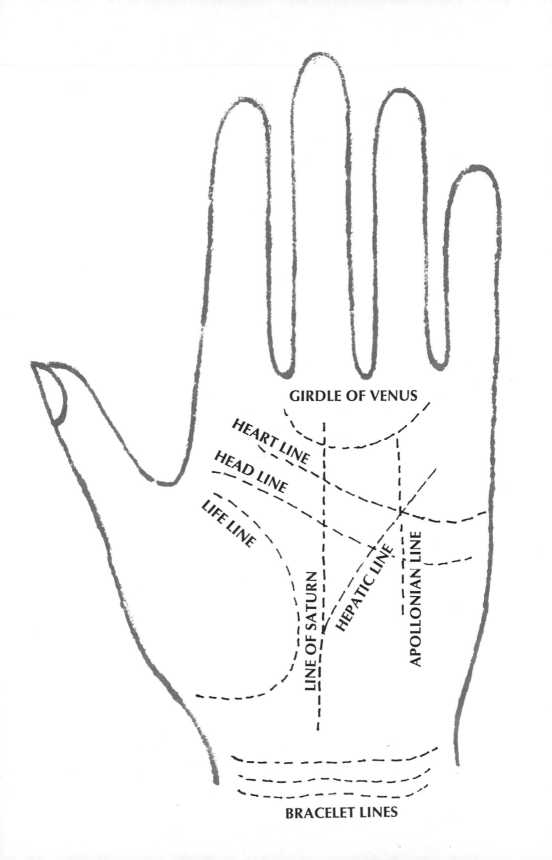

GIRDLE OF VENUS

HEART LINE

HEAD LINE

LIFE LINE

LINE OF SATURN

HEPATIC LINE

APOLLONIAN LINE

BRACELET LINES

ity. If the line forks around the Mount of Saturn (below the middle finger), the subject may be more emotionally reserved and perhaps even sexually inhibited, although he may have many lighthearted affairs. Breaks in the Heart Line show a weakness of affection, too, as well as a lack of interest in the

4. The Line of Saturn: Often called the Fate Line, this is *the* fortune-telling line. Study it carefully. Its relation to the other lines and to the mounts indicates the course of the subject's future.

If it rises at the wrist and is heavy, the subject will have hard times in early life but later comfort. If it rises from the Life Line, he will have to work hard to excape a closed-in early environment. If it rises from the Head Line, he will have to work hard to escape a closed-in early environment. If it rises from the Head Line, he will have fulfillment very late in life. If it rises at or near the Mount of Venus, he will be able to count on the support of those who love him. Near the Mount of Luna, he'll have a varied, exciting life, full of adventures but lacking a home base.

Note also where the Fate Line ends. If the end curves from the Mount of Saturn toward the Mount of Jupiter, the subject will acquire great power in life. If it ends nearer the Mount of Apollo, fame or money will be more likely. If it ends lower down, at the Head Line, the subject may fail in life through being too careless; at the Heart Line, he may be disappointed in romance.

5. The Hepatic Line: The name comes from the Greek *hepar,* meaning liver. This line is the barometer of the subject's health. If it touches the Life Line, the blood or heart will be adversely affected. When the two lines are well separated, the subject will have a long life. A twisted Hepatic Line forecasts a history of headaches; breaks indicate stomach trouble.

6. The Apollonian Line: This is the fame-and-fortune line, and like fame and fortune, it's not easy to locate. It usually rises down near the lower end of the Life Line, and moves up toward the Mount of Apollo. A strong Apollonian Line going right up into the Mount indicates success at the very least; if it's a double line, fame will come, too. If it's vague or broken, it foretells a lack of purpose, uncertainty about careers.

7. The Bracelet Lines: These horizontal lines are across the wrist below the palm. Three of these lines indicate wealth and good health. If they are chainlike, the subject will have to work hard for success.

Compare the bracelets of both hands. If the left-hand ones are stronger, the subject will have an active life, though he may be foolishly impulsive. If the right-hand bracelets are stronger, he'll display great organizational power and force of will.

8. The Girdle of Venus: This is a small, curving line above the Heart Line, looping from between the index and middle fingers to between the third and little fingers. The Girdle of Venus, especially if clear and deep, indicates a deeply passionate nature. Sometimes it is missing altogether, but when it is present, it always means a degree of passion. The passion need not be sensual, though that is its most usual form; but it may express itself in an intense devotion to a cause.

For palmists in earlier times, when strong sexuality was disapproved of, the Girdle of Venus was taken as a sign of instability and infidelity; nowadays it may be interpreted to mean *healthily* robust sexuality.

216

HOW MANY TIMES WILL A PERSON FALL IN LOVE?

Lines of Affection. These lines are on the far edge of the palm below the little finger. Turn the hand sideways to see them better. These lines represent love affairs, marriages, and marital complications. A *strongly* marked line denotes a marriage or an important attachment. *Vertical* lines touching these lines indicate the number of children.

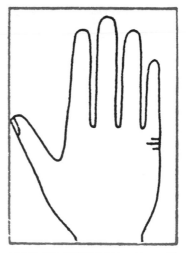

LINES OF AFFECTION: *"You will marry (count the strong lines) that many times and have so many affairs (count the weaker lines)."*

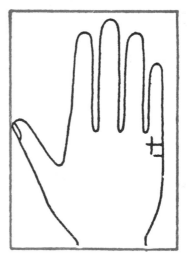

VERTICAL LINES CROSSING LINES OF AFFECTION: *"This could mean you'll be divorced, separated, or have a very unhappy love affair."*

MOOD SETTERS FOR YOUR PALM READING

1. A small interesting lamp to spotlight the hand but leave the surrounding area darkened. An Art Deco gooseneck would be marvelous.

2. Use a large magnifying glass to read the hand. Find the most interesting one around. Something antique and mysterious looking with a carved ivory or silver handle—if the budget will allow it. (It would be a handsome thing to have around in any case.) But for a small sum, Bamboo handled glasses are obtainable in many of the oriental novelty shops around town.

3. Prepare in advance tracings of the two hand charts in this book. Use a red or purple fine-line marker. Prepare at least one set for each sitter. Fill in the details of your reading in black, so that it will show up well against the outline color. Sign and date each chart and give them to your sitter. If you are doing the hand prints we've mentioned, they will make a very handsome and frameable set.

THE METHOD

Now that you have this basic information, you'll need some technique to go with it. I've talked earlier about the preliminaries—putting your subject at ease, taking the hand, manipulating it so that the lines are as evident as possible. Remember to structure the reading: chirognomy first, chiromancy second. The over-all structure of the hand will give you character insights that will illuminate the fortune-telling meanings of the lines.

For instance, I recently read a palm that showed great upheavals in the Heart Line—many breaks and chains, suggesting a whole series of romantic difficulties. But I was aided in my reading by knowing that the hand I was looking at was definitely the Philosophical type. No matter what problems that subject had in his love life, he would never let them disrupt his reasonable, ordered life, and would continue to find pleasure in intellectual commitments. He was not in danger from his possibly disastrous love life—as any number of others might have been—and that insight considerably changed the tone of the reading.

The best method for developing a knowledge of palmistry is constant practice—at parties, with friends, at work. Just keep looking at hands. At first, it really isn't necessary to do readings. Just check out basic hand shapes on people at work, on buses, and so on. See if the hand on the typewriter next to yours is Philosophical, Elemental, Artistic, or what—take a look at the nails, the joints of the fingers, the placement of the thumb, the size and shape of the palm. All those things are perfectly visible if you're within a few feet, and you can get very good at basic chirognomy by this kind of casual observation.

For chiromancy, of course, you will need the upturned palms of your lovers, friends, relatives, and acquaintances whom you feel comfortable with (or want to get closer to). Actually, the best people to begin with are those whose life histories you already know. By tracing their major lines, and filling in with your own personal knowledge, you can begin to discover how the lines in the hand correspond to the experience of the life. Then, when you're up against a *stranger's* hand, you'll be able to read the life in the hand itself.

RANDOM LINES

These formations of lines are to be found on every hand, but not always in the same combinations or all at once. Their importance depends on their size, definition, and upon the mounts they appear near or on. This chart shows what they mean in various positions.

218

NEAR OR ON THE MOUNT OF	✳ STAR	✕ CROSS	△ TRIANGLE	卄 SQUARE	井 GRILL
VENUS	*Center: powerful sex drive; near wrist; trouble in sex; near thumb: ong happy relationship*	One, definite: love for life; many: lots of lovers	Shrewd & calculating about sex	Carefree sex life	
MOON	Danger in travel	Danger in travel	Success, fame, money	Travel without danger	Tension & melancholy
JUPITER	Unlooked-for success	Marriage with money	Executive ability	Success	Dominating character
SATURN	Catastrophe threatens		Trouble-shooter	Financial security	Introspective, goalless
APOLLO (THE SUN)	New & influential friend	Disappointment, loss	No-hassle fame & fortune	Good reputation	Vanity, a preener
MERCURY	Academic success, promot on	Treachery among friends: beware	Friendly, loyal	Free of tension	Sly, possibly dishonest
UPPER MARS		Danger		Safety	Danger
LOWER MARS		Danger	Physical prowess; success in combat	Danger, but no harm	Danger

HOW TO TAKE HAND PRINTS

The practice of taking hand prints for leisurely reading was not widespread until Cheiro began to take prints of the famous and the notorious for his files. He wanted permanent records so that he could check his predictions against the future lives of his subjects, and so that he could make more detailed analyses of the hands.

A hand print will allow you to practice palmistry without having the palm around permanently. Once you've made the print, you can study it any time. Of course, when you're more adept, you may want to use the prints as Cheiro did—for detailed analysis and future reference, to check on your own divination.

Hand prints make good gifts, too, framed and accompanied by an analysis and fortune. The black-on-white palm print looks quite striking matted in black and framed in chalk white. Parents especially love to receive a hand print of a growing child, and a tactful divination would be a lot of fun for him to read later!

To make a hand print, you'll need the following materials:
linoleum-cut ink (ask for it at your art-supply store)
a five-inch roller
a sheet of glass at least 12 in. square (framing glass will do nicely)
sheets of good-quality white paper (8 x 11 is fine, but bigger if you'd like to frame it later)
a rubber pad (like the one under your typewriter at the office) at least 12 inches square.

1. Cover the roller with ink. (You can use a glass or ceramic plate to hold the ink; roll the roller in it as you would a paint roller in paint.)

2. Prepare the paper to receive the hand print by laying it on the rubber pad to steady it. (If you think you might have placement problems with an inked hand, ask the subject to put his *clean, uninked* hand down on the paper first, and make a couple of light pencil marks to indicate where you'll want the hand when it's inked.)

3. Coat the glass with ink, rolling it out as evenly as possible, and re-inking the roller if necessary.

4. Now, press the hand you're printing onto the inked glass, very firmly and steadily, so that every part of the hand is inked.

5. This is the tricky part. Take the inked hand and press it onto the paper, making sure that it doesn't shift or slide in any way. (If it does, you'll get a blurred image, with unclear lines.) Then let the subject raise his hand from the paper in one smooth motion while you hold the paper firmly in place.

6. Wait for the ink to dry *thoroughly,* then sign the paper with your name and the subject's (or have *him* sign it) and the date.

Don't be discouraged if your first efforts end in smudged prints or blurred and unrecognizable marks. If you try three or four the first time around, your fifth or sixth effort will probably be perfect. Just be sure you have a good supply of paper, so that the first print or two isn't crucial. You'll soon have enough confidence and skill to produce perfect prints every time.

VICTORIAN PHYSIOGNOMY
BEAUTY SPOTS

The Victorians believed that you could tell someone's character and future from every physical detail about him—his hair, nose, eye color, even the moles that are sometimes called beauty spots. To give you an idea of the *certainty* of the Victorian physiognomist, here are the detailed readings that they derived from beauty spots:

1/On the lip: languid sensuality, love of all life's pleasures—especially the sexual kind.

2/On the outside corner of the eye: a calm, quiet, even prissy personality.

3/On the cheek: a life of moderate means, neither rich nor poor.

4/On the chin: success in business, and not by shady means. This person will be looked up to by his peers in the world of business.

5/On the right side of the forehead or temple: some chance happening will bring money and prestige, but care will be needed to prevent extravagant spending of the new-found wealth.

6/On the left side of the forehead or temple: sudden downfall, loss of money and position.

7/On either eyebrow: marriage and domestic contentment, many children, happy old age.

8/On the nose: a smooth-sailing life without many jolts or surprises. Success, but nothing extraordinary.

9/On the ear: dangers arising from jealousy, greed, and gossip. But if the person can rise above these faults, he will be troubled by no other problems.

10/On the side of the neck: an overly cautious life, leading to missed opportunities. But a sudden inheritance may make up for these.

11/At the center of the throat: an accident-prone, hysterical, but enjoyable life.

12/On the left breast: a lifelong ability to seduce those of the opposite sex. Troubles will arise from too much lovemaking, not enough attention to stability.

13/On the right breast: a marriage of convenience, which will nevertheless be happy.

14/Between the two breasts: a banal life.

15/Over the heart: kindness and sincerity, gregariousness, and love of good companions of the same sex will make this person's life fulfilled.

16/On the stomach: greed that brings misfortune.

17/On either hip: many children, who will be healthy and devoted to their parents.

18/On the right thigh: great wealth.

19/On the left thigh: great poverty.

20/On either ankle: fashionableness carried to extremes will cause a wasted life.

PHRENOLOGY

Do you have an irresistible urge to *giggle* at the thought of phrenology? Some people do—they mutter something about "bumps on the head," and go off into uncontrollable gales. It's an interesting phenomenon, because phrenology has a quite respectable pedigree. It began as part of the great classifying urge of the nineteenth century, when it was believed that to define a thing was to bring it somehow under civilized control. The study of physiognomy—a systematic attempt to discover what the various structures of man's appearance means to his life—was taken very seriously. Although it did not yield the great results that its devotees hoped for, it left us several extremely interesting and useful remnants: the Bertillon system of skull measurement, which was, until the advent of the fingerprinting system, the most dependable method of physical identification; the fingerprinting system, which is still, of course, in use all over the world; and phrenology, which continues to find practitioners and subjects.

Still, why the giggles? Why is the head, which houses the brain and all the major organs of sense, often an object of laughter and even ridicule? Well, I have a theory. I think people laugh at phrenology out of sheer nervousness. The head is just too important to be talked about, to be considered a subject for even the most serious study, let alone a method of *fortune-telling*. We live in an age when it's possible to replace a heart or a cornea, to substitute artificial limbs and veins for real ones, to reconstruct a face hopelessly disfigured in an accident. Terrible damage can be inflicted on the body—yet it can survive.

But the brain is where our personalities lie, perilously close to the surface, protected by the bony structure of the skull. We all know that brain activity is the measure of life. When the brain ceases to function, even though heartbeat and respiration are artificially sustained, the personality—what we know as *ourselves*—is dead. And we know enough about emotional disorders and brain diseases to be frightened at the thought that we might change, become someone else, if our minds or brains were damaged. So it's no wonder that one of the chief reactions to phrenology is a nervous giggle and perhaps a hand brushed over the top of the head—the subject reminds us, unconsciously, of the fragility of this all-important area.

So when you begin the study of phrenology, be aware that many people will have strange reactions, which you may find hard to classify. Don't ignore them, exactly, but do press on with a serious, good-humored effort to observe what their heads are like, and from that, what *they* are like.

WHAT IT'S ALL ABOUT

Begun as a serious discipline in the very early nineteeth century by a German doctor named Franz Josep Gall, phrenology is based on the notion that the formation of the brain affects the case that surrounds it, the skull. Phrenology measures and classifies that effect by locating skull parts that correspond to the inner brain structures that produced them. After finding these outer structures (those famous "bumps"), phrenologists "read" them—interpret their influence on character.

Phrenology was once a great craze—especially in America—and like most crazes, it died a fast and very thorough death. It had its zenith in the 1820's, when there were twenty-nine phrenological journals in the United States and Britain, and was suddenly eclipsed by spiritualism in the 1840's. But Gall and his followers had meticulously documented their studies, and many people have continued to believe and practice phrenology.

Preliminaries

The phrenologist begins his studies by learning the basic divisions into which

222

the skull is divided, and the mental faculties to which they correspond; then he is ready to begin the study of individual heads to discover their variations, what makes them unique and gives each a separate character.

Because the brain has two lobes, each of its traits is represented by two areas—one on either side of the head. That means that you can use both hands to more easily find the bumps, analyze their size and shape.

Don't rush into a phrenological reading—you may meet with a good deal of resistance. And since your subject will have to sit quite still for a fairly long time while you run your fingers through his hair, you will want him in a co-operative and easy-going frame of mind.

One warning: Sensitive wearers of wigs or hairpieces are *not* candidates for phrenology. No matter how much he may want to know his future, there is almost no hairpiece-wearer who will casually take it off while you check out his bumps. Women are usually not quite so sensitive—after all, many have two wigs, a fall, and perfect confidence in their real hair as well (but you'd do well to steer clear of them when the wig is in place). And as for the kind of woman who still has a *set* once a week—well, don't give her another thought! Approach those with loose, un-fussed-over heads of hair— in fact, the more vigorous and unruly the hairdo is, the more likely a candidate for phrenology the person will be.

Once you have someone's head under your hands, remember that this is his more precious possession—the *real him*. Use your hands gently, and don't make sudden or jerky movements. If you take a great deal of time with a reading, run your hands down his neck with a massagelike motion and give the head gentle support from time to time, to help prevent fatigue and provide reassurance.

You must also remember that even the relative positions of the subject and the phrenologist can be threatening. The subject must sit down; the phrenologist stands (*behind* him most of the time) and holds the head with her hands. Now, that is a very vulnerable position for the sitter, a very powerful one for the reader. Don't abuse that power—be tactful, chat easily, talk about the weather, the room, anything (think of how your hairdresser relates to you)—until you're ready to present your findings. Don't become a distant, silent, and therefore ominous presence. Humanize yourself to keep phrenology from being a slightly shaking experience for the sitter.

You can even further disarm your subject's anxieties by sitting directly in front of him at first, and meeting his eye. Then tell him how you're going to proceed—starting with a first over-all view of the head, then moving to an analysis of specific areas. *Everyone* is reassured by knowing just what is going to happen—so be explanatory, chatty, unhurried. It will make for a much better session, one in which you don't feel rushed by your sitter's uneasiness.

THE BASIC DIVISIONS OF THE HEAD

One of the great popularizers of phrenology, George Combe, is now generally recognized as the most reliable. The text most English-speaking phrenologists now use is Combe's *System of Phrenology*. Combe divided the bumps on the head into four basic groups: The *first* reveal the *essential qualities* of the sitter; the *second*, his *feelings*; the *third*, his *perceptions*; and the *fourth* (which Combe called the "reflective areas") indicate *reason* and *organization of knowledge*. In all, there are thirty-seven areas, and each has a place in one of the major groups. As you read the following explanations of

223

each bump, check the chart (page 285) for its position on the head. (Remember that there will be a corresponding bump on the other side.)

ESSENTIAL QUALITIES

1 SEXUALITY: If small or hard to locate, it means lethargic erotic drives. If very large it suggests nymphomania or satyriasis—a powerful, distorted sexual drive that disturbs its owner. Usually you'll find a medium-sized formation—healthy sexuality.

2 SELF-PRESERVATION: If it's very small, the subject may be self-destructive, even suicidal. Very large: The sitter may be a coward, is certainly over-cautious, leery of risks.

3 PARENTHOOD: The larger this bump, the greater the subject's desire for children. But his desire can be sublimated into work that helps take care of all mankind—the "catcher in the rye" syndrome.

4 DOMESTICITY: Underdevelopment in this area will be found in on-the-town types, or the girl who changed jobs eight times in five years and spends her summers touring Northern Africa or Turkey. It is well developed in homebodies, married or not, and especially large in people with a mindless obsession with fidelity.

5 FRIENDSHIP: The larger this bump is, the more loyal and trustworthy will the sitter be. If neither this bump nor the domestic bump is well developed, the subject is probably a Don Juan or a pathologically fickle woman.

6 COMPETITIVENESS: Overdevelopment of this bump produces ruthless industrial giants and executives who have a jungle morality. Of course, a lack of *any* development here is a sign that the sitter will be a loser, at least in the world of business and commerce.

7 IMPATIENCE: Overdeveloped, it suggests harshness and imbalance. If it's medium-sized, the sitter will just be unwilling to tolerate unnecessary impediments to his progress. An insignificant development suggests total passivity—or an Eastern-style ability to shrug at the workings of fate.

8 SECRETIVENESS: Tact and an ability to respect a confidence are foretold by an average-sized bump here. Too small? The subject is insensitive, brutally honest. Too large? He's a liar or super-sly, or both.

9 ACQUISITIVENESS: This, along with a well-developed competitive bump, will almost always indicate success in business. But when this one is large out of all proportion, the sitter may be a real snarler and biter, possibly even a thief.

10 APPETITE: Normally developed, it suggests a healthy hunger and gusto at the table, even a refined palate. If it's overdeveloped, the sitter may be a compulsive eater; underdeveloped, he'll show a lack of vitality, a tendency to ignore fleshly pleasures.

11 ACHIEVEMENT: This is the bump of the artist and the craftsman, of getting-it-together. If it's too large there will be a tendency to overreach; if too small, the sitter will be a chronic underachiever.

FEELINGS

12 SELF-ESTEEM: This bump should be easily discernible. If you can't find it, you've got a bad case of inferiority feelings on your hands; if it's over-large, an inflated ego.

13 DESIRE FOR APPROVAL: Vanity and petty self-importance are indicated by a too-large bump. If it's small, the sitter is probably a genuine flower child, with no need to feel success or failure; or an irrationally confident type who can't stand interference or suggestions from others.

14 PRUDENCE: This formation, when too large, indicates the kind of person who'll start asking about pension plans at twenty. Too small? Watch out! He's the sort who says, "Speed doesn't kill; it's incompetence."

15 BENEVOLENCE: Too small a bump here indicates monumental selfishness; but too large a one will lead to a kind of sentimentality that ignores real problems in favor of mindless good will.

16 RESPECT (usually for authority): If the bump is very small, your sitter may have been a Weatherman in the sixties (or a loyal member of the Nixon Administration); if it's too large, he is likely to be a Uriah Heep, who abases himself before *everyone,* especially the boss.

17 DETERMINATION: If you find a small formation, you will have a real nebbish sitting for you. On the other hand, determination isn't *always* positive—a very large bump here may indicate a will so stubborn that it can be stupid.

18 CONSCIENTIOUSNESS: Sitters who have large bumps here tend to be guilt-ridden; amoral high-fliers are *not* well developed in this area.

19 OPTIMISM: Too large a development suggests gullibility. A minuscule bump means the sitter is a full-time alarmist.

20 BELIEF (refers to religious faith): A moderately developed bump here indicates a balanced religious belief, or an intelligent interest in the occult. If it's too small, the sitter is a skeptic, or weakly credulous; too large, and you have the common garden-variety fanatic with you.

21 BEAUTY: A normal appreciation of beauty if suggested by proportionate development here. Too large? The sitter is a hyper-aesthete, perhaps an artist. Too small? You probably knew from his clothing and the way he put ashes on your Chinese rug that he is oblivious to appearances.

22 HUMOR: Those without this development share the usual dilemmas of the humorless person. The too-large bump of humor reflects vitriolic wit or—heaven forbid—practical jokes.

23 EMULATION: Normal development indicates the ability to see-and-learn, and a capacity for expressing admiration. Too large a development indicates lack of self-assertion, fear of standing out in a crowd, copycat faddism.

PERCEPTION

24 OBSERVATION: This area reflects the ability to make a general assessment of your environment, to take in what is going on around you. Overdeveloped, it suggests a spying, petty character; underdeveloped, it is typified by the type who, when asked to describe someone, is likely to say, "She's very spiritual . . . and somewhere between four and seven feet tall."

25 SHAPE: If highly developed, this bump suggests mathematical ability, and a possible aptitude for sculpture. If too small, the sitter is likely to go around bumping into things.

26 SIZE: This area denotes a sense of proportion—not just physically, but in the larger aspects of life. The subject has a good sense of priorities if the area is developed normally. If it's too small, he's a nitpicker and worrier; too large, he has grandiose ideas with no substance.

27 WEIGHT: Moderately developed, the area indicates athletic skill, understanding of natural forces, and a well-balanced mind. Over-large? He'll have a ponderous personality. Underdeveloped? He's light-minded, likely to underestimate the consequences of his behavior.

28 COLOR: Well developed in painters and lovers of the country, this bump also indicates sensuality. Underdeveloped, it might suggest color-blindness or a general drabness of personality.

29 PLACE MEMORY: With a well-developed bump in this area, the sitter might be a sports-car-rally navigator or a novelist; he's certainly an enthusiastic traveler. If the bump is underdeveloped, he'll remember what he ate at that terrific little restaurant but won't be able to remember whether it was on the east side of town or the west side..

30 NUMBERS: Skill in calculation, general shrewdness, typify the person with a well-developed bump here. For those in whom it's undeveloped, the pocket calculator and computer-dating were devised.

31 ORDERLINESS: Proportionately developed? His check-book is balanced to within a dollar, and his desk usually neat. Overdeveloped? The compulsive takes over, with each color pen in exactly the same place at all times. Underdeveloped? The sitter is about to be sued by the creditors whose bills are lost on his desk.

32 MEMORY FOR EVENTS: A good development in this area means that the sitter is likely to be able to remember his eighth birthday party; if it's overdeveloped, he will probably *tell* you about his eighth birthday party; if it's underdeveloped, he'll forget that he was not only invited to Truman Capote's ball at the Plaza, but *went.*

33 TIME SENSE: You know about this one. If he's forty-five minutes late for your session and doesn't *know* it, don't even bother feeling for the bump. If he breezes in with just twenty-seconds to spare and says, looking at his Rolex chronometer, "Yes, the elevator took just forty seconds less than I thought it would," he's a bit overdeveloped. A normal development simply means that he *usually* gets to work on time. (You can also read rhythmical sense from this bump.)

34 MELODY: Along with a well-developed time-sense bump, a good development here indicates real musical ability. Otherwise, he just has a happy tendency to sing in the shower or appreciate Schubert *Lieder*. If the area is totally undeveloped: He knows two tunes, "Yankee Doodle" and the other one.

226

35 VERBAL EXPRESSION: This is the bump of the con man, the orator, and the writer, when well-developed: in other words, Norman Mailer. If the area is overdeveloped, he may be a demagogue or petty tyrant of some kind. If it's underdeveloped, he may be the strong silent type to an almost *maddening* degree.

REASON

36 COMPARISON: This bump shows how well he forms judgments about the relative importance of people, places, events, ideas. Normally developed, it shows a capacity to conduct his life with a sense of rational priorities. Overdeveloped, it indicates an excessively analytical mind, obsessed with objectivity. Underdeveloped? He has a general tendency to be unable to cope, difficulty in setting priorities and finding a real goal in life.

37 CAUSALITY: If well developed, this bump suggests logical skill, the ability to argue rationally to a conclusion and to spot holes in an argument. Underdeveloped, it may indicate anything from a powerfully primitive personality to the village idiot. Overdeveloped, the subject is a veritable whirlwind of debating tactics, or may even have complex paranoid (but *logical*, in a sense!) explanations for everything.

READING THE BUMPS

Whew! Thirty-seven bumps is a *lot*. And because they may be neither very high nor very well defined (in fact, to call them *areas* is more genuinely descriptive), you'll have to practice (try your *own* head) for a while before you can even be certain that you *are* feeling them (and know where they ought to be).

When you finally feel competent to work with a sitter, pick a *tolerant* friend for the first attempts! (The most important initial step—identifying the bumps and their placement on the head—may take a while.)

Next, you must discover the *relative* sizes of your sitter's bumps, seeing how each relates to the others, to produce a likely reading of the future through his character. This is, of course, a reasonably complicated undertaking, since you are dealing with subtle physical formations. The easiest plan—and, because it is of such interest to subjects, the best working method—is to tear out one of the charts on page 285. Use this page as a worksheet while you do your reading. As you find the bumps on your client's head, list next to each faculty the relative size of the bump, using a code: L for large, M for medium, S for small, and N for non-existent. When you've completed the chart, you can manipulate the information in various ways. For instance, list all the bumps that are marked L for large, to get a picture of your subject's very strongest capacities and drives. These will be the most powerful determiners of his future.

Another tip: You certainly don't have to analyze *all* thirty-seven bumps for each sitter. Once you know roughly where they are on a head, you can read the ones most likely to answer a particular question. ("Will I get this raise?" Check bumps number 6 (Competitiveness), 7 (Impatience), 9 (Acquisitiveness), and 11 (Achievement)—perhaps along with 17 (Determination) and 18 (Conscientiousness), or some of the Perception and Reason qualities that would be desirable in his particular job.) Using *selected* readings, you can tailor the analysis to almost any subject the sitter wants a prediction for.

Afterward, give him your chart as a souvenir of this intimate—and enlightening—encounter between you and his gorgeous head.

GRAPHOLOGY

Although handwriting is not, strictly speaking, a *part* of the body, graphologists insist that it is as distinctive as the lines in the palm of the hand or the bumps on the head, and can be used just as validly to read character and tell the future. Certainly it is a production—the most *intimate* production—of what Aristotle called "the organ of organs," the human hand.

Of course, some people dispute that handwriting is *that* individual; but they have been proved wrong again and again. In spite of the incursions of printing in the public schools, the ascendancy of the typewriter, and the assumption by most of us that it's easier—if not cheaper—to phone than to write, handwriting remains stubbornly our own from the time we learn to form the letters until we write out our last shaky signature. Even a single stroke of a person's handwriting is distinctive. If you analyze a series of strokes from several samples of the same hand, the downstrokes of the g's, for instance, will resemble each other more closely than they resemble any other marks in the world. And all factors taken together—the different strokes, the pressure applied to the pen, the slope of the lines—make up a perfectly unique evocation and expression of the writer.

SAMPLES
Graphology is one of the few methods of fortune telling in which you are dependent on your subject for more than his presence. You'll need a sample of his handwriting—and, to be thorough, a sample of his signature, too. The best sample is one that is not specially written for you, but obtained at random. You might ask him to bring a memo—if he's given to dashing them off by hand—or a not-too-intimate diary entry, or even a personal letter if he can borrow one from a recipient. A full-page sample is better than a snippet jotted on a scrap of paper. His signature *can* be written on the spot, since that's not likely to vary under pressure. And you might also, for purposes of comparison, ask him to write a few lines for you while he's sitting there. It's often enlightening to see the differences between an un-self-consciously produced sample and one that is done under the stress of observation.

Treat your samples with respect: It is a way of showing that you understand that the handwriting is an extension of the body. Lay them out carefully on a table, and examine them with a certain gentleness of touch, as if you were touching the body of your subject. Unless you're alone, don't make notes on the sample—it may seem like a violation to the subject, even though he's *given* you the sample. Remember, some people have trouble throwing away old grocery lists if they're handwritten. Be careful.

PRELIMINARIES
Handwriting may seem to you at first to be a much more *objective* way to judge another person than looking at his palm or reading his head—but consider a couple of curious facts. Not only is it quite difficult to forge anyone else's handwriting, it is exquisitely difficult to change one's own—try it and see. The patterns of childhood are engraved in the synapses of the brain, and

228

cannot be erased except by the most diligent practice. Almost everyone can recognize his own handwriting immediately, and feels a curious fondness for it. (The poet W.H. Auden once said that he was grateful for the invention of the typewriter, because if he had read his poems only in his own handwriting, he'd *never* have known how bad some of them were. He called the cold and objective typewriter a "great critic.")

Try to remember all this when you're working out an analysis of someone's writing. It may *seem* like a separate entity. But actually you are dealing with a very intimate extension of his personality and body—one over which he has even less *conscious* control than he has over his hands and feet. In automatic writing, only the *content* matters; in graphology, you look for content on the surface, in the forms of the handwriting itself. (Somehow that scrutiny is even *more* threatening to some people—it makes them feel helpless.) So when you look at someone's handwriting and begin to analyze, try to see the person *himself* in every stroke, and realize that you are not just looking at marks on a piece of paper.

Before you begin, you'll need to know the age and sex of the writer. You'll probably know much more, but graphologists are willing to work with that information alone.

THE METHOD

Begin, as always, by taking an over-all look. Inspect the samples to see if there are any general patterns. Here are some to look for:

Placement on the Page: There are two elements here, *margins* and *directions of lines*. If you have a full-page sample, examine the margins. Are they wide, with the writing placed in a neat block in the center? This person is especially artistic. If the placement looks overly *calculated*—a tiny bit of writing dramatically studding an almost *blank* sheet, the writer may be overly self-conscious and hyper-concerned with appearances. Writing that *floods* the page, bursting up against the edges of the paper and crowding down to the *very* bottom, suggests an impulsive person with a quick mind, someone who thinks faster than he can talk. He may also fear that people don't *listen* to him. A writer who hangs back from the right-hand margin but crowds the left is probably negative, fearful of advancing into the world or expressing strong opinions. A wide left margin and crowded right one indicates an outgoing, confident, even *pushy* character.

Graphologists assume that the right-hand side of the page represents energetic direction and optimism, while the left hand stands for melancholy and withdrawal. So study the width of each margin.

Now look for direction. If the lines run *straight* and *regular,* you can assume that the writer is well balanced and even tempered. If the lines *wander* up and down, with no established pattern from line to line or word to word, the writer may feel unstable, lacking purpose or goals in life. *Drooping* lines as an over-all pattern (the line sinks toward the right) are a sign of chronic depression and lack of self-esteem. *Rising* lines indicate optimism and happiness, though perhaps a tendency to the manic. A line that *sags* in the middle and then rises again suggests an up-and-down temperament, perhaps even a manic-depressive type of personality.

Legibility: This is a very important over-all characteristic. A person with a cryptic, indecipherable handwriting may be secretive, neurotically unwilling to reveal himself, even when he is committed to do so by the act of writing. A very clear script signals, "Look at me! I have nothing to hide."

Pay attention, also, to whether the script is conventional or highly individualized. No matter how the writer may have changed his writing from the conventional style, *any* change is significant. It indicates that he was unwilling to let well enough alone, and has transformed himself in some way. For this portion of the analysis, it helps to know just what method the writer was originally taught. If he started out on Palmer Method, he is likely to show change by printing some letters, or inventing unorthodox capitals. If he was taught printing, the changes will show up as an effort to make letters in a more flowery and connected fashion.

Instrument and Pressure: Take a look at the amount of *pressure* the writer has applied in writing, and at the type of instrument he has used. (His instrument will, of course, *affect* the pressure—it's impossible to bear down as hard with a Pentel or a fountain pen as with a ballpoint.) If he *skitters* across the page, hardly touching the surface enough to leave his mark, he is showing timidity, an oversensitive personality, a fear of making impact on the world because he's scared of retaliation. A *moderate pressure,* with just as much speed, indicates that the writer is agile and flexible, able to take advantage of situations and ideas as he happens on them. *Heavy pressure,* evenly applied, shows a persistent personality, perhaps obstinate and rigid. He has considerable energy, though it may be misapplied. If the pressure is so great that it holds back the flow of the writing, it may show great uncertainty expressing itself as slow carefulness; or the writer may be so inflexible that no amount of pressure can alter his course.

The choice of instrument is, I believe, more important than many graphologists have noticed. Of course, this is in part a historical problem. The only two instruments common fifty years ago were the fountain pen and the pencil; and most people were taught to write formally with a pen. Now there are a number of kinds of writing instruments. The writer may choose one that fits his style and that he finds congenial for other reasons. For instance, the ballpoint is perfect for the heavy-pressure writer—you can bear down hard without destroying its point, and it produces a firm, no-nonsense line. The fountain pen has become almost archaic. Those who use it can be seen as preserving a way of writing they were taught as children—a way they probably think of as more elegant, more correct, than writing with a ballpoint or a marker. Felt-tip pens are especially suited to someone with a swooping, light-pressure hand. They lend themselves to people with large-looped, easy-going writing (or people who *wish* they wrote that fluidly). Writers of great precision will choose special instruments: an Osmiroid pen with a draftsman's point that makes dramatic changes from thick lines to thin; a particularly finepointed Parker; or some such personally chosen and crafted pen. The graphologist should pay attention to these choices; they indicate not merely how the writer performs but, very often, how he wishes he could perform. (I know more than one really sloppy penman who uses good pens in the hope that the instrument will improve the product.)

Circularity: Look also for the over-all roundness or lack of it in the writing. *Full curves, fat loops,* show a high degree of imagination. If exaggerated, the writer is a dreamer, a big planner with little to show for his fantasies. *Angular* writing shows a great capacity for logic, clarity, and a love of the abstract. *Wide, full lower loops*—on g's and p's, for instance—show sensuality, a sexually active character. *Thin,* or *unlooped* descenders show coldness and unresponsiveness.

Slope: *Upright:* The writer is independent, reserved, likes taking initiative

230

and power, is highly self-sufficent. *Sloping right:* He has an eagerness for contact, but may be too other-directed. He can't make a decision without advice or influence from another, or some pressure from the outside world. *Sloping left (backhand):* This suggests introversion, moodiness, withdrawal, loneliness—or an immense ego that play-acts these feelings in order to gain attention. *Change of slope:* If the angle of the writing changes noticeably anywhere in the sample, take note of what it has changed from and what it has changed to. (For instance, writing that starts out upright and then slopes toward the right may suggest that the writer tries to be independent but, when off guard or relaxed, wants to move toward others.) A changeable writing is always an important indication of character.

backhand

sloping right

three zones

Circularity

Angular writing

Upright

DETAILS TO WATCH FOR

Zones: Graphologists divide the line of writing into three zones. (See sample specimen.) The *middle* zone is on the line (or imaginary line)—*c's, m's,* and so on; the *lower* zone falls below the line (the descenders on *p's* and *z's,* for instance); and the *upper* zone rises above (the ascending loops on *h's* and *l's,* for instance). Each zone corresponds to a level of human existence: the middle is practical; the lower is earthy, sensual; and the upper is spiritual.

A handwriting that emphasizes the *upper* zone, with high-flying, dramatic upper loops, is that of an exalted and spiritual person, concerned with the meta-physical, artistic, and philosophical aspects of life.

The *middle* zone, which makes up the bulk of everyone's handwriting, shows how the writer handles his everyday, how his ego is adjusted to his environment. If he has a balanced middle zone, with well-organized ascenders and descenders, he has struck a good compromise between his needs and those of others. If the middle zone is overemphasized—large, for instance, with relatively small upper and lower loops—he is overbearing and ego-involved, with little thought for the others in his life. A small middle zone indicates a crushed ego, or at least a withdrawn and observant personality. A widely fluctuating middle zone indicates instability, an ego that desperately adapts to the needs of other people.

A dominant *lower* zone suggests a writer with strong sensual appetites, a love of the down-to-earth and the sexual.

Notice particularly any dramatic differences in size in the three zones. For instance, a writer whose middle-zone letters are tiny but who makes enormous lower loops may be trying to overcompensate for feelings of worthlessness by an obsession with sexuality.

Connections: The way letters are linked (or not linked) will tell you a great deal about the details of a writer's true character. For one thing, the connections are not *necessary* to the formation and legibility of the letters, so they indicate the general tendencies of the personality, the ways in which the writer can let himself go. He *must* form the letter with *some* care, and its form is to some extent arbitrary; but he can always fail to connect letters, or, if he prefers, connect them very strongly and idiosyncratically. Look to them for the quirks and quibbles of a writer's personality.

Garlands are the loops that connect the downstroke of one letter with the upstroke of the next. If they are well formed, they show that the writer has confidence in moving forward. He does not fear extending himself into the world, and believes in the possibility of progress. Firm garlands, clear and written with some pressure, indicate openness to society and friends. Less firm, but still clear, they mean the writer is passive, but highly sympathetic and receptive. Hesitant and weak garlands indicate a Milquetoast quality, an unwillingness to make commitments.

Angular connections between letters do not have the rounded curves

angular

connections

232

Arcades

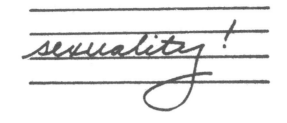

sexuality!

Garlands

Separations

of the garland. They are less fluid, and show someone ill at ease in the company of others. Usually, this trait is matched by great determination of will, so that the very social unease it indicates can be overcome—but at some cost to the writer, who is likely to be irritable and touchy, not the easiest of friends and lovers.

Separations are simply connections omitted—and they're very significant _if_ the handwriting you are analyzing is one of the standard forms. Some people learned a form of printing in childhood, and their letters are forever after separated by habit, to the despair of graphologists. But if in an otherwise normal handwriting you find a great number of separated letters, the subject is likely to be solitary, a loner—either by choice or circumstance. He will tend to get caught up in the details of his own life and be unable to see the forest for his own trees. He will reject relationships or find fault with them, will have difficulty committing himself to another person or even to work that deeply involves others.

On the other hand, some writers go to great lengths to connect each letter of a word, even when, as between the small _e_ and _a_, it's easier to drop the connection. They are very subject to social pressure, likely to do just about anything to win approval, and therefore aren't very trustworthy. They don't have an internal gyroscope that keeps them in tune to their _own_ feelings, emotions and ideas.

Arcades are an unusual formation—a series of arches connecting the tops of letters. This is a highly self-conscious structure, covering the writing like a colonnade, and covering the writer's personality, too—but in a highly decorative and even charming fashion. The arcaded writer is likely to be formal, controlled, someone who expects the total environment to conform neatly to what he *wants* it to be. Because he values social connection, he'll often hide this manipulative tendency behind a facade of outgoingness.

Individual Letters: Although the graphologist looks for the over-all tendencies in any handwriting, the indications provided by certain letters have been found to be so important that analysts always look closely at them. The *dot over the small* i, for instance, is considered a strong indicator. If it is a dash with an upward slant, the writer is impatient, forward-looking, and eager; if the slant is downward, but vigorous, it indicates melancholy and a powerful temper—a dangerous combination. The use of a circle for a dot is very interesting. It is often made by those who want to impress, and who have the ability to do so. These people are charming, witty, quick, and intelligent. They are likely to have an artistic temperament even if they are not artists, and to be happily ambitious. A *floating* dot—placed very high—indicates some confusion about a life-plan, vagueness in decisions.

The *bar of the small* t is another good indicator of character. A strong bar indicates great determination; one that slants downward from left to right is a sign of a terrible temper (the stronger the stroke, the more violent); an upward slant from left to right means that the writer is overeager, and often overreaches himself. Notice where the horizontal bar is placed on the vertical part of the t. The *lower* it is with relation to the rest of the writing, the more impatient and demanding the writer is. A high t-bar, or one that misses the t altogether, indicates an ethereal or unrealistic personality, which will run into trouble with career and ambition unless it keeps to ivory towers. The middle-ground t-bar is often very conventional—he was taught to place that bar carefully and precisely, and he is still doing what he was taught.

Descenders and risers—that is, the parts of the letter that are below and above the middle line—are always a good indication of character. This is especially true of the decorative descenders that often form the flourishes and details of a handwriting. The figure-eight g is considered an almost infallible sign of the artistic personality, the real creator. Well-looped and rounded descenders are also signs of creativity.

Unlooped descenders indicate a strong, impatient, not very sexy character . . . the C.P.A.'s of this world.

Unlooped risers show energy and determination. Very rounded upper loops show imagination and concern for others—an ability to empathize, often creatively—in writing or acting.

The Signature

You must consider the signature a completely different case than the rest of the handwriting. It should be analyzed *after* you've done an analysis of the writing itself, as a comment on the rest. Because that is what a signature is most likely to be. The signature is a statement to the world, *This is who I am.* Even if the writer would prefer not to say who he is, the situation of writing his name—the one set of letters that identifies him to himself and to others— traps him into a statement. The contrast between his signature and his other writing is perhaps the single most important indication of character you're likely to see.

Since the signature is an indication of how a writer sees *himself*, any marked difference between his signature and his handwriting indicates that his self-image differs from the self he shows to the world.

Look at the *size* of the signature in comparison to the rest of the writing.

An over-large signature is a sign of a desire to impress. Check the upper loops of the letters in the signature; if they're small compared to the rest of the large signature, you'll know at once that he's hiding inferiority feelings. On the other hand, if the ascenders are large with relation to an apparently shrinking signature, you can bet he's hiding a big ego behind a modest facade.

An exaggerated first name suggests a shield, as if the writer wanted to hide behind the gregariousness of the Big Hello. His ego may be developed to the point of narcissism. If the last name is emphasized, he'll have a strong sense of family and tradition. On the whole, the first name stands for the private person, the last for the public one. A good balance in size between the two indicates social ease and a relatively serene inner life. The greater the difference between the two, the greater the social difficulties of the writer.

A writer is much more likely to develop flourishes and idiosyncracies in his signature than he is in normal writing, and the details are important. A *dot after the signature,* for instance, means a decisive but often negative character—there he is, telling you to STOP. If he ends his signature with a strong *dash to the right,* you can expect him to be full of energy—a sixteen-hour-a-day person, with a little left over at the end. A *line curving upward* is a fine sign—the writer is happy, unambitious, quirkily individualistic, and generally a joy to others, a cockeyed optimist. If an *end-stroke doubles back on the name,* or *cuts through it,* the writer is negating himself. (Any stroke cutting through his name anywhere is a bad sign.) But a *line under the name* does just what it might suggest—it underlines the writer's sense of himself, is an indication of a strong will and powerful determination to succeed on his own terms. A *flourish* that *becomes a line around a name* means you can take *years* getting to know the writer—he has fenced himself off from normal human contact, and no matter how genial he may appear (he is often ambitious and so wants to seem friendly), he will prevent you or anyone else from getting to him.

Then of course there is the problem of the *illegible signature.* No matter that doctors and great executives are said to be immediately recognizable by their unrecognizable signature—there is nothing good about this trait. The writer is unsure of himself, wants to hide from the world, has an exaggerated and unrealistic notion of privacy and self-importance, and is likely to be megalomaniac. Of course, that may be a definition of the fifty-thousand-a-year man, but we can hope for the state of big business that it isn't so.

A zonal analysis of the signature will be helpful, since even the smallest element in this piece of writing is likely to be important. The *middle* zone is where to look for the real strength of character. If an elaborate signature proves to have all its strong strokes in the risers and descenders, with a weak middle zone, you can assume that it is a defensive structure, indicates a poor sense of reality and a weak ego. The stronger the *upper* zone, the more guilt-ridden and morality-laden the subject will be. He is full of social consciousness, but probably lacks a sense that he needs to fulfill *himself.* He'll do what he feels he *ought to do,* and then wonder why he's unhappy.

The *lower* zone of the signature is the indicator of sensuality and sexual fulfillment. Sometimes light and airy flourishes in this zone indicate that the writer has a terrific fantasy life, but wouldn't be caught dead acting it out . . . his dreams are probably *great.* Bold and energetic descenders are a sign of the real thing—sexual desire often fulfilled and openly avowed. If there is a descender at the end of the name and the writer emphasizes it with a flourish, you can be certain that his sexiness is something he knows about and *approves* of. Beware, though, of the writer who drags mid-zone letters into the lower zone—like the lower curves of small *m's* and *n's.* He will be obsessive sexually, and unlikely to put his desires in a healthy, balanced perspective.

The placement of the signature on the page is important. Remember that the right-hand side of a page is the optimistic, energetic side; the left-hand, melancholy and introverted. A signature very *low* on the page indicates depression (and if it's very low and to the *left,* you might ask some tactful questions about whether the writer is seeing his friendly neighborhood psychotherapist). A signature placed very far from the body of a letter or other writing indicates that the writer senses a deep disparity between the two selves.

ANALYSIS
Now, of course, you have to put all this information *together.* The best way is to *study* handwriting wherever you see it. Much of the art makes quite logical sense, and soon you'll be able to tell a lot at a glance. Samples abound—you shouldn't have any trouble getting them. Ask friends, whose personalities you already know, to give you samples; then you can double-check your accuracy by thinking, "*Is* my friend Alice really negative and shrinking?" Try the famous-people route, too. Go to the library and look up the signatures of celebrities you're interested in—or better yet, copies of letters—and then analyze their handwriting. You'll discover the most *fascinating* reflections of, and contradictions of, their public personalities. They will suddenly be *very* private people to you.

We've included samples here, too—along with analyses to give you an idea of how to string together your observations in a coherent way. Don't try to *hurry* your first efforts. Take samples from friends, and then make notes in private. You'll begin soon enough to spot the really significant things about a handwriting.

Darling, —
I'm desperately sorry that I couldn't make it this afternoon, but on the way to the Plaza, my taxi fell into a pothole and I was lucky to escape with my life.

Hal

L. H. _____

236

The subject whose sample is shown above is a man of thirty-three, a professor of psychology, married.

His writing is small, clear but not noticeably well formed, and slopes slightly to the right.

The vertical strokes in the capital *D* and *P* are strong, unequivocal; combined with the slight forward slope, this would indicate that the writer has more determination and ego strength than his small handwriting would betray immediately.

There is a strong intellectual bent here, and perhaps a repressed spiritual one—the ascenders (see the *l's, d's,* and, especially, small *f's*) are very powerful and full. The descenders indicate some sort of fear or repression in the sensual sphere—they are short and straight, not very decisive . . . there are few open loops.

There are several uncompleted letters—the *g* in *Darling,* the first *I,* the *d* in *desperately*—and they may indicate a holding back, a lack of certainty confirmed by the way the writing shrinks toward the left margin. This judgment is reinforced by the somewhat indecisive shapes of the vowels.

The most interesting single formation, however, is the *t* in *it* in the second line. The cross-bar is formed without lifting the pen from the paper after forming the vertical bar—as if the writer were unwilling to let the paper—or the letter—go. It shows a definite conservatism, innate and perhaps unconscious; an unwillingness to let go and take the next step; and perhaps a deeply fearful side to the personality. Interestingly, this is not the *normal* way for the writer to form his *t's*—notice the difference between this *t* and the others.

In general, one might say that the writer is successful intellectually, even overweening, but that he has resisted some of his most spiritual and generous instincts, and is cramped in his sensuality. He is unlikely to be happy unless he acknowledges his passion for values that he himself sometimes finds half laughable—justice, unity, brotherhood; and yet he is too determined and clear of mind to fail altogether.

His signature confirms the analysis—the ascenders strong, the middle zone weak or even slightly unreadable. Notice that he turns the *c* in the *Mc* into an ascender—as if there were not enough in his life that was aspiring to what he really wants.

I am aware of several things, including the fact that I have not your Manhattan address, except for one which I don't depend on. But I just became aware of a new thing: I can send this care of V. Bully! Writing begets thinking. Vice versa?

John Wylie

P.S. Best to Veronica

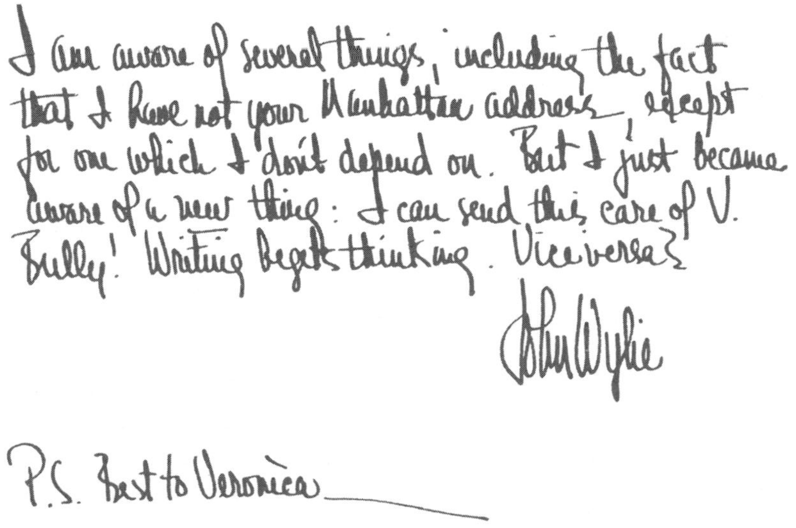

This handwriting is that of a quite extraordinary man in his late forties, an actor. It is remarkably legible and strong, moving across the page with even pressure and complete symmetry. Yet there are energetic flourishes everywhere—in the round upper loop of the small *f* and *h*, which indicates a powerful empathy with others; in the figure-eight *g*'s, which are a strong sign of the creative personality; and in the strong, no-nonsense *t* bars, which show an energy and decisiveness that can back the creativeness and give it power.

Notice the remarkable *uprightness* of the hand—his energy is contained and put to constant daily use, neither held back nor impatiently urging forward. He has a great sense of his own ego, his own *rightness*, which can sometimes make him seem stiff-necked.

The middle zone is relatively large—indicating an essentially practical nature that his creative power has not stamped out.

The signature is quite consistent with the rest of the handwriting. The large initial letters indicate an even more pronounced ego than we'd at first supposed, and the strong but undecorative descender on the *y* suggests a suppressed sexual drive and a creative urge that is sublimated in work, not dissipated in play.

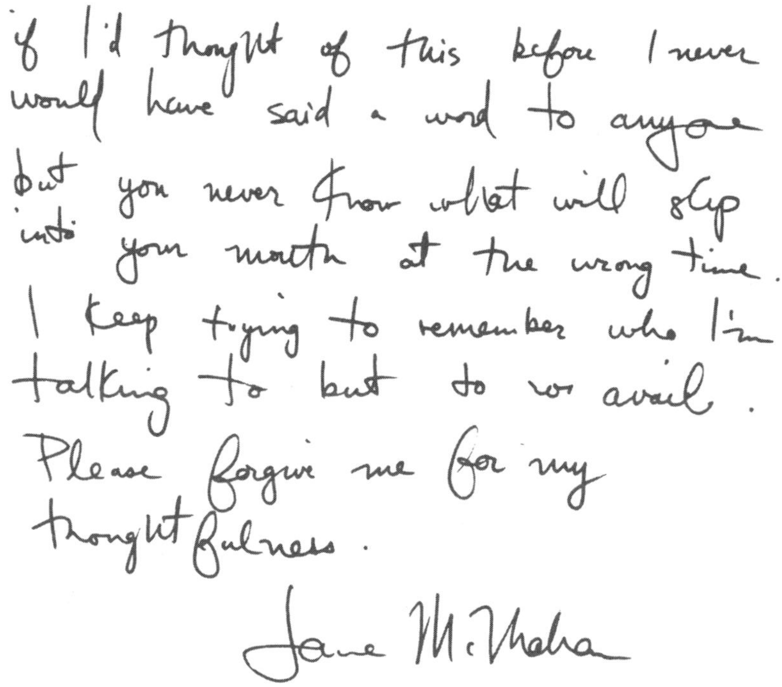

If I'd thought of this before I never would have said a word to anyone but you never know what will slip into your mouth at the wrong time. I keep trying to remember who I'm talking to but to no avail. Please forgive me for my thoughtfulness.

Jane McMahon

This is the handwriting of a young woman of twenty-five, quiet and even girlish on the surface, but determined enough about her life to want a career as a concert singer; she has been married four years.

The straightness of the hand is striking; it is almost entirely vertical, except for the impatient forward motion of some *l*'s and *t*'s, and the *m* at the end of the fifth line. She pushes the writing far to the right, and keeps the left margin moving forward—the need to have a curb in her life is quite clear.

Both the dots of the *i*'s and the periods show impatience and determination. They are solid and well formed, but they occur well forward—beyond the sentence, in the case of the periods; and above and beyond the letter, in the case of the dot. The dots seem to float—that is, they are farther above the *i* than is normal, almost unconnected to it in some cases. (See the *i* in *trying* in line five.) The subject is clearly determined to do what she wants, but occasionally doubts her own ability—drifts off from the mark.

The strong verticals are very significant. The capital *I*'s are single slashes, as are the vertical bars of the *t*'s. The cross-bars of the *t*'s are slightly inconsistent, varying from high on the letter to the middle—but they are always decisive and strong. No matter what the subject feels, it is likely to be powerful, even if, as her cross-bars suggest, it is likely to be anything from a commitment to what she's been taught to a determination to achieve a life goal of her own. The simple, strong vertical of the *l* is especially hopeful—it is a sign of a healthy ego and an impatience with fooling around (even by herself).

The descenders—especially on the *f*'s in the last two lines—indicate a strongly sensual nature. But those same *f*'s have equally full and strong ascenders. The balance is clearly very good, although the solid determination of the verticals indicates that calculation and ambition may eventually win out over passion.

The only disturbing elements in this essentially strong character are the erratic, slashing, and uncertain *k*'s (lines three, five, and six), which change with each formation and show a conflict between the strong vertical and the uncertain horizontal. Also, the tiny single *a* in the second line and, generally, the uncertain shape of the vowels lead the analyst to believe that, though the subject will have no trouble getting what she wants, she may have a long row to hoe in finding out what it *is*.

The signature bears out the general conclusions of the analysis: The determined, no-nonsense upper stroke of the *J* is balanced by a large and sensual descender; but the *a* of the *Jane* is much larger and more defined than the *a*'s of *McMahan*; and the two *n*'s are almost unreadable—she irons them out as if she wanted to hide them. The final *n* is especially interesting—it shows both impatience ("There, I've written my name, now let's get on with it") and a real uncertainty about goals. ("What will I do after *this* is finished?")

The prediction: That the subject will achieve what she wants, after a considerable *struggle*.

The sample above is from a woman thirty-three years old. She is unmarried and makes her living as a freelance writer; she is intelligent and independent.

The writing is rather forward-looking, and occasionally spurts into the right margin; the left margin drags slightly to the left as the writing moves down the page. These points suggest that she is tentative in her extroversion, and tends to withdraw somewhat. But the handwriting is full of energy and life; she doesn't stop to make careful forms, in the desire to say what she means. Similar zest shows in some incompleted and unconnected letters. Notice the interesting tendency to make full lower loops—a very sensual sign—but then to drag the end of the final lower-looped letter straight across, instead of back up into the middle zone. It's as if this woman *liked* the lower zone so much, she hated to leave it!

See, though, how most of the other letters tend toward middle-zone size. (The *we'll* in the first line, for instance, and the *and* in the fourth line, are good examples.) The writer is clearly a practical person, who likes to reduce all matters to reason, common sense, technical skill. She will never get carried away with a religious cult, or allow her sexuality, strong as it is (those looped descenders) to overshadow the rest of her life.

The signature, with its strong initial *A,* shows a secure sense of self-importance. But it is not dramatically larger or smaller than the rest of the writing. This means that the writer has a well-integrated idea of her public and private selves: no delusions of grandeur, no shrinking back from the eyes of the world.

This woman's future will certainly be full of energetic work, but she won't drive herself to the point where her social and sexual life is neglected. She will probably succeed at whatever she undertakes—if she can conquer a tendency to be aloof and withdrawn. (She just *may* become a total *hedonist!*)

Chapter Nine
"ESP"
PSYCHIC READING
AND
CLAIRVOYANCE

Traditionally, the occult "reader" has been a gypsy sitting behind a small shawl-covered table in a booth at the county fair. She used no professional equipment—just her own mysterious character, her deep and penetrating eyes, and the claim that she could tell all without ever having laid eyes on you before. Usually, sophisticated people dismissed her as a fast talker with a line of simple and flattering tricks: What woman doesn't want to hear that she's going to meet a dark and handsome man? What mother isn't thrilled to learn that all her children will grow up to be rich and famous? And for that matter, who doesn't desire (just a little) to be threatened with a mysterious "danger" in his life? If anything like what the reader said came true, the subject decided she was right; if what she said didn't come true, it was just forgotten. A nice game.

Psychic researchers and clairvoyants (the mediums and seers who have visions of the future and past) hold a much more powerful reputation—but a much less innocent one. They are, or believe they are, making serious attempts to explore areas that science has sneered at (because most scientists just haven't agreed that "psychic phenomena" exist). And if psychic researchers and clairvoyants are fooling with the nonexistent, they're either charlatans or fools, and certainly to be shunned by the intelligent and sensible person. Right?

Well, not exactly. For one thing, there is a huge body of tradition behind research into psychic phenomena. And very few people are willing to deny completely that the tradition is groundless. That's why even the most rationalist type will enjoy some of the fortune-telling methods described in this book. They are not just pleasant and emotionally stimulating games—they are also part of an ancient body of knowledge that everyone finds subliminally believable. The psychic researchers are trying to find out what is believable in fact; the clairvoyants simply act upon their faith that what they believe must exist in fact. And so we have a great controversy—and a fascinating new world for you to explore.

THE PSYCHIC READER

Because the claims of the psychic reader have been so vague and, therefore, so modest, it has been possible to examine just *what* she does and *how* she does it with much less brouhaha and controversy than has surrounded other explorers into occult territory.

Psychic readers claim that by *looking* at you they can tell your future.

242

Until recently that sounded pretty dopey, but very tempting—and what did anyone have to lose? After all, the claim didn't involve anything threatening, like a belief in reincarnation or a prophecy about the end of the world. You only had to believe that the reader knew what would happen to you in the next week—could *see* it with her dark gypsy eyes. Now, though, we're realizing that she has long been using methods that can be employed by responsible sociologists, psychotherapists, experimental psychologists, and students of cultural attitudes. The psychic reader was using these methods before there was any name or scientific rationale for them, and foretelling the future with their help.

Body Language

The Secret Weapon of the psychic reader is body language. That's really *all* she has to work with. The subject enters the booth, or comes in to her office, and she is faced with a total stranger who may not be willing to tell her his name. But he is *there*—in the flesh, moving as he normally does, revealing himself with every gesture, every tic or graceful swoop of his hand. So she watches carefully, and begins to see the kind of person he is. Of course, she is also looking for other signs—how he's dressed, whether he's had a haircut recently, what objects he carries with him, whether he's wearing a wedding ring. This combination of physical characteristics and give-away indirect clues makes it possible to understand him and—by projection—his future.

Of course, a good many psychic readers also have *clairvoyant* powers that may very well allow them to see *directly* into the future. But we can't *assume* that about ourselves—we can only hope that we have some measure of it and go on to use all the *other* commonsense tricks of the trade as well as we can. So, in this section, we'll talk about ways to read body language to tell your subject's fortune in the most *direct* way of all.

THE MYSTIC MOOD

The secret of this mood is intimacy—as it is with all the directly physical methods—and *intensity*. Your subject must be convinced that your passionate attention is wholly fastened on *all* of him. With palmistry, phrenology, and graphology, your attention was directed toward one *part* of the subject's body, or toward his handwriting—and you had some leeway to be a little kittenish, playfully seductive. But the psychic reader must use her total body, mind, emotions, to absorb the subject's personality and win his confidence. Relaxation is not so necessary here—*concentration* is the key, and the intensity that goes with it.

Black, deep red, a jewellike purple—these colors will be as intense as the mood. Your dress should be dramatic, a powerful indication of the power you expect your subject to believe in. And your figure should be just a bit overpowering, too! If you've never worn a Merry Widow, now might be the time to try one. It will accentuate everything—push up your breasts, exaggerate your hips a bit, cinch the waist. Don't be afraid to overdo slightly—or even not so slightly (a *deep* cleavage . . . glittering boots with your long dress . . . hair in a great controlled mane down your back . . . enormous rings, earrings to the collar-bone, long red fingernails, a crescent-shaped beauty mark on the inside of your wrist. . . .

Make-up should match the overheated quality of the costume—it should be *almost* theatrical. Use liner around eyes . . . and then add a touch of white *inside* the liner. Use a pale red lipstick with an outline in a lusher shade. Try metallics on your eyes—gold, silver, or bronze shadow; then hollow above the lid with dark mauve. Don't hesitate to emphasize your brows—they should be almost *heavy,* and darker than your hair shade.

Arrange your apartment as carefully as a stage set—you want nothing left to chance, and a minimum of outside influences. The windows should be heavily draped. If your curtains are light, find some deep-colored velveteen and pin it over them. There should be pillows everywhere. However, you won't sit too close to your subject. (If possible, arrange two comfortable armchairs, facing one another.) Use candles, but not in twos or threes— you'll need at least a dozen. (If you have a candelabra, now is the time to polish it, and put in very long tapers.) Make sure you've hidden or removed all signs of the frivolous or humorous from the environment. (That happy-face poster will have to go, and the bright ceramic piggy-bank you bought in Acapulco.) Don't play music—it will be a distraction. If you use incense, burn it for about an hour before the subject arrives, then remove it—so that only the scent remains in the air, mysterious and sourceless. Serve drinks, of course, but no food (schedule the reading for *after* dinner), and remember to make a small ceremony of the serving process, with a carefully arranged tray and your best glasses.

One of the chief goals of this mood-setting is to keep the subject riveted on *you*—while you are carefully, coolly, with all your intelligence and quickness, watching *his* every move, his costume, his jewelry, his way of holding that drink you hand him. You are practicing the old art of indirection, so that what you tell him about himself will seem to come, not from simple observation, but from some deep mysterious and spontaneous well of psychic knowledge.

THE METHOD

With almost every other method we've discussed, the more you know about your subject in advance, the better off you are. You've learned to use your knowledge openly—to help personalize an interpretation of cards, tea leaves, or whatever. But with this method, you should know—or *admit* to knowing—as little about the subject as possible beforehand. All your wisdom should *appear* to have occurred to you at that moment, as the result of his *vibrations* reaching you from across the room. So play down what you've already found out—that he comes from Chilicothe, or has nine brothers and sisters, or is indifferent to his job. Of course, it's a great mistake to *lie* in a situation like this: The whole point of fortune-telling is the full appearance of truth, and even a small fib can destroy a subject's confidence in you. So if you and he have spent an hour discussing your small-town childhoods, don't try to come on suddenly as the Mysterious Lady who knows everything and has been told nothing. Surprise him instead with your *memory* of what he's told you, and with what you can add.

For the subject, the reading will begin when the two of you sit down, he poses questions or problems, you begin to tell him their solutions and explain to him what you see in his future. But for you, the reading must begin the moment he walks in the door—and with every memory of him that you can dredge up.

Aside from previously known facts, you have two basic sources of knowledge about your subject—his *body* (and how he uses and dresses it), and his *words* (and how he speaks them). Of these two, the visual is by far the more important, because he will be much less aware of it as a source of clues.

The Greeting: Pay attention to the way he chooses to *arrive*. (For everyone, this moment has a bit of theater in it, and everyone, no matter how basically confident, is a *little* nervous upon first entering a room.) Does he stand at the door and wait for you to invite him in? (Your mind should click—"Possibly a *passive* fellow.") Does he keep his coat on (or his hat or umbrella or briefcase in his hand) until you ask to take it, or is he whipping out of it before you have the door closed? Does he wear gloves? (Of course, if it's mid-winter in Minnesota, he will *have* to, but often they are an indicator of someone who wants to *limit* his contact with the world.) In winter, is he well protected (hat, muffler, heavy gloves, overcoat), or does he seem just to dash from car to building, heedless of the weather? Overshoes? (These can be very important. Many people who wear overshoes are conscious of poverty, though not necessarily poor—they don't want to ruin a good pair of shoes. On the other hand, the man with no overshoes in a driving snowstorm would rather buy new shoes and risk his death of cold than appear klutzy and overcautious.)

Does he touch you when he comes in? This behavior differs with men and women, but for both, the question it answers is the same: Do they *like* bodily contact or not? People who like to touch will use a greeting as an *excuse* for it. Someone who's known you for one whole evening previously, or for a quick drink, or not at all (perhaps a friend is bringing him along to see you) may take your hand, kiss your cheek, or touch your forearm as you take his coat. It's a perfect opportunity, and he won't miss it if he likes to touch—nor will his female counterpart. But if he's shy about touching, or repelled by it, he'll *use* the fact that he doesn't know you well to *avoid* contact, to hold off, edging past you in the foyer, *hanging* his coat over your arm rather than handing it to you, perhaps even not meeting your eyes. Of course, there are many subgroups within these two, and you must be on the watch for them. Does he just like generalized touch, or is he on the Seduction Trail from the beginning? Is she touching you because she's a warm person, or is she really trying to prove something, to gain some kind of ascendancy over you?

From Standing to Sitting: This is a crucial point, and will let you determine a great deal about your subject's character—and therefore, later, let you speculate fruitfully about his future. Does he immediately take over the room, finding the most comfortable chair and commandeering it, observing that the drinks are in the antique icebox and that he'd like Scotch with one cube thank you, and asking which door is to the bathroom—finding everything that will make him comfortable in thirty seconds flat? Because if he does, you've got an executive on your hands, and/or a very anxious person. Either he just naturally takes over, physically dominating the room and its appurtenances, or he is desperately upset to be on unfamiliar terrain and is doing everything he can to *seem* at ease, to control a situation he fears might master him. (After all, at *his* place, he *knows* where everything is—and maybe he just doesn't feel safe until he has that knowledge about *every* place he's in.)

You'll be able to tell the difference right away. Confidence and anxiety may *talk* the same, but they move differently. For instance, the truly confident man will stand at ease, almost leaning back on his heels, while he looks things over. The nervous type will lean forward on the balls of his feet, trying to take everything in for safety's sake; that one bodily subtle gesture gives the game away.

Of course, the truly shy person may handle his tension in any number of ways. One of the most obvious is the non-sitter. He just can't manage to sit down—even after *you're* in your chair. After all, if he sits, he's *committed*. His indecision keeps him feeling safe, as if he could bolt from the room at any moment (though he is probably too shy to *consider* such a daring move). Or he will sit down very quickly, almost before you've indicated a chair, and accept a drink, which he'll hold in front of him like a tiny shield, watching you even as he sips.

The movement from standing (not-quite-being-here-yet) to sitting (I-have-arrived) isn't totally a matter of shy versus confident. There is also the question of territory. Some perfectly confident people aren't takers-over. How *do* they treat the space? You'll find that some will look first at you, then at the surroundings, then back at you. They are interested in how *you* occupy your *own* space. They don't want to usurp it; they want to *observe* you in it. These people will be hard to read—because they'll be reading *you*.

Then there's the Prowler. You may never get him into a chair. He wants to be sure that he's Lord of the Jungle; and if you let him, he'll spend all evening roaming the peripheries of the apartment, full of energy and with no place to put it. His female counterpart often picks up bibelots and peers at them, as if she wants to know where everything *came* from. Actually *she's* just being territorial, too, trying to work off a bit of her excess energy—but she hasn't the same social permission that a man has to prowl. (At least, she didn't until recently. Have you noticed how fussy gestures are dying off in women? Well, *now* is the time.) Watch for these and the many other ways that a person settles down for the evening—they can be dead giveaways of hopes, fears, and character.

The Offer: One of the reasons we've suggested that you serve only drinks is that the interaction will give you a single and isolated example of how your subject responds to an offer. Look carefully at how he reacts to the simple question, "Would you like a drink?" (Keep the question that simple to allow lots of room for interpretation.) Does he seem to take the offer as his due? Or does he act surprised that you'd give him anything? Does he immediately offer to mix it himself? Or ask what you *have*?

Listen for all the overtones. If he asks what you have available, does he do it because he's trying to tell you how fastidious he is? Or does his tone imply that he thinks you might have a *small* selection and he wouldn't want to embarrass you by asking for Irish whisky? Suppose he says, "I don't drink." Look at that one carefully. Is he a defensive alcoholic? An aggressive puritan? Why did he *assume* you were offering him *alcohol*? The overenthusiastic responder is another case. Does he still think that he is illustrating his sophistication by showing great ardor for alcohol? Or is it just a sign of age? (Remember William Powell's almost hysterical reaction to every drink in *The Thin Man*? That was really a *cultural* reaction to the repeal of Prohibition, and there are still some old dudes suffering from it.)

Once the drink—with or without alcohol—is mixed, observe how he takes it from you. (If he's mixed it himself, it may be a sign that he can't stand being *given* anything—he must *take over* the raw materials.) Do you have to *hand* it to him, or bring it to him? Or does he come to you? Does his hand linger on the glass, half touching your hand? Or does he make a quick grab and clutch the glass to himself? Once he has it, how does he hold it? In a firm death-grip, as if it would get away from him? Or does he sip and set it down? (The latter usually shows a good deal of confidence—he believes his drink will *be* there when he reaches for it again. At the other extreme is a woman I once saw at a party, who takes her drink to the *bathroom* with her.) Some people always *gesticulate* with their drink. They seem to lose track of the fact that they're holding a *glass* with *liquid* in it, and begin to use it as if it were a baton, to conduct themselves and others in conversation. If they don't spill very often, that would seem to indicate that they're not *hopelessly* out of touch with physical reality and their own bodies.

Now, consider the question of seconds: Does he ask for another, or wait to be given it? How does he take your offer of a second drink? Is he by now confident enough simply to mix his own *without* an exchange? Does he even offer to mix you one?

A very interesting response to your offer of seconds is the "Who, me?" reaction. He behaves as if you'd never offered him the *first* drink, as if the glass in his hand or at his elbow were a mysterious object that had grown there unheeded. Usually people who do this are deeply manipulative. They don't trust any straightforward situation and have a great desire to *deny* the *facts* in order to recast them closer to their hearts' desire. Often they don't even know that they want something different from what they've got. They simply can't leave any situation as it is, but must alter it in their mind's eye. Like all manipulative people, this person usually succeeds in confusing the situation. When he answers your offer of seconds with "Who, me?", you're apt to feel, "Was the first drink all wrong? Am I rushing things? What is going on?" In this situation, you must avoid questioning like that, either aloud or in your head. You're there to analyze *his* behavior not to agonize over your own. There is an element of calculation in the psychic reader. She can't afford normal social reactions, but must continue to observe even when her own role as hostess is called into question.

The Primary Encounter: This moment comes when the settling-down has taken place, when you and your subject are seated and drinks are in hand, and the preliminaries are all over. You must face *each other,* no longer buffered by coat-taking and drink-offering. *This moment is probably the greatest single revealer of character in the whole evening.* Some people will avoid it altogether—will never meet your eye, will not let the conversation change in tone from the greeting at the door, will continue to prowl the room ceaselessly. They just don't want *contact,* and will go to considerable social lengths to avoid it. It's actually *hard* to sit opposite someone and not let eyes meet, but they'll manage it. Arms will stay crossed even though a cigarette manages to appear in one hand; the drink will be used as a shield, or even as a weapon if you come too close.

At the other extreme is the person who has been *waiting* for this moment. He doesn't come around to people's houses to *avoid* anything—he wants just what an invitation implies, real connection. He will let a silence fall after the first sip in his drink and then look up and into your eyes quite deliberately. Even if this is a ploy of some kind, it is genuine. If he hated contact, he'd avoid that particular ploy and find another.

This is the time when you'll begin to look carefully at facial expressions and listen to conversation. Often there is a dramatic difference between the expression of a face and the sound of a voice, or between the expression and the posture of the body. That difference will say more about character and possibility in someone than almost anything they'd tell you about themselves consciously. Are there conflicts between what he's saying and what he feels? Does his face look friendly, his body terrified? Are the words kind and the tone harsh?

The *tensions* here are what you're looking for—or, in rare cases, *lack* of tension. I once knew a former college athlete of immense physical size and strength, who would try to disarm his companions by throwing his legs wide and spreading his arms along the back of a couch. But his smile had all the ease and comfort of a jackal's; and the opener his body posture got, the quieter *he* got. Probably everyone has met the kind of woman (again, she's likely to go back a generation or two) who talks brightly and looks you right in the eye while embracing herself tightly with both arms, her legs crossed viselike, her shoulders hunched. Her messages are different, and there's bound to be conflict in anyone who's conveying two at once.

The Proposal: Most likely, you've told your subject that you will give him a reading, so he's not totally unprepared. Still, there is bound to be a reaction when he knows that *this* is the moment, that you are about to tell him his future, to read his character. Whether or not he *believes* you have any power to do so, his attitude toward the bare *possibility* is bound to be revealing. And his feelings about your confidence that you can do it will tell you a good deal. Is he *careful* to be amused? Or genuinely so? Does his bluff response of "nothing to hide" make you feel immediately that there is a lot he hopes you don't know? Does he get the shifty look of the loser, as if he is certain there won't be anything terrific in his future? Or is he just frankly curious—about the experience, about your abilities, about his own future?

Notice how much of what he says is belied by his posture. Does he unconsciously shrink at the idea of a reading? Or does he lean forward eagerly? This is the moment when you're most likely to discover whether there is a *specific* problem bothering him. Often, you can see a worried look spring up in someone's eyes, as if perhaps the future could solve a present trouble, or make it even worse. It is from this clue that you can say later, "There is something worrying you, a very specific problem . . ." and get credit for *real* second sight.

DELIVERING THE READING

The most important thing to remember about delivering a psychic reading is that *you must not reveal the nature of your sources*. Never say, "Because you were five minutes getting your coat off when you came in and then couldn't decide whether to hand it to me or hang it over a chair, I believe that you have a problem with indecision." *No.* Your pronouncements must be genuinely *oracular*, full of authority, and come from some spontaneous (or seemingly spontaneous) arousal of your second sight, or preternatural perception. We live in a world where we're constantly asked to give *reasons* for everything we say; we're expected to *justify* our reactions, *explain* our statements, *understand* and *analyze* our insights. Well, the whole power of the psychic reading lies in *not* doing any of those things. *You just know.* You've really drawn the conclusion from observation, from intuition, from just plain listening, or in fact from a source in your subconscious deeper than you can understand—but you mustn't say a word about where it comes from. If you remember that as an iron-clad rule, you will halfway toward a really persuasive reading every time.

While you will speak with that oracular authority, use a little personal modesty at the same time. Hesitate a bit; let the subject do some of your work for you. If you say, "I believe you have children . . ." and trail off, chances are he will say, "Yes, two, a boy and a girl." Or, "I think that you were for a long time involved with one woman . . . though perhaps not sexually . . ."; if your guess about his personality is right, he might say for you, "I lived with my mother for years." From here it's not far to the *prediction:* "You have had trouble finding a woman to replace her, and it is doubtful that you will. Perhaps you will be happier knowing many women than trying to settle with one." *There*—from your observation and his revelation, you have made a likely prediction; mama's boys really do have trouble finding other women, and often don't, or can't, settle down. You may very well have truly predicted the course of his life.

Remember to keep talking . . . with pregnant pauses to let him respond, but in a flow that convinces him that you are thinking all the time, always just a breath away from the next phrase, the next sentence. Here your carefully calculated atmosphere will be invaluable. The mood of intensity is very important to his confidence in your perfect concentration on him and his future, and in his conviction that you have the powers you claim and hope to reveal. The combination of this very *obvious* intensity and the very *mysterious* source of your knowledge creates the most provocative reading.

Don't be afraid to get caught up in your own spell, at least after you have made all your observations and are well into the reading. Your reactions are part of the atmosphere, and if you are too dramatically detached, you'll seem phony. Keep your antennae out, your full powers of observation at work; but draw on your own emotions, and have confidence in your observations. If things are going well do take a chance or two. That mama's boy we were talking about earlier, for instance: Is he gay or not? You might talk vaguely about the "polymorphous quality of true sexuality" or about "universal bisexuality" and see if you get a reaction. It might be worth taking the plunge and saying quite flatly, "You have only been in love with men." Or, to a man who is married but looks thoroughly worried, "You love someone other than your wife and are tortured by it." It's never a good idea to take a *complete* shot in the dark—to be totally wrong will shoot your credibility to hell—but when you decide to make a plunge based on some observations you've made, it's no use pussyfooting.

Of course, you also have *carte blanche* to make specific *future* predictions. They may or may not come true, but trying a few will test both your confidence and the possibility (which you shouldn't discount) that you really *can* unconsciously tell the future. If you predict a journey, concentrate hard and try to sense whether you believe your subject will meet someone. Then try to see a set of initials. If you have even the briefest flash, mention it. If the meeting should happen, you'll have a reputation for being uncanny; if not, the prediction will probably be forgotten. Of course, it might mean that when your subject goes to Puerto Rico next July, he'll spend his entire vacation looking for a tattooed woman whose initials are M. F.—but after all, that's a good conversation-starter, isn't it? You may actually *improve* his vacation.

In general, move from the *sure* (what you know you've observed) to the *probable* (deductions from your observations) to the *unlikely but not impossible* (not all mama's boys are homosexuals, or vice versa .but . . .) to the *frankly predictive, unlikely, and oracular.* Your clues about when, or whether, you can go on to the next level, will come from the subject himself, who is bound to be either more or less convinced as you go along. If he gains confidence and shows that he believes in you, be *bolder* or he'll begin to feel you're hedging. But if he is uncertain, you mustn't jump head-long into belief-defying predictions that he will make a round-the-world one-man sailing voyage before he's forty. Build each prediction on his reaction to the last, and you'll succeed in convincing him that you (and perhaps you *alone*) have a line to the future . . . *his* future.

CLAIRVOYANTS AND PROPHETS

There is no true distinction between the clairvoyant and the prophet. Usually the prophet is just a clairvoyant who makes statements about *public* as well as private events. These two types are the aristocrats of the fortune-telling world—and its most controversial figures. They claim a direct descent from the prophets of the Old Testament and the oracles of antiquity; they believe that their inner vision is preferable to the most sophisticated modern methods of analysis and prediction; and they are most often attacked as charlatans, con men, and rip-off artists.

Of course, much of what you believe about modern prophets depends upon whether you believe there is even a *possibility* that they may be right. Rationalists who see the universe as totally random are not likely to be convinced by the most sincere and passionate prophet; and deeply religious people are often offended by what seems to them a frivolous claim to divine powers. To those who are agnostic, mildly skeptical, and secretly intrigued, however, the public and private prognostications of various clairvoyants and seers remain fascinating, even if evidence of their actual powers remains controversial.

What is it that these people claim? And can any—or all—of us partake to any extent in the powers they believe themselves to possess? On the latter question, there are two totally opposed schools of thought. One says that the power to see the past *and* the future is available to all of us, that it is a normal human ability fallen into disuse through generations of rationalist discouragement. Others are convinced that clairvoyance is a *gift,* the province of a few chosen ones, who are themselves often puzzled by it and sometimes unworthy of it.

But acquirable or not, what *is* it? Well, the word *clairvoyant* is French, and simply means "clear." That is as good a definition as any. A clairvoyant is one who can see clearly what has happened in the past and what will happen in the future. For believers in reincarnation, the ability to see into the past is the primary one. But, for most of us, the past is over and done with; the future is what holds both hope and terror—and that is what we'd like to know more about.

How the seer looks into the future and comments on it differs drastically. Often one man's method is another's anathema. Basically, there are two types of seers. The *visionary* witnesses future events through dreamlike experiences in either a trance state or in what appears to be deep sleep. The *medium* speaks with the voice of another, someone in the spirit world who has access to knowledge of the future and who passes it on *through* the medium. The famous American visionary Edgar Cayce is an example of the former type; and Madame Helena Blavatsky, the celebrated Russian mystic, typifies the latter. Both types sometimes claim they don't understand the mechanism by which they work. Often, they disarm critics by saying flatly that they have no idea of the source of their powers or of their ultimate value, and maybe are just talking gibberish, who knows? The scholars will have to come along and find out. Madame Blavatsky said, "Me? I am just a simple Russian peasant woman. It is my disciples who know what I am doing."

ESP AND THE NEW RESEARCH

Jeane Dixon claims that she can foretell the future; Edgar Cayce's followers say that he correctly diagnosed over four thousand physical and mental ailments (and cured some) while in a trance state; the Israeli psychic Uri Geller is supposed to be able to bend spoons, fix broken watches, and transport all sorts of objects from place to place by sheer *mental* powers. They seem exotics, strange in a modern world which for years insisted that the mind would only think, the body could only act, and the twain were certainly not likely to meet.

But attitudes are changing. The phenomenon of biofeedback is experimentally established. (It's *proved* that the mind can control the body, right up to the point of being able to *determine* its own blood pressure.) We now know that acupuncture works to relieve pain—though Western scientists agree that they don't know *how*. And the ability of certain individuals to "read" with uncanny accuracy the symbols on hidden cards continues to be debated hotly.

This may not sound entirely relevant to fortune-telling, but it is— profoundly. These scientific developments suggest not only that we can *foretell* the future—which was the most that seers expected to do in the past—but *control* it. It is one thing to say that I know my blood pressure will rise twenty points in the next two hours; it's quite another to say that I can *decide* whether or not it will.

During the 1970's, there has been an explosion of interest in extranormal powers. Deep concern with the religions of the East, which sprang up in the 1960's, has led to concern with the physical and psychic disciplines of those religions, and a new desire to prove that the powers of Eastern gurus and wise men are real. Experiments with LSD and other mind-expanding drugs have led a great many people to believe that the rationalistic and materialistic bias of our scientific establishment is a closed-mindedness that is itself antiscientific. One scientific popularizer says, "Modern science should indeed arouse in all of us a humility before the immensity of the unexplored and a tolerance for crazy hypotheses."

What is certainly of deep interest to anyone interested in the occult, or in one of its practical uses like fortune-telling, is the possibility that the hundreds of years of tradition behind a book like the *I Ching* or a set of images like the Tarot might prove to be more than just amusing sociological material, but could come to be the cornerstones of a new understanding of how the brain works and affects the body.

For instance, it is now thought that the term "extrasensory perception" (ESP) should not be taken to mean the ability to perceive with an extra sense, or outside the senses; it should be understood to mean that the senses themselves have something *extra* that has not yet been fully explored and defined. With large flash cards showing geometrical symbols, experiments are being conducted to find out if the normal senses we already have can predict which cards will turn up in a random sequence. (If you'd like to experiment with this notion, make a set of cards by drawing geometric shapes—circle, triangle, etc.—on some white cardboard.) An American at Barnard College in New York and, more recently, a team of Russian doctors have bent their efforts to proving that both color and shape can be perceived by the fingertips—that one sense can do duty for another.

There's some evidence that *if* these abilities exist, they will be much more likely to appear if they are seriously believed in and treated with

251

respect. In other words, what you're not looking for, you can't find. And this idea is one of the best arguments for experimenting with psychic phenomena yourself. If you have an experience or two that convinces you that you or someone you know has gone beyond the bounds of what you've been taught to think of as "normal," you may be open to a whole range of experience that was always *there*, but just never *acknowledged*. The process may be a little like the "discovery" of orgasm in women. Until fairly recently (this century—your time span gets a lot bigger when you're immersed in occult traditions), all the best authorities said that "normal" women didn't *have* orgasms. Nymphomaniacs had orgasms; normal women were "fulfilled" or "satisfied" or something vague and pleasant like that, but they didn't have anything as definite and definable as an *orgasm*. And guess what? Most of them *didn't*. And the ones who did weren't talking. Or didn't *know* that those exciting sensations of tension and release were called orgasm, or *could* be called that if anyone knew that women could have them. And then a few liberated souls—researchers like Kensey, women with a lot of passion, and psychologists like Albert Ellis with savvy and compassion—began to insist that indeed women *did* have orgasms, and that they were just as intense and definable as a man's (although not so *visible*). After a flurry of denials and complacent statements from people who didn't believe that respectable women would *want* to even if they could, Masters and Johnson appeared with a massive and beautifully documented and researched study proving that the female orgasm is a real doozer—measurable, definable, repeatable, and inarguably *there*.

If the orgasm, why not the higher consciousness? An open-minded friend of mine, now a successful novelist, used to have long conversations on the phone with *her* friend Dolores. They'd heard about experiments with ESP cards, and they began a series of small games of their own. My friend would draw a shape, and ask Dolores to guess—over the phone—what it was. Then they'd go on to another shape, Dolores guessing and my friend keeping score of the times right and the times wrong. Dolores had a *fantastic* record—she would just *know* what the shapes were. They were both a little spooked. And then Dolores tried drawing the shapes and my friend guessing. And . . . either Dolores was rotten at sending, or my friend at receiving, because the results were plenty poor; not any better than simple chance. They've no idea what happened, but they are both convinced that *something* happened. And with that knowledge, they are open to any number of capacities in themselves that they weren't prepared to find before. Perhaps they are winding up to a sort of *psychic* orgasm. In any case, it's a wider world because they played that telephone game.

And that's probably the best argument for experimentation with the occult, for attempts to foretell the future by whatever methods come to hand. You may discover things in yourself that none of your teachers, bosses, friends, parents, or even lovers could ever have told you about.

THE REAL THING: Talking with a Clairvoyant
When Ethel Myers was four years old, she grew irresistibly curious about her father's mirror. It sat on the bureau in his bedroom, and no one in the house but he could see into it. ("My mother was a *tiny* woman," she said.) So, after long thought and much tactical planning, she managed to screw the piano stool into its highest position, haul it up to the bureau, and, making use of a handy bedside table as well, climb all the way up to stand face to face with

the mirror. She was gazing into forbidden territory, and very excited! "But at that point," she says, "I suddenly felt that the eyes I was looking into were no longer mine—even the color was different. And my nose looked so much bigger! I couldn't take my face down from the mirror—even though I could move the rest of my body—and I panicked and turned over the piano stool, taking a terrific tumble." Later, she discovered from a family album that the face she had seen—had hypnotized herself into seeing—was that of her paternal grandfather, who had died long before she was born.

That was just the first of Mrs. Myers's long line of experiences as a psychic and medium. She was certainly not encouraged in them for many years. Her father was deeply interested in the occult, and her mother had a definite bend for psychic work, especially for automatic writing, but had been frightened by her trance states. ("Sometimes she would be unable to come out and would cry 'Help!' " Mrs. Myers says. "It *was* very frightening.") Naturally, the mother did not want her daughter to be subject to the same fear, and there seems to have been a family conspiracy not to take Ethel's paranormal experiences seriously. She was simply treated as if she were a normal child, and life went on. In time, she studied for a singing career, and became a singing teacher (a career she still has).

In 1944, though, events occurred that were to change the whole tenor of Mrs. Myers's life. Her husband, the cellist Albert Rosenthal, died. (She is now remarried.) In life, she says, he had been a true "realist," open-minded about occult experiences but unconvinced that they represented any real contact with a world beyond, that they had any power to foretell the future or affect human life. Nevertheless, she says that he appeared to her a week to the hour after his death, to reassure her that he was still with her and that he believed her life would be successful. From then on, she has taken her occult powers for granted, and for some time now has given readings professionally.

When I talked to Mrs. Myers in her studio apartment in a soaring thirties-modern building on New York's West 73rd Street, she had just finished an hour with a singer she is coaching, and was to follow her hour with me with a young man whose psychic reading indicated to her that he'd had a prior life in Florida. (She had given him clear details about it and what his name had been. He told me later that the person he was supposed to have been did indeed exist, and that the resemblances were remarkable.) She is a colorful and articulate woman in her sixties, who looks as if she puts her wardrobe together with verve and an eye on current fashion, but no great slavishness. She was wearing a bright nylon-knit jersey print with a rope of fake-gold beads and earrings to match, and lipstick-red leather clogs. Her hair was piled on top of her head in a pleasantly vague way. Her studio is full of pictures of her students, and dominated by a grand piano on which rest several photographs of her strikingly handsome late husband.

The interview was not routine! She began by telling me that she had been talking the night before with a woman who has had a long, involved battle over land rights on behalf of some put-upon landowners. Suddenly, seemingly out of nowhere, Mrs. Myers said: "And then *he* said—he makes naughty jokes all the time—'They're the kind of people who'd spend a dime for nipples so that they could become better suckers.' He was beautifully educated, of course, and a descendant of Francis Bacon. . . ." I asked Mrs. Myers who was the "he" she was talking about. "Oh, that's Elliot Bacon, this lady's late husband," she said. "He advises her." It was clear that to Mrs. Myers, Mr. Bacon is a very *present* personality, and the best person to advise

253

his wife about her legal affairs. I asked how she contacted such spirits. She told me that originally she spoke only to her husband (who is still her "contact," bringing her information about other spirits), but recently she has allowed other voices to speak *through* her. "Although," she says, "it's a strange experience to hear such different voices from my body, and to hear them say things that I sometimes think sound *crazy*, just crazy."

Crazy-sounding or not, she has had some remarkable successes. One of her clients was a retired teacher and C.P.A. who had a salt-box house in Connecticut, which he thought of as his last home on earth. "No," pronounced Mrs. Myers one day, "I don't see you living there for very long." "What do you mean? Am I going to die soon?" "No—I see you in the southwest, raising imported cattle and, eventually, horses too." He trusted Mrs. Myers, but thought that in this case she had connected with the wrong future. Within six months, a relative of his died and a cousin insisted that he come to New Mexico to look at a ranch. There was a fast sale of the house in Connecticut, and a new career as a rancher, raising imported cattle and, eventually, horses.

Not all predictions are so dramatic, of course, and Mrs. Myers doesn't claim one-hundred per cent accuracy. In fact, she doesn't claim anything at all, saying that it still startles her to have a connection with the future and with life beyond death. She believes in both, but feels that her role is truly that of *medium*. She's not in direct touch, but has, through her husband, developed a network of spirits from whom she receives messages—which she is often at a loss to interpret. Certainly for a woman artist I know, her predictions proved tidily correct: She was to meet a man whose initials were E. T., who was a writer, and they were to have a long affair. That is exactly what happened, and my friend believes to this day that Mrs. Myers is in touch with *something*.

Whatever her contact with the world beyond has brought to her clients, Mrs. Myers believes that continuing to know her dead husband has given her a "working philosophy," allowing her to succeed where she failed before. She'll tell about her life as a medium and seer in a book to be published in November 1974, *The Spirit That Moves*. Meanwhile, she goes on teaching singers and seeing into a future that for the rest of us remains murky. When I asked Mrs. Myers if I might return for a reading of my own, she said pertly, "Certainly—if you think you can take it!" I wonder. . . .

EXPERIMENTING IN A MEDIUM'S WORLD

It was clear to me from talking to Mrs. Myers that divination through direct contact with the spirit world is a *gift*—and, if the experience of her mother is any indication, not always a *welcome* gift. So it's obvious that for someone with no spontaneous experience, an attempt at trance or a conversation with spirits who haven't been previously forthcoming is probably doomed to failure.

I was impressed, though, by Mrs. Meyers's descriptions of many of her trance states as very much like *free association,* and her statement that her first fully acknowledged occult experience—the one after her husband's death—had come to her through automatic writing. And probably the closest the interested amateur can come to fortune-telling in the manner of the true clairvoyant is by experimenting with a kind of *automatic speech*—free association, the verbal counterpart of automatic writing. As with direct readings from the subject's body and character, the free association technique requires the greatest self-confidence and minimum self-consciousness. The psychic reader uses *intellectual* tools as well as unconscious ones. But the "automatic speaker" is using the deepest level of her unconscious (in the case of the *true* clairvoyant, an unconscious taken over by the spirit of another personality entirely). Whereas the psychic reader must keep her wits about her at all times, the free-associater must "lose" her wits, go deep into her unconscious, and *experience* her subject in order to read his future.

The Method

The most important instrument for this method is the tape recorder. If you're to speak freely and without the usual trappings of coherent conversation, you'll need to record *exactly* what you've said. Then you can listen, interpret, and if necessary *reinterpret*. Of course, a friend with a knowledge of shorthand could take down your utterance, but in free association often the tone is more important than the words themselves, and the silences most important of all. Also, only a tape recorder can give an exact replay of what you *really* said if there is some dispute. So, borrow a tape recorder if you don't own one already, then prepare yourself for the unrehearsed sound of your own voice.

Of course, this method even more than for any other, relaxation is essential. The same exercise that you used for the Tarot will work here. (See page 62.) In this case, the breathing is especially important; your voice-production mechanism must be completely relaxed and ready to respond when you begin talking. After you've completed the exercise, take a series of deep breaths and let them out while *vocalizing*—just let an inarticulate syllable follow your breath. Usually it comes out "Ah-h-h"—or sometimes like a long, groan-like sigh. Try it several times, just to get used to what your voice can do when you're not brightly *projecting*.

Now you're ready for work with the tape recorder. Of course, in a session with friends or with a subject, you will first "take a reading" of the vibrations in the situation, and decide from that, as you did with automatic writing, whether to go on. But during practice, just follow exercises with tape sessions, mood or no mood. You'll begin to *love* the sound of your own voice, and to be quite amazed at your perception about yourself and your friends. (But you'll also find yourself remarkably candid—so *do* erase the tapes!) *Never* pursue a session with others, though, unless the vibrations are *just* right. The voice is a very intimate instrument, and you can't in any way *censor* yourself once you've begun, or you miss the point of the whole method. Be certain that those you're working with (or, in the case of your subject, *for*) are prepared for anything. As Mrs. Myers says, they have to be able to "take it." Otherwise, you'd better stick to some method that allows for *tact* as well as honesty.

Now, sit down with the recorder at hand. The perfect way to sit is on an old-fashioned *chaise longue*, which allows you to relax with your feet up; but remain in an upright position. A good compromise is the sofa—with your feet up, just half-reclining. Don't *hold* the microphone of the tape recorder. Put it somewhere near your head, unless your instrument has a microphone with a necklace attachment. Be sure and do a couple of test sentences so that you know it's picking up your voice. Then lean back, relax, half-close your eyes, and begin.

If you're working to establish a fortune for a subject in the room, it's often best to begin by saying his name over and over. Then say the things that come into your head along with the name—whatever you associate with him, his life, his circumstances. If you get stuck, describe him to yourself. If he has a specific problem he wants help with, or a situation he wants enlightenment about, let your mind rest on that, and then begin associating to it. Don't expect everything to make sense; in fact, don't even listen to yourself—that's what the tape recorder is for. Just let the words fall where they will, without bothering about syntax or sense. *Trust yourself.*

Count on the subject to trust you, too. He must fully understand that you are, as long as you're recording, at the mercy of your own unconscious. You're not making an effort to be nice, or socially acceptable, but to find out what the deepest level of your perceptions know or can divine about your subject. Of course you must not abuse this power and freedom. As long as the tape recorder is running, you must be honest, and your associations must be truly free—but no fair using the occasion to make *conscious* statements that you've been withholding socially. *That* can be a very destructive trip, and is typical of people who use psychic experimentation to hurt other people. (I had a friend—or so I thought her—who used to come to dinner with my lover and me and recount her quite remarkable, deeply colorful dreams. They were full of bright banners, threatening demons, dark caverns, the three of us on spiritual journeys. I became so fascinated with them that I failed for a long time to notice that their one recurring element was a pitting of my lover's talents and passions against *my* seeming lumpishness. After a while I was less fascinated by her dreams and a lot more interested in her intentions toward the man.) Try to keep the associations free of your own conscious interference—even if you are a *tiny* bit tempted to say in a low, sepulchral tone that you've just had a vision of the two of you in Morocco in December. That's cheating!

Here, as with automatic writing, the question of when to stop is a delicate one. Sometimes it's very easy—you suddenly begin to hear the sound of your own words too clearly, and you realize that you're back on the ordinary conscious, conversational level. But often fatigue will decide—your voice will get tired, your audience will become restless, or a certain limit of perception will be reached. For whatever reason, you'll probably be able to feel the moment when you should stop. Experiment in private with your own staying power—you'll know fairly soon what your energies are.

Once the recording is made, the most difficult task of all follows: interpreting what you've said. Here you have a small *social* difficulty—you must listen with objectivity and honesty to your own voice, to opinions and feelings that might embarrass *you* more than they do your subject or anyone else in the room. (Mrs. Myers gave me the impression, for instance, that her "naughty" contact Mr. Bacon used language and made jokes that *she* would never think of articulating in her own private life. You may have a similar experience: "I thought of *that?*") Practice sessions will accustom you to the freedom of your own thoughts and the sound of your own voice expressing them. When the time comes to *interpret,* you can then listen impassively and give a reading based on what was really said, what you *might* have said.

Don't expect a clear, coherent, and grammatical version of anything—past, present, or future. In the unconscious (as you'll remember from the earlier chapter on dreams), there *is* no time sense, and past-present-future will be mixed together. Your job is to do the sorting out. (Mrs. Myers explained that clairvoyance always works both ways—into the past and into the future. It takes a considerable level of concentration to find out which you are dealing with.)

Remember, too, that you are using a highly verbal method, and that words play *tricks. Very* revealing tricks, often. One woman whose lover was the subject of a reading found a long, associative run on the tape that started out with the end of their dinner: "Chocolate mousse . . . soft and sweet, sticky, soft . . . dessert . . . life's dessert, the end of all good things . . . a good thing at the end? . . . desert . . . dry, cold, hot . . . dessert . . . pudding 'n' tame, I'll kiss you again . . . pudding . . . junket . . . Saratoga . . . the old hotel." Of course she was thinking of lovemaking, but the *dessert* that turned into a *desert* was disturbing, and then the *junket* that turned into a trip to Saratoga. She realized that she was afraid her lover would go to one of their favorite weekend places without her, would *desert* her. She concluded, after examining the rest of the tape, that she really didn't have any reason to be afraid of losing him, and then suggested that the two of them go up to Saratoga for the weekend. He thought it was a fine idea.

So be certain that you examine everything you've said for its *ambiguity*. Think over every possible meaning for a word, and don't discount any until you've listened to the tape several times. Each word may have two or more meanings, and you'll have to fit them into a coherent fortune for your subject. Be sure to query him about *private* meanings the words have for him. Your own unconscious may have picked them up. (It is remarkable how much we hear in other people's speech and thought patterns without realizing it.) By the time you've done a careful analysis of your automatic speech, you should come up with some interesting information for your subject. And, though it may not come from sources quite as mysterious as Mrs. Myers's, it will nevertheless have its own fascination, since *you* were the source.

THE MYSTIC MOOD
Automatic speaking—the trance without a trance—requires a wholly different atmosphere from the psychic reading. After all, the dramatic mood and costume of the psychic reader are based on her terrific authority; she might or might not *know* the sources of her delphic powers, but is very, very certain of them, and that they are truly *powers*, not just ravings from the unconscious. But as Ethel Myers says, sometimes the true medium sounds *crazy*—her powers control *her*, not the other way around. Your task is to convince your subject that you and he will move through unknown territory. He must believe that he is safe, and that *you* may need protection from the forces working through you.

The watchword for this method is still *sensual*—but it must be protectable, vulnerable. You may never have thought of wearing a pastel before—well, try it now. And not a pastel *print;* this is the time for the palest of powder blues, the faintest of pinks, the most dawn-like yellow. You can be just as revealing of your body as you are in all the sensual methods—but you must do so innocently, as if provocation could not even *occur* to you. Eyelet, pale blue satin ribbons, masses of dimity ruffles . . . the sweetest *nightgown* look. You're fresh, untouched, just a *little* bit untouchable. You may want to leave your hair down, or better yet, to wear it in a long braid down your back, plaited with ribbons and flowers.

Bare feet for anyone past puberty are a little too wanton to seem truly innocent, so go *demure*—wear old-fashioned Capezio flats in pastels to accent your dress.

Your face must be flowerlike, too—with the palest, rosiest tone your complexion will take, and the whole palette of innocence helping you: rose tones in blusher and lipstick, pastels and white for the eyes. Mascara should be brown or navy—not a touch of black or even *dark* brown anywhere. Avoid the matte finish; you should look dew-touched, shiny new.

Although the practice of speaking out, or speaking deep, as some call it, sounds exotic enough for the depths of night, this is the time to have a daylight session, if you can . . . let all the sun in! Bowls and bowls of fresh flowers, open windows, fruit juice (even if it's laced with gin or vodka), and a general sense of innocent good health and good *sense* are necessary. And arrange for an *uninterrupted* session. (Turn off the phone, or put it in a closet under a pillow.)

Remember that you want to appear innocent, not dotty. You mustn't give the impression that because you're willing to delve into your unconscious for clues to the subject's future, you're not quite *bright*. In fact, the real point is that you are certain enough of your own goodness to take a considerable chance, but one worth taking. You aren't—and mustn't appear to be—operating out of ignorance, but from a position informed enough to know the dangers of the unconscious and still find it valuable.

And of course you *are* taking a chance—because this method makes demands on your honesty and your willingness to say what may not be *exactly* what your subject is ready to hear. The openness of your surroundings and dress is designed to make it clear that you are without guile, under the compulsion of this method to speak out. And that is just the truth.

Chapter Ten

FUTURE-CASTING WITH ASTROLOGY

Professional astrologists tend to be a bit snobbish about the use of astrology to predict the future. They like to mutter about scientific methods, basic characterological data, free will, and are rather defensive about the respectability of their profession. They dislike being lumped with gypsies and occultists, and would prefer to be considered somewhere between an astronomer and psychiatrist.

But the evidence is clear: Most people are interested in astrology not because they want to know if they are basically tempestuous or lethargic, or are likely to have blue or brown eyes, but because they want to know what will happen to them tomorrow. Will that man call? Will the job tension ease? Will a handsome stranger appear at the party on Saturday night? The avid reading of daily horoscopes in newspapers—which are based on the roughest information and are notoriously vague—confirms that people are interested in astrology for one overriding reason: to know the future.

I don't see anything shifty about using astrology to make specific predictions about the future. The astrologists who object usually want to keep their business untainted by the irrational—but as you probably know if you've read the earlier chapters in this book and tried some of the methods, fortune-telling lays no claim to being rational or scientific. Quite the reverse! It aims to give you access to irrational, psychic forces that bear no relation to the laws of physics or to logical cause-and-effect. And very often, it works!

So, if you can believe that the random fall of cards, coins, dice, candle-drippings, or apple peels can tell the future . . . if you accept the premise that our lives are foreshadowed in the lines on our palms and the bumps on our skulls . . . you should have no trouble at all accepting the far more likely possibility that the sun and its planets give off forces that affect our bodies and minds from the moment we're born, and that these forces powerfully influence the way we act and feel.

Probably you already know a lot about astrology. The reticent English used to criticize us nosy Americans for asking, when we've been introduced to someone, "What do you do?" But now a very common getting-to-know-you question is probably, "What's your sign?" You doubtless know that the question refers to your sun sign—the zone of the zodiac in which the sun was when you were born. In fact, I wouldn't be surprised if you have a fairly sophisticated knowledge of your qualities as a Scorpio girl with Libra rising and her moon in Aquarius, or whatever. It's hard to escape an astrological education when the facts are all around you—in the newspapers, in Cosmopolitan and other magazines that print a monthly horoscope, and in the many marvelous books on the subject. So, what we're not going to do in this chapter is explain to you all the qualities of each sun sign. For that information—as well as many more details about casting and interpreting a horoscope and so on—we refer you to the books and magazines listed on page 275. Some are quite seriously professional; others are frankly for fun . . . and we recommend them all (or as many as you care to read).

What this chapter will do is tell you how to use the information in those books, in your own head and insights, and in the pages to come, in order to read a fortune for someone—much like the fortunes you've learned to tell with other methods. Ready?

THE MYSTIC MOOD

By all means use the techniques we'll teach you to delight your lover and friends . . . but this is *one* case where we're not going to suggest that you plan a special evening to show off your powers. Astrology is *so* popular that some people are a bit fed up with talk of signs and aspects and retrogrades, and would just as soon be invited over for an evening of taped speeches by the treasurer of your city council. Furthermore, the idea of an astrological décor, with a sun-and-planets mobile and you in a dress hand-painted with the signs of the zodiac, is a little junior-high, don't you think? Instead, we suggest that you lie in wait with your skills—and then *spring* them on the most receptive subjects some evening when you're sitting around talking about each other's personalities or futures.

Do keep the necessary materials on hand. Most useful is a current ephemeris—a chart showing exactly where each planet is at every moment of the month ahead, and exactly the hour and minute at which it moves from one sign to another. (Monthly horoscope magazines, available on every newsstand for about fifty cents, give you this table, along with a bonus of information about what the motions of these planets will *mean*. (For instance, "Venus parallel Mars . . . 10:23 A.M. Eastern Standard Time . . . Temperamental precedents should not be set in any interpersonal relationship.") The entries give the times in all the Standard Time Zones, and tell how long the prediction or advice should be taken note of. These little books are a marvelous bargain—far more complete, naturally, than the ones which supposedly forecast your entire *year*. They also include horoscopes for each sun sign for each day of the month, plus heaps of other information.

You might also keep on hand a longer-range ephemeris (see page 284), useful for checking the sun signs of people who don't know theirs. (Since the planets are in a *slightly* different position at the beginning of each year, the standard sun-sign categories—Aries, March 21 through April 20, and so on—are not always precise, depending on the *year* you were born.) With a long-range ephemeris, you can also find the signs that *all* the planets were in at the person's moment of birth—assuming he *knows* his moment of birth. With *those*, you can get even more detailed information from astrology books.

Finally, by all means have at least one of the comprehensive books on astrology that you'll find listed on page 284.

You might strew these rather *carelessly* around your apartment—on the coffee table alongside *The New York Times* and the latest Simenon novel, or beside your bed for a late-night consultation. Be casual about introducing the subject. If people are interested—and they probably will be when they notice the books containing untold clues about their fascinating selves—they'll probably ask you what the stars foretell for them that month. Then, you charmingly oblige with a fortune—and if you're wearing a star-stenciled T-shirt or a twinkly crescent-moon necklace, so be it!

THE QUICKIE SUN-SIGN LOVE-WORK FORTUNE

People born under a particular sun sign *do* share basic characteristics. And even though those characteristics may be modified by the positions of the other planets, the *place* of birth, and all the environmental factors that shape a human personality, a sun-sign prediction is (claims astrologer Linda Goodman) eighty to ninety percent accurate. So you can tell a helpful, insightful fortune on sun-sign data alone . . . and if you *know* the subject, your intuition may make up the remaining ten or twenty per cent!

Now, the most common questions put to astrologers have to do with *love* and *work*. From sun-sign information alone, you can get a fairly sound idea of how an individual will behave under stress in either of those areas. (A Capricorn, for instance, is a plodder. In an office, he or she will be the one who cleverly revises the entire filing system after thinking through all the problems for six months; and while Capricorns may not be shooting stars, they're inexorably ambitious, moving slowly but sure-footedly up the professional ladder. In a difficult situation, they dig in, and take each setback as a position from which to launch a new upward bound. A chart of their progress might look like something you'd see at a stockbroker's, full of zig-zags—but the over-all result is *progress*.)

So, given a few facts about the basic reactions of each sun sign in each area of prime concern, you can formulate a fortune in answer to a specific question. On pages 263 to 270, we've given you a summary of these tendencies. Here's a sample of how you might use it:

Your friend Mara, a Capricorn, has been seeing a man who's a Cancer, and the sexual sparks have been lighting up her life (and, vicariously, *yours*!) She comes to you in tears, having just discovered that her lover is seeing another woman, a long-standing love. He has confessed this to Mara and suggested that they split, because the situation is "unfair" to her. How should Mara react? What will happen?

You consult the readings for Love for Capricorn and Cancer. You find that Capricorns are tremendously vulnerable and need *masses* of affection, but tend to put up a brave front and feign total independence. They also like to "come first" in a lover's life. Cancer, you find, is incurably romantic and domestic, believes in "true love" with all the trimmings—and cries real tears when disappointed (yes, even if he's a man!) But perversely, he'll edge away if he feels pursued—like his zodiac symbol, the crab.

From these simple facts, it shouldn't be too hard to construct a helpful fortune—though not a very encouraging one. Mara's man is obviously

262

hooked into his old girlfriend for some sentimental, Gatsby-ish reason, and for however long it lasts, he'll be under that spell. Mara, however, is likely to react by pleading sweet reason with him, suggesting that he see them both—What could be more sensible?—and that she wouldn't mind a bit. But she *will* mind, eventually—she'll want to come first in his life. What should Mara do, then? Accept her own desire for love, and admit that right *now* this man won't be capable of giving it. If she retreats with dignity, she may find that Cancer's interest will be piqued; his sign is the Crab, and he moves emotionally the way a crab erratically lumbers across the beach—pursuing an object until it notices him, then skittering away, then moving back toward it again. However, since Capricorns tend to be emotional and loving *without* being sentimental, it's unlikely that this relationship will ever prosper. Mara will have contempt for her Cancer's sloshy moods, and he will probably resent her genuine desire for independence, preferring a more *clinging* girl.

Now, if you have some *personal* insights into your friend's character and emotions, by all means toss them into the fortune-mix. They can only add to its accuracy.

When asking the Love-Work Fortune, be sure your subject asks a question about a *specific* situation. "What should I do with my life?" will *not* yield a helpful reply . . . and for that question, you should send him to a professional astrologer for a complete horoscope. (Or learn to chart one yourself, and give it to him for his birthday!) Instead, encourage the subject to ask questions that apply to particular problems in the areas of love and work: "Will I get a raise soon?" "How can I handle my jealousy over my lover's new friend?"

QUICK
LOVE-WORK
READINGS
FOR THE TWELVE SUN-SIGNS

These readings will guide you to your subject's tendencies to behave in certain ways under stress, when conflict strikes. Most people are likely to ask for a fortune that will help them resolve a current problem. These analyses are vital keys to how each sign of the zodiac will react under pressure in the all-important areas of love and work.

ARIES MARCH 21-APRIL 20
LOVE / Aries people were born in the *first* sign of the zodiac, and they remain emotional babies all their lives. They want—now! Cross them at your own risk. If they flare up, they'll cool off with equal ease; but insult their pride and they *walk*. Aries is too direct to be bothered with the strategies of mating—your Aries lover will never lie or manipulate. They're romantics, try to be faithful

263

and expect the same in return, may even *deceive themselves* to cling to true-love illusions. *As pursuer:* Aries is happiest taking the lead. *Pursued:* Aries loses interest. *When it's over:* Aries will *say* so—icily.

WORK / Aries people go bonkers if they feel their hands or minds are tied in an uncreative, subservient job. They're natural leaders, pioneers, love the heat of intellectual battle. (An Aries can back-talk the boss and win!) *Office politics:* Aries is too direct to be shrewd politician—always blurting out the truth, incapable of biding time. *Money:* An Aries will probably never strike it rich or inch his way to a corporate presidency by being responsible and reliable. But he'll end up with the most exciting, creative job in the company—and may bolt suddenly to a top job through his powerhouse energy and ego.

TAURUS APRIL 21-MAY 21

LOVE / Taurus is a stay-at-home. His devotion is the flip side of his stubbornness. Tauruses make wonderfully faithful lovers—and when they sense a change in the direction of the romantic winds, they dig in their heels and produce incredible staying power. Never *push* a Taurus—the stoicism may suddenly *give,* and a seemingly insignificant final straw will incite a fierce attack. *As pursuer:* Taurus would rather not, may even be sexually passive. *Pursued:* if flattered, Taurus will entertain your advances—but doesn't like to *noodged. When it's over:* Tauruses clam up, cross their arms, wait for the rejected one to get the idea. If *they're* being rejected, it takes a while to sink in.

WORK / Tauruses deliberately, slowly *accumulate* their power and possessions and privileges, will put in long hours for a desired promotion. They don't crave action particularly—flash and drive aren't part of their style. *Office politics:* Taurus's best negotiating weapon is his take-it-or-leave-it attitude . . . but he had better remember that the answer will sometimes be "Okay, I'll leave it." He's good at the waiting game and probably won't get embroiled in the tackier forms of political intrigue unless someone attacks him *personally.* Then he'll lash out—usually from a position of power. *Money:* Taurus people are savers, and love security too much to let themselves get strapped for funds. If a sudden wipe-out occurs, Tauruses may really crack.

GEMINI MAY 22—JUNE 21

LOVE / Geminis in love are *infuriating*—now you see them, now you don't. Broken dates are not a sign of cooling passion, just part of Gemini's changeable nature. They love excitement, challenge, fun, get itchy at expressions of deep passion or overseriousness. They play the field, may even be promiscuous—but won't lie about their activities, and are rarely jealous. *As pursuer:* Geminis like to be tantalizing. They give and then take back, get a charge out of *confusing* the object of their affections. *Pursued:* Geminis bore easily, and respond best to someone whose merry-go-round temperament is like their own. Seem single-minded and kiss dear Gemini good-bye. *When it's over:* Motives are always obscure with this will-o'-the-wisp sign. Sarcasm from them usually suggests love is on the wane.

WORK / The charm, creativity, and flash of Geminis conceal very little actual *drive.* They hate routine and time-clock-punching, and try to cut corners (sometimes dishonestly!) They're goof-offs—great for office morale but undependable in a crisis. They may take hold brilliantly, or they may flee to Nassau for two weeks—you never know. *Office politics:* Geminis are the glibbest members of the zodiac, could talk Las Vegas out from under Howard Hughes. They are likely to have a series of office affairs going—which may provide them with loyal allies *or* disgruntled former lovers just waiting to get revenge. *Money:* Too restless to build an empire, Geminis don't *have* to . . . they can talk money out of anyone. They also write a lot of bad checks!

CANCER JUNE 22—JULY 23

LOVE / Cancers are the mushiest, soppiest, most romantic members of the zodiac. They believe in True Love, Fidelity, Little Houses with Picket Fences Just Built for Two, and all the other old-fashioned virtues . . . which doesn't mean they aren't extremely sexy! Emotional conflict sends them crashing into a truly depressed mood . . . Cancers cry passionately (even *male* Cancers!) But when the moon changes, they're up again, laughing that infectious lunar giggle. They want to be loved, gentled, but left *alone* when they hurt; they don't like to reveal their emotions very profoundly to anyone. *As pursuer:* Cancer plays a to-and-fro game, just like the crab scuttling along the beach. He'll chase you as long as you pretend not to notice. He will *lunge* only if it looks like some rival may seize the prey. *Pursued:* Cancer skitters away, but may return if left alone. *When it's over:* Cancers go all weepy, have trouble breaking off because they *identify* so with the rejected one. They usually delay so long that it is usually the *other* party who has to deliver the *coup de grâce.*

WORK / Cancer people work to build up security and respect in their chosen profession. They have terrible trouble letting go—tend to hang in there and try to save an unsalvageable situation. Self-doubt nags at them—usually unjustifiably. *Office politics:* Cancers are oversensi-

tive, can disrupt the office with pouting resentments if they feel misused. Pettiness is a weak spot—the worker who keeps a secret dossier of a rival's every tiny mistake and presents it to the boss at bonus-time is likely to be a Cancer. *Money:* Conservative Cancer is a hoarder; generous but never a spendthrift, he's saving to buy property or Pollack paintings, and is unlikely to take financial risks.

LEO JULY 24—AUGUST 23

LOVE/ Vulnerable to flattery, the lion wants to be adored. Leos always seem to be in love, or picking up the pieces of a shattered romance. They like to do the courting—showering the beloved with expensive gifts, lavish compliments. In return, they demand fidelity, and jealousy is the chink in their shiny armor. *As pursuer:* Leo loves the role of teacher and mentor, is a marvelous guide through the world of passions. But these proud people are a little suspicious if they don't meet at first with a display of resistance. They like the process of winning out after a brisk round of fireworks. Then they demand submission. *Pursued:* Leos lap up the flattery, then go for someone more challenging. *When it's over:* Scenes and reconciliations are his *meat,* but when Leo is truly finished he'll make a proud exit—setting up the situation so it will seem that *he* is the one with the initiative and the upper hand.

WORK / Leos adore importantsounding titles and positions of authority. They thrive on expense accounts and deference. When they're asked to take charge, their egos *insist* that they measure up. *Office politics:* Leos can't bear to be criticized or—what is worse—ignored. They hate secret intrigues, *must* know what's going on. When crossed, they'll bring all their power to bear—and it may be considerable. Leos generally have allies—thanks to their charm—but should look out for resentful underlings of whom they've been too demanding. *Money:* Leo workers may sacrifice a raise for a title with the word "Director" in it. They're given to grand gestures with money, like to be lavish in order to make themselves feel important. That Leo who's always taking twenty people to dinner on his expense account isn't trying to *buy* love—he's enjoying himself, while knowing that the courting will probably pay off. Small change doesn't interest him—Leos forget that they borrowed cab fare from the receptionist, they buy her a cashmere sweater-set for her birthday.

VIRGO
AUGUST 24-SEPTEMBER 23
LOVE / Virgos are afraid of being dependent on anyone, and don't open up easily. They are unsentimental, and often frightened by people who overemote. Romantic crises do not seem to move them; they are cool, until they decide to declare themselves. Once they do, they're loyal and thoughtful, rarely promiscuous. *As pursuer:* Virgo will clearly state his case—simply and honestly. *Pursued:* If Virgo isn't interested, he'll be stony and aloof— and *no* tactics will change his mind. The only way to catch a Virgo is by being *perfect*—smart, together, serene—and placing yourself casually in his line of vision. *When it's over:* Virgo makes clean breaks— honest and kind. The poor things do *suffer* afterward, but try not to let on and never use their pain to manipulate others.

WORK / Virgos are practical, unbelievably good at details, and get nervous if they think they're being promoted beyond their abilities. (Who ever heard of anyone doing *that*?) They don't like insecurity, and are the best people for checking facts and planning elaborate campaigns

where short-cuts would be disastrous. In a crisis, Virgo will be the one who knows exactly what to do—he's been meticulously studying the situation for months. *Office politics:* Virgos are too ethical to play devious games, and often find themselves at a loss when the infighting gets rough. Generally they've done their job so well that they're immune to attack—lucky them, since they're too outspoken to play underhanded tricks to get ahead. *Money:* Virgos are almost *unnaturally* fair-minded about money, and will expect to be paid in exact proportion to what they accomplish. They get edgy at the thought of the unemployment line, and may tend not to take risks that might bring them a financial windfall. They hate accepting favors, will have to be practically on skid row before asking for a loan.

LIBRA
SEPTEMBER 24-OCTOBER 23
LOVE / Their symbol is the Scales, and Libras are not so much *balanced* in their emotions as always engaged in the act of weighing advantages and disadvantages. "Maybe we should get married. On the other hand, it might be more wise to separate." That's mind-boggling Libratalk . . . and you can imagine how helpful it is in a crisis! Since Libra is ruled by the planet Venus, it's the most seductive sign in the zodiac; and all Libras are romantic charmers, skilled at every game in the book of love. They play the field with gusto. *As pursuer:* Libras let you *think* you're the active partner. If you resist, be prepared for a watertight argument fit for presentation in the Supreme Court. *Pursued:* Love *offered* is just as interesting to a Libra as the love he seeks out. But if the affair gets rocky, Libra won't hesitate to remind you, with unflappable logic, that *you* started it. *When it's over:*

Libras can forget easily, go merrily on to the next love with almost *insulting* ease. A few are susceptible to manipulators who threaten suicide if abandoned, and will often stay unhappily tied.

WORK / Libra workers are brilliant strategists and negotiators, have lots of creative ideas that need to be weighed and selected. But they get unsettled by adverse office conditions—a cranky secretary, a phone that won't give a dial tone, a mudbrown carpet. They can make enemies by brilliantly demolishing someone else's ideas without realizing that *hurt* is being inflicted by their devastating points. *Office politics:* Like Geminis, Venus-ruled Libras may get embroiled in sex-in-the-office trouble. They are too nervous to enjoy overt friction and yelling, but may plunge into an ideological disagreement with zest for driving home a few rational points. Libras rarely hold grudges. *Money:* Fair-minded with money, as with everything, Libras rarely have financial troubles. They do like to spend on beautiful surroundings and party-giving, dress fashionably, and then balance the checkbook neatly.

SCORPIO
OCTOBER 24-NOVEMBER 22
LOVE / Scorpio is the most sexual sign of the zodiac, and its passions run from the spiritual to the morbidly decadent. Scorpio people are sensual and explosive, sometimes cruel, and madly jealous. They do not flatter—they *take* what they want. Under pressure, they cannot bear to lose, muster all their courage, and *never* crumple in self-pity. *As pursuer:* Scorpios may project an icy cool, while secretly plotting the best attack. They often tease, as a prelude to conquering. Another Scorpio ploy is to strip the sought-after-one of all defenses, while preserving his own

dignity and safety. When rejected, Scorpios sometimes turn sadistic, say brutal things. *Pursued:* It's hard to catch a Scorpio unaware, but he may be tempted by someone who seems superior and forbidden-fruit mysterious. *When it's over:* Scorpios sever relationships as passionately as they form them. They conceal disappointments, but can seethe with anger for *years* if denied the satisfaction of crushing anybody who displeases them.

WORK / Even if they're employed by a large corporation, Scorpios work for their own reasons, and strike out unmercifully at anyone who thwarts their plans. They're loyal—as long as nobody asks them to sacrifice for the greater good of the company. Scorpios are so fearless that they can calculate exactly when to demand what they want—and aren't afraid to call a bluff. After all, they *can* always leave. *Office politics:* Scorpios are often the *instigators*—ruthless and cunning, though they're smart enough to *conceal* those qualities. But they'll also take an amazing amount of guff from people they need as allies. Scorpios are like brilliant poker players—with all the odds calculated in advance. *Money:* With that far-seeing plan for the future, Scorpio is unlikely to be in want. Whatever he decided to do, he'll come out at the top of the heap. He *never* forgets a debt—it gets repaid double.

SAGITTARIUS
NOVEMBER 23-DECEMBER 21
LOVE / Sagittarians are not the *smoothest* lovers in the zodiac. But they are always sincere, idealistic, and filled with boundless enthusiasm. It's easy to mistake their ardor for more than it actually *is*— free and casual. Sagittarians don't conceal their true feelings on

purpose—they couldn't; under pressure, they trip over their tongues and utter some tactless version of the truth; but they often seem to be leading a lover on, because they *assume* everyone is as flirtatious as they are. *As Pursuer:* Sagittarians seek variety—not just sex, but intellectual companionship, someone who'll be a pal in high-spirited adventures. But they're rarely *looking* to settle down. They don't crush easily, and if rejected will sail blithely off in pursuit of friendlier game. *Pursued:* Nothing turns off Sagittarians more than claustrophobic encroachments on their freedom. But you can follow them anywhere and they'll put up with you—as long as you keep a lighthearted temperament and don't puncture their enthusiasms. Sagittarians need a lot of rope—and prefer companions who are just as easygoing. *When it's over:* Sagittarius says so—with blunt tenderness. If you've been a pain in the neck with recriminations and possessiveness, he may be a touch *acid*.

WORK / Their rambunctious idealism and almost *nosy* curiosity make Sagittarians highly visible in any office. Under pressure, they don't fall apart—instead they ask millions of questions that drive everyone else to distraction, and then come up with a bold solution that may be the biggest flub *ever* . . . or a dramatic save-the-day success. Sagittarians don't think *small*. But they should beware of a tendency to promise what they can't deliver. *Office politics:* Because Sagittarians are so indiscreet, they occasionally set off tremors that could have been avoided. Other co-workers find themselves trailing around patching up Sagittarian blunders. But this sign has too much integrity to be petty or unethical, and will openly attack office shrewdies with all the righteousness of a Grand Inquisitor. *Money:* Gambling may

be Sagittarius's downfall. And even a financially conservative Sagittarian will always choose the free-and-easy life of temporary jobs to riches and security that hamper his liberty and wanderlust.

CAPRICORN
DECEMBER 22-JANUARY 20
LOVE / Capricorns don't like to show their vulnerability. But underneath their cool, shy exteriors, they're loving and passionate, and need affection. Under emotional pressure, they pretend not to care what happend, and cultivate a cynical veneer. That's a clue that they're feeling exposed and sensitive. Just because Capricorns don't find it easy to show affection doesn't mean they don't feel it—*au contraire. As pursuer:* Capricorns love to feel independent and in control, but are incapable of being totally forthcoming about their emotions. They need a little help. *Pursued:* Most Capricorn people succumb to flattery and verbal expressions of love, since they find it so hard to give these. They may cover their embarrassment and delight by a display of casualness, but expect others to *understand. When it's over:* Capricorns are no better at sounding off *negatively* than at making passionate declarations of love. They sulk and act contemptuous until the unwanted presence disappears.

WORK / The symbol of Capricorn is the goat, and that animal's nimble ability to leap from crag to crag just about sums up Capricorn's career pattern. Sure-footed, looking carefully before leaping, Capricorns move upward, step by step. Each setback or advance is consolidated firmly before another jump is made. Capricorns are intolerant of incompetents, maybe because they're so good at conscientious work and hair-splitting details. They get awfully upset if they make a mistake—

and usually don't. *Office politics:* Capricorns see political intrigues as time-wasting, inefficient annoyances. They keep aloof from squabbles, and growl impatiently if distracted from duty by tales of who's nibbling at whose heels in the race for creative director. Capricorn already *knows* who'll win out—probably himself. *Money:* Most Capricorn people work more for status and professional esteem than for cold cash. They need respect most of all. Some are stingy, but respond generously to anyone in *real* need.

AQUARIUS
JANUARY 21-FEBRUARY 19
LOVE / Aquarians hate to conform, and generally have the most liberated relationships of anyone in the zodiac. Nothing is too far-out for the Aquarian personality—group sex, multiple love affairs, homosexuality, platonic intimacies, even marriage—though most avoid the latter like poison. Mystery is a potent erotic scent for an Aquarian. They're pretty mysterious themselves, too—always holding back their feelings until the right moment, which may be twenty years later. Aquarians aren't tormented by jealousy, but may arouse it in others easily, since they make friends everywhere. *As pursuer:* Aquarius people seem to look right into your soul. But they don't let on whether the interest is purely academic, or something more torrid. They often lose someone they love because they are so inscrutable about their feelings, and the someone finally shrugs and moves on. *Pursued:* You can't fool an Aquarian with love-games; he knows you too well, and see through every trick. The best approach is total honesty, with lots of emphasis on *friendship.* Aquarians will answer a direct question once, but have little patience with disingenuous ploys. *When it's over:* Aquarian people are the ones who say, "Can't we still be friends?" And they mean it!

WORK / Aquarians have marvelous minds and very little ambition. They are great tinkerers, dabblers, job-changers—love learning a skill, working their way to the top, and moving on to a new field. But while they're around, they're conscientious and perceptive. They may seem remote for a few weeks—then, when pressure hits, they emerge with some dazzling idea for saving the company three million dollars or re-engineering the water-cooler to increase efficiency. *Office politics:* Aquarians really can't be bothered with such worldly matters. Besides, they'd never give away a secret, rarely make enemies, and are on their way to some new job or profession long before power-struggles can set in at the *old* place. *Money:* This commodity is well down on the Aquarian's list of priorities. He may invent a new kind of color film and forget to register the patent, or sacrifice to the bone in order to become the first human to wrap the Empire State Building in cellophane. You'll see Aquarians in the newspapers, but not at the bank.

PISCES
FEBRUARY 20-MARCH 20
LOVE / Because Pisces is the twelfth and last sign of the zodiac, it's an enigmatic blend of all the others. So a Pisces person is never easy to understand. In love, they're romantic to the point of impracticality—always rushing off to island idylls without a thought of the bill, suggesting marriage and babies when neither partner has a steady job. Pisces people have many friends of both sexes, which can make a lover somewhat *jealous;* but usually when a Pisces actually lies, he's just doing it to keep you on your toes. *As pursuer:* A Pisces is not as self-confident as ap-

pearances suggest. He covers up his fears and insecurities with a smile, and seduces others with a compassionate willingness to hear their problems. *Pursued:* Good cheer, admiration, and encouragement will attract a Pisces. So will any dramatically romantic gesture—like sending flowers to a *male* Pisces, or sending a female Pisces a really *gushy* love letter. Never succumb to a Pisces's invitation to lay all your woes on his shoulders—he'll secretly be depressed by your presence. *When it's over:* Pisces people know the word "Maybe," but rarely commit themselves to "Yes" or "No."

WORK / Pisces people have dreamy visions of their place in the world. They want to accomplish something great and socially useful—and they end up as Albert Schweitzer or the man who rolls round the coffee wagon at 10 A.M. They can miss out on opportunities because of their indecisiveness. *Office politics:* Pisces people shrink from competitive situations with horror. But they may unthinkingly drop a secret, and create an unintentional mess. *Money:* Nobody in his right mind would give Pisces a high credit rating! Pisces people are so other-worldly that the value of money *escapes* them.

THE JAPANESE ZODIAC

Here's an interesting variation on the more familiar Western horoscope. The signs refer to twelve-year cycle; so you can do a simple horoscope just by knowing the *year* of someone's birth.

Japanese legend has it that on one New Year's Day, Buddha announced that every animal to come and pay respects to him would receive a special gift: a year would be named after it. Twelve animals came:

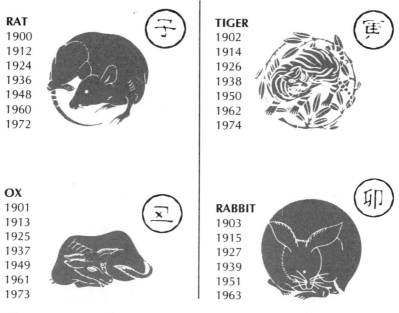

RAT
1900
1912
1924
1936
1948
1960
1972

TIGER
1902
1914
1926
1938
1950
1962
1974

OX
1901
1913
1925
1937
1949
1961
1973

RABBIT
1903
1915
1927
1939
1951
1963

270

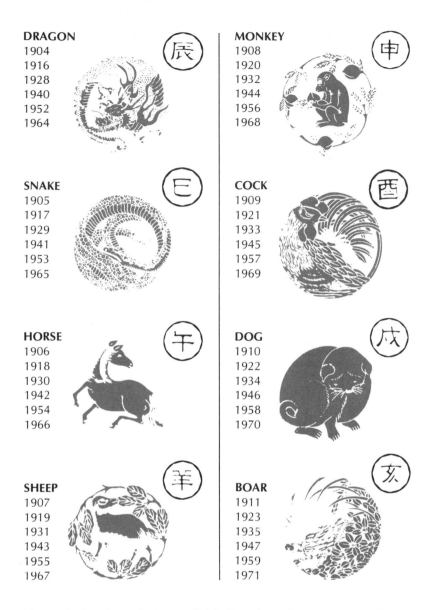

DRAGON
1904
1916
1928
1940
1952
1964
辰

MONKEY
1908
1920
1932
1944
1956
1968
申

SNAKE
1905
1917
1929
1941
1953
1965
巳

COCK
1909
1921
1933
1945
1957
1969
酉

HORSE
1906
1918
1930
1942
1954
1966
午

DOG
1910
1922
1934
1946
1958
1970
戌

SHEEP
1907
1919
1931
1943
1955
1967
羊

BOAR
1911
1923
1935
1947
1959
1971
亥

The predictions for each sign are divided into three phases, corresponding to phases in the person's life-span. These are not limited to an arbitrary number of years, but refer to general trends in the subject's life.

THE YEAR OF THE RAT

First phase: Good fortune, but a tendency to be gossipy and selfish will limit friendships. **Second phase:** A wild gamble or a love affair in which too much is risked will cause Rat People to lose money they have saved. **Third phase:** A comfortable, easy life, in which the subject learns to be generous by deeply loving another person.

Best lovers: Dragon, Monkey, or Ox People.

THE YEAR OF THE OX

First phase: A happy, easy-going time, marked by success achieved through patience and reticence. **Second phase:** Stubborness and a reluctance to admit failure will cause others to lose respect for the Ox Person. Also, since these people are emotionally cool, unwilling to understand the feelings of others, they will have love and family problems during this time. **Third phase:** Mellow years, in which the subject may rise quite high in a field that requires eloquent public-speaking.

Best lovers: Snake, Cock, and Rat People.

THE YEAR OF THE TIGER

First phase: Occasional struggles with authority, but in general a fortunate time. (The Japanese believe Tiger People are extemely lucky, since the tiger represents the greatest worldly power.) Credit may be given undeservedly. **Second phase:** The Tiger Person's short temper, suspiciousness, and indecision will cause trouble that may carry over into the third phase. **Third phase:** Careful handling of problems will win the Tiger Person great admiration from colleagues.

Best lovers: Horse, Dragon, or Dog People.

THE YEAR OF THE RABBIT

All three phases of the Rabbit Person's life tend to be quite calm and happy, although they can succumb to fits of melancholy for insubstantial reasons. They should take care not to be too gossipy. They make good businessmen, since they combine a shrewd gift for gambling with a conservative care for detail. Rabbit People, however, are somewhat emotionally detached all their lives, need to learn reaching out.

Best lovers: Sheep, Bear, and Dog People.

THE YEAR OF THE DRAGON

First phase: Overcautiousness may keep Dragon People from achieving much at this time. They don't like to admit that they need help, or express their feelings. And they hold back from emotional involvements. **Second phase:** Good and bad fortune will come and go repeatedly, giving the subject much concern about when his life will settle *down*. Overexcitability, tempestuousness, stubbornness need to be rooted out. Temptations to follow an evil way of life must be resisted. **Third phase:** Great peace and accomplishment. Dragon People will be much loved by others in later life, though they may never marry.

Best lovers: Rat, Snake, Monkey, or Cock People.

THE YEAR OF THE SNAKE

First phase: Snake People are born beauties. (In Japan, it is considered a great compliment to a woman to tell her she is *mi-bijin*—a Snake Beauty.) But they must learn not to be so selfish and vain about their good fortune. **Second phase:** Snake People are determined to succeed, but their intensity and ambition leads them to *overdo*. They are very wise, but must learn not to doubt everyone *else's* opinions. **Third phase:** This is the worst stage for a Snake Person. Marital or family troubles may cause great upheaval.

   Best lovers: Ox and Cock People.

THE YEAR OF THE HORSE

   First phase: Many projects will fail, and the Horse Person will become extremely impatient. He may also break away from his family too early, in an unwise grab for total independence. **Second phase:** Blind passions and an unwillingness to take advice cause further trouble. **Third phase:** Final success will come. Horse People like to be around the theater or other public entertainments, and act like superstars themselves. But their skill in financial matters will blend with these interests for a solid career. And Horse People *always* win at love.

   Best lovers: Tiger, Dog, and Sheep People.

THE YEAR OF THE COCK

   First phase: Up-and-down fortune and an over-eagerness for independence will bring troubles. **Second phase:** Cock People like to seem adventurous and devil-may-care, but aren't equipped for this sort of life, and become disappointed when they over-reach themselves. They may make absurd plans that are doomed to fail. **Third phase:** Cycles of wealth and poverty may occur, but Cock People obtain the esteem of others for their direct speech and exciting personalities.

   Best lovers: Ox, Snake, and Dragon People.

THE YEAR OF THE DOG

   First phase: Dog People are born with a deep sense of loyalty, responsibility, and honesty. They will have to conquer an immature tendency to be sarcastic and critical. **Second phase:** Money will always be available, although Dog People care little for it. They will spend much of their time battling for idealistic goals. They'll have trouble in emotional and social relationships, as they tend to be withdrawn and aloof. **Third phase:** Good fortune and the high regard of others will inspire the Dog Person to succeed either in business or in some work that serves others.

   Best lovers: Horse, Tiger, and Rabbit People.

THE YEAR OF THE SHEEP

   First phase: Shy and negative, the people born in this year will suffer emotional problems in early life. **Second phase:** Sheep People, with their elegant manners and generous natures, will be very popular, but will still feel indecisive about what to do with their lives. Nevertheless, they will never lack material security. **Third phase:** Extemely good luck will help Sheep People achieve a career that is highly satisfying—probably in the arts—and a passionate love life.

   Best lovers: Rabbit, Boar, and Horse People.

THE YEAR OF THE MONKEY

First phase: This person's eccentric, endearing charm will make him well loved, though he's easily discouraged when he doesn't succeed at a task. **Second phase:** This is the worst time in life for Monkey People. Plans won't work out, and confusion about a direction for life will set in. Love affairs will not go smoothly. **Third phase:** Great skill at manipulating money, facts, and other people will bring success in almost any field. Great fame may even come to these people. Their love affairs will be passionate and quite numerous.

Best lovers: Dragon and Rat People.

THE YEAR OF THE BOAR

First phase: Difficulties will arise—a scarcity of friends, a shyness that must be overcome. Boar People don't like asking for help and will unwisely try to solve their problems alone. **Second phase:** Emotional problems with a loved one will occur, but the Boar Person's tremendous inner strength will help him survive. An unethical rival may also take advantage of him in business or in a lawsuit. **Third phase:** Peace and contentment will come as a result of intellectual studies and a few very close friends. An affectionate, loving circle of companions and family will surround the Boar Person, rewarding his courage and kindness.

Best lovers: Rabbit and Sheep People.

BOOKS AND
PARAPHERNALIA

On the following pages, you'll find a list of sources for reading and other materials, arranged by chapter. One of the problems with finding books on these subjects is that so many of the good ones are out of print, or at least difficult to come by. (Most of the books listed here are easily available and in print, but I couldn't resist including a few of the more fascinating ones that aren't.) If you have trouble finding a particular book at your local stores or library, your best bet is to write to Samuel Weiser, Inc., 734 Broadway, New York, N.Y. 10012. Weiser's deals exclusively in books on the occult, and has, as well, a selection of fortune-telling gear, such as a large range of Tarot packs. Their complete catalogue will be sent to you on request.

Another good (and sometimes very amusing) source of both books and paraphernalia is the Zolar Publishing Co., Inc., 333 West 52nd Street, New York, N.Y. 10019. Zolar bills himself as the World's Most Popular Astrologer. His line includes a number of books that are highly detailed, if somewhat primitive, and a lot of other items that are almost irresistible: Gambler's Spray, Love Soap, and, of course, crystal balls in a number of sizes. His catalogue is available on request, too.

General Reading
The following books will give you an overview of the world of fortune-telling; and most cover details that we have not talked about in the text . . . on the assumption that we've *thoroughly* whetted your appetite for the mystic arts and that you'll continue to explore at least *some* in depth!

The Complete Gypsy Fortune Teller, by Kevin Martin. Putnam (N.Y.), 1970; $3.50 (hard cover).

A Dictionary of Symbols, by J. E. Cirlot. Philosophical Library (N.Y.), 1962; $12.00 (hard cover). This book is especially useful if you are interested in the symbols of fortune-telling, many of which are common to several methods. Cirlot lists them alphabetically and traces their origins in the art and archeology of various cultures, as well as in numerous occult methods.

A Manual of Occultism, by Sepharial. Weiser (N.Y.), 1972; $4.00 (hard cover).

The Mysteries and Secrets of Magic, by C. J. S. Thompson. Olympia Press (N.Y.), 1972; $1.45 (paper).

Oriental Fortune-Telling, by Jimmei Shimano. Tuttle (Rutland, Vt.), 1965; $3.25 (hard cover).

Psychomancy and Crystal Gazing, by William W. Atkinson. Yoga Publication Society (Des Plaines, Ill.); $1.00 (paper).

Raphael's Book of Fate. Tower (N.Y.), 1966; $.75 (paper).

Romany Magic, by Charles Bowness. Weiser (N.Y.); $4.50 (hard cover).

Sex and the Supernatural, by Benjamin Walker, Harrow Books (N.Y.), 1973; $1.25 (paper).

Simple Lessons in Fortune Telling, by Zolar. Zolar Publishing Co. (N.Y.), 1972; $.75 (paper).

Soothsayer's Handbook: A Guide to Bad Signs and Good Vibrations, by Elinor Horwitz. Lippincott (N.Y.), 1972; $1.75 (paper).

The Sybil Leek Book of Fortune Telling, by Sybil Leek. Collier (N.Y.), 1969; $2.95 (paper).

More Information
If your interest blossoms past the point where reading satisfies, there exists in New York City a unique school for the teaching of fortune-telling—all the methods discussed in this book, in far more detail than I've been able to cover—plus various forms of magic and other occult sciences. (The Tarot and astrology, for instance, are each taught in three semesters—beginning, advanced, and a workshop.) You can learn from professionals about color symbolism, ceremonial magic, ESP, palmistry, graphology, the *I CHING,* occult anatomy, number vibrations, and more. The school's president is Vera Scott Johnson, and you can have a brochure by writing her at InnerVision, 235 East 22nd Street, New York, N.Y. 10010.

Chapter One
TEA LEAVES AND OTHER
RANDOM SIGNS

Books
The Art of Tea Cup Fortune Telling, by Minetta. Wehman (Hackensack, N.J.); $1.95 (paper).

The Master Book of Candle Burning, by Henri Gamasche. Wehman (Hackensack, N.J.); $2.50 (paper). Potions and spells as well as wax divination.

Signs, Omens and Superstitions, by Astra Cielo. Gale (Detroit), 1974 (reproduced from a 1918 edition), $11.00 (hard cover). A lengthy catalogue of many signs and omens—physiological, natural, and random—that our ancestors *lived* by.

Tea, by Thomas Eden. Humanities Press (N.Y.); 1965; $8.00 (hard cover). A really exhaustive and fascinating account of the history and tastes of teas—a must if you want to move on from the tea bag to the mysteries of loose tea, its various origins and flavors.

Tea and Coffee

For excellent teas and coffees by mail, shipped anywhere in the United States or abroad, write for a catalogue to McNulty's Tea and Coffee Co., 109 Christopher Street, New York, N.Y. 10014. They are equipped to provide you with Turkish-ground coffee (it's much finer than the finest drip grind) in any blend you choose from an extensive list.

If you don't want to send off for your Eastern-style coffee, look for Venizelos brand Greek-style pulverized stone-ground demitasse coffee. It comes in small eight-ounce tins, and has full instructions on the label.

More Information

Available to consult if you develop a real passion for the subject: the Tea Council of the U.S.A., Inc., 230 Park Ave., New York, N.Y. 10017; and the Coffee Brewing Center, 120 Wall St., New York, N.Y. 10005.

Chapter Two
CARTOMANCY—PLAIN AND FANCY

PLAYING CARDS

The only equipment you need for these methods is the pack of cards. I suggest that you use a regular dime-store deck—not those fancy bridge sets decorated on the back with photos of kittens or *art nouveau* designs, which will only distract you and the client.

Books

How To Tell Fortunes with Cards, by Wenzell Brown. Sterling (N.Y.), 1963; $3.50 (hard cover).

How To Tell Fortunes With Playing Cards, by Zolar. Zolar Publishing Co. (N.Y.), 1973; $.75 (paper).

THE TAROT
Cards

There are at least a dozen versions of the pack of Tarot cards. I recommend the Rider Pack (designed by Edward Arthur Waite and drawn by Pamela Colman Smith) as the most authentic, but you may find yourself taken with the style of one of the other versions. *Always* specify which pack you want when ordering; you'll find that you like some and hate others.

The Rider Pack is available from the following sources: University Books, Inc. (New Hyde Park, N.Y. 11041); and U.S. Games Systems, Inc. (468 Park Avenue South, New York, N.Y. 10016). Both supply cards along with booklet of instructions for $5.00. The latter source, U.S. Games, also carries a wide variety of other Tarot packs (Marseilles, Egyptian, Witches', other reproductions of antique decks), along with Tarot games and posters, *I CHING* and palmistry games, gypsy card games, and other occult materials. Write for their illustrated catalogue.

The Simplified Tarot, a modern design by Martha Everts, is also available. For information, write the designer at 249 E. 48th St., New York, N.Y. 10017.

Books

How To Read Tarot Cards, by Doric C. Doane. Funk & Wagnalls (N.Y.), 1968; $1.25 (paper).

The Pictorial Key to the Tarot, by Edward Arthur Waite. University Books, Inc. (New Hyde Park, N.Y.), 1960; $7.50 (hard cover).

Sexual Key to the Tarot, by Theodor Laurence. Citadel Press (N.Y.), 1971; $5.95 (hard cover).

The Tarot, by S. L. Mathers. Weiser (N.Y.); $1.00 (paper).

Tarot Classic, by Stuart R. Kaplan. U.S. Games Systems (N.Y.), 1972; $5.95 (hard cover).

Tarot: Origins, Meanings, and Uses of the Cards, by Alfred Douglas. Penguin (N.Y.), 1973; $1.45 (paper).

The Tarot Revealed: A Modern Guide to Reading the Tarot Cards, by Eden Gray. Bell (N.Y.), 1960; $3.95 (hard cover). Expanded interpretations of cards.

Chapter Three
SPOTS BEFORE YOUR EYES:
CLEROMANCY

Books

Dominoes: Five-Up and Other Games, by Dominic C. Armanino. McKay (N.Y.), 1959; $5.95 (hard cover).

Fortune-Telling by Cards and Dice, by LeNormand. Wehman (Hackensack, N.J.); $1.00 (paper).

Popular Domino Games, by Dominic C. Armanino. McKay (N.Y.), 1961; $2.50 (paper).

Other Materials

Dice and dominoes are, of course, available in almost any dime store or toy store. If you want something a bit more elegant than the plastic versions, try your local department store; they'll probably have stunning ones at a variety of prices (designed for gambling, but no one says you must *use* them for that!) Dice with a dice cup may also be obtained from U.S. Games Systems, Inc. (468 Park Avenue South, New York, N.Y. 10016); price $7.50.

And don't forget your casino-look table! Buy green felt in the fabric department to glue to the table or sew into a round cloth.

Chapter Four
PLAYING THE NUMBERS:
FORECASTING WITH NUMEROLOGY

The books we've listed here are technical—that is, they are designed to explain the ways numerology works, and how you can become more adept at finding numerological bases for your actions and those of others.

Cheiro's Book of Numbers, by Cheiro. Wehman (Hackensack, N.J.), 1964; $.95 (paper).

Numerology, by Sybil Leek. Collier's (N.Y.), $2.95 (paper).

Secret Power of Numbers, by M. Anderson. Weiser (N.Y.); $1.00 (paper).

The Secrets of Numbers, by Vera Scott Johnson and Thomas Wommack. The Dial Press (N.Y.), 1973; $8.95 (hard cover). Although somewhat murkily written, this book is useful because it contains a sample "numeroscope," which you can use to chart the important numbers in a person's life.

Chapter Five
THE I CHING AND
OTHER MAGICAL TEXTS

THE I CHING
Books
The authoritative text is the Bollingen Series translation: *The I Ching, or Book of Changes,* translated by Richard Wilhelm and rendered into English by Cary F. Baynes, with a Foreword by Carl Jung; Princeton University Press (Princeton, N.J.), 1967; $8.50 (hard cover). Even if you can't afford to buy this book, you should take a look at it in a bookstore or the library, because it is both very informative and a beautiful book that will give you a sense of the *spirit* of the I Ching.

The Complete I Ching, by Edward S. Albertson. Sherbourne (Los Angeles), 1969; $2.50 (paper).

How To Consult the I Ching, by Alfred Douglas. Berkley (N.Y.), 1972; $1.25 (paper).

Secrets of the I Ching, by Joseph Murphy. Prentice-Hall (Englewood Cliffs, N.J.), 1970; $2.45 (paper).

Coins
If you'd like to use three authentic Chinese pierced coins for the throw, they are available at under five dollars for the set of three from Joe D. Coen, Inc., 39 West 55th Street, New York, N.Y. 10019 (write him for current prices), or from your local numismatist.

Other Oriental Supplies, Including Foods
The following stores can supply you with materials to make your *I Ching* readings truly Oriental:

Chen, Joyce, P.O. Box 3, Cambridge, Mass. 02138: mail-order foods.

Kwong On Lung Co., 686 N. Spring St., Los Angeles, Cal. 90012: mail-order foods.

Oriental Country Store, 12 Mott Street, New York, N.Y. 10013 (Write to them for a catalogue of Oriental spices, cookware, and gourmet delicacies.)

Takashimaya, 509 Fifth Avenue, New York, N.Y. 10036 (New York's largest Oriental store, Takashimaya has a fine selection of all sorts of supplies—clothing, cookware and serving dishes, chopsticks, whatever exotic atmosphere-enhancers you desire. Their Christmas catalogue is available in the late fall.)

Cookbooks

If you have an urge to *cook* Chinese, rather than merely to buy Oriental delicacies, you'll need one of the following books:

Craig Claiborne's Chinese Cookbook, by Craig Claiborne, with Virginia Lee. Lippincott (N.Y.), 1973; $12.50 (hard cover). Written in collaboration with a Chinese, this is the *New York Times's* food editor's account of his romance with Chinese cooking, and the recipes that resulted. Chatty, informative, not as authentic or as amusing as the Chao book below, but perhaps more immediately available to Western palates.

How to Cook and Eat in Chinese, by Buwei Yang Chao. Random House (N.Y.), 1949; $6.95 (hard cover). This is a charming and completely authentic book, whose author is informative in a wonderful and literate, though discernibly Chinese, style.

OTHER MAGICAL TEXTS

The Old Testament makes a perfect random text, but be sure that the edition you use is the King James Version. None of the others—the Catholic Douay, any of the various Jewish translations, or the Revised Standard version—have the sonorous poetry or the mysteriousness of tone that the older translation has. Just ask your bookseller for a "King James Version," and be *very* firm about it.

The books listed below are translations of various short and lovely Greek lyrics that can be used in the same way as the Sappho poems quoted in the chapter. (The Mary Barnard translation listed below is the one we used.)

Sappho, a New Translation, by Mary Barnard. University of California Press (Berkeley, Cal.), 1965; $1.25 (paper).

Greek Lyric Poetry, translated by Willis Barnstone. Bantam (N.Y.), 1967; $.60 (paper).

Greek Lyrics, translated by Richmond Lattimore. The University of Chicago Press, Phoenix Book (Chicago), 1963; $1.35 (paper).

Chapter Six
DREAMS: UNCONSCIOUS FORTUNES

THE PSYCHOLOGICAL METHOD

The Handbook of Dream Analysis, by Dr. Emil A. Gutheil. Fawcett (N.Y.), 1967; $.60 (paper).

The Interpretation of Dreams, by Sigmund Freud. Avon (N.Y.), 1968; $1.65 (paper).

THE TRADITIONAL METHOD
The Encyclopedia and Dictionary of Dreams, by Zolar. Zolar Publishing Co. (N.Y.), 1974; $3.95 (paper). *Enormous* listing of dream symbols.

The Gypsy-Witch Dream Book. Stein (Chicago), $1.00 (paper).

Three Wise Men Dream Book, by Zonite. Wehman (Hackensack, N.J.), 1971; $1.25 (paper).

Chapter Seven
THE OUIJA BOARD AND
AUTOMATIC WRITING

The Ouija Board itself is available from Parker Brothers, 190 Bridge Street, Salem, Mass. 01970. But you should have no trouble finding one at your local toy or department store.

Madame Helena Blavatsky was the most noted practitioner of the methods described in this chapter. Her published works run into dozens of volumes. A beginning book might be: *Practical Occultism.* Theosophy Publishing House (N.Y.), 1967; $.75 (paper).

Chapter Eight
READING THE BODY:
THE SENSUAL METHODS

PALMISTRY
The literature on palmistry is extensive. If I had to recommend any one book, or set of books, it would be those by Cheiro, who made "palmistry" a word with more than gypsy-tent connotations.

Cheiro's Language of the Hand: The Classic of Palmistry. Arco (N.Y.), 1968; $.95 (paper).

Complete Book of Palmistry, by Joyce Wilson. Bantam (N.Y.), 1971; $1.00 (paper).

Palmistry Made Easy, by Elizabeth P. Hoffman. Simon and Schuster (N.Y.), 1971; $1.00 (paper).

You and Your Hand, by Cheiro. Berkley (N.Y.), 1971; $1.25 (paper).

PHRENOLOGY
How To Read Character: A New Illustrated Handbook of Phrenology and Physiognomy, by Samuel R. Wells. Tuttle (Rutland, Vt.), 1971; $1.80 (hard cover).

Observations on Mental Erangement, by Combe and Walsh. Scholar's Facsimiles & Reprints (Gainesville, Fla.); $20.00 (hard cover). This is the most authoritative text in phrenology, being a facsimile of the 1861 edition of the English classic. It is very long, very expensive, and really interesting more as a historical curiosity than as a practical modern guide. If you are seriously interested however, it is a *must,* even if you have to take your notes at the library.

Phrenology, by Howard V. Chambers. Sherbourne (Los Angeles), 1968; $2.50 (paper).

Phrenology, by Sybil Leek. Collier (N.Y.), 1970; $2.95 (paper). This book is especially useful to the beginner because it includes a head chart with a detailed list of the information necessary for a long-term reading.

Phrenology: Fad and Science, by John Davies. Shoe String (Hamden, Conn.), 1971; $6.50 (hard cover).

GRAPHOLOGY
Here, too, the literature is extensive, and there are several schools of thought. I've concentrated here on the American school.

Books
Encyclopedia of the Written Word, by Klara G. Roman. Ungar (N.Y.), 1968; $12.50 (hard cover). You'll probably never see this outside a library, but it is fascinating—full of information about the history of handwriting as well as about its analysis.

Graphology and Palmistry: Language of the Hand, by Henry Frith. Steiner (N.Y.); $1.95 (paper).

A Graphology Student's Workbook, by Ruth Gardner. Llewellyn Publishers (St. Paul, Minn.), 1973; $3.95 (paper).

Key to Handwriting Analysis, by J. S. Meyer. Wehman (Hackensack, N.J.); $1.00 (paper).

You Are What You Write, by Huntingdon Hartford. Macmillan (N.Y.), 1973; $7.95 (hard cover).

Other Materials
To find a pen that really suits your handwriting personality, check your local artists' supply store. Two with flair are the Osmiroid pen, which comes with a booklet explaining the Italic style; and the Rapidograph, in numerous point sizes.

Chapter Nine
"ESP": PSYCHIC READING AND CLAIRVOYANCE

This is an overwhelmingly large field. There are mediums, prophets, psychic readers, seers, ESP experts from universities, and everybody in between running around declaiming theories about the powers of the mind over the material world. The occult section of any bookstore will have a wide selection of books on these subjects; below, I've listed some that follow up on the chapter.

The Call to Glory, by Jeane Dixon; Bantam (N.Y.), 1973. $1.25 (paper). The autobiography of the famous prophet and mystic.

Change: The I Ching and the Edgar Cayce Reading, by the editors of ARE Press (Virginia Beach, Va.), 1971; $1.50 (paper). Especially fascinating because it recounts the meeting of the ancient Chinese oracle and the modern prophet.

Clairvoyant Women, by Robert Tralins. Popular Library (N.Y.), 1972; $.75 (paper).

The Complete Guide to Oracle and Prophecy Methods, by Joseph J. Weed; Parker Publishing (West Nyack, N.Y.), 1971; $6.95 (hard cover). A good working account of the most famous prophets and their methods, with a detailed guide for developing latent clairvoyant gifts.

ESP and the Clairvoyants, by Raymond van Over. Universal Publishers and Distributors (N.Y.), 1970; $.75 (paper).

Fifty Years a Medium, by Estelle Roberts. Avon (N.Y.), 1972; $.95 (paper). Fascinating because it's a first-hand account.

How to Develop Clairvoyance, by W. E. Butler. Weiser (N.Y.), 1971; $1.00 (paper).

Jeane Dixon: Prophet or Fraud?, by Mary Bringle. Tower (N.Y.), 1970; $.95 (paper).

Modern American Spiritualism, by Emma Hardinge. University Books (New Hyde Park, N.Y.), 1970; $12.50 (hard cover).

Mysteries and Romances of the World's Great Occultists, by Cheiro. University Books, Inc. (New Hyde Park, N.Y.), 1972; $7.95 (hard cover).

Twentieth Century Prophecy: Jeane Dixon and Edgar Cayce, by James Bjornstad. Bethany Fellowship (Minneapolis); 1969 (paper).

Voice of the Silence, by Helena Blavatsky. Theosophy House Publications (N.Y.); $1.75 (paper). A small handbook by the famous medium and seer, whose published works run into dozens of volumes.

What I Believe, by Edgar Cayce. ARE Press (Virginia Beach Va.), 1946; $1.25 (paper). This book and the one above are especially interesting because they are first-person accounts of the ideas and visions of two of the most widely-believed-in occultists of the twentieth century.

Chapter Ten
FUTURE-CASTING WITH ASTROLOGY

Astrology is by now so popular that it would be impossible to list comprehensively what is available on the subject. Here, then, is a selection of materials for following up on the chapter.

Magazines
Dell Horoscope, published monthly and available at newsstands for $.50 or from Box 4800, Marion, Ohio 43302 ($6.00 for a one-year subscription). A comprehensive horoscope for each of the signs, plus columns and articles on investments, world affairs, and lucky numbers. There is a special section each month on that month's sign.

Books

A number of publishers, including Dell, New American Library, and Simon and Schuster, put out annual horoscopes in paperback form—one for each sign. Look for these in your bookstore, five-and-ten, or even supermarket! They make good gifts for I-was-just-thinking-about-you moments.

Basic Principles of Astrology, by American Federation of Astrologers. Llewellyn Publishers (St. Paul, Minn.), 1962; $1.00 (paper).

Casting the Horoscope, by Alan Leo. Weiser (N.Y.), 1968; $7.50 (hard cover). For the ambitious who want to learn how to make a chart.

Chinese Zodiac Book, by Kim Hai Song, Simon and Schuster (N.Y.); $3.00 (hard cover). A Chinese version of the zodiac, with analysis of each sign.

Ephemeris, 1890-1950, by Metz, Llewellyn (St. Paul, Minn.), $12.00 (hard cover). The essential tables of the positions of the planets for these years—necessary for casting a horoscope from scratch. A solid investment if you plan to take up astrology seriously.

It's All in the Stars, by Zolar. Fawcett (N.Y.), 1962; $.95 (paper). A complete account of each sun sign; also includes sun signs of famous persons, compatibility charts, and lucky numbers.

The Japanese Fortune Calendar, by Reiko Chiba. Tuttle (Rutland, Vt.), 1965; $2.95 (hard cover). A charmingly designed book on colored paper with red cloth covers and Japanese drawings, explaining the Japanese version of the zodiac in more detail.

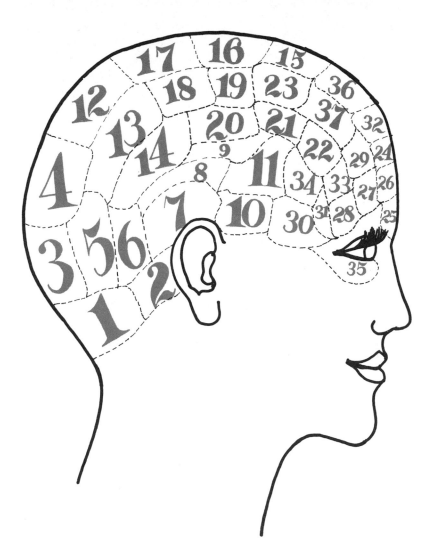

ESSENTIAL QUALITIES
1. Sexuality
2. Self-Preservation
3. Parenthood
4. Domesticity
5. Friendship
6. Competitiveness
7. Impatience
8. Secretiveness
9. Acquisitiveness
10. Appetite
11. Achievement

FEELINGS
12. Self-Esteem

13. Desire for Approval
14. Prudence
15. Benevolence
16. Respect
17. Determination
18. Conscientiousness
19. Optimism
20. Belief
21. Beauty
22. Humor
23. Emulation

PERCEPTION
24. Observation
25. Shape

26. Size
27. Weight
28. Color
29. Place Memory
30. Numbers
31. Orderliness
32. Memory for Events
33. Time Sense
34. Melody
35. Verbal Expression

REASON
36. Comparison
37. Causality

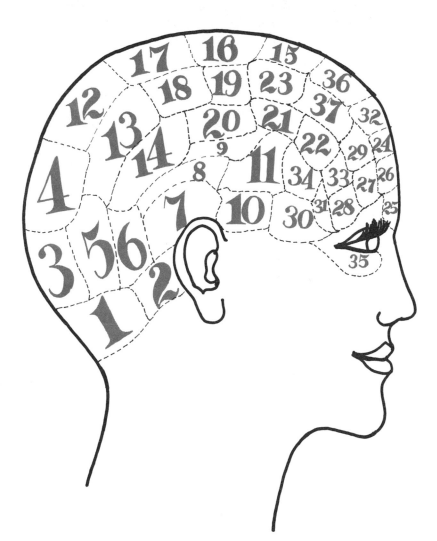

ESSENTIAL QUALITIES
 1. Sexuality
 2. Self-Preservation
 3. Parenthood
 4. Domesticity
 5. Friendship
 6. Competitiveness
 7. Impatience
 8. Secretiveness
 9. Acquisitiveness
10. Appetite
11. Achievement

FEELINGS
12. Self-Esteem

13. Desire for Approval
14. Prudence
15. Benevolence
16. Respect
17. Determination
18. Conscientiousness
19. Optimism
20. Belief
21. Beauty
22. Humor
23. Emulation

PERCEPTION
24. Observation
25. Shape

26. Size
27. Weight
28. Color
29. Place Memory
30. Numbers
31. Orderliness
32. Memory for Events
33. Time Sense
34. Melody
35. Verbal Expression

REASON
36. Comparison
37. Causality

This book is set in 9 point Optima with 2 points leading, with Optima demi bold and italics. The Optima face is designed by Herman Zapf, of Nürnberg, Germany. Zapf is also the designer of Melior, Palatino and many other internationally known types.

The display face used for titles and initials is Broadway.
The Title is set in Photolettering Broadway Condensed.

Book design and covers by Dorris Crandall

Editorial Coordinator: Cheryl Johnson
Assistant Coordinator: Nancy Jessup